Introducing AutoCAD® 2010 and AutoCAD LT® 2010

Introducing AutoCAD® 2010 and AutoCAD LT® 2010

GEORGE OMURA

WILEY

Wiley Publishing, Inc.

Senior Acquisitions Editor: WILLEM KNIBBE
Development Editor: KIM WIMPSETT
Technical Editor: PAUL R. RICHARDSON III
Production Editor: DASSI ZEIDEL
Copy Editor: LIZ WELCH
Editorial Manager: PETE GAUGHAN
Production Manager: TIM TATE
Vice President and Executive Group Publisher: RICHARD SWADLEY
Vice President and Publisher: NEIL EDDE
Book Designer: CARYL GORSKA
Compositor: CHRIS GILLESPIE, HAPPENSTANCE TYPE-O-RAMA
Proofreader: REBECCA RIDER
Indexer: JACK LEWIS
Project Coordinator, Cover: LYNSEY STANFORD
Cover Designer: RYAN SNEED
Cover Image: MAIN COVER IMAGE: FREDERIC CIROU / GETTY IMAGES, INC.; BOTTOM ROW IMAGES: ISTOCKPHOTO

For general information on our other products and services or to obtain technical support, please contact our Customer Care Department within the U.S. at (877) 762-2974, outside the U.S. at (317) 572-3993 or fax (317) 572-4002.

Wiley also publishes its books in a variety of electronic formats. Some content that appears in print may not be available in electronic books.

Library of Congress Cataloging-in-Publication Data

Omura, George.
  Introducing AutoCAD 2010 and AutoCAD LT 2010 / George Omura. — 1st ed.
    p. cm.
  ISBN 978-0-470-43867-1 (paper/website)
 1. Computer graphics. 2. AutoCAD. 3. Computer-aided design. I. Title.
  T385.O4753 2009
  620'.00420285536—dc22
                  2009021672

10 9 8 7 6 5 4 3 2 1

Dear Reader,

Thank you for choosing *Introducing AutoCAD 2010 and AutoCAD LT 2010*. This book is part of a family of premium-quality Sybex books, all of which are written by outstanding authors who combine practical experience with a gift for teaching.

Sybex was founded in 1976. More than 30 years later, we're still committed to producing consistently exceptional books. With each of our titles, we're working hard to set a new standard for the industry. From the paper we print on, to the authors we work with, our goal is to bring you the best books available.

I hope you see all that reflected in these pages. I'd be very interested to hear your comments and get your feedback on how we're doing. Feel free to let me know what you think about this or any other Sybex book by sending me an email at nedde@wiley.com. If you think you've found a technical error in this book, please visit http://sybex.custhelp.com. Customer feedback is critical to our efforts at Sybex.

Best regards,

Neil Edde
Vice President and Publisher
Sybex, an Imprint of Wiley

To my friends Richard and Spencer: What a long, strange trip...

Acknowledgments

I'd like to thank Willem Knibbe for giving me the opportunity to work with Sybex, an imprint of John Wiley & Sons, on this project. I'd also like to thank Kim Wimpsett for keeping the project moving along. Paul R. Richardson III offered his AutoCAD expertise while checking all the details. Thanks to Dassi Zeidel for handling the production end of things and to Liz Welch for carefully copyediting each chapter.

At Autodesk, Jim Quanci once again gave his full support for our work and cheerfully answered all our questions. Thanks to Shaan Hurley and Kathy O'Connell for graciously opening the doors to the AutoCAD beta program so early in the process. And thanks to Denis Cadu, who is always more than willing to help us in our times of need.

Thank you all for making this book possible.

About the Author

George Omura is a licensed architect, Autodesk Authorized Author, and CAD specialist with more than 20 years of experience in AutoCAD and more than 30 years of experience in architecture. He has worked on design projects ranging from resort hotels to metropolitan transit systems to the San Francisco Library project. George has written numerous other AutoCAD books for Sybex, including *Introducing AutoCAD 2009 and AutoCAD LT 2009*, *Mastering AutoCAD 2010 and AutoCAD LT 2010*, and *Mastering AutoCAD 2009 and AutoCAD LT 2009*.

CONTENTS AT A GLANCE

Contents

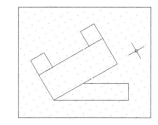

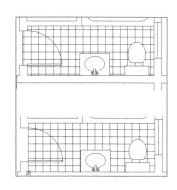

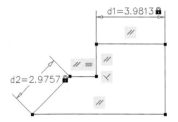

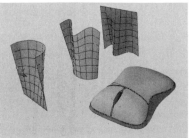

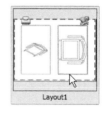

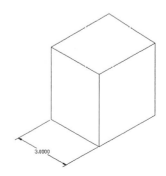

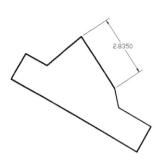

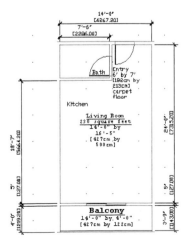

Introduction

If you're involved in any way with the design and manufacturing industry, you've probably had to work with AutoCAD drawings. Autodesk AutoCAD has become the standard program for producing technical drawings of all types. It has the depth and range of features that enable the expert user to create nearly any type of technical drawing.

But not everyone needs to be an expert at AutoCAD. Many AutoCAD users really need to know only a few of its vast array of tools. Still others use AutoCAD only from time to time to review existing drawings and make minor changes. If you're someone who doesn't need or want to be an AutoCAD power user but wants to be able use AutoCAD proficiently, this book is for you. You may have taken an AutoCAD course and forgotten most of what you've learned, or you might be a project manager who has to work with AutoCAD drawings only occasionally. Or perhaps you have had a job that has taken you away from AutoCAD and you want to get back into using the latest version. You want a resource that gets to the point and lets you find what you need fast without wading through volumes of information. If this sounds like you, you've come to the right place. *Introducing AutoCAD 2010 and AutoCAD LT 2010* is designed with you in mind.

How to Use This Book

Introducing AutoCAD 2010 and AutoCAD LT 2010 covers the basic drawing and editing tools that most users will need to produce high-quality AutoCAD drawings. You won't find information about every last feature. Instead, this book presents AutoCAD's essential features through a combination of tutorials and reference material to give you a concise, easy-to-use companion for your work with AutoCAD. It's designed so that you can quickly learn the tools you need when you need them.

Most chapters start with tutorials covering basic concepts on a particular topic so that you can understand how AutoCAD works in a general way. Later parts of the chapter provide reference material to help you with specific tasks. For example, in Chapter 9, a tutorial at the beginning gives you the basic steps for creating and formatting text. After that, the chapter goes into more depth to show you how to use other features, such as how to import text, how to size and scale text, and how to create tables. Once you've learned the basics from the beginning tutorial, you can pick and choose from those topics later in the chapter as the need arises.

The book assumes you have a working knowledge of the Microsoft Windows operating system. You should also know how to locate files on your computer and how menus and toolbars work in a general way. Experience with other graphics programs also helps but is not essential.

If you are wondering whether your computer has the capacity to run AutoCAD 2010, here is a rundown of the minimum system requirements:

- Windows XP Home or Professional, or Windows Vista
- 2GB free disk space
- 1GB of RAM (2GB if you are using Windows Vista)
- Pentium V or better processor

What You'll Find

To help you get the most from AutoCAD, the chapters in *Introducing AutoCAD 2010 and AutoCAD LT 2010* are organized into general topics such as "Drawing 2D Objects" or "Laying Out and Printing Your Drawings." Within each chapter, I discuss specific tasks in detail, such as drawing circles or choosing a printer paper size.

The first three chapters serve as an introduction to the AutoCAD way of doing things. If you're new to AutoCAD, you'll want to pay special attention to these chapters. In Chapter 1, "Getting Familiar with AutoCAD," you'll be introduced to AutoCAD and how it's organized. You'll learn where to find features and the purpose of the various parts of the AutoCAD screen. Chapter 2, "Understanding the Drafting Tools," gets into more detail regarding the way AutoCAD works. You'll learn how to set up a drawing and how to use AutoCAD's basic drafting tools, such as the grid and the coordinate system. Chapter 3, "Drawing 2D Objects," discusses the most common AutoCAD drawing and editing tools. Here you'll find out how to draw lines, arcs, and circles, as well as how to add hatch patterns and how to lay out a drawing.

The next two chapters are concerned with editing in AutoCAD. Chapter 4, "Editing AutoCAD Objects," describes the general methods for editing drawings in AutoCAD. This is another good chapter to read if you are new to AutoCAD. Or if you're an old hand, you'll want to look here for information on the new parametric features in AutoCAD 2010. Chapter 5, "Editing with the Modify Panel Tools," shows you how to use specific tools to make changes to your drawing. Here you'll learn how to join, move, scale, and stretch objects, as well as how to perform many other operations.

Chapter 6, "Creating 3D Drawings," introduces 3D modeling in AutoCAD. You'll learn about the basic concepts for creating and viewing 3D models in AutoCAD. You'll also learn about the new Mesh Modeling features.

Chapter 7, "Getting Organized with Layers," shows you how you can use a feature called layers to organize your drawing. You'll see how to create and use layers and how to manage large lists of layers. You'll also learn how to employ AutoCAD object properties such as color and lineweights to help visually organize your drawings. Chapter 8, "Using Blocks, Groups, Xrefs, and DesignCenter," shows you how to work more efficiently by grouping objects into assemblies. Here, you'll also learn how to use existing files as backgrounds for new projects. If you work with PDFs, you'll want to read this chapter's coverage of AutoCAD's PDF support.

Textual notation plays a major role in technical drawing, and AutoCAD provides some excellent tools to help you with your notation tasks. Chapter 9, "Creating Text," shows you how to create and edit text. You'll learn how to scale text properly for your particular drawing and how you can use AutoCAD's table feature, which works just like a spreadsheet. Chapter 10, "Using Dimensions," shows you the dimensioning tools you'll need to add and display crucial dimensions of your drawing.

One of the greatest features of AutoCAD drawings is the amount of information they hold. Chapter 11, "Gathering Information," shows you how to extract the types of information available from an AutoCAD drawing. You'll learn how to find basic types of information, such as distances and areas, plus you'll learn how to search for text and other named components.

Eventually, you'll need to print your drawings, but the nature of technical drawings means that AutoCAD's printing and plotting feature is a bit more complex than your word processor's. Chapter 12, "Laying Out and Printing Your Drawings," guides you through the process of getting the output you want on the media you need. Chapter 12 also shows you how to use AutoCAD's layout feature to lay out and organize the components of your drawing on a printed sheet.

How to Contact the Author

The idea for this book came from the growing number of casual users of AutoCAD I've observed over the years. Instead of wanting to become experts, they want to know how to perform certain tasks with the least amount of fuss. I've tried to incorporate the essential information most users need, but if you have ideas about how I can improve the book or if you think I've omitted an essential feature while covering nonessentials, you can email me at the following address. If you think you need more information than this book provides, you should consider Sybex's *Mastering AutoCAD 2010 and AutoCAD LT 2010*.

You can also contact this book's publisher, Sybex, an imprint of John Wiley & Sons, regarding general questions about this and other AutoCAD publications at www.sybex.com. Thanks for choosing *Introducing AutoCAD 2010 and AutoCAD LT 2010*.

—George Omura

gomura@yahoo.com

CHAPTER 1

Getting Familiar with AutoCAD

If you are totally new to AutoCAD, you'll want to read this chapter. It provides an overview of AutoCAD's layout and shows you what to expect when you start to use it. Even if you've had an AutoCAD class or used an older version of AutoCAD, you'll find this chapter helpful because it covers the new AutoCAD interface.

You'll start by taking a tour of the AutoCAD window to become familiar with the menus and other components. You'll then get a chance to try your hand at drawing, and in doing so, you'll be introduced to the way AutoCAD's commands work. You'll also learn how to use the Zoom and Pan tools to help you get around in a drawing. And you'll look at the ways you can view your drawing by using the layout feature. Finally, you'll be introduced to the Help system for those times when you forget to have this book on hand.

This chapter covers the following topics:

- **Understanding the AutoCAD window**
- **Starting commands**
- **Starting a drawing**
- **Panning and zooming to adjust your view**
- **Understanding the Layout view**
- **Understanding how command options work**
- **Getting help**

Understanding the AutoCAD Window

Autodesk has redesigned AutoCAD 2010's interface. If you've used a version prior to AutoCAD 2009, it will appear as though AutoCAD has completely changed.

Don't worry; the underlying program still behaves in much the same way as before. Through AutoCAD's workspace feature, you can easily change AutoCAD's interface to display the old, familiar toolbars that are seemingly missing from this latest version. In this section, you'll look at AutoCAD's newest interface options.

> The ⏎ symbol in this book denotes the Enter key. Whenever you see it, press the Enter key, also known as the Return key.

AutoCAD works like most other Windows-based graphics programs, but it also has a few quirks. This section gives you an overview of AutoCAD's layout. Although many elements will be familiar, a few will be new to you.

To start, you'll see the two ways that AutoCAD displays a drawing. Then, for the rest of this chapter, you'll focus on the 2D drawing environment. After installing AutoCAD, take the following steps to get to the 2D workspace:

1. Choose Start → All Programs → Autodesk → AutoCAD 2010 → AutoCAD 2010. (LT users will click AutoCAD LT 2010 in place of AutoCAD 2010 in the previous menu selection.) You can also double-click the AutoCAD 2010 icon on your Windows Desktop.

   If this is a new installation, you will see the Initial Setup dialog box. This dialog box lets you set up a workspace for the type of file you want to work with. Everything from Architectural to Manufacturing to Structural Engineering is offered. For the purposes of this book, you can click the Skip button in the lower-right corner of the dialog box. You can always open this dialog box through the User Preferences tab of the Options dialog box. After closing the Initial Setup dialog box, you'll see a greeting, called a *splash screen*; then, if this is a new installation, AutoCAD displays the Workspaces message box. This message box offers an option to select 2D Drafting & Annotation, 3D Modeling, or AutoCAD Classic.

2. Click 2D Drafting & Annotation. You'll see the AutoCAD window with a blank default document named Drawing1.dwg, as shown at the top of Figure 1.1. If this is a new installation, you will also see the New Features Workshop window. If this happens, select Maybe Later, and then click OK.

AUTOCAD 2010 VS. AUTOCAD 2010 LT

AutoCAD 2010 and AutoCAD 2010 LT are essentially the same program, with some differences both large and small. The LT version has limited 3D capabilities and no 3D workspace. Customization features too are limited in the LT version. With the exception of the 3D features, you should be able to use the features discussed in this book when using AutoCAD 2010 LT.

Quick Access toolbar

InfoCenter

Application menu

Ribbon

Drawing area

UCS

Command window

Status bar

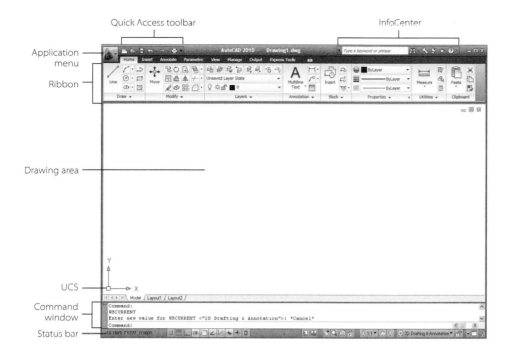

Figure 1.1

AutoCAD when opened into a 2D Drafting & Annotation workspace

> In some installations, you might see a Startup dialog box. If this happens to you, click Cancel, and AutoCAD will display the blank default document.

3. The default document appears to be an empty 2D space. You'll also see a special tool palette, called the Ribbon, along the top, as shown in Figure 1.1. This is a set of 2D drafting and annotation tools that gives you ready access to the most common drafting functions.

If you are using AutoCAD 2010, try the following exercise to see how to get to the 3D Modeling workspace (this workspace is not available in AutoCAD 2010 LT):

1. In the lower-right corner of the AutoCAD window, you'll see a gear-shaped icon. This is the Workspace Switching tool. Click it to open a list that shows 2D Drafting & Annotation, 3D Modeling, and AutoCAD Classic. If you selected an option in the Initial Setup dialog box, you will also see the Initial Setup Workspace listed.

> If you're feeling adventurous, you can go to Chapter 6 to find out more about AutoCAD's new 3D tools. LT users will not have the 3D functions.

2. Select 3D Modeling from the list.

The current default file, Drawing1.dwg, is set up for 2D drafting, but you can open a new file by using a file template already set up for 3D modeling.

3. On the Quick Access toolbar, click New. The Select Template dialog box appears (Figure 1.2).

4. Select acad3D.dwt from the list, and click Open. A new file, called Drawing2.dwg, appears. Notice that this drawing is in a 3D space (Figure 1.3). You'll learn more about 3D modeling in Chapter 6.

Figure 1.2

Opening the Select Template dialog box

Click New in the Quick Access Toolbar.

The Select Template dialog box appears.

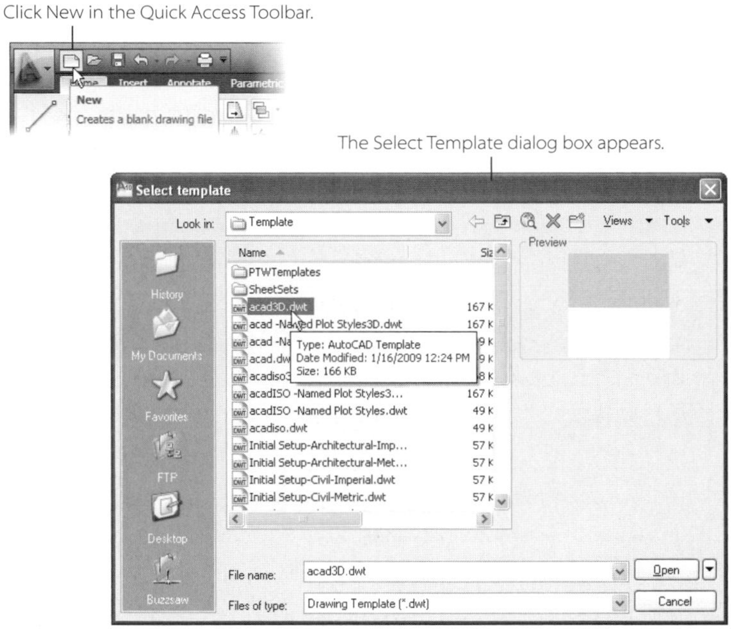

Figure 1.3

The AutoCAD window set up for 3D modeling

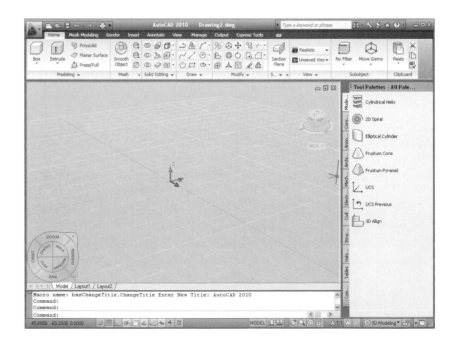

5. Click the Workspace Switching tool, and click 2D Drafting & Annotation in the Workspaces toolbar. You'll be working in this workspace for most of this book.

6. Exit the 3D `Drawing2.dwg` file by clicking the Close icon in the upper-right corner of the drawing area. The Close icon looks like an X.

Even though the default 2D file looks completely different from the new 3D file you created by using the `acad3D.dwt` template, they really are basically the same. They just have different display settings turned on. You can learn more about the various ways to display drawings in Chapter 6.

You now have AutoCAD set up for 2D drawing, so you'll take a more detailed look at the AutoCAD window. You'll find that, for the most part, it is a typical Windows-style graphics program window with a few twists.

Getting to Know the Window Components

Your AutoCAD window should look like the earlier Figure 1.1, which shows the default configuration for a new AutoCAD installation. Since AutoCAD is so easy to customize, you might not see exactly the same layout, but the basic components should be there. The AutoCAD window offers several controls to the program:

Ribbon The Ribbon contains most of the common functions you'll need to use (see Figure 1.4). The Ribbon contains several panels, each of which contains tools for drawing and editing. The set of panels changes depending on which Ribbon tab is selected. The Ribbon panels can be moved with a click and drag of their title bars, and the entire Ribbon can be set up to stay hidden until you need to use it.

When Ribbon panels are away from the edge of the window and appear "free floating," they are said to be floating, as opposed to docked. You'll learn more in the "Using the Ribbon" section of this chapter.

Figure 1.4

The Ribbon and its components

Quick Access toolbar The Quick Access toolbar offers the most commonly used Windows functions, such as Save, Undo, Redo, and Print.

Application menu If you click the AutoCAD logo in the upper-left corner of the window, you open the Application menu, which offers general file-related tools (see Figure 1.5). At the top of the Application menu, you see the Search tool. This enables you to find a specific tool by name just by typing the name into the search input box. Just below and to the left of the Search tool are two icons that offer Recent Documents and Open Documents. If you click Recent Documents, the panel to the right lists the most recent files you've opened. Each file has a pushpin icon to the right, enabling you to lock the item in the list. If you click Open Documents, you'll see a list of documents that are currently open in AutoCAD. You'll learn more in the "Using the Application Menu" section of this chapter.

Figure 1.5

The Application menu

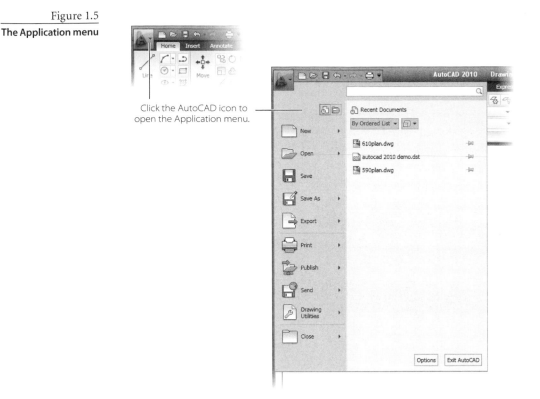

Click the AutoCAD icon to
open the Application menu.

Drawing area In the middle of the AutoCAD window is the drawing area where you'll do
your actual drawing. You'll learn more in the "Getting Familiar with the Drawing Area"
section of this chapter.

UCS icon The UCS icon is the L-shaped icon you see at the lower-left corner of the drawing area; you'll learn more in the "Checking the UCS Icon" section.

Status bar At the bottom of the screen is the status bar, which provides information
about many of the settings you'll use in AutoCAD. The status bar also offers controls over
many of the different drawing modes in AutoCAD.

Command window Just above the status bar is the command window, which is almost
unique to AutoCAD. The command line is a text window that displays commands as you
use them, as well as your keyboard input. Messages often appear here that prompt you
to perform a step in a command. You'll learn more about the command line a bit later in
this chapter; see the "Using the Command Line" section.

InfoCenter In the upper-right corner of the AutoCAD window you'll see the InfoCenter.
This is where you can get help about AutoCAD features or find current information
about AutoCAD on the Internet. You'll learn more in the "Staying Informed with the
InfoCenter" section of this chapter.

Another unique item in AutoCAD's window is the set of tool palettes shown in Figure 1.6. You can use these palettes to keep your favorite tools and drawing components in one convenient place for quick access.

The Properties palette shown on the left and the AutoCAD tool palettes shown on the right of Figure 1.6 might not appear in your AutoCAD window by default, but you can open the tool palettes by clicking the View tab in the Ribbon and selecting Tool Palettes from the Palettes panel.

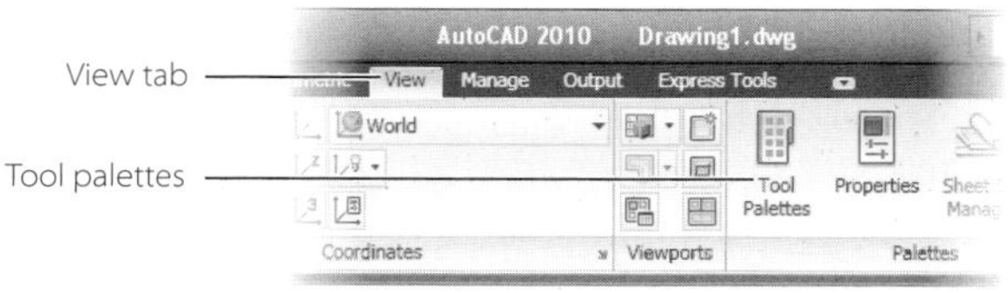

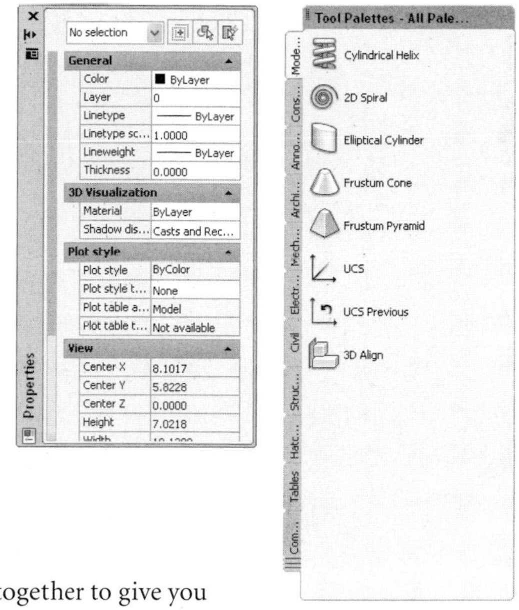

Figure 1.6

The Properties palette (at left) and the tool palettes (at right)

The drawing area, the status bar, and the command line work together to give you feedback while you create and edit your drawing. As you move your cursor over the drawing area, you'll see the cursor appear as a crosshair cursor. If you click the drawing area, a pair of numbers and a selection window appear. Click again, and the selection window disappears.

With the crosshair cursor, you can point to portions of the drawing area, and the numeric display, known as the *Dynamic Input display*, tells you your XY coordinate within the drawing area. The selection window lets you select objects in the drawing area. You'll learn more about coordinates in AutoCAD in Chapter 2, and you'll look at selection windows a bit later in this chapter.

If you don't see the Dynamic Input display, go to the status bar at the bottom of the AutoCAD window, and click the Dynamic Input tool.

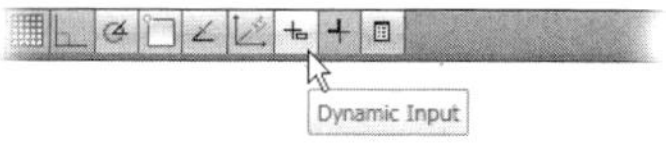

Along with the Dynamic Input display, the command line and status bar just below the drawing area provide feedback as you work with AutoCAD commands (see Figure 1.7). You can also see the XY coordinate in the far left of the status bar in the lower-left corner of the AutoCAD window.

Figure 1.7

The status bar and the command line work with the drawing area to give you feedback as you draw.

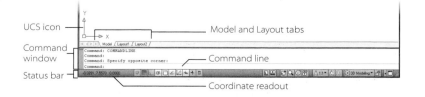

CONTROLLING THE STATUS BAR DISPLAY

To the far right of the status bar, you'll see a down-pointing triangle, or *arrow*; click this arrow to open a menu that controls the display of the status bar. You can also just right-click in a blank area of the status bar to display this menu. You use this menu to turn the items in the status bar on or off. A check mark by an item indicates it is currently on.

If for some reason you do not see all the buttons mentioned in the preceding discussion, check this menu to make sure that all the status bar options are turned on. Note that the LT version does not have an Otrack option in the status bar.

Using the Ribbon

If you've used the latest version of Microsoft Office for Windows Vista, you'll be familiar with the Ribbon. The Ribbon is a bit like a super toolbar that offers quick access to the most commonly used tools. In addition, the Ribbon offers a lot of helpful information in the form of expanded tooltips.

Specifically, the Ribbon is a collection of tools that invoke commands. These tools are grouped into several *tabs*. Each tab contains a set of *panels*, and each panel contains a set of icons representing tools and showing their function (see the earlier Figure 1.4). The tools also offer *tooltips* that provide a lot of information, including a description that helps you understand what the icons represent.

If the Ribbon does not appear on the screen, you can click in the command window and then type **ribbon.↵** to restore it to the window.

If you move the cursor onto one of the Ribbon panel tools and leave it there for a moment, you'll see a tooltip appear just below the cursor, giving you a brief description of the tool. Leave the cursor there a bit longer, and the tooltip expands to show even more information on how to use the tool (see Figure 1.8). As a new user, you'll find these tooltips very helpful.

Throughout the book, when I ask you to select a tool from the Ribbon or from a toolbar, I'll use the name shown in the tooltip. For example, if you hover your cursor over any icon tool in the Ribbon, you'll see the name of the tool at the top of the tooltip that appears (as shown in Figure 1.8).

In most cases, you'll be able to guess what each tool does by looking at its icon. The icon with an arc in the Draw panel of the Ribbon, for instance, indicates that the tool draws arcs; the one with the circle shows that the tool draws circles; and so on. But for further clarification, the tooltip gives you the name of the tool.

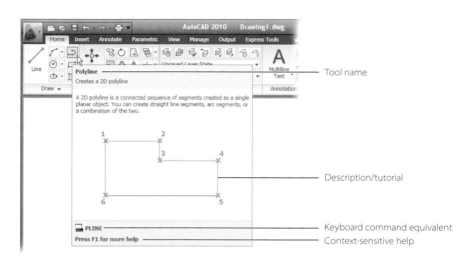

Figure 1.8

A tooltip showing the name of the tool, a brief tutorial-like graphic, and the command name associated with the tool

Tool name

Description/tutorial

Keyboard command equivalent

Context-sensitive help

Finding Hidden Panels and Tools

In the "Getting Familiar with the Drawing Area" section, you'll start to work in the drawing area by drawing some lines. Before you do that, though, take a moment to examine the left part of the Ribbon, where the Draw panel of the Ribbon resides. You will be instructed to use the tools in this Ribbon panel frequently throughout this book, so it will be helpful for you to get a feel for their arrangement and what they contain.

Besides the visible tools, a few tools are hidden from view. Click the Blocks and Reference tab just above the Ribbon. The row of Ribbon panels changes to a new set of panels. Click the Home tab above the Ribbon to return to the previous set of panels.

> As you work through exercises in this book, I'll abbreviate the name of the Ribbon tabs to simplify the Instructions. For example, I'll say "On the Home tab's Draw panel" to refer to the Draw panel on the Home tab of the Ribbon.

If you see a triangle next to the title on the Ribbon panel title bar, you can expand the panel to reveal more tools. To do this, click the panel title bar (Figure 1.9). The panel will expand downward. Once you click in the drawing area, the panel returns to its normal view. If you want to lock the expanded panel so that it stays open, click the pushpin icon on the left side of the expanded panel's title bar.

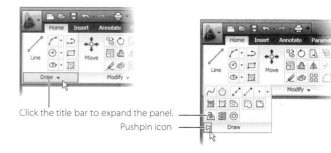

Click the title bar to expand the panel.

Pushpin icon

Figure 1.9

Expanding a Ribbon panel

> From now on, when you see the term *expanded panel*, you should expand the Ribbon panel by clicking the panel's title bar.

Figure 1.10

Opening a flyout

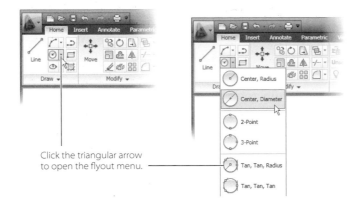

Click the triangular arrow to open the flyout menu.

You might also notice that some of the tools have triangular arrows next to them. You can click these arrows to open *flyout* menus that contain options related to the tool with which they are associated. For example, you can click the triangle next to the Circle tool to open a flyout that offers different ways to draw a circle (Figure 1.10). You'll get a chance to use these features in Chapter 3.

Switching to Floating Ribbon Panels

Return panels to ribbon

Toggle orientation

Figure 1.11

A Ribbon panel in its floating appearance, showing its controls

If you find that you use one particular Ribbon panel a lot, you can "tear off" the panel and have it available as a floating Ribbon panel. To do this, click and drag the panel title bar toward the drawing area. The panel's appearance changes slightly to offer some controls (see Figure 1.11). These controls disappear when you are not pointing inside the panel, but they reappear when you hover over the panel with your cursor.

Tooltips appear when you hover over the controls, and they describe what each control does. The Toggle Orientation control is a little misleading because it only controls the display of the title bar.

Using the Application Menu

The AutoCAD Application menu provides a familiar means of finding file- and print-related commands. You can open the Application menu by clicking the AutoCAD icon in the upper-left corner of the AutoCAD window (shown earlier in Figure 1.5).

In the Application menu, you'll see many of the standard Windows menu options, such as Open, Save, Save As, and Print, as well as a few that are specific to AutoCAD. Many of the options show arrowheads that indicate a cascading menu. Open the Application menu, for example, and click the arrowhead to the right of the Export option. You'll see a list of options that are related to exporting AutoCAD drawings.

Figure 1.12

The Recent documents and Open documents tools at the top of the Application menu

Recent documents

Open documents

As mentioned earlier, you can view a list of recently opened drawing or currently opened drawings by clicking either of the two tools at the top of the Application menu (Figure 1.12).

While viewing the drawing list, you can hover your cursor over a drawing name to view a thumbnail of the drawing. You can also click the File View tool above the list to change the list from names to images (Figure 1.13).

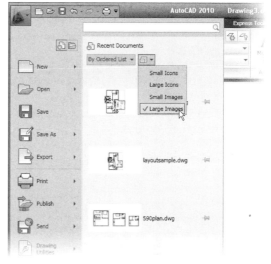

Getting Familiar with the Drawing Area

As you might imagine, the drawing area in the middle of the AutoCAD window is the space where you'll be spending a lot of time. It pays to get a feel for how it behaves early on. As your introduction to the drawing area, try the following exercise:

Figure 1.13

Changing the list from names to Large Images

1. Move the cursor around in the drawing area. As you move the cursor, notice that the coordinate readout in the status bar gives the X and Y coordinates and adds the Z coordinate.

2. Click in the middle of the drawing area. You have just selected a point. Move the cursor, and a rectangle follows. This is a *selection window*; if any objects appear in the drawing area, you can select them for editing. A coordinate display appears at the cursor, showing your coordinates in an X, Y format. Also notice the words *Specify opposite corner* in the Dynamic Input display. This tells you that you have started a selection window and you need to select the opposite corner for the window.

3. Move the cursor a bit in any direction; then click again. Notice that the selection window disappears. Had there been objects within the selection window, they would be selected. This is similar to the way the cursor behaves on the Windows Desktop; however, in Windows, you have to drag the cursor to create a selection window.

4. Try selecting several more points in the drawing area. Notice that as you click, you alternately start and end a selection window.

As you click the drawing area, you might notice that, depending on whether you click to the right or to the left of the preceding point, the selection window displays a different color. If you click from left to right, the selection window appears blue. From right to left, it's green. These colors indicate a different mode of selection, which you'll learn about in Chapter 4.

If you right-click, a context menu appears. Just as with most other Windows applications, a right-click frequently opens a menu that contains options that are *context sensitive*. This means that the contents of the context menu depend on where you right-click as well as on the command that is active at the time of your right-click. You'll learn more about these options as you progress through the book. For now, if you happen to open this menu by accident, press the Esc key to close it.

Finally, as with any window, you can expand the drawing area or contract it into a smaller window by clicking the Restore Down icon in the upper-right corner of the drawing area.

When the drawing area is in the Restore Down position, it appears as a separate window within the AutoCAD window. You can then resize the window to any rectangular shape you need. This is helpful when you have multiple AutoCAD drawing files open. To maximize a drawing to fill the AutoCAD window, double-click the drawing window title bar.

Minimize
Restore Down
Close

Checking the UCS Icon

The UCS icon is the L-shaped icon you see at the lower-left corner of the drawing area (shown earlier in Figure 1.1). It helps you see your orientation at a glance by pointing to the positive X and Y directions. UCS stands for *user coordinate system*. That name is a hint that you can create and use other coordinates besides the default one that exists in new drawings. By default, the X direction is from left to right, and the Y direction is from bottom to top; but with AutoCAD you can alter your view orientation as well as include additional coordinate systems that can be oriented in different directions. The UCS icon is especially helpful when you start to use these other coordinate systems and display modes, but right now, just be aware that it is there to help you get your bearings.

You might notice a small square at the base of the UCS icon. This square tells you that you are in the world coordinate system, which is the base coordinate on which other coordinate systems can be built. You'll learn more about the UCS in Chapter 6.

Using the Command Line

The horizontal window at the bottom of the AutoCAD window is called the *command window*. Besides the drawing area, this is where you can get feedback from AutoCAD. As you work in AutoCAD, the command activity appears in the bottom line of the command window and scrolls upward.

When AutoCAD is waiting for input, you'll see the word Command: at the bottom of the command window. This is the *command prompt*. As you click a point in the drawing area, you'll see the message Specify opposite corner in the command line. Simultaneously, a selection window appears in the drawing area. Click another point without selecting anything; the selection window disappears, and the command prompt returns.

You'll want to pay close attention to the command window as you start using AutoCAD because it tells you what AutoCAD expects you to do. It also lists information when you query AutoCAD for certain types of information, which you'll learn about in later chapters.

In addition to getting feedback from the command window, you'll also see the command prompt at the cursor whenever you have the Dynamic Input display turned on.

The command window is a little like a chat window when you're online. You "chat" with AutoCAD by responding to messages that appear in the command line. When AutoCAD asks for specific data, the command line allows you to enter data using the keyboard. It is also an area that provides information about your drawing when you request it.

"CHATTING" WITH AUTOCAD

AutoCAD communicates its needs to you in messages in the command line. These messages often tell you what to do next or offer options, usually shown in square brackets. Commands often display a series of messages, which you answer to complete the command. If you aren't sure what to do, check the command line for clues.

As an additional aid, you can right-click to display a context menu. If you are in the middle of a command, this menu provides a list of options specifically related to that command. For example, if you right-click before selecting the first point for the Rectangle command, a menu appears, offering the same options that are listed at the command prompt, plus some additional options.

Note that AutoCAD allows you to customize the right mouse button, and many users will set up this button as an Enter key. This is a holdover from the very earliest versions of AutoCAD, and many users still prefer it to the context menu function.

Starting Commands

Working with commands is fairly straightforward, but you have a few options in AutoCAD that you won't find in other Windows programs. You can use tools in the Ribbon to start a command with a simple click and then use the command window to get feedback from AutoCAD. Try the following to see firsthand how this works:

1. Click the Dynamic Input tool in the status bar to turn off Dynamic Input display mode. When it is off, it is gray. You'll start your exploration of commands with this feature turned off so you can get a clear view of your activity. You'll get a chance to try the Dynamic Input feature in later chapters, starting with Chapter 2.

2. Click the Rectangle tool in the Draw panel. Notice that the command line at the bottom of the window now shows the following prompt:

   ```
   Specify first corner point or [Chamfer/Elevation/Fillet/Thickness/Width]:
   ```

   AutoCAD is asking you to select the first corner for the rectangle, and also, in brackets, it is offering a few options that you can take advantage of at this point in the command. Don't worry about those options right now. You'll have an opportunity to learn about command options in Chapter 2.

3. Click a point roughly in the lower-left corner of the drawing area, as shown in Figure 1.14. Now as you move your cursor, you'll see a rectangle follow the cursor with one corner fixed at the position you just selected. You'll also see the following prompt in the command line:

   ```
   Specify other corner point or [Area/Dimensions/Rotation]:
   ```

4. Click another point anywhere in the upper-right region of the drawing area. A rectangle appears (see Figure 1.15). You'll learn more about the different cursor shapes and what they mean later in this chapter.

Figure 1.14

Selecting the first point of a rectangle

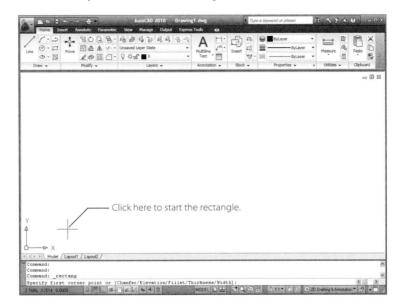

Figure 1.15

Once you've selected the first point of the rectangle, you'll see a rectangle follow the motion of your mouse.

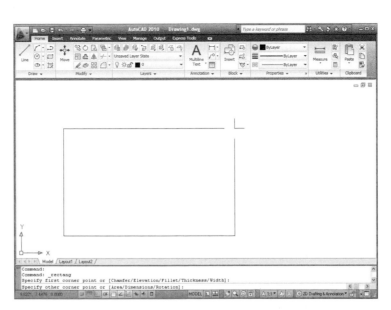

Next, try deleting the rectangle you just drew:

1. Place the cursor on top of the rectangle, but don't do anything yet. Notice that as you pass the cursor over the rectangle, it is highlighted. In a crowded drawing, this highlighting can help you determine exactly what will be selected when you click an object.

2. With the cursor on the rectangle and the rectangle highlighted, click the rectangle. The rectangle is selected, and the Quick Properties dialog box opens. This dialog box gives you access to the properties of the selected object.

3. Close the Quick Properties dialog box by clicking the X in its upper-right corner. You'll see a message box asking whether you want to "turn off the Quick Properties panel for all future selected objects."

4. Click the answer that says "Turn off for all future selected objects." You can easily restore the Quick Properties panel feature at any time by clicking the Quick Properties Panel tool in the status bar.

> You'll learn more about the Quick Properties panel in Chapter 4.

5. The rectangle is still selected, so press the Delete key to delete it. This removes the rectangle from the drawing.

In step 1, AutoCAD shows you exactly what the cursor is pointing to by highlighting objects that will be selected with the next click.

When drawing and erasing the rectangle, you were exposed to the most common processes you need to know about to work in AutoCAD: you selected a command from the menu bar, and then you selected points in the drawing area while following the messages in the command line. Commands from the toolbars work in the same way, as you'll see next.

UNDERSTANDING THE COMMAND-TOOL-OPTION RELATIONSHIP

One of AutoCAD's greatest assets is its ability to adjust to your way of performing tasks. If you prefer using toolbars, you can switch to the AutoCAD Classic workspace, which shows the older style toolbars and menu bar. If you stay with the 2D Drafting & Annotation workspace, the Ribbon offers the most commonly used functions in AutoCAD. Experienced users know how to use the command line and know nearly all the commands by heart.

The AutoCAD commands are really at the heart of its operations. Menu bar options, the Ribbon, and the toolbar buttons are just different ways to invoke AutoCAD commands. When you click a Ribbon tool or a menu option, you are really initiating a command through AutoCAD's menu system, sometimes with predetermined options already selected. In fact, if you watch the command line as you click an Application menu option or Ribbon button, you'll see that the messages in the command line are the same regardless of where you invoked the command.

For this reason, I'll often intermix the terms *tool, option,* and *command,* because at a practical level they are all the same. Just be aware that the Application menu options and Ribbon buttons invoke commands.

Starting a Drawing

What you do to start a new drawing in AutoCAD is a little different from what you do in other programs, so let's create a new file to see how it's done:

1. From the Application menu, choose File → Close to close the current file. When the message box appears asking you to save changes, click No. Notice that the toolbars disappear and that the AutoCAD drawing window appears blank when no drawings are open.

2. From the Quick Access toolbar, click the New tool to open the Select Template dialog box.

3. Select the acad.dwt template file, and then click Open to open a blank drawing window.

4. To give your new file a unique name, choose File → Save As from the Application menu to open the Save Drawing As dialog box.

5. Enter **My First Drawing**. As you type, the name appears in the File Name text box. By default, the file will be saved in the My Documents folder.

6. Click Save. You now have a file called My First Drawing.dwg, located in the My Documents folder. Of course, your drawing doesn't contain anything yet. You'll take care of that next.

The acad.dwt template file you selected in step 3 is really just an AutoCAD drawing file that has been set up with standard settings. AutoCAD uses those settings to create a new file. As you saw in the Select Template dialog box, you can choose from several such templates.

The new file you just created shows a drawing area roughly 31 units wide by 13 units high. The units can be inches, meters, or millimeters. You determine what the units are equivalent to through the Drawing Units dialog box, which you will learn about in Chapter 2.

The drawing area you're presented with initially is your workspace, although you're not limited to the 75 by 45–unit area in any way. No visual clues indicate the size of the area, so to check the area size for yourself, move the crosshair cursor to the upper-right corner of the screen, and observe the value in the coordinate readout in the lower-left corner of the AutoCAD window. This is the standard AutoCAD default drawing area for using the acad.dwt drawing template for new drawings.

> The coordinate readout won't show exactly 75 units by 45 units, because the proportions of your drawing area are not likely to be exactly 7.5 by 4.5. Factors such as the size and resolution of your display and the shape of the AutoCAD window affect the dimensions of the drawing area.

SWITCHING BETWEEN OPEN DRAWINGS AND THE MODEL AND LAYOUT VIEWS

As with most Windows programs, you can have several drawings open at one time. AutoCAD offers the Quick View Drawings tool in the status bar, with which you can easily navigate among multiple drawings.

When you click the Quick View Drawings tool, you will see a row of drawing preview panels just above the status bar. These panels show the contents of the currently open drawings.

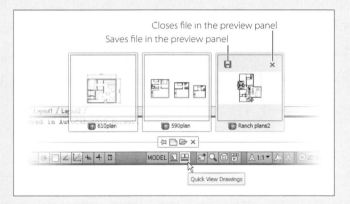

You can then click a preview panel of a drawing you want to switch to; the selected drawing appears in the drawing area. Click in the drawing area to make that drawing current.

When you hover over a preview panel with your cursor, additional preview panels appear, showing you the model and layout views of the drawing to which you are pointing.

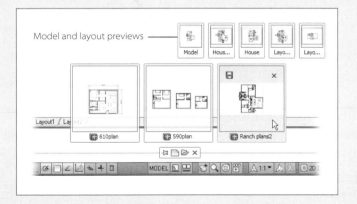

You can then click in a model or layout preview to have it display in the drawing area. Click in the drawing area to make the selected view the current one.

Next, try drawing a couple of objects just to get comfortable with drawing in AutoCAD. In the following exercise, you'll draw a rectangle; then you'll add a circle:

1. Click the Rectangle tool in the Draw panel. Remember that you can use the tooltips to help you locate a tool. You can also type **Rec⏎**.

2. Click a point in the lower left of the drawing area, as shown in Figure 1.16. Don't worry about the exact location. You're just practicing right now. After clicking, you'll see that one corner of the rectangle follows the cursor.

3. Click a point in the upper right of the drawing area, as shown in Figure 1.16. Again, it's not important if you don't pick the exact location. The rectangle is now in place.

Figure 1.16

Drawing a circle

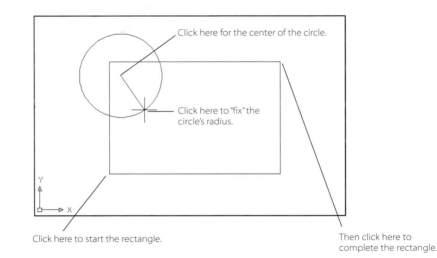

Click here for the center of the circle.

Click here to "fix" the circle's radius.

Click here to start the rectangle.

Then click here to complete the rectangle.

Now add a circle to the drawing:

1. Click the Circle tool in the Draw panel.

2. Click the location shown in Figure 1.16 to place the center of the circle. Now as you move the cursor, a circle appears whose radius follows the location of the cursor.

3. Click another point as shown in Figure 1.16 to "fix" the circle's radius in place. If you prefer, you can enter an exact radius value for a circle instead of clicking another point to "fix" the circle radius.

You now have a circle and a rectangle. As you can see, you create objects by placing key points of their geometry within the drawing area. For the rectangle, it was two corners; for the circle, it was the center and a location on the perimeter.

Once you've placed objects in the drawing, you can use a variety of tools to edit them. In later chapters, you'll learn more about those editing tools. In the following section, you'll learn how to get around in your drawing.

WHEN YOU NEED TO UNDO

The AutoCAD User Group International (AUGI) has conducted a survey to identify the most commonly used features in AutoCAD. The group found that the Undo feature and the Esc key were at the top of the list. Everyone makes mistakes, and it would be impossible to get any work done if it weren't for these two features. But Undo and the Esc key are just two of a set of features you can use to reverse something you have done. If you find you've done something unintentionally, you can use the following options to get out of trouble:

Backspace If you make a typing error, press the Backspace key to back up to your error, and then reenter your command or response.

Esc When you need to exit a command or a dialog box quickly, without making changes, just press the Esc key in the upper-left corner of your keyboard.

Undo If you accidentally change something in the drawing and want to reverse that change, click the Undo tool (the left-pointing curved arrow) in the Quick Access toolbar. You can also enter **U↵** at the command prompt. Each time you do this, AutoCAD undoes one operation at a time, in reverse order. The last command performed is undone first, then the next-to-last command, and so on. The prompt displays the name of the command being undone, and the drawing reverts to its state before that command. If you need, you can undo everything back to the beginning of an editing session.

Redo If you accidentally undo one too many commands, you can redo the last undone command by clicking the Redo tool (the right-pointing curved arrow) on the Quick Access toolbar. Or enter **Redo↵**.

Panning and Zooming to Adjust Your View

One of the greatest features of AutoCAD is its ability to draw accurately through a wide range of scales. For example, you can draw a football field, zoom into a blade of grass, and draw its cell structure. With such a broad range of views to work with, you need to be familiar with AutoCAD's view features. The Zoom and Pan commands are the most frequently used view features, so you'll want to become familiar with them right away.

If you have a typical mouse with a scroll wheel, you can use the wheel to zoom in and out of your drawing view. You can also use it to pan across your drawing. To zoom, scroll the wheel. To pan, click and drag the scroll wheel. You can obtain just about any view you need by using this method. You'll also want to know about several other view-related tools.

If you have a mouse that uses special drivers, you might not be able to use the wheel to control pans and zooms.

Try the following exercise to see how the Zoom tool works:

1. Click the magnifying glass icon in the View tab's Navigate panel to open the Zoom flyout.

2. Select Window from the Zoom flyout (Figure 1.17).

3. Click the first point indicated in Figure 1.18. You don't have to be too accurate.

4. Click the second point indicated in Figure 1.18. The area you selected expands to fill the drawing area. Notice that the transition to the zoomed view is smooth. This helps you keep track of exactly where in the drawing the zoom occurs.

5. Right-click and select Pan. Notice that the cursor changes to a hand icon.

6. Click and drag the cursor in the drawing area. Notice how the view moves as you drag the cursor.

7. Press Esc to exit the Pan command. You can also right-click and choose Exit from the context menu.

8. Finally, to get your original view of the overall drawing, open the Zoom flyout again as you did in step 1 and select Previous.

Figure 1.17

The Window tool on the Zoom flyout

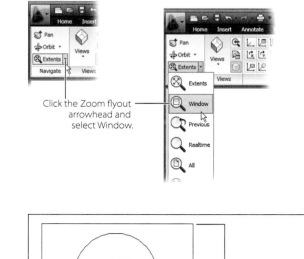

Click the Zoom flyout arrowhead and select Window.

Figure 1.18

Selecting a Zoom window

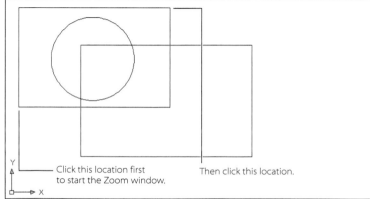

Click this location first to start the Zoom window.

Then click this location.

Several other Zoom- and Pan-related commands exist, but those you've just tried are the ones you'll use 90 percent of the time. You can try the other Zoom and Pan options that you saw in the magnifying glass icon flyout in the Utilities panel. You'll also find options in the Zoom command-line options list:

```
[All/Center/Dynamic/Extents/Previous/Scale/Window/Object] <real time>:
```

Here is a list of the options you'll find in the magnifying glass icon flyout:

Extents This displays a view that encompasses all the objects in your drawing. This option ignores the limits of your drawing.

Previous This displays the previous view, just as Undo does for the Zoom command.

Realtime This is the default Zoom option. It displays a magnifying glass cursor. With this option, you can click and drag up or down to change your magnification in real time. You can right-click to access the other Zoom options, including Exit and Cancel.

All This displays the area of your drawing defined by the drawing limits plus any part of your drawing that falls outside the limits.

Dynamic This changes the display to an overall view. A rectangle also appears, which lets you select an area to which to zoom in. To change the size of the rectangle, click the rectangle. You can adjust the size of the rectangle and thus change the size of the zoom area. Click again to fix the rectangle size. Right-click, and choose Enter to zoom in to the selected area.

Scale This lets you zoom in or out by a specific value. It allows you to enter a specific view scale.

Center This allows you to center a location on the screen.

Object This lets you select a view area based on the area occupied by an object. For example, if you want to zoom in so that a particular object fills the display area, use this option.

In This is the same as using the Scale option and entering **2x** to magnify your view two times.

Out This is the same as using the Scale option and entering **0.5x** to view twice the current view area.

> You can also start a zoom or pan by clicking the magnifying glass icon or hand icon in the status bar, or right-click and select Zoom or Pan at any time. You can right-click in the middle of a zoom to switch to a pan, and vice versa.

You've just about completed your first look at AutoCAD. You'll want to know about just a couple of other features. In the next section, I'll introduce a display feature in AutoCAD that helps you set up your drawing for printing.

ACCURATE PANNING

Realtime Pan is a great tool for quickly getting around in a drawing, but sometimes you need to pan in an exact distance and direction. A version of the Pan command lets you "nudge" your view to an accurate distance.

Type **-pan**↵ and you'll see the following prompt:

```
Specify base point or displacement:
```

This is the prompt you'll see for the Move or Copy command, though in this case you're not affecting the objects in your drawing. When you select a point at this prompt, you'll see a rubber-banding line in conjunction with the next prompt:

```
Specify second point:
```

The rubber-banding line indicates the direction and distance of your pan. As with any other command that displays a rubber-banding line, you can select points to indicate distance and direction, or you can enter coordinates. This enables you to specify exact distances and directions to pan your view.

Understanding the Layout View

Aside from the command prompt, you've probably noticed that AutoCAD behaves like most other Windows programs. But in one of its features AutoCAD is a little different from other Windows graphics programs. Specifically, at the bottom of the AutoCAD window, you'll see some tabs.

The Model tab is currently active, telling you that you are in what is called *model space*. If you have followed the exercises in this chapter, you've been working in model space all along. Model space is the display you'll use to do most of your drawing. It's like your main workspace.

Clicking the Layout1 tab opens a view that is like a page preview with the added advantage of enabling you to draw within the preview. This preview is called a *paper space layout*. Besides previewing your drawing, Layout1 also gives you control over the printed scale. You can have multiple paper space layouts for different printed versions of your drawing. For example, you can have one layout for an 8½ by 11–inch sheet and another layout for an 11 by 17–inch sheet. Or, if you use multiple printers, you can have a layout set up for each printer.

The terms *paper space* and *layout* are often used interchangeably, which can cause a lot of confusion to new users. One way to think of these two terms is to say that "paper space is where you lay out your drawing." It's called *paper space* because it is where your drawing is translated into the paper shape, size, and layout of your drawing before you actually commit the drawing to paper.

Another way to look at paper space layouts is to think of them as a drawing mock-up area. Using a paper space layout, you can set up multiple views of the drawing you create in model space. You can also add a title to your drawing and include borders or other graphic design features.

Since paper space layouts are labeled with the "layout" prefix, as in Layout1, I'll just use the term *layout* in this book.

Try the following exercise to see firsthand how layouts work:

1. Click the Layout1 tab at the bottom of the drawing area.

   The drawing area changes to show your drawing, plus some additional display elements, as shown in Figure 1.19. The layout view shows how your drawing will look when it is printed.

2. Move the cursor over the rectangle that immediately surrounds the rectangle and circle drawing that you created earlier in the chapter.

3. Click the highlighted rectangle, and then press the Delete key. Your drawing disappears.

4. Click the Model tab to return to model space. You'll see that the objects you drew are still there.

5. Click the Undo tool in the Quick Access toolbar twice to return to the Layout1 view and undo your deletion of the outer rectangle. The view of the rectangle and the circle returns.

6. Click the Model tab to return to the original drawing area.

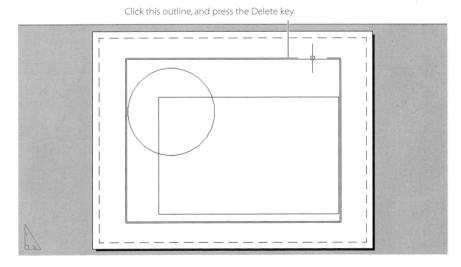

Click this outline, and press the Delete key.

Figure 1.19

Your drawing as it appears in one of the layout views

In step 3, your entire drawing disappeared when you deleted the outer rectangle. This is because that rectangle is really a *viewport* into the drawing you created in model space. When you are in a layout view, a viewport acts like a window into your drawing. By default, AutoCAD creates a single viewport to show your drawing, but you can have multiple viewports of various sizes, each displaying different parts of your drawing. When you deleted that viewport, you essentially closed your view into your drawing in the model space, so your rectangle and circle disappeared from view. They didn't really go anywhere—it's just that your view of them was deleted.

You might have also noticed that a layout displays a white area over a gray background. This white area represents the area of the paper onto which your drawing will be printed.

The white area also shows a dashed line close to its edge. This dashed line represents the printable area of your paper. The current default printer connected to your computer determines both the paper area and the dashed line.

If you have a printer that accepts paper of different sizes, you can select a different sheet size, and the new sheet size will be reflected in the white area shown in the layout. You'll learn how to control sheet sizes and layouts in Chapter 12.

As you might guess, you use the layout to lay out your drawing for printing. You can print from the model space if you want, but you have much more control over your printer output from a layout.

TURNING OFF THE LAYOUT TABS

AutoCAD can be set up to hide the model and layout tabs at the bottom of the drawing area. To hide the tabs, right-click any tab, and select Hide Layout and Model Tabs. With the tabs hidden, you can still switch from model space to a layout by clicking the Model or Layout1 tools that appear in the status bar.

Model   Layout1

If you have multiple layouts, you can use the Quick View Layouts tool just to the right of the Layout1 tool in the status bar to switch between layouts.

Quick View Layouts tool

To turn the tabs back on, right-click the Model or Layout1 tool, and then select Display Layout and Model Tabs. The tabs will appear below the drawing area.

For more on the Quick View Layouts tool, see "Switching Between Layouts" in Chapter 12.

Understanding How Command Options Work

Nearly every AutoCAD command offers a set of options shown at the command-line prompt. These options let you alter the behavior of a command to suit your current drawing. To see how command options work, and to get a feel for the drawing process in general, in this exercise you'll draw an arc and then place it exactly in the inside corner of the rectangle:

1. Click the Arc tool in the Draw panel.

   The prompt Specify start point of arc or [Center]: appears, and the cursor changes to a crosshair cursor.

2. If you examine this Specify start point of arc or [Center]: prompt, you'll see that the start point contains two options. The default option is stated in the main part of the prompt: Specify start point. If other options are available, they appear within brackets, as in the [Center] option that appears in the Arc tool's command prompt. This [Center] option tells you that you can also start your arc by selecting a center point instead of a start point. If multiple options are available, they appear within the brackets and are separated by slashes (/). The default is the option AutoCAD assumes you intend to use unless you tell it otherwise.

3. Enter **C↵** to select the Center option. The prompt Specify center point of arc: appears. Notice that you had to enter only the C and not the entire word *Center*.

   When you see a set of options in the command line, note their capitalization. If you choose to respond to prompts by using the keyboard, these capitalized letters are all you need to enter to select that option. In some cases, the first two letters are capitalized to differentiate two options that begin with the same letter, such as LAyer and LType.

4. Now select a point for the center of the arc, as shown in Figure 1.20. The prompt Specify start point of arc: appears. You'll also see a rubber-banding line from the center point you just selected to your cursor.

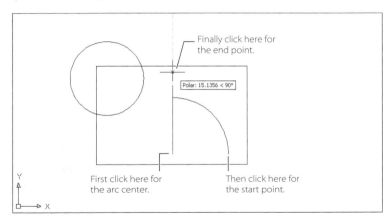

Figure 1.20

Using the Arc command

If you point directly to the right, you'll see that the rubber-banding line snaps to an exact horizontal orientation, and you'll see a tooltip appear at the cursor. This is a feature called *polar tracking vector*, and it helps you draw in exact horizontal and vertical directions, much like a T square and a triangle. The tooltip shows your cursor's location relative to the center point you just selected. It displays this information in what is known as a *polar coordinate*. You can learn more about polar coordinates in Chapter 2.

5. With the rubber-banding line pointing to the right, click to select a point, as shown earlier in Figure 1.20. The prompt Specify end point of arc or [Angle/chord Length]: appears.

6. Move the mouse, and a temporary arc appears, originating from the start point of the arc that you just selected and rotating about the center of the arc.

   As the prompt indicates, you now have three options. You can enter an angle, a chord length, or the endpoint of the arc. The prompt default, to specify the endpoint of the arc, lets you select the arc's endpoint. The cursor is in Point Selection mode, telling you it is waiting for point input. To select this default option, you need only select a point on the screen indicating where you want the endpoint.

7. Move the cursor so it points vertically from the center of the arc. You'll see the polar tracking vector snap to a vertical position, as shown in Figure 1.20.

8. Click any location with the polar tracking vector in the vertical position. The arc is now fixed in place.

As you can see, AutoCAD has a distinct structure in its prompt messages. You first issue a command, which in turn presents options in the form of a prompt. Depending on the option you select, you get another set of options, or you are prompted to take some action, such as selecting a point, selecting objects, or entering a value. The prompts offer a great deal of help by "prompting" you to take an action.

Getting Help

AutoCAD provides a good set of help options that can answer most of the questions you might have while working on a drawing. If you're stuck with an AutoCAD problem, give the AutoCAD help options a try.

To get more familiar with the AutoCAD Help window, try the following:

1. Press F1 to open the AutoCAD 2010 Help window.

2. Click the Contents tab, which contains a table of contents. The other two tabs, Index and Search, provide assistance in finding specific topics (Figure 1.21).

3. Scan down the screen until you see the topic Command Reference, and double-click it. Both panels of the Help window change to show more topics.

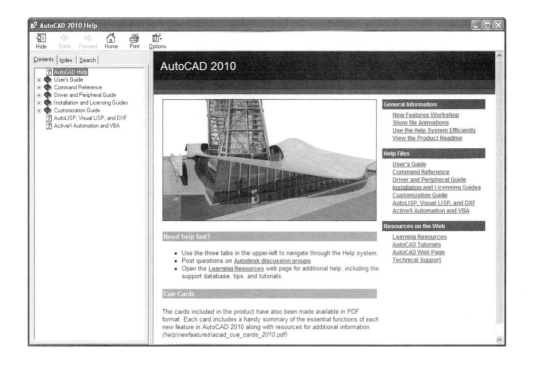

Figure 1.21

The AutoCAD 2010 Help window

4. Expand the Commands list, and then click the item labeled *C* near the top of the command listing. The panel to the right changes to display a list of command names that start with the letter *C*.

5. Look down the list, and click Copy. A description of the Copy command appears.

You also have the Concept, Procedure, and Quick Reference tabs along the top of the panel on the right. These options provide more detailed information about how to use the selected item. If you want to back up through the steps you have just taken, click the Back button on the toolbar.

Using the Search Tab

If you're a beginning AutoCAD user looking for help, the Help window's table of contents might not be as useful as it could be. To use it, you have to know a little about what you want to find. Sometimes it's quicker to use the Search feature of the Help window:

1. Click the Search tab in the left panel. If this is the first time you've selected the Search tab, you might see a message telling you that AutoCAD is setting up an index for searches.

2. Enter **Change** in the text box at the top of the Search tab, and then click Ask or press ↵. The list box displays all the items in the Help system that contain the word *Change*.

In this example, the list that is returned is quite large. You can use Boolean AND, OR, NEAR, and NOT in conjunction with other keywords to help filter your searches. Once you've found the topic you're looking for, select it from the Select Topic list, and then click the Display button to display the topic information.

The Index tab lets you find specific topics in the AutoCAD Help system by entering a word in a list box.

Using Context-Sensitive Help

AutoCAD also provides context-sensitive help to give you information about the command you are using. To see how this works, try the following:

1. Close or minimize the Help window to return to the AutoCAD window.

2. Click the Move tool in the Modify panel to start the Move command.

3. Press F1 or choose Help from the menu bar to open the Help window. A description of the Move command appears in the panel on the right (Figure 1.22).

4. Click the Close button, or press the Esc key.

5. Press the Esc key to exit the Move command.

If you gain some confidence with AutoCAD's Help window, you can go far in helping yourself learn basic AutoCAD commands. But if you really get stuck, this book will help you get past your barriers.

Figure 1.22

The Help window showing information on the Move command

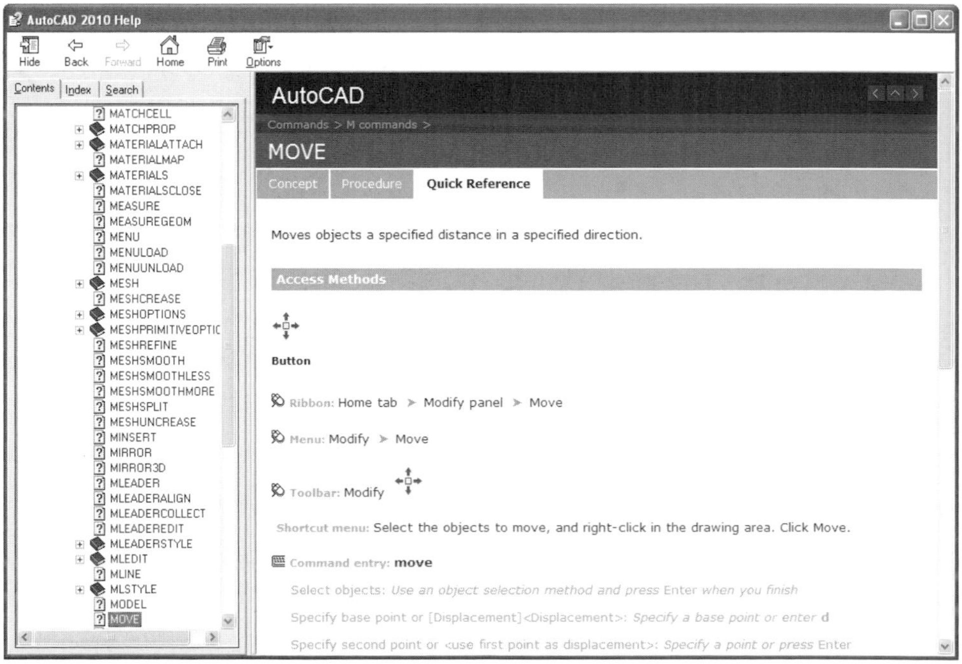

![Screenshot of the AutoCAD 2010 Help window showing the MOVE command Quick Reference, with the Contents tree on the left and command details on the right]

Staying Informed with the InfoCenter

Nearly every major Windows program is somehow linked to the Internet to offer the latest news and updates for software. AutoCAD provides the InfoCenter, which appears as a bar in the upper-right corner of the AutoCAD window.

The InfoCenter provides a way to stay informed about the latest software updates and support issues for AutoCAD. Enter a keyword or phrase in the input box and then click the binoculars icon to get a list of sources for your query.

You can then select a topic from the list to find the information you need. If you click the InfoCenter's Communication Center tool, the one that looks like a satellite dish, you'll open a list of general topics available.

The list is divided into main topics shown as gray title bars. You can click the arrow to the right of a title bar to close or open a topic.

Finding Additional Sources of Help

The Help window and the InfoCenter are the main source for reference material, but you can also find answers to your questions through the other options in the Help menu. To open the Help menu, click the arrowhead to the right of the question mark icon in the InfoCenter.

Here is a brief description of the other Help menu options:

Info Palette (AutoCAD 2010 LT only) The Info palette is a pop-up window that offers immediate help with the command you are using. It's helpful for first-time users. When you issue a command with the Info palette open, you will see an option or a list of options in the palette. These options offer a brief tutorial or other information about the current command.

New Features Workshop This option provides descriptions and tutorials focused on the new features found in AutoCAD 2010. You can update this unique support tool through the Autodesk website.

Additional Resources This options provides online help from Autodesk's website, including a support knowledge base, online training resources, and the Developer Center. There is also a link to the Autodesk User Group International website.

Send Feedback Click here to open a web page that allows you to send comments about AutoCAD directly to Autodesk.

Customer Involvement Program This program tracks your use of AutoCAD and its interaction with your computer system. This information is used to help determine future changes to AutoCAD. You can participate anonymously or supply contact information.

About This options provides information about the version of AutoCAD you are using.

Summary

AutoCAD is a rare example of a program that has successfully made the transition from a text-based DOS program to a fully Windows-compliant one. The trick to using AutoCAD is in learning how to use it to input exact distances and directions. Once you've mastered the input methods AutoCAD offers, you're well on your way to producing accurate drawings. If you find you have questions along the way, this book will provide the right amount of help, but don't forget the AutoCAD Help system. It is full of great information and can be a real lifesaver.

That does it for your introduction to AutoCAD. You might want to practice what you've learned thus far. When you're ready to get down to some serious drawing, check out the next chapter. There you'll be introduced to the drawing tools you'll need to produce accurate drawings.

CHAPTER 2

Understanding the Drafting Tools

A lot of programs let you draw lines, circles, and arcs, but AutoCAD lets you draw with a level of precision that goes way beyond most other drawing programs. To take advantage of that precision, however, you need to know how to use the drafting tools.

This chapter covers the tools that allow you to place objects exactly where you want them. You'll start by learning about the AutoCAD coordinate system, which is fundamental to your understanding of precision in AutoCAD. You'll then learn how to set up a drawing and how AutoCAD uses units of measure. The last half of this chapter covers the tools that let you select points in your drawing accurately. You'll learn how to select exact endpoints or midpoints of lines, for example, and how to align one object with another.

This chapter includes the following topics:

- **Understanding the AutoCAD coordinate system**

- **Setting up a drawing**

- **Using a digital T square and triangle**

- **Getting a visual reference with the Grid mode**

- **Snapping to the grid or other regular intervals**

- **Changing the grid and snap settings**

- **Selecting exact locations on objects**

- **Aligning objects using object snap tracking and tracking points**

- **Using the temporary tracking point feature**

Understanding the AutoCAD Coordinate System

Before you get too far into your use of AutoCAD, you'll want to know a little about its coordinate system. Coordinates are important because they allow you to specify exact locations in your drawing. You'll use coordinates frequently to set the size and location of objects, to move and copy objects, and to align objects relative to each other.

AutoCAD uses a standard XY Cartesian coordinate notation with a horizontal x-axis and a vertical y-axis (see Figure 2.1).

In a new drawing, AutoCAD shows the positive X and Y range of coordinates with the 0,0 coordinate, or *origin*, placed in the lower-left corner of the drawing area. The origin is an important coordinate location because you can use it as a reference for multiple drawings. For example, you can use the origin in a set of house plans to coordinate locations among a site plan drawing, a landscape drawing, and a floor plan.

Many AutoCAD commands ask you to choose a location by entering a point. For example, if you start the Line command, you'll see the following prompt:

```
Specify first point:
```

You can specify exact coordinates by entering the X and Y coordinates separated by a comma. You give the X coordinate first and then the Y coordinate. For example, you enter a location that is 5 units in the X direction and 4 units in the Y direction as 5,4 (shown in Figure 2.1). If you want to include the Z coordinate for a 3D location, you include it at the end of the list with a comma, as in 5,4,2; in this case, 2 is the Z coordinate. When you enter coordinates in this way, you are said to be using *absolute* coordinates, since these are exact locations in the overall coordinate system.

Figure 2.1

AutoCAD's coordinate system

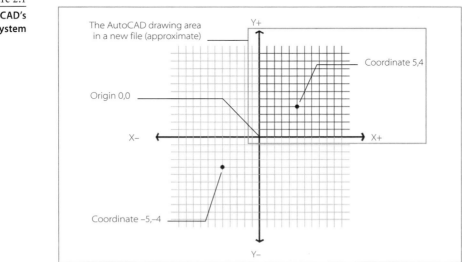

But for the most part, you won't be entering absolute coordinates to specify locations in a drawing. Usually, you'll want to specify locations that are relative to a point you select in the drawing area. You can specify a distance and direction from a selected point by using *relative* coordinates.

You specify relative coordinates in the same way you specify absolute coordinates, with one major exception—you must precede the coordinate with the @ sign. The @ sign means "from the last point selected." For example, suppose you want to draw a horizontal line 3 units long in a random location in the drawing. You can start the Line command and then at this prompt

```
Specify first point:
```

you can select a point anywhere on the screen by clicking the drawing area. The next prompt asks for the next point of the line:

```
Specify next point or [Undo]:
```

At this point, you enter **@3,0**. This tells AutoCAD to draw a line that is 3 units in the X coordinate and 0 units in the Y coordinate from the last point selected.

Another way to specify distance and direction is to use *polar* coordinates. With polar coordinates, you specify a distance and an angle. For example, if you want to specify a point that is 40 units from another point and at a 45° angle, you enter **@40<45**. Here, the @ sign tells AutoCAD that you want to select a point relative to the last point selected, the 40 is the distance, and the <45 is the angle, as shown in Figure 2.2.

Figure 2.2

Drawing a line at a 45° angle

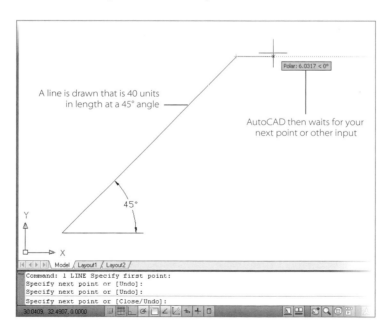

A line is drawn that is 40 units in length at a 45° angle

AutoCAD then waits for your next point or other input

You won't have to use coordinates for everything you draw. You can accurately select locations on objects using *object snaps*, or *osnaps* for short. Osnaps are a way of selecting exact locations on existing objects in a drawing, such as the endpoint or midpoint of a line or the intersection of a line and a circle. See "Setting Up Osnap Locations" later in this chapter for more about osnaps.

Experimenting with Coordinates Using Lines

The preceding explanation of AutoCAD's coordinate system, though brief, can serve as a reference as you work with AutoCAD. If you need some additional practice, try the following to see firsthand how to use the coordinate methods. You'll use the Line command as a practice tool. These exercises will also help you become more familiar with the way AutoCAD works in general; so if you are totally new to AutoCAD, it is a good idea to do the exercises in this section.

> Throughout the rest of the book, I'll be asking you to select tools from a Ribbon panel. Instead of showing you the entire panel, I'll show the tool as a margin icon next to the step that uses the tool, as shown in step 3 of the following exercise. If you need to refresh your memory of the locations of the Ribbon panels, see Figure 1.4 in the preceding chapter.

To begin a line, follow these steps:

1. Start AutoCAD, and from the Quick Access toolbar, select New.

2. In the Select Template dialog box, select the acad.dwt template. Make sure you are in the 2D Drafting & Annotation workspace.

3. Make sure the Dynamic Input option is off by clicking the Dynamic Input tool in the status bar. It should appear with a gray background. You'll get a chance to use this feature later.

4. Click the Line tool on the Home tab's Draw panel, or enter **L↵** to start the Line command. AutoCAD responds in two ways. First, in the command line, you'll see this message asking you to select a point to begin your line:

        Specify first point:

    The cursor has also changed its appearance; it no longer has a square in the crosshairs. This is a clue telling you to select a point to start a line (see Figure 2.3).

5. Click to select a point on the screen a little to the left of center. As you select the point, AutoCAD changes the prompt to the following:

        Specify next point or [Undo]:

First point   Rubber-banding line

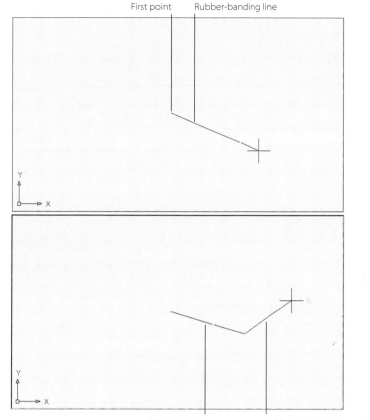

Figure 2.3

**A rubber-
banding line**

Line segment   Rubber-banding line

Now as you move the cursor, notice a line with one end fixed on the point you just selected and the other end following the cursor (see the top image in Figure 2.3). This action is called *rubber-banding*.

If you move the cursor to a location directly to the left or right of the point you clicked, you'll see a dotted horizontal line, along with a message at the cursor. This action also occurs when you point directly up or down. In fact, your cursor will seem to jump to a horizontal or vertical position.

Polar: 6.5192 < 0°

This feature is called *polar tracking*. It helps restrict your line to an exact horizontal or vertical direction as a T square and a triangle would. You can turn polar tracking on or off by clicking the Polar tool in the status bar. If you don't see it, it's probably turned off.

Now continue with the Line command.

6. Click a point below and to the right of the center of the drawing area. The first rubber-banding line is now fixed between the two points you selected, and a second rubber-banding line appears. (See the bottom image in Figure 2.3.)

7. If the line you drew isn't the exact length you want, you can back up during the Line command and change it. To do this, click Undo (the left-pointing curved arrow) in the Quick Access toolbar, or enter **U↵**.

Now the line you drew previously will rubber-band as if you hadn't selected the second point to fix its length. You've just drawn, and then undrawn, a line of an arbitrary length. The Line command is still active. Two items tell you that you are in the middle of a command. If you don't see the word Command at the bottom line of the command window, a command is still active. Also, the cursor will be the plain crosshairs without the box at its intersection.

> From now on, I will refer to the crosshair cursor without the small box as the Point Selection mode of the cursor. If you look ahead to "Interpreting the Cursor Modes and Understanding Prompts," you'll see all the modes of the drawing cursor.

Specifying Exact Distances

Next, you will draw a simple rectangle 10 units wide by 2 units high. By drawing a rectangle to a specific dimension, you'll get a chance to specify exact distances. You can use either relative polar coordinates or Cartesian coordinates to draw in AutoCAD. You'll start by using relative polar coordinates, which is the most common method for distance input.

Specifying Polar Coordinates

To enter the exact distance of 10 units to the right of the last point you selected using polar coordinates, do the following:

1. Click the Line tool in the Home tab's Draw panel again, and then click a point just left of the center of the drawing to start the line (see Figure 2.4).

2. Enter **@10<0**. As you type, the characters appear at the command prompt.

3. Press ↵. A line appears, starting from the first point you selected and ending 10 units to the right of it (see Figure 2.4). You have just entered a relative polar coordinate.

Remember, you specify polar coordinates by starting with the @ sign followed by the distance, a less-than symbol (<), and finally the angle.

> If you are accustomed to a different method for describing directions, you can set AutoCAD to use a vertical direction or downward direction as the 0 angle. See "Using Other Drawing Unit Options" in this chapter.

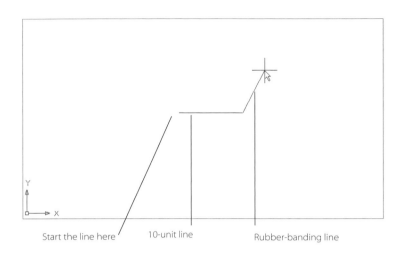

Figure 2.4

Notice that the rubber-banding line now starts from the last point selected. This tells you that you can continue to add line segments.

Start the line here   10-unit line   Rubber-banding line

Angles are given based on the system shown in Figure 2.5, in which 0° is a horizontal direction from left to right, 90° is straight up, 180° is horizontal from right to left, and so on. You can specify degrees, minutes, and seconds of arc if you want to be that exact.

Figure 2.5

AutoCAD's default system for specifying angles

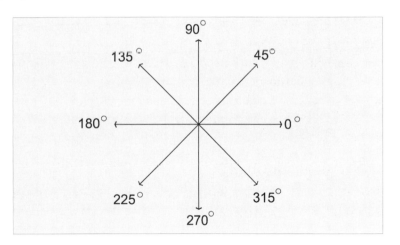

Specifying Relative Cartesian Coordinates

For the second line segment, let's try the Cartesian method for specifying exact distances. Follow these steps:

1. Enter **@0,2↵**. A line appears above the endpoint of the last line.

   As in the polar coordinate method, @ tells AutoCAD that the distance you specify is from the last point selected. But, in this step, you're giving the distance in X and Y values. You give the X distance, 0, first, followed by a comma, and then the Y distance, 2. This is how to specify distances in relative Cartesian coordinates.

2. Enter **@-10,0↵**. The result is a drawing that looks like Figure 2.6.

    The distance you entered in this step was also in X,Y values, but here you used a negative value to specify the X distance. Positive values in the Cartesian coordinate system are from left to right and from bottom to top (see Figure 2.7). (You might remember this from your high-school geometry class!) If you want to draw a line from right to left, you must designate a negative value.

3. Enter **C↵**. This *C* stands for the Close option of the Line command. It closes a sequence of line segments. AutoCAD draws a line connecting the first and last points of a sequence of lines (see Figure 2.8), and the Line command terminates.

Figure 2.6

These three sides of the rectangle were drawn using the Line tool. You can specify points using either relative Cartesian or polar coordinates.

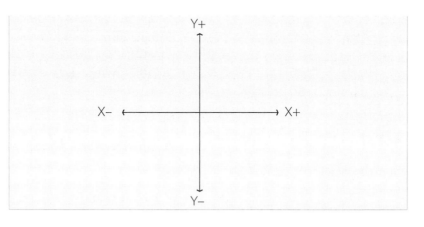

Figure 2.7

Positive and negative Cartesian coordinate directions

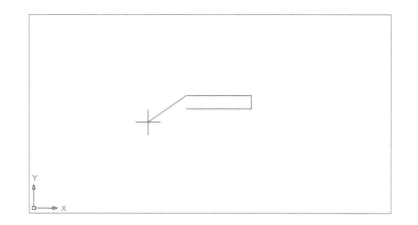

Figure 2.8

The finished rectangle

To finish drawing a series of lines without closing them, you can press Esc, ↵, or the spacebar.

You can also use these methods when you need to specify distances when moving or copying objects or anytime you need to specify a distance and direction.

Using the Direct Distance Method for Quick Relative Coordinates

A third way to enter distances is to simply point in a direction with a rubber-banding line and then enter the distance from the keyboard. For example, to draw a line 5 units long from left to right, click the Line tool on the Draw panel, click a start point, and then move the cursor so that the rubber-banding line points to the right at some arbitrary distance. While holding the cursor in the direction you want, enter **5**↵. The rubber-banding line becomes a fixed line 5 units long.

Using this method, called the *direct distance method*, along with polar tracking, can be a fast way to draw objects of specific lengths. Use the standard Cartesian or polar coordinate methods when you need to enter exact distances at angles other than those that are exactly horizontal or vertical.

A slight variation on the direct distance method is to first enter an angle, such as **<30**↵, and then point in the direction you want and enter the distance.

Using the Dynamic Input Option

Many users find it bothersome to have to look at the command window while drawing and entering data. AutoCAD provides the Dynamic Input option, which offers a kind of "heads-up" display for the command window. Dynamic Input displays the command window prompts at the cursor so that you don't have to look down to see them. It also offers yet another method for entering distances and directions. Try the following exercise to see how Dynamic Input works:

1. Click the Dynamic Input tool in the status bar to turn on Dynamic Input. The tool should have a blue background, telling you it is turned on. Make sure the Polar Tracking tool is also turned on.

2. Click the Line tool in the Draw panel. Now as you move the cursor, you'll see the `Specify first point:` prompt at the cursor. You'll also see the coordinate readout, as shown in Figure 2.9.

3. Click a point below the left corner of the rectangle you just drew. Now as you move the cursor, you'll see the actual dimension of the rubber-banding line as well as its angle near the cursor. You'll also see the `Specify next point or` prompt at the cursor, and the length dimension is highlighted, as shown in Figure 2.10.

Figure 2.9

The prompt and coordinate readout

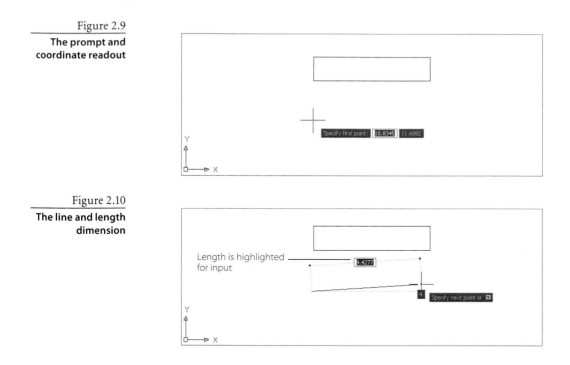

Figure 2.10

The line and length dimension

Length is highlighted for input

4. The length dimension being highlighted tells you that you can enter a value for that dimension. Enter **10**, and then press the Tab key. As you enter 10, it appears in the horizontal dimension. Once you press the Tab key, the line remains fixed at a length of 10 units, while the angle continues to follow the cursor, as shown in Figure 2.11.

5. Notice that the angle value is now highlighted. Enter **0**↵ to fix the angle at 0°. The line is now fixed in place, and the next line segment is ready to be entered.

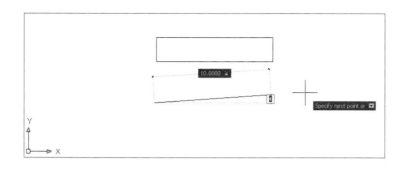

For the next line segment, try entering the angle first:

1. Press the Tab key. Notice that the angle value is now highlighted without affecting the length dimension.

2. Make sure the cursor is somewhere above the previous line; then enter **90** and press the Tab key. The angle is fixed at 90°, but the length is still variable. After you press the Tab key, the length dimension is highlighted, as shown in Figure 2.12.

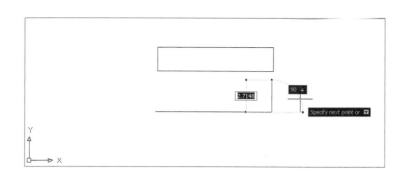

Figure 2.12

The length of the next line segment is highlighted.

3. Enter **2↵** for the length. Now you have a vertical line segment 2 units long.

   Next, try entering a Cartesian coordinate.

4. The length value is now highlighted again, ready for another line segment. Enter **−10,0↵**. A line segment is drawn from right to left. Notice that you didn't have to include the @ sign. With Dynamic Input turned on, AutoCAD automatically assumes you want to specify the object's dimension rather than a coordinate in the overall coordinate system. This applies only to points you enter after the initial point you select to start the object. If you prefer, for consistency, you can still use the @ sign while entering relative coordinates with the Dynamic Input display.

5. Enter **C↵** to close the set of lines.

6. Turn off the Dynamic Input tool by clicking the tool in the status bar.

As you worked through the exercise, you might have noticed a little down-pointing arrow in the command line at the cursor. This tells you that you can press the down arrow key to access command options. The options are the same as those inside the square brackets in the command line.

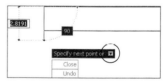

The Dynamic Input tool offers yet another method for drawing and editing objects. As you can see from this example, you can enter a value for an object's dimension and then use the Tab key to move to the next value displayed by the cursor. If you prefer, you can use the Tab key to move to a different value from the currently highlighted value without entering anything, or you can just enter distances in the usual way, using Cartesian or polar coordinates.

Other commands, such as Rectangle and Circle, offer different dimension values that are more appropriate to the object being drawn, but the process is still the same: enter a value for the highlighted dimension by using the cursor, and then use the Tab key to move to the next dimension value. If you want to enter relative Cartesian or polar coordinates, you don't have to include the @ sign, though you can if you want to for consistency. You can also use the direct distance method mentioned earlier, with the added benefit of using the angle readout of the Dynamic Input display. Use the Dynamic Input display's angle readout to point the rubber-banding line at the desired angle, and then enter the length you want, followed by ↵. AutoCAD will draw the line at the length you specify and at the indicated angle.

If you want to enter an absolute coordinate from the Dynamic Input display, use a number sign (#) in place of the @ sign.

Now that you have some general practice, you're ready to set up an actual drawing.

For the rest of the book, unless I'm specifically discussing the Dynamic Input tool, I will assume that it is turned off. Although it is a great tool, it can create some confusion for new users and can create some visual clutter in some of the exercises and examples. You might also be receiving help from others who are not familiar with the Dynamic Input option, which would create further confusion for you as a new user. As you become more accustomed to using AutoCAD, you might want to turn it on and experiment with it on your own. I'll also explain other features of the Dynamic Input option in later chapters.

Setting Up a Drawing

When you first open AutoCAD, you are presented with a default drawing called Drawing1. You can start drawing right away in Drawing1 without having to set up a drawing area or determine the drawing units you want to use. And even if you do set up a drawing for a particular area and type of drawing unit, you can always change them at any time. So as you learn how to set up a drawing, keep in mind that you can alter, expand, and modify the setup at any time.

Selecting the Drawing Units

Though not absolutely essential, it is helpful to set up the drawing units in AutoCAD before you start your drawing. Eventually, you'll want to set up the drawing units, so you might as well make a habit of setting them up first.

You'll most likely use either an imperial or metric measurement system, although you are not limited to those two systems. You can regard the base AutoCAD unit as anything you want as long as you are consistent in your use of that unit.

The most commonly used system in the United States is the imperial system of inches and feet. Since the imperial system has some special requirements, AutoCAD provides additional options when you're using it.

To select a drawing unit, you use the Drawing Units dialog box.

If you want to just start drawing right away without setting up the drawing units, you can assume that the basic unit is the inch. Metric users can decide to use millimeters, centimeters, decimeters, or meters, but whichever you choose to be the basic unit, make sure you stick with it throughout the drawing. You can tell AutoCAD what you want that unit to represent later by using the Drawing Units dialog box.

1. From the Application menu, choose Drawing Utilities → Units to open the Drawing Units dialog box (see Figure 2.13).

2. In the Length group, click the Type drop-down list, and then select the option that best represents the unit of length you will be using in your drawing. (See Table 2.1 for a description of these options.) If you are creating an architectural drawing using imperial units, select the Architectural option. This will let you specify distances in feet and inches.

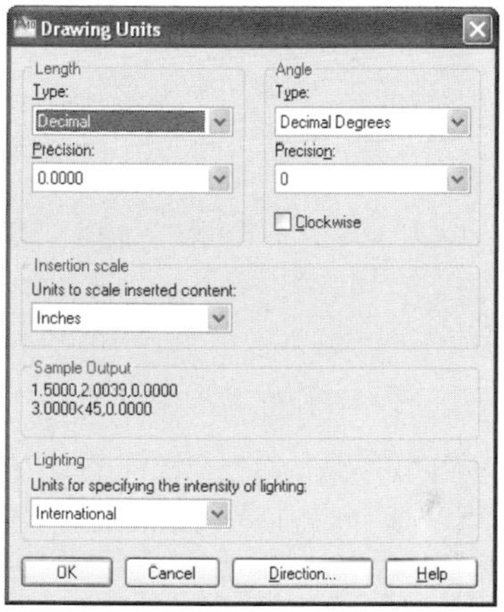

Figure 2.13

The Drawing Units dialog box

As you select an option in the Type drop-down list, you'll see a sample of the type in the Sample Output box at the bottom of the dialog box.

3. In the Angle group, click the Type drop-down list, and then select the option that best represents the type of angle you plan to use. (See Table 2.2 for a description of these options.) The Decimal Degrees option is the most commonly used angle option for most drawings, but if you are drawing a site plan, you can select Surveyor's Units to use a "metes and bounds" style of distance measurement.

4. Click OK.

Once you've set up the drawing units, you can use that unit as you specify distances in AutoCAD. For example, if you select Architectural, you can specify distances in feet and inches. The Engineering option lets you specify distance in feet and decimal feet. If you are using a metric system, stick with the default Decimal option.

TYPE	DESCRIPTION
Architectural	Feet, inches, and fractional inches, as in 12'6½". You would enter this as **12'6 1/2"** with a space between the 6 and the 1/2.
Engineering	Feet and decimal inches, as in 12.5' or 12'6.5". You would enter this as **12'6.5"**.
Decimal	Whole and decimal units that can be anything (metric distances, decimal inches, decimal feet, or decimal miles, for example).
Fractional	Whole and fractional units that can be anything (fractional metric distances, fractional inches, feet, or miles, for example).
Scientific	Scientific notation for distances. Units can be anything (meters, angstroms, miles, astronomic units, parsecs, or light-years, for example).

Table 2.1

The Length Options

Table 2.2

The Angle Options

TYPE	DESCRIPTION
Decimal Degrees	Whole and decimal degrees of angle.
Deg/Min/Sec	Degrees, minutes, and seconds of angle.
Grads	Angles specified in grads. For example, you would specify 45° of an angle by entering **50g**.
Radians	Angles specified in radians. For example, you would specify 45° by entering **0.785r**.
Surveyor's Units	Angles specified in degrees from north or south to east or west, as in N45dE.

Using Other Drawing Unit Options

You might want to know about a few other options in the Drawing Units dialog box. The following options are not as important as the type of length and angle you want to use, but they might play an important role in your work at some point:

Precision The Precision option lets you control how AutoCAD reports length and angle values. This option does not actually affect the precision of the objects in the drawing. For example, if you select Decimal as the length type and 0.0 for the precision, AutoCAD displays a distance of 1.2 for the true distance of 1.167. If you choose 0.000 for the Precision option, you will see the full distance of 1.167 whenever AutoCAD displays a distance.

Direction By default, AutoCAD assumes that 0° is a horizontal direction from left to right. For example, 90° is directly vertical, and 180° is a horizontal direction from right to left. Angle values increase from 0° in a counterclockwise fashion. Figure 2.5 (earlier in this chapter) shows the cardinal directions and their degree values in a default AutoCAD setup.

If your drawing requires a different direction for 0°, you can use the Direction option to choose an angle. When you click the Direction button, the Direction Control dialog box opens. Click one of four radio buttons to select the 0° direction from the four cardinal directions. If your desired 0° direction does not conform to the cardinal directions, you can specify an angle numerically or graphically by selecting the Other option.

Clockwise By default, angle values increase counterclockwise, but you can change this to clockwise by selecting the Clockwise option in the Angle group of the Drawing Units dialog box.

Insertion Scale AutoCAD can automatically scale an inserted drawing.

If you draw an object in inches but you later need to import that object into a drawing created using millimeters, AutoCAD can automatically scale your object so it is the correct size in the metric drawing. To take advantage of this feature, you must specify the type of unit you are using for the current drawing in the Insertion Scale drop-down list. For example, if the current drawing uses feet and inches, select Inches from the list.

Lighting When creating 3D models, you can add light sources and control their intensity. This option determines the standard used for measuring light intensity.

Determining the Drawing Area

One important concept you need to know is that AutoCAD's drawing area is virtually limitless. Although your view of a new drawing might show you an area that is only 31 units by 13 units, you are not confined to that area. If you like, you can include the entire Western Hemisphere of the world in your drawing area, even if you are only drawing a plan of your backyard.

With such a limitless area to work with, you need to set boundaries. To set up your drawing area, think of a reasonable area for the drawing you are about to start. You don't have to be too precise because you can always change it.

Drawing a Reference Rectangle

The first step is to determine what the drawing unit represents and then think of the area you want in real-world terms. You can go about this in a number of ways. This example uses a rectangle to help you see the drawing area more easily.

Suppose you are starting a drawing of a house plan. You know that the lot size is 100′ by 50′. First, set up your drawing units to be Architectural, and then do the following:

1. From the Application menu, choose Drawing Utilities → Units to open the Drawing Units dialog box, select Architectural from the Type drop-down list, and click OK.

2. Choose Rectangle from the Home tab's Draw panel. In the command window, you'll see the following prompt:

   ```
   Specify first corner point or [Chamfer/Elevation/Fillet/Thickness/Width]:
   ```

3. Enter **0,0**. This tells AutoCAD you want the first corner of the rectangle at the origin of the drawing, which is the lower-left corner of a new drawing. If you remember your high-school geometry, you'll know that 0,0 is the coordinate for the origin of an XY graph. You'll see the next prompt:

   ```
   Specify other corner point or [Area/Dimensions/Rotation]:
   ```

4. Enter **100′, 50′** to draw a 100′ by 50′ rectangle. The value you entered (100′, 50′) is an absolute coordinate that is 100′ in the X direction and 50′ in the Y direction.

5. The rectangle is larger than the display of a new drawing, so to view the entire rectangle, choose Extents from the Zoom flyout on the View tab's Navigate panel.

You've now set up your view to include the entire area enclosed by the rectangle. This is a quick way to set up your drawing area, and it gives you the visual reference of the 100′ by 50′ rectangle.

Using Limits to Set Up the Drawing Area

In the previous section, you saw how to use a rectangle to set up a drawing area. Another tool for setting up the area is the Limits command. Unlike drawing a rectangle, the

Limits command just defines an area. No visual clues show you what that area looks like, but you can choose All from the Zoom flyout on the View tab's Navigate panel to display the area set by Limits. You can also type **Z↵ A↵** to display the limits of a drawing.

Here's how to set up the limits of a drawing:

1. If you did the previous exercise, delete the rectangle from the drawing. To do this, select the rectangle and press the Delete key or click the Erase tool in the Modify panel.

2. Type **Limits↵**. You'll see the following prompt:

   ```
   Reset Model space limits:

   Specify lower left corner or [ON/OFF] <0'-0",0'-0">:
   ```

3. Press ↵ to accept the default location for the lower-left corner, which is the origin of the drawing. You'll then see the following prompt:

   ```
   Specify upper right corner <1'-0",0'-9">:
   ```

4. Enter a coordinate value representing what you want to use for your drawing. It should be the actual area at full scale. To use the example of the site plan from the previous section, enter **100′, 50′**. Once you've entered a value, it will appear as though nothing has happened.

5. Choose All from the Zoom flyout on the View tab's Navigate panel or type **Z↵ A↵**. Again, nothing apparently has happened. However, now as you move your cursor to the upper-right corner of the drawing area, you'll see that the coordinate readout in the lower left of the AutoCAD window shows a coordinate of about 100′ by 50′.

The drawback to the Limits command is that it does not give you any visual feedback. So, why use it? Well, it provides the following features that can be quite useful:

- You can choose All from the Zoom flyout on the View tab's Navigate panel or type **Z↵ A↵** to quickly display the area set by the Limits command.

- You can use the On/Off option of the Limits command to force your drawing to stay within the boundary set by the Limits command.

- The Grid feature, which displays a grid of dots, displays only within the boundary set by the Limits command. (This is important if you plan to use the Grid feature.)

If you find that you use the same drawing setup repeatedly, you can create template files that are already set up to your own customized way of working. To do this, choose Save As from the Application menu, and then, at the Save Drawing As dialog box, select AutoCAD Drawing Template (*.dwt) from the File of type drop-down list. Enter a name for your file in the File name input box, then click Save.

Using a Digital T Square and Triangle

Before CAD became so prevalent in drafting rooms, most people used T squares and triangles to draw horizontal and vertical lines. AutoCAD provides two features that perform the same function as these hand-drafting tools: Ortho mode and polar tracking.

Using a Quick T Square Function with Ortho

Ortho mode is the simpler of the two—it forces the cursor to point in either a vertical direction or a horizontal direction. You can use Ortho mode in two ways. If you just need to temporarily restrain a rubber-banding line to a vertical or horizontal orientation, hold down the Shift key while selecting points. This is a common method found in many drawing programs. You can also click the Ortho tool in the AutoCAD status bar to lock Ortho mode on.

Once you've turned Ortho mode on in the status bar, your cursor will be continually constrained to a vertical or horizontal orientation as you draw objects or move, rotate, or copy objects.

Using an Adjustable Triangle with Polar Tracking

Another T square like tool is *polar tracking*, which also helps restrain the cursor to horizontal or vertical motion. Polar tracking is much more flexible than Ortho mode, because it doesn't force you to point in strictly a horizontal or vertical direction. Instead, it causes the cursor to "snap" to a horizontal or vertical orientation as your cursor approaches such an orientation.

Try the following exercise to see how polar tracking works:

1. Click the Line tool in the Home tab's Draw panel.

2. Click the Polar Tracking tool in the AutoCAD status bar to turn it on. Notice that the Ortho tool turns off since their functions overlap.

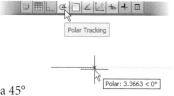

3. Click a point on the screen to start the line.

4. Point the cursor so that the rubber-banding line is at a 45° angle, and then slowly rotate the rubber-banding line to a horizontal orientation. Notice that as the rubber-banding line comes close to being horizontal, it snaps to a horizontal orientation. You'll also see a tooltip that displays the length and direction of the line.

5. Try pointing the rubber-banding line vertically. It snaps into a vertical orientation.

6. Press the Esc key to exit the Line command without drawing anything.

Modifying Polar Tracking's Behavior

Polar tracking is not limited to vertical and horizontal orientations. You can set it to allow for other angles as well, much like an adjustable triangle in hand drafting. You can change the behavior of polar tracking through the Drafting Settings dialog box. To open the Drafting Settings dialog box, do one of the following:

- Right-click the Polar Tracking tool in the status bar to open the context menu, and then choose Settings.

- Enter **DS**⏎ at the command prompt, and then select the Polar Tracking tab (see Figure 2.14).

With the Drafting Settings dialog box open at the Polar Tracking tab, you can set polar tracking to snap to any angle you need. First, select the Track Using All Polar Angle Settings option from the Object Snap Tracking Settings group. Then select an angle from the Increment Angle drop-down list, which is in the Polar Angle Settings group.

Figure 2.14

The Polar Tracking tab of the Drafting Settings dialog box

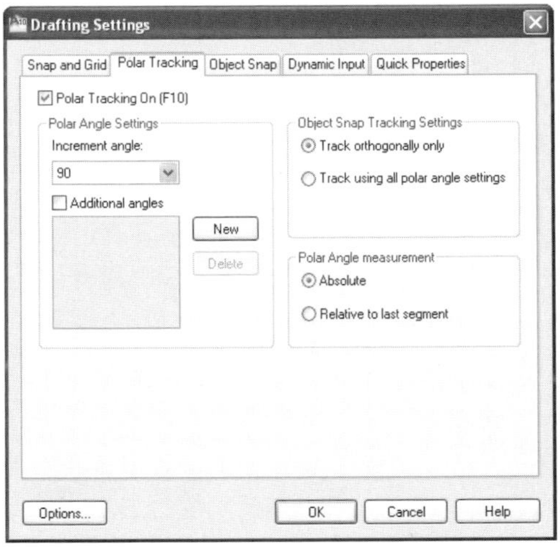

INTERPRETING THE CURSOR MODES AND UNDERSTANDING PROMPTS

The key to working with AutoCAD successfully is understanding the way it interacts with you. You need to become familiar with some of the ways AutoCAD prompts you for input. Understanding the format of the messages in the command window and recognizing other events on the screen will help you learn the program more easily.

The command window aids you with messages, and the cursor also gives you clues about what to do.

INTERPRETING THE CURSOR MODES AND UNDERSTANDING PROMPTS
(continued)

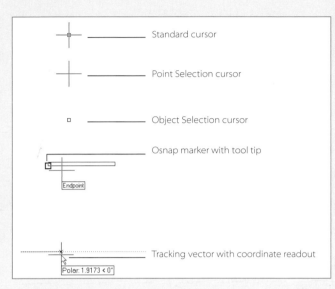

The standard cursor tells you that AutoCAD is waiting for the initiation of a command through a toolbar click, a menu selection, or a keyboard entry of a command name. You can also edit objects using grips when you see this cursor. Grips are squares that appear at endpoints and midpoints of objects when they are selected. (You might know them as work-points from other graphics programs.)

The Point Selection cursor appears whenever AutoCAD expects point input. It can also appear in conjunction with a rubber-banding line. You can either click a point or enter a coordinate using the keyboard.

The Object Selection cursor tells you that you must select objects—either by clicking them or by using any of the object selection options available. The osnap marker appears with the Point Selection cursor when you invoke an osnap and the cursor nears an osnap location. The polar tracking vector appears when you use the polar tracking or osnap tracking feature. Polar tracking aids you in drawing orthogonal lines, and osnap tracking helps you align points in space relative to the geometry of existing objects. Osnap tracking works in conjunction with an osnap.

If you don't see the angle you want in the drop-down list, you can enter the value in the list. You can also include an exact, fixed angle that is not incremental by turning on the Additional Angles option. Click New, and then enter an angle in the list box. Table 2.3 shows the polar tracking options and their functions.

Table 2.3

Options on the Polar Tracking Tab of the Drafting Settings Dialog Box

SETTING	PURPOSE
Increment Angle drop-down list	These are angles that a rubber-banding line will snap to in increments. For example, an incremental angle of 10° will cause the rubber-banding line to snap to the angles of 10°, 20°, 30°, and so on. You can use the existing angles shown in the list or enter a custom angle in the list.
Polar Angle Settings	You can set a fixed, absolute angle to which polar tracking will snap with these settings.
Object Snap Tracking Settings	Use the settings you choose in the Polar Angle Settings group by selecting the Track Using All Polar Angle Settings option.
Polar Angle Measurement	Set polar angles relative to the base coordinate system in AutoCAD or to the angle of the last line segment created.

Getting a Visual Reference with the Grid Mode

If you're a CAD user, chances are you've used grid paper to help sketch an idea for one design or another. Grids can help you get an idea of proportion or approximate distances when you don't have a scale.

AutoCAD's Grid mode displays an array of nonprinting dots within the drawing area. These dots can give you a reference for distance or location. You can set the spacing of the dots and easily turn them on or off by using one of the following methods:

- Click the Grid tool in the status bar.

- Press F7 or Ctrl+G.

You can also enter **Grid↵ on↵**. An array of dots appears in the drawing area, as shown in Figure 2.15.

You can turn off the grid by repeating the operation you used to turn the grid on, or you can enter **Grid↵ off↵** at the command prompt.

You might also see a grid that appears only in a small area, as shown in Figure 2.16. This happens when the Display Grid Beyond Limits grid setting is turned off. You'll learn about the grid settings in the next section.

Figure 2.15

An AutoCAD grid

Figure 2.16

The grid as it appears when the limits of the drawing are smaller than the current display

As was described in "Using Limits to Set Up the Drawing Area," earlier in this chapter, you can choose All from the Zoom flyout on the View tab's Navigate panel or type **Z**↲ **A**↲ to adjust the display so that the limit of the drawing roughly equals the display area. If parts of the drawing are outside the limits of the drawing, choosing All from the Zoom flyout displays the limits of the drawing and any parts of the drawing that fall outside the limits.

You can make a wide range of settings for the way grids display. See "Changing the Grid and Snap Settings" later in this chapter for more information.

Snapping to the Grid or Other Regular Intervals

Depending on the type of drawing you are doing, it can be helpful to have the cursor snap to the grid. Snap mode in AutoCAD forces the cursor to snap to regular intervals. For example, if you are drawing an object whose dimensions fall exactly within 1-unit increments, you can turn on Snap mode and set it to 1 unit. When you then start to draw, the cursor jumps to 1-unit increments.

Units can be inches, metric measurements, or any unit of measure you choose.

To control Snap mode, do one of the following:

- Click the Snap Mode tool in the status bar.
- Press F9 or Ctrl+B.

You can also turn on Snap mode by entering **Snap**↲ **on**↲ at the command prompt.

To turn off the Snap mode, repeat the operation you used to turn it on. You can also enter **Snap**↲ **off**↲ at the command prompt.

By default, the spacings in grid and snap are the same; so if you turn on the grid and snap at the same time, the cursor appears to snap to the grid points. It is possible to set the grid and snap spacings to different values. For example, you might want the grid to show at a 12-inch interval while the snap spacing is set to 1 inch.

If Snap mode does not seem to have an effect, the snap spacing might be set to a value too small to be noticeable in relation to your current view. For example, if your view encompasses an area the size of a football field and your snap spacing is set to ½ inch, you won't notice the effects of the Snap mode.

In a new drawing, the snap interval is set to 0.5 units. (This is 0.5 inches if you are using the Architectural or Engineering unit type in the Drawing Units dialog box.) The snap spacing can be anything you want, plus you can rotate the snap interval orientation, have a different X and Y snap spacing, or set the snap intervals to align with a specific location such as the corner of a box or the center of a circle. You'll learn how to make these adjustments in the next section.

Changing the Grid and Snap Settings

Grid mode and Snap mode have a wide range of settings. You can modify their spacing and rotation and even set up a grid for 2D isometric drawing. To edit these settings, you use the Drafting Settings dialog box, which you can open by doing one of the following:

- Right-click the Grid or Snap tool in the status bar, and choose Settings from the context menu.

- Enter **DS**↵ at the command prompt to open the Drafting Settings dialog box, and then select the Snap and Grid tab (see Figure 2.17).

From here, you can adjust both the grid and snap settings. The following sections describe the settings in this dialog box.

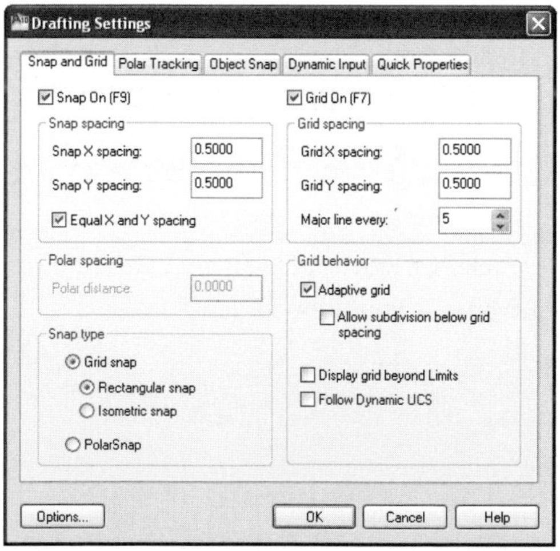

Figure 2.17

The Snap and Grid tab in the Drafting Settings dialog box

Adjusting the X and Y Spacing

You can set the X or Y grid spacing for either the grid interval or the snap interval by using the Snap X Spacing and Snap Y Spacing text boxes in the Grid and Snap Spacing groups. The Y-spacing value automatically adjusts to match the X-spacing value for both Snap and Grid settings. For example, if you enter **4** for the Grid X Spacing value, the Grid Y Spacing value automatically changes to 4. To set the X and Y spacing to different values, first set the X-spacing value, and then set the Y-spacing value. If you have the Isometric Snap setting turned on, the X-spacing and Y-spacing values are always the same.

> The grid spacing automatically follows the snap spacing if you set both Grid X Spacing and Grid Y Spacing to zero.

Setting Up for Isometric 2D Drawing

Using isometric drawings is a common drafting method for drawing a 3D view of an object. Lines are drawn at 30° increments to simulate a 3D look. If you want to use the grid or snap to help you draw an isometric drawing, select the Isometric Snap option (see Figure 2.18) in the Snap Type group of the Drafting Settings dialog box.

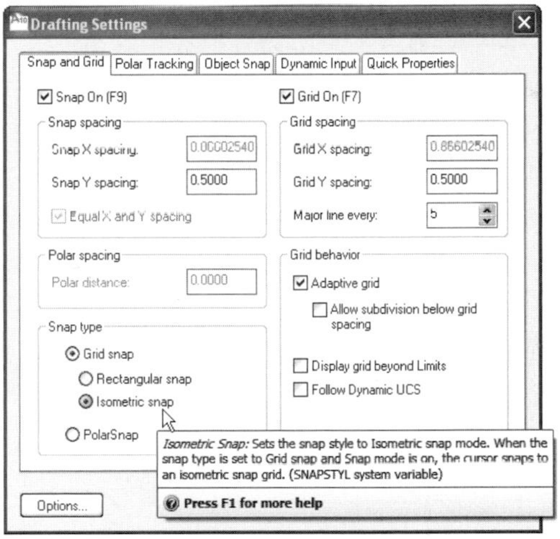

With the Isometric Snap option turned on, the grid changes to an isometric pattern, and the cursor changes to conform to the grid. To further aid in drawing an isometric view, you can toggle the cursor orientation between the left, right, or top Isoplane mode by pressing F5 or Ctrl+E. Figure 2.19 shows the cursor orientation for each Isoplane mode.

Figure 2.18

The Isometric Snap option

Since this is still a 2D drawing, the cursor's Isoplane mode is only an aid to help you visualize your 3D surface and does not affect the objects you draw.

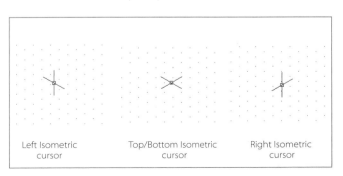

Left Isometric cursor   Top/Bottom Isometric cursor   Right Isometric cursor

Figure 2.19

The isoplane cursors

Rotating the Grid, Snap, and Cursor

At times, it's helpful to temporarily rotate your grid to draw objects at an angle. For example, you might need to draw an assembly of rectangular-shaped objects at a 30° angle to the screen orientation, as shown in Figure 2.20. AutoCAD lets you rotate not only the grid but the cursor and snap points as well, facilitating the construction of such a drawing.

You can rotate the grid by using the user coordinate system (UCS). Here's how it works:

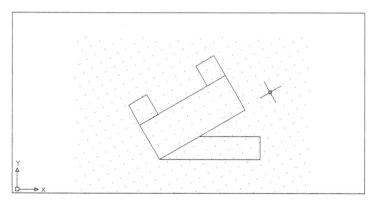

1. From the View tab's Coordinates panel, click the Z tool.

2. At the `Specify rotation angle about Z axis <90>:` prompt, enter the angle you want for your snap and grid. The grid displays at the angle you indicated in step 2.

You can also indicate an angle visually in step 2 by clicking two points. For example, to align the grid to a line you've drawn at an angle, use Endpoint object snaps (discussed in "Selecting Exact Locations on Objects" later in this chapter), and select the two endpoints of the line, as shown in Figure 2.21.

To return to the standard grid orientation, choose World from the View tab's Coordinates panel. You will learn more about the UCS in Chapter 6.

Figure 2.20

A rotated grid and lines

Figure 2.21

Using osnaps in conjunction with the UCS to align the grid to an object

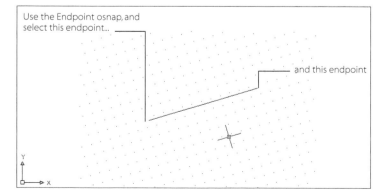

Use the Endpoint osnap, and select this endpoint...

and this endpoint

Aligning the Grid to an Object

In addition to rotating the grid, you can align the grid's origin, or *base*, to an object. This is useful when you want to use the grid to propagate from a specific location in a drawing, such as the corner of a room or the center of a hole (see Figure 2.22).

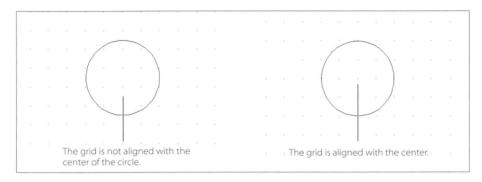

The grid is not aligned with the center of the circle.

The grid is aligned with the center.

Figure 2.22

The grid at the left is not aligned, but the grid on the right was aligned with the center of the circle using Snapbase.

To align the grid or snap to an object, do the following:

1. At the command prompt, enter **Snapbase**↵.

2. At the `Enter new value for SNAPBASE <0.0000,0.0000>:` prompt, select a location that you want to use as the base of the grid or snap, or enter a coordinate for the base.

3. Enter **Re**↵ to reset the grid location.

As the command's name indicates, Snapbase sets the base for the snap. It also sets the base for the grid, even if the grid is set to a different X and Y interval from the Snap setting.

Selecting Exact Locations on Objects

One of the main reasons for using AutoCAD is to create accurate representations of your designs. And one of the most important tools you'll use to draw accurately is the object snap, or *osnap*. Osnaps enable you to select specific locations in your drawing as you draw or edit objects. For example, you can draw a new line from the exact endpoint of another by using object snaps. Or you can quickly start or end a line from the exact center of an arc or circle.

These examples might sound trivial, but they reflect some of the most common activities you'll do in AutoCAD. Therefore, understanding osnaps is vital to using AutoCAD successfully.

Setting Up Osnap Locations

You can set up AutoCAD to automatically snap to endpoints, midpoints, and a variety of other locations on objects in your drawing. This exercise shows how this works:

1. Open a new AutoCAD drawing.

2. Type **Ds**↵, and then select the Object Snap tab. You can also right-click the Object Snap tool in the status bar and select Settings.

3. Click the Clear All button at the right of the dialog box to turn off any options that might be selected.

4. Click the Endpoint, Midpoint, and Intersection check boxes so that they contain a check mark (see Figure 2.23).

Figure 2.23

Selecting the End-point, Midpoint, and Intersection check boxes

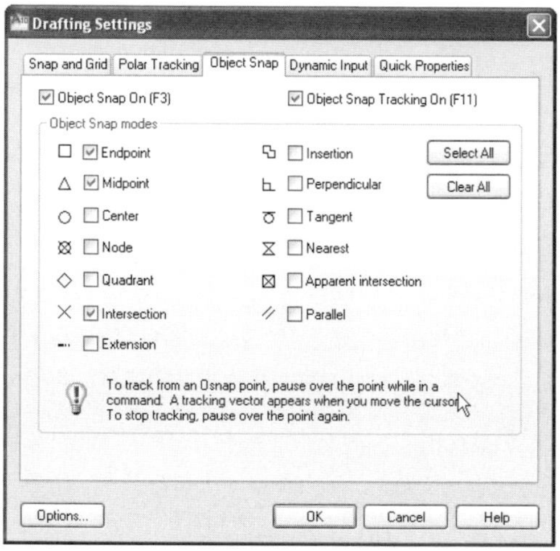

Automatically Snapping to Locations
==

Automatically Snapping to Locations

After setting up osnaps as in the previous example, you are ready to use them. You can turn on Osnap mode so that AutoCAD automatically selects the nearest osnap on an object as you approach the osnap location. This is called a *running osnap*. The following exercise shows how a running osnap works:

1. First turn on Osnap mode by clicking the Object Snap tool in the status bar.

2. Click the Rectangle tool in the Home tab's Draw panel, and then draw a rectangle in the drawing area about the size and at the location shown in Figure 2.24. You'll use this rectangle to test the osnap settings.

3. Start the Line command, and place the cursor at the lower-left corner of the rectangle, but don't click yet. Notice that the cursor snaps to the corner and that a square appears. Also, a tooltip appears after a moment, showing you the name of the osnap that is active, Endpoint.

4. Click the mouse while the Endpoint osnap is displayed. The line is now fixed to the corner of the rectangle.

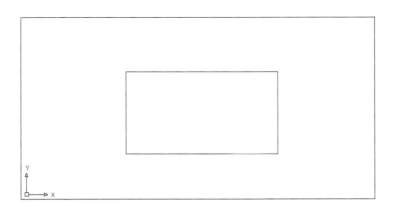

Figure 2.24

Draw this rectangle to practice using osnaps.

5. Move the cursor to the middle of the right side of the rectangle, as shown in Figure 2.25. The Midpoint osnap appears. This time you'll see a triangle that gives you immediate feedback as to which osnap is active. Leave the cursor there for a moment, and you'll see the Midpoint tooltip.

6. Click the mouse while the Midpoint osnap is displayed. The line is now fixed between the lower-left corner and the midpoint of the right side.

7. Move the cursor to the upper-left corner, click when you see the Endpoint osnap marker, and then press ↵ to exit the Line command.

As you can see, with osnaps you can quickly select a location on an object without too much intervention on your part.

> When you see an osnap marker on an object, press Tab to move to the next osnap point on the object. If you have several Running Osnap modes on (Endpoint, Midpoint, and Intersection, for example), pressing Tab cycles through those osnap points on the object. This feature can be especially useful in a crowded area of a drawing.

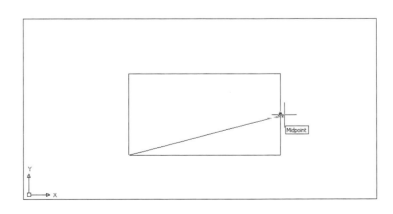

Figure 2.25

Using the Midpoint osnap

Selecting Osnaps on the Fly

As helpful as osnaps are, they can get in the way. In a crowded drawing, osnaps can cause you to accidentally select a point you don't want to select. In these situations, you can turn off Osnap mode. When you then need to select an osnap, you can do so from a Shift+right-click menu. This lets you be more selective in the osnap you choose. The following exercise shows how this method works:

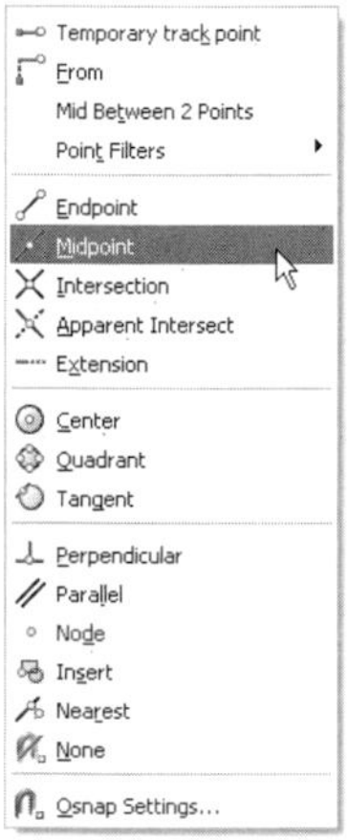

1. If you don't already have a rectangle in the drawing, start a new drawing, and place a rectangle roughly in the middle of the drawing area.

2. Make sure the Osnap tool in the status bar is turned on. If it isn't, click the Osnap tool, or press F3.

3. Click the Line tool, hold down the Shift key, and right-click. A menu appears at the cursor, displaying a list of osnap options (see Figure 2.26).

4. Select Midpoint, and then place the cursor near the midpoint of the line at the bottom of the rectangle. The Midpoint osnap marker appears.

5. Shift+right-click again, and select Endpoint from the shortcut menu.

6. Move the cursor to the upper-right endpoint of the rectangle. This time the Endpoint osnap marker appears.

7. Click the corner while the Endpoint osnap marker is still visible.

8. Press ↵ to exit the Line command.

> If you accidentally select too many objects, you can remove them from your selection by holding down the Shift key and clicking the objects.

Figure 2.26

Osnap options

Understanding the Osnap Options

In the previous exercise, you made several of the osnap settings automatic so that they were available without having to select them from the Osnap shortcut menu. Another way to display the osnap options is to press their keyboard equivalents while selecting points or to Shift+right-click while selecting points to open the Osnap context menu.

The following is a summary of all the Osnap options, including their keyboard shortcuts. You've already used many of these options in this chapter and in the preceding chapter. Pay special attention to the options you haven't yet used in the exercises but might find useful to your style of work. The full name of each option is followed by its keyboard shortcut in brackets. To use these options, you can enter either the full name or the abbreviation at any point prompt. You can also select these options from the shortcut menu that is displayed when you Shift+right-click.

Sometimes you'll want one or more of these options available as the default selection. Remember that you can set running osnaps to be on at all times. Type **Ds↵** to open the Drafting Settings dialog box, and then click the Object Snap tab. You can also right-click the Osnap tool in the status bar and choose Settings from the shortcut menu.

Apparent Intersection [app] Selects the apparent intersection of two objects. This is useful when you want to select the intersection of two objects that do not actually intersect. You will be prompted to select the two objects.

Center [cen] Selects the center of an arc or a circle. You must click the arc or circle itself, not its apparent center.

Endpoint [end] Selects the endpoints of lines, polylines, arcs, curves, and 3D face vertices.

Extension [ext] Selects a point that is aligned with an imagined extension of a line. For example, you can select a point in space that is aligned with an existing line but is not actually on that line. To use that point, enter **ext↵** during point selection, or select Extension from the Osnap context menu; then move the cursor to the line whose extension you want to use, and hold it there until you see a small, cross-shaped marker on the line. The cursor also displays a tooltip with the word *extension*, letting you know that the Extension osnap is active.

From [fro] Selects a point relative to a selected point. For example, you can select a point that is 2 units to the left and 4 units above a circle's center. This option is usually used in conjunction with another osnap option, such as From Endpoint or From Midpoint.

Insertion [ins] Selects the insertion point of text, blocks, xrefs, and overlays.

Intersection [int] Selects the intersection of objects.

Midpoint [mid] Selects the midpoint of a line or an arc. In the case of a polyline, it selects the midpoint of the polyline segment.

Mid Between 2 Points [m2p] Selects a point midway between two points.

Nearest [nea] Selects a point on an object nearest the pick point.

Node [nod] Selects a point object.

None [non] Temporarily turns off running osnaps.

Osnap Settings [os] Opens the Object Snap tab of the Drafting Settings dialog box to allow you to make osnap setting changes.

Parallel [par] Lets you draw a line segment that is parallel to another existing line segment. To use this option, enter **par↵** during point selection, or select Parallel from the Osnap context menu; then move the cursor to the line that you want to be parallel to, and hold it there until you see the cross-shaped osnap marker on the line (you might have to move the cursor a bit to see the marker). The cursor also displays a tooltip with the word *Parallel*, letting you know that the Parallel osnap is active.

Perpendicular [per] Enables you to specify that an object should be perpendicular to another object. You can use this osnap for the start point of a line. The line will then be constrained to a perpendicular direction to the selected object.

Point Filters [.x, .y, .z, .xy, .xz, .yz] Opens an additional set of options that you can use to select just the X, Y, or Z coordinate of a point or a combination of any pair of these coordinates, such as X and Z or Y and Z. This feature is most useful in creating 3D models.

Quadrant [qua] Selects the nearest cardinal (north, south, east, or west) point on an arc or a circle.

Tangent [tan] Selects a point on an arc or a circle that represents the tangent from the last point selected.

Temporary Track Point [tt] Allows you to use the osnap tracking feature "on the fly." See "Using the Temporary Tracking Point Feature" later in this chapter.

Fine-Tuning the AutoSnap Feature

When you click the Options button on the Object Snap tab of the Drafting Settings dialog box, you'll see the Drafting tab of the Options dialog box. This tab provides options pertaining to the AutoSnap feature (see Table 2.4). AutoSnap looks at the location of your cursor during osnap selections and locates the osnap point nearest your cursor. AutoSnap then displays a graphic called a *marker* showing you the osnap point it has found. If it is the one you want, simply click to select it.

You can also get to this tab by choosing Options from the Application menu and then selecting the Drafting tab.

	OPTION	USE
Table 2.4	Marker	Turns the graphic markers on or off
The AutoSnap Settings on the Drafting Tab of the Options Dialog Box	Magnet	Causes the osnap cursor to snap to inferred osnap points
	Display AutoSnap Tooltip	Turns the Osnap tooltip on or off
	Display AutoSnap Aperture Box	Turns the old-style osnap cursor box on or off
	AutoSnap Marker Size	Controls the size of the graphic marker

Aligning Objects Using Object Snap Tracking and Tracking Points

Osnaps are great for selecting exact locations directly on existing objects, but what if you want to find a point that is aligned with an object but not necessarily on the object? *Object snap tracking*, or *osnap tracking*, is like an extension of object snaps that enables you to align a point to the geometry of an object instead of just selecting a point on an object. This alignment point is referred to as a *tracking point* since the cursor "tracks" from the selected osnap point.

With osnap tracking you can select a point that is exactly at the center of a rectangle. In the following exercise, you'll place a circle in a rectangle to see how osnap tracking works firsthand.

> The osnap tracking feature is not available in AutoCAD LT 2010. If you are using LT, you can use the temporary tracking feature described later in this chapter.

First, make sure running osnaps are turned on and that they are set to the Midpoint option. Then make sure osnap tracking is turned on. The following steps describe how to do this:

1. Right-click the Object Snap Tracking tool in the status bar, and choose Settings from the context menu to open the Drafting Settings dialog box (see Figure 2.27) at the Object Snap tab.

2. Make sure the Midpoint option in the Object Snap Modes group is checked. Other osnap modes might also be checked. You can leave them on.

3. Also make sure that Object Snap On and Object Snap Tracking On are both checked. Click OK.

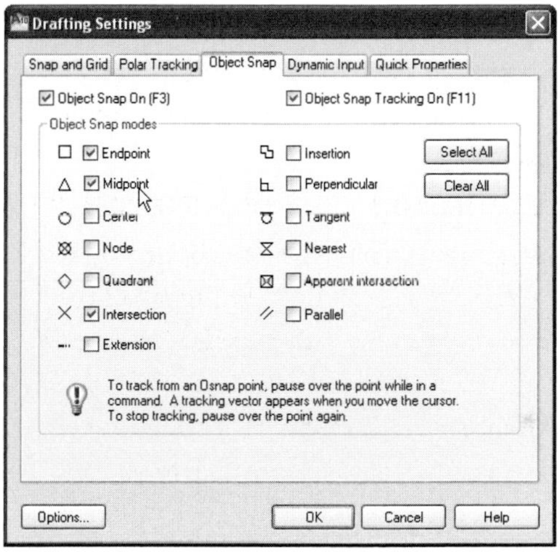

Figure 2.27

The Drafting Settings dialog box

Now you're ready to draw:

1. Draw a rectangle large enough to fill most of the drawing area with some margin around the outside, as shown in Figure 2.28.

Figure 2.28

Draw this rectangle to practice using osnap tracking.

2. Click the Circle tool in the Home tab's Draw panel, or enter **C**↵.

3. At the `Specify center point for circle or [3P/2P/Ttr (tan tan radius)]:` prompt, enter **C**, or right-click and choose Center from the context menu.

4. Move your cursor to the top horizontal edge of the rectangle, until you see the Midpoint tooltip.

5. Move the cursor directly over the Midpoint osnap marker. Without clicking, hold the cursor there for a second until you see a small cross appear, as shown in Figure 2.29. (Look carefully because the cross is quite small.) This is the osnap tracking marker.

Figure 2.29

The osnap
tracking marker

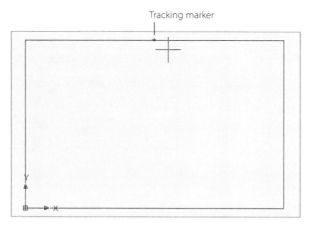

You can alternately insert and remove the osnap tracking marker by passing the cursor over it.

Now as you move the cursor downward, a dotted line appears, emanating from the midpoint of the horizontal line. This line is called a *tracking vector*. The cursor also shows a small *x* following the dotted line as you move it.

6. Move the cursor to the midpoint of the left vertical side of the rectangle. Don't click, but hold it there for a second until you see the small cross. Now as you move the cursor away, a horizontal tracking vector appears with an *x* following the cursor, as shown in Figure 2.30.

7. Move the cursor to the center of the rectangle. The two tracking vectors appear simultaneously, and a small *x* appears at their intersection, as shown in Figure 2.31.

8. With the two tracking vectors crossing and the *x* at their intersection, click to select the exact center of the rectangle.

9. At the `Specify radius of circle or [Diameter]:` prompt, click a point anywhere to finish the circle. The radius doesn't really matter here. The circle appears in the exact center of the rectangle, as shown in Figure 2.32.

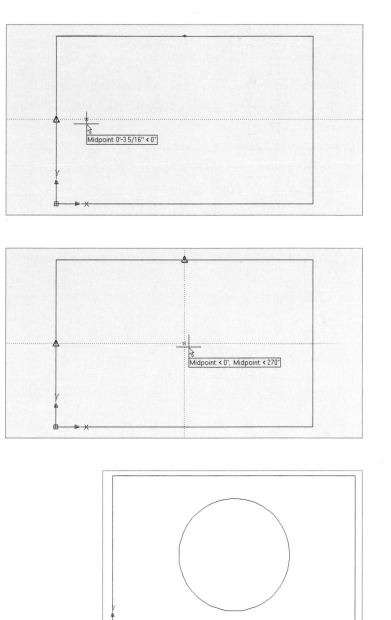

Figure 2.30
**The tracking vector
appears.**

Figure 2.31
**The tracking vectors
cross in the middle
of the rectangle.**

Figure 2.32
**The completed
circle centered on
the rectangle**

Although you used the Midpoint osnap setting in this exercise, you are not limited to only one osnap setting. You can use as many as you need to in order to select the appropriate geometry. You can also use as many alignment points as you need, although in this exercise, you used only two. If you want, erase the circle and repeat this exercise until you get the hang of using the osnap tracking feature.

As with all the other tools in the status bar, you can turn osnap tracking on or off by clicking the Otrack tool. You can also press F11.

Using the Temporary Tracking Point Feature

The osnap tracking feature described in the previous section automatically selects tracking points for you when you momentarily hold the cursor on a location. Osnaps must be turned on for this feature to work. But what if you want to use osnap tracking on the fly when osnaps are turned off?

The *temporary tracking point* feature lets you specify tracking points even if osnaps are turned off or if your current osnap settings do not include an osnap that you want to use as a tracking point. For example, what if you want to use the Endpoint osnap for a tracking point but you have only Midpoint turned on for your running osnaps?

The following exercise demonstrates how you can use temporary tracking points to use any osnap option you need on the fly:

1. If you haven't done so already, draw a rectangle large enough to fill most of the drawing area with some margin around the outside, as was shown in Figure 2.24 earlier in this chapter.

2. If you did the exercise in the previous section, erase the circle you drew in the center of the rectangle by clicking it and pressing Delete.

3. Turn off the Object Snap tool in the status bar.

USING OSNAP TRACKING AND POLAR TRACKING TOGETHER

In addition to selecting as many tracking points as you need, you can also use angles other than the basic orthogonal angles of 0°, 90°, 180°, and 270°. For example, you can locate a point that is aligned vertically to the top edge of the rectangle and at a 45° angle from a corner.

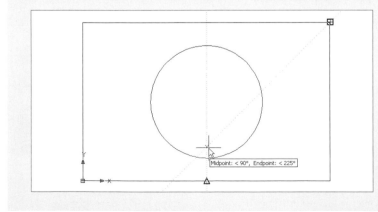

Midpoint: < 90°, Endpoint: < 225°

USING OSNAP TRACKING AND POLAR TRACKING TOGETHER *(continued)*

To do so, use the settings on the Polar Tracking tab of the Drafting Settings dialog box. (See "Modifying Polar Tracking's Behavior" earlier in this chapter.) If you set the increment angle to 45° and turn on the Track Using All Polar Angle Settings option, you will be able to use 45° in addition to the orthogonal directions.

Now you're ready to try the temporary tracking point feature:

1. Click the Circle tool in the Home tab's Draw panel, or enter **C⏎**.

2. At the `Specify center point for circle or [3P/2P/Ttr (tan tan radius)]:` prompt, Shift+right-click, and choose Temporary Track Point.

3. Shift+right-click again, and choose Midpoint.

4. Move your cursor to the top horizontal edge of the rectangle, until you see the Midpoint tooltip, and click that point.

5. Shift+right-click, and choose Temporary Track Point again.

6. Shift+right-click, and choose Midpoint.

7. Move the cursor to the midpoint of the left vertical side of the rectangle, and click that point.

8. Move the cursor to the center of the rectangle. The two dotted lines or tracking vectors appear simultaneously, and a small *x* appears at their intersection, as shown in Figure 2.33.

9. With the two dotted lines crossing and the *x* at their intersection, click to select the exact center of the rectangle.

10. At the `Specify radius of circle or [Diameter]:` prompt, click a point anywhere to finish the circle. The radius doesn't really matter here.

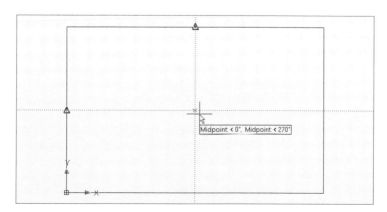

Figure 2.33

Using the temporary tracking point feature to locate the center of the rectangle

When a drawing gets crowded, running osnaps might get in the way of your work. The temporary tracking point feature lets you access the osnap tracking vector without having to turn on running osnaps.

The temporary tracking point feature and the other tools that use tracking vectors take a little practice to use, but once you understand how they work, they are indispensable in your drawing.

Summary

The drawing area and drawing units are often the most mystifying aspects of AutoCAD, if only because they have few limits. Once you understand how to set up drawings for area and units, you can start to draw with more confidence.

Next, you'll want to brush up on your high-school geometry so you can understand the way AutoCAD determines the location of objects.

Since AutoCAD is all about drawing accurately, you'll want to become intimately familiar with the tools that help you maintain accuracy, such as osnaps and osnap tracking. This chapter covered all the osnap methods, but if you focus on just knowing how to get to them through the context menus, you'll have all you need to make good use of osnaps.

CHAPTER 3

Drawing 2D Objects

Drawing 2D objects is one of the basic topics covered in this book, and many users will jump in and start to draw without needing to consult this chapter. Still, some tools and tool characteristics might not be obvious or might trip you up as you begin to draw. If you find you need a little extra help when you draw something, you should review this chapter.

When you draw in AutoCAD, you are creating AutoCAD objects: lines, circles, arcs, ellipses, and hatch patterns. Each and every object has a set of properties. Geometric properties include the endpoints of a line or the center and radius of a circle. Also, some properties are not directly related to the geometry of an object, such as its color or its layer assignment. (See Chapter 7 to find out what layers do.)

When you draw objects, you are really specifying their geometric properties. The other properties are assigned by whatever defaults are currently in place, such as the current color and layer assignments. You can set these defaults in the Home tab's Properties panel. You can always change the properties of an object (see Chapter 4), so don't think you need to be too careful when you're drawing.

This chapter includes the following topics:

- ■ **Working with the Draw panel**
- ■ **Drawing straight lines**
- ■ **Drawing circles and arcs**
- ■ **Drawing curves**
- ■ **Drawing parallel lines**
- ■ **Drawing revision clouds**
- ■ **Working with hatch patterns and solid fills**
- ■ **Drawing regular polygons**
- ■ **Using objects to lay out your drawing**

Working with the Draw Panel

Figure 3.1

**The Home tab's
Draw panel**

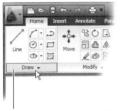

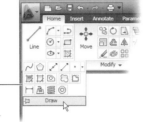

Click the title bar to expand the panel.

You'll be using the Home tab's Draw panel frequently in this chapter, so you should keep a couple of facts in mind. You can expand the Draw panel to show additional tools by clicking the panel title bar, as shown in Figure 3.1.

You'll also want to be aware of the flyout menus in the Draw panel. You might recall from Chapter 1 that the flyout menus are the ones that appear when you click the triangular arrow to the right of an icon tool (shown in Figure 1.10 of that chapter). In this chapter, you'll use several tools in those flyout menus.

Drawing Straight Lines

The basic object in AutoCAD is the *line*. If you worked through the exercises in earlier chapters, you've already used lines. Drawing lines consists of four basic steps:

1. Click the Line tool in the Home tab's Draw panel, or enter **L**↵ at the command prompt.

2. Click a start point, or enter a coordinate.

3. Continue to select points, either by clicking them or by entering coordinates, to place a series of contiguous line segments.

4. Press ↵ to exit the Line command, or enter **C**↵ to join the last line endpoint with the first.

When you draw a series of contiguous line segments using the Line command, each line segment behaves like an individual object. You can move the segments separately or change their individual properties.

You typically don't just draw a line and leave it alone. Lines tend to get edited a lot. Some of the most commonly used editing commands for lines are Trim, Extend, Fillet, and Offset. Trim and Extend either trim lines to intersecting lines or extend lines to other objects. Fillet joins two lines exactly end to end or adds an arc between them. Offset makes a parallel copy of a line at a specific distance.

As useful as lines are, you might find that you need your contiguous line segments to behave as a single object instead of as a series of individual lines. Another type of object called a *polyline* is just such an object. Using the Polyline command, you can draw a series of line segments, and they will behave as a single object. In fact, the rectangle is really a polyline that is closed. So are regular polygons created by the Polygon command, described later in the "Drawing Curves with Polylines" section.

To draw a polyline, click the Polyline tool in the Home tab's Draw panel, or type **Pl**↵. Then start selecting points just as you would with the Line command. Press ↵ when you finish drawing your lines.

When you click a polyline, instead of just selecting a line segment, you select the entire polyline. You can "break down" a polyline into its constituent parts by using the Explode command. (See Chapter 5 for more about Explode.)

Polylines can help you construct some types of objects quickly. Figure 3.2 shows some examples of polylines that have been created from standard AutoCAD commands or edited to form complex shapes.

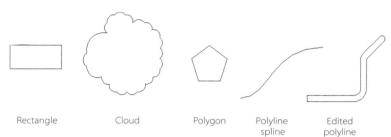

Rectangle Cloud Polygon Polyline spline Edited polyline

Figure 3.2

Although different commands were used to create them, these objects are all polylines and can be edited as such.

Drawing Circles and Arcs

Next to lines, *circles* and *arcs* are the easiest objects to draw. But like everything else in AutoCAD, they offer a wide range of options to enable you to draw them in nearly any situation.

Using the Circle Options

Click the Circle tool in the Home tab's Draw panel, click the location for the center, and then click a point to indicate a radius or enter a radius value. You can use osnaps to select points on objects to determine the center and radius. You can also specify the diameter instead of the radius by typing **D↵** after selecting a center point.

Using the 2P Option to Indicate Diameter

If you want to draw a circle based on two points, you can do so by using the 2P option. Here's how it works:

1. Click the Circle tool in the Home tab's Draw panel, or enter **C↵** at the command prompt.

2. Enter **2P↵**. You can also right-click and select 2P from the context menu.

3. At the `Specify first end point of circle's diameter:` prompt, click the first point.

4. At the `Specify second end point of circle's diameter:` prompt, click the second point. A circle appears using the two selected points to determine the circle's diameter.

You can select 2-Point from the Circle tool flyout in the Ribbon to automatically issue the 2P option in step 2, as shown in Figure 3.3. Use osnaps to select points on objects in steps 3 and 4.

Figure 3.3

Select 2-Point from the Circle flyout.

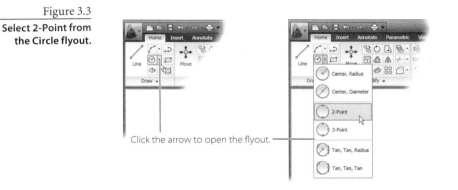

Click the arrow to open the flyout.

Using the 3P Option to Specify Three Points on the Circle

If you know you want a circle to pass through three points but you don't know the center point or radius, you can use the 3P option. This lets you select three points to indicate the location of the circle.

1. Click the Circle tool in the Home tab's Draw panel.

2. Enter **3P↵**, or right-click and select 3P from the context menu.

Figure 3.4

Drawing a circle tangent to a circle and two arcs

3. Select three points through which you want the circle to pass.

You can also choose 3 Point from the Circle tool flyout in the Ribbon, to automatically issue the 3P option in step 2. Use osnaps to select points on objects in step 3.

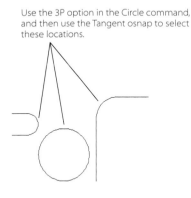

Use the 3P option in the Circle command, and then use the Tangent osnap to select these locations.

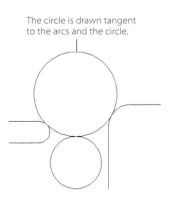

The circle is drawn tangent to the arcs and the circle.

One use of the 3P option in conjunction with osnaps is to draw a circle tangent to three other circles or arcs. Choose 3-Point from the Circle flyout on the Home tab's Draw menu, and then use the Tan osnap to select a circle or an arc. Repeat using the Tan osnap to select two arcs or circles (see Figure 3.4).

Using the Tan Tan Radius Option to Select Tangent Objects and a Radius

You can also draw a circle tangent to two objects. You must also specify a radius:

1. Click the Circle tool in the Draw panel.

2. Enter **ttr↵**, or right-click and select Ttr (tan tan radius) from the context menu.

3. Select two objects to which the circle is to be tangent, and then enter a radius value (see Figure 3.5).

AutoCAD does its best to draw a circle to your specifications, but if it's impossible, don't expect miracles.

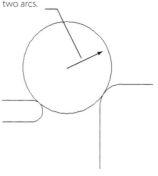

Use the 2P option of the Circle command, and then use the Tangent osnap and select these arcs.

Specify a radius that allows a circle to be drawn that is tangent to the two arcs.

Figure 3.5

Drawing a circle tangent to two objects

Using the Arc Options

The default method for drawing an arc consists of these steps:

1. Click the Arc tool in the Draw panel, or enter **A↵**.

2. Select the start point.

3. Select a second point through which the arc is to pass.

4. Select the endpoint.

If this default method for drawing arcs does not fill your needs, you can use several other AutoCAD methods. The first option, 3-Points, is the default just described. Figure 3.6 shows you how the other options work.

The Continue option, shown at the bottom of the menu, lets you continue an arc from the last line or arc drawn. You might notice that there isn't a Continue option in the Arc command prompt. To continue an arc, choose Continue from the Arc flyout on the Draw panel or start the Arc command, and then press ↵ instead of selecting a point or entering an option. The arc begins from the last line or arc that was drawn.

Figure 3.6

The methods for drawing an arc. The numbers indicate the order of point selection.

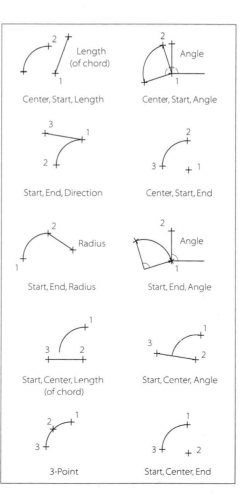

Center, Start, Length

Center, Start, Angle

Start, End, Direction

Center, Start, End

Start, End, Radius

Start, End, Angle

Start, Center, Length (of chord)

Start, Center, Angle

3-Point

Start, Center, End

You can draw an arc by first drawing a circle and then crossing the circle with two lines or other objects. Use the Trim command to trim the arc back to the crossing objects. This method is useful for constructing an arc that is connected to another object. See Chapter 5 for more about the Trim command.

Drawing Curves

Not everything you draw will consist of straight lines and perfect circles. For those more complex curves, AutoCAD offers some additional objects. *Ellipses* and *elliptical arcs* are two objects that are self-explanatory. *Splines* are specially designed to draw smooth curves that are mathematically accurate.

Polylines are the all-purpose object that let you draw anything from a closed irregular polygon to contour lines on a topographical map. If you think you'll need to draw any of these types of objects, check out the following sections.

Drawing Ellipses

When drawing an ellipse, remember that it has a major axis and a minor axis, as shown in Figure 3.7. You'll see prompts that ask you to select an axis. It doesn't matter which axis you select first; it can be either the major axis or the minor axis.

The default method for drawing an ellipse is to select two points defining one axis and then select a third point defining the other axis. Here are the steps:

1. Click the Ellipse tool in the Draw panel, or enter **el**↵. You can also choose Axis, End from the Ellipse tool flyout on the Draw panel.

2. At the Specify axis endpoint of ellipse or [Arc/Center]: prompt, click the first point defining one end of an axis of the ellipse, as shown in Figure 3.7.

3. At the Specify other endpoint of axis: prompt, click another point for the axis, as shown in Figure 3.7. You'll see an ellipse that is "fixed" at the two points you've selected. As you move the cursor, the ellipse changes shape to follow the cursor.

4. At the Specify distance to other axis or [Rotation]: prompt, click another point to complete the ellipse.

Figure 3.7

Drawing an ellipse

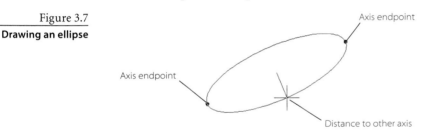

You might notice the Rotation option in the prompt in step 4. Selecting this option lets you simulate the way a circle looks on the side of an isometric or other 3D view. If you enter **R↵** in step 4 instead of clicking a point, you can enter a value indicating the angle from which you are viewing the circle.

> You might use osnaps to determine the location of the points on the ellipse.

If you need to place the center of an ellipse at a specific location, you can use the Center option of the Ellipse command:

1. Enter **el↵**.

2. Enter **C↵** (or right-click, and choose Center from the context menu), and then select a point for the center of the ellipse (see Figure 3.8). A rubber-banding line emanates from the point you select.

3. At the Specify endpoint of axis: prompt, select a point to define one axis of the ellipse.

4. At the Specify distance to other axis or [Rotation]: prompt, select a point to define the other axis of the ellipse.

Figure 3.8

Drawing an ellipse from a center point

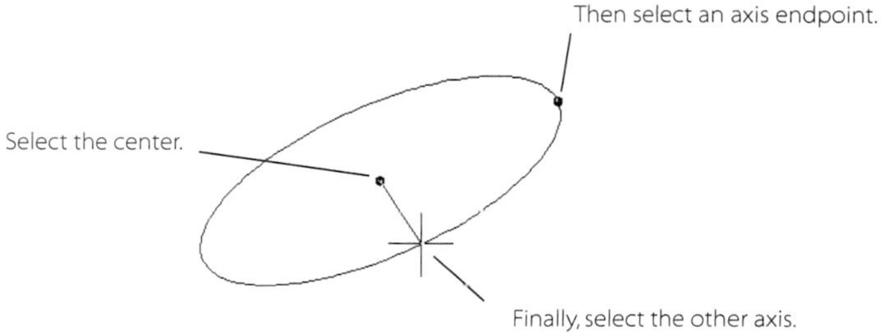

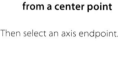

Then select an axis endpoint.

Select the center.

Finally, select the other axis.

Drawing Elliptical Arcs

You draw elliptical arcs using the Ellipse command. In the Ellipse tool flyout in the Draw panel, you'll find an Elliptical Arc tool. Drawing an elliptical arc is the same as drawing an ellipse with the addition of prompts that ask you for beginning and end angles defining the arc. Here's how it works:

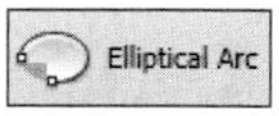

1. Click the Elliptical Arc tool in the Ellipse tool flyout of the Draw panel.

2. At the Specify axis endpoint of elliptical arc or [Arc]: prompt, click the first point defining one end of an axis of the ellipse, as shown in Figure 3.9.

3. At the Specify other endpoint of axis: prompt, click another point for the axis. Once this is done, you'll see an ellipse that is "fixed" at the two points you've selected. As you move the cursor, the ellipse changes shape to follow the cursor.

Elliptical Arc

Figure 3.9

Drawing an elliptical arc

Start as if you are drawing an ellipse.   Then indicate a start angle…   And an end angle.   The completed elliptical arc.

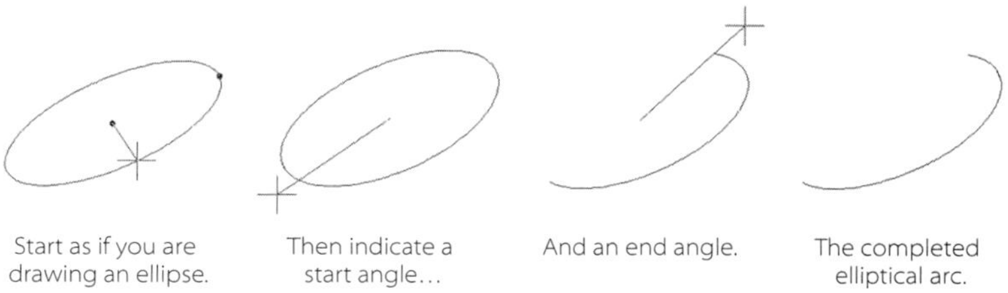

4. At the `Specify distance to other axis or [Rotation]:` prompt, click another point to indicate the overall ellipse shape that defines the arc.

5. At the `Specify start angle or [Parameter]:` prompt, notice that a rubber-banding line emanates from the center of the ellipse. This helps you visualize the beginning of the arc. Click a point to determine its beginning.

6. At the `Specify end angle or [Parameter/Included angle]:` prompt, notice that an elliptical arc now appears from the location you selected in the previous step. As you move the cursor, the arc expands or contracts depending on the cursor location. Click a point to fix the arc in position.

Drawing Smooth Curves

Whether you're a naval architect drawing a ship's hull or a civil engineer drawing map contours, you'll eventually need some way to draw smooth curves. AutoCAD provides two commands that do just that. Splines let you draw curves that conform to NURBS. Polylines are a general-purpose line object that can simulate a smooth curve.

If you need accurate curves, use the Spline command to generate NURBS curves (see Figure 3.10).

To draw a spline, do the following:

1. Click the Spline tool in the expanded Draw panel. You can also type **Spl**⏎.

2. At the `Specify first point or [Object]:` prompt, select a point to start the spline.

3. At the `Specify next:` prompt, select another point.

4. At the `Specify next point or [Close/ Fit tolerance] <start tangent>:` prompt, continue to select points. As you select points, a curve appears that passes through each point. When you complete your curve, press ⏎.

5. At the `Specify start tangent:` prompt, you'll see a rubber-banding line emanating from the spline's starting point. This lets you adjust the tangent angle of the beginning

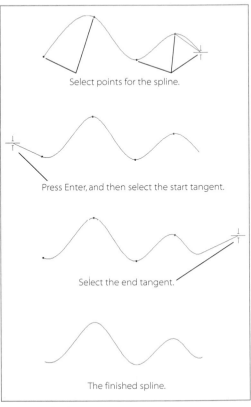

Select points for the spline.

Press Enter, and then select the start tangent.

Select the end tangent.

The finished spline.

Figure 3.10

Drawing a spline curve

of the spline. Press ↵ to accept the default angle, or indicate a direction with the rubber-banding line and click. You can always change it later if you want.

6. At the Specify end tangent: prompt, you'll see a rubber-banding line emanating from the spline's endpoint. Here, you can adjust the tangent angle of the end of the spline. Press ↵ to accept the default angle, or indicate a direction with the rubber-banding line and click. You can always change the tangent angle later if you want.

By default, AutoCAD draws the spline through the points you select. You can change the Fit Tolerance option as you draw so that the points you select indicate a direction for the curve rather than a point along the curve. In step 4 of the previous exercise, you'll see two options in the command prompt: Close and Fit Tolerance. If you enter F↵, you can enter a value to indicate the amount of "pull" the selected points have on the curve. A value of 0 "pulls" the curve through the point, and a value greater than 0 draws the curve toward the point but not through it, as shown in Figure 3.11.

Figure 3.11

The effect of the Fit Tolerance option on a spline

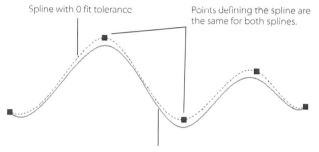

Spline with 0 fit tolerance

Points defining the spline are the same for both splines.

Spline with fit tolerance of 1

> The Fit Tolerance value affects all the points along the spline, not just the currently selected point.

Drawing Curves with Polylines

If you don't need the most accurate spline curves, you might want to draw your curves using the Polyline command. Polylines are the most versatile object type in AutoCAD because they can be shaped and duplicated quickly. You can quickly find the area enclosed by a polyline, and you can "explode" a polyline to smaller components when the need arises, which is something you cannot do to a spline.

To use a polyline to draw a curve, follow these steps:

1. Click the Polyline tool in the Draw panel, or enter **pl**↵ at the command prompt.

2. At the Specify start point: prompt, select a point.

3. At the Specify next point or [Arc/Halfwidth/Length/Undo/Width]: prompt, continue to select points. A line appears between each point you select.

4. Press ↵ when you finish selecting points, or right-click and choose Enter.

Your polyline doesn't look like much of a curve, but you can alter the way it's drawn using the Pedit command:

1. Choose Edit Polyline from the Home tab's expanded Modify panel, or enter **pe**↵.

2. At the `PEDIT Select polyline or [Multiple]:` prompt, select the polyline you just drew.

3. At the `Enter an option [Close/Join/Width/Edit vertex/Fit/Spline/Decurve/Ltype gen/ Reverse/Undo]:` prompt, enter **S↵** to select the Spline option. The straight lines of the polyline change to form a curve, as shown in Figure 3.12.

Notice that the spline version of the polyline does not pass through the points selected to generate the polyline. Instead, the curve is "pulled" toward the points without passing through them. This is similar to the behavior of a spline drawn with the Fit Tolerance option set to 1.

Another way to turn a straight-line polyline into a curve is to use the Fit option in the Pedit command. Instead of using the Spline option in step 3 of the previous exercise, enter **F↵** to use the Fit option, which changes the straight-line polyline into a set of arcs, as shown in Figure 3.13.

Since arcs are used, the curve is not as smooth, but the polyline passes through each point that defines the corners of the original straight-line polyline.

If you've created a spline curve using the Polyline command but you decide you'd rather have a true spline, you can convert it using the Spline command. This lets you apply some of the spline-editing options to a curve generated using polylines.

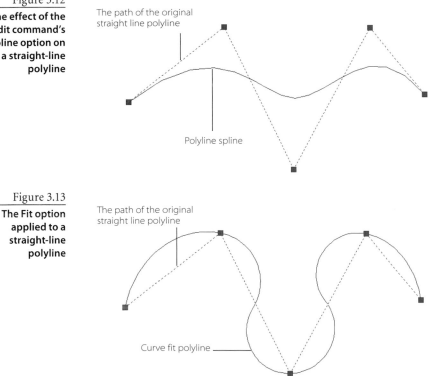

Figure 3.12

The effect of the Pedit command's Spline option on a straight-line polyline

The path of the original straight line polyline

Polyline spline

Figure 3.13

The Fit option applied to a straight-line polyline

The path of the original straight line polyline

Curve fit polyline

To convert a polyline spline curve into a true spline curve, use the Object option in the Spline command:

1. Click the Spline tool in the Draw panel, or type **Spl**↵.

2. At the `Specify first point or [Object]:` prompt, enter **O**↵, or right-click and choose Object.

> **WHAT ARE MULTILINES?**
>
> Multilines are objects that appear as multiple parallel lines. You can use them in any situation where you need to quickly draw a set of lines such as in cavity walls or fancy borders. You can also customize multilines to display solid fills, centerlines, and additional linetypes. You can save your custom multilines as multiline styles, which are in turn saved in special files for easy access from other drawings.
>
> Multilines are not flexible and are difficult to work with, so you might not encounter them often. If you do encounter multilines and find you need to edit them, you can explode and edit them using the standard AutoCAD editing tools. When a multiline is exploded using the Explode command, it is reduced to its component lines. Linetype assignments and layers are maintained for each component. If you are working as part of a team, you will want to consult with your team members before you explode multilines in an AutoCAD drawing. (See Chapter 5 for more about the Explode command.)

3. At the `Select objects:` prompt, select the spline-fitted polyline curves you want to convert.

4. Press ↵ to finish your selection. You can also right-click and choose Enter. The polylines are converted to splines.

These steps will work only on spline-fitted polylines. You will get an error message if you try to do this on other types of polylines.

Drawing Parallel Lines

Another common CAD function is to draw parallel lines. You frequently want parallel lines when drawing the walls of a floor plan or when drawing a cross section of a flat metal assembly, for example. In AutoCAD, you can do this in two ways. You can use the Multiline command, which draws parallel lines and arcs, and you can use the Offset command to copy objects to a set distance. The overall effect of the Offset command is to draw a line parallel to an existing one.

The Offset command makes parallel copies of objects and is the most flexible way to draw parallel lines. It works with lines, arcs, circles, splines, and polylines, so you can produce just about any parallel line you might need (see Figure 3.14). Since it works with splines and polylines, you can easily draw complex parallel curves.

No matter what type of object you're trying to make parallel copies of, the operation is the same. Here are the steps to use the Offset command:

1. Click the Offset tool in the Home tab's Modify panel, or enter **O**↵ at the command prompt.

2. At the `Specify offset distance or [Through/Erase/Layer] <Through>:` prompt, indicate a distance by either entering a distance through the keyboard or selecting two points in the drawing area. You can use osnaps to indicate distances based on existing objects in the drawing.

3. At the `Select object to offset or [Exit/Undo] <Exit>:` prompt, select the object you want to copy.

4. At the `Specify point on side to offset or [Exit,Multiple/Undo] <Exit>:` prompt, select the side of the object where you want the copy to appear. AutoCAD creates a parallel copy at the distance you specified in step 2.

5. Repeat steps 3 and 4 for more parallel copies, or press ↵ to exit the Offset command.

You might notice the Through option in step 2. If you enter **T**↵ at the prompt in step 2 to invoke the Through option, AutoCAD prompts you with `Specify through point:` at step 4. You can then select a point through which the parallel copy is to pass. This option is useful when you know where the parallel line is to pass but you do not know the distance.

Drawing Revision Clouds

Revision clouds are common in all types of technical documents. They draw attention to areas of a drawing that have been modified or updated since the last official version of a drawing, as shown in Figure 3.15.

AutoCAD lets you use two types of revision clouds: normal and calligraphy style, as shown in Figure 3.16. The *normal* style uses lines of uniform thickness, and the *calligraphy* style varies the lineweight to simulate a hand-drawn appearance.

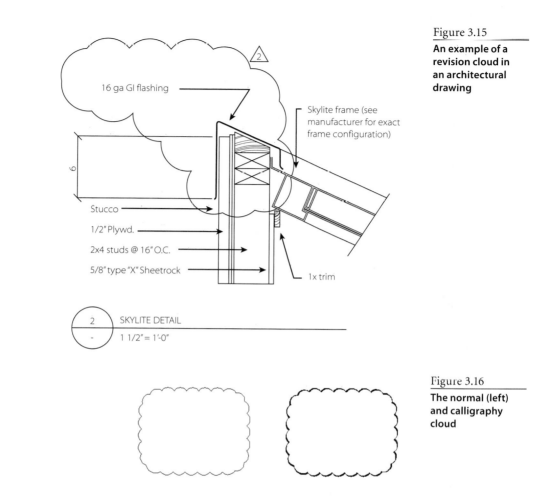

Figure 3.15

An example of a revision cloud in an architectural drawing

16 ga GI flashing

Skylite frame (see manufacturer for exact frame configuration)

6

Stucco

1/2" Plywd.

2x4 studs @ 16" O.C.

5/8" type "X" Sheetrock

1x trim

2

SKYLITE DETAIL

1 1/2" = 1'-0"

Figure 3.16

The normal (left) and calligraphy cloud

Drawing Freehand Revision Clouds

The following describes the default "freehand" method for drawing revision clouds:

1. Click the Revision Cloud tool in the expanded Draw panel. You can also enter **revcloud**↵ at the command prompt. In the command window, you'll see the following message:

   ```
   Minimum arc length: 0.5000
   Maximum arc length: 0.5000
   Style: Calligraphy
   ```

2. At the Specify start point or [Arc length/Object/Style] <Object>: prompt, click a point in the drawing area to start the revision cloud. You'll see the following message:

   ```
   Guide crosshairs along cloud path...
   ```

3. Start to move the cursor to encircle the revision area in your drawing. As you move the mouse, the revision cloud appears.

4. As you come full circle to the starting point of the revision cloud, the cloud automatically closes, and you'll see the following message:

   Revision cloud finished.

Drawing Revision Clouds Based on the Shape of an Object

Figure 3.17

The Cloud tool
in the expanded
Draw panel

If you want to place your revision cloud more carefully, you can draw a closed polyline or a circle around the area you want to cloud and then use the Object option of the Revcloud command:

1. Click the Revision Cloud tool in the expanded Draw panel, as shown in Figure 3.17. You can also enter **revcloud**↵ at the command prompt.

2. At the Specify start point or [Arc length/Object/Style] <Object>: prompt, press ↵ to select the default Object option, or right-click and select Object.

3. Click the object that defines the path of the cloud, such as a closed polyline, spline, or circle. A revision cloud replaces the object you select. You'll also see the following prompt:

   Reverse direction [Yes/No] <No>:

4. You can reverse the direction of the revision cloud by entering **Y**↵, or you can press ↵ to accept the cloud as it is. You can also right-click and select Yes or No from the context menu.

As you draw the revision cloud, you might find that the individual arcs that make up the cloud are too small or too big. You can adjust the size of the revision cloud arc by using the Arc Length option:

1. Start the Revcloud command, and then at the Specify start point or [Arc length/ Object/Style] <Object>: prompt, enter **A**↵, or right-click and choose Arc Length.

2. At the Specify minimum length of arc <2.5722>: prompt, enter a size for the arc.

3. At the Specify maximum length of arc <1.0000>: prompt, you can press ↵ to accept the default maximum arc length, which is equal to the minimum, or you can enter a larger value to vary the arc size.

4. Draw the revision cloud, or press Esc to exit the Revcloud command.

You might find that the revision cloud does not stand out enough in your drawing. You can change the way the arcs are drawn by changing the revision cloud style:

1. Start the Revcloud command, and then at the Specify start point or [Arc length/ Object/Style] <Object>: prompt, enter **S**↵, or right-click and choose Style.

2. At the Select arc style [Normal/Calligraphy] <Normal>: prompt, enter **C**↵. You'll see the following message:

   Arc style = Calligraphy

3. Draw the revision cloud, or press Esc to exit the Revcloud command.

You can change back to the regular style by taking the same steps, but instead of entering **C**↵ in step 2, enter **N**↵.

Revclouds are really polylines, so you can edit them just as you edit any polyline. If you use the regular Revcloud style, you can use the Pedit command to adjust the thickness of the Revcloud arcs. See Chapter 5 for more about editing polylines.

Working with Hatch Patterns and Solid Fills

Just about every drawing program has a Paint Bucket tool that lets you fill a closed area with a color or a pattern. AutoCAD has a tool that performs a similar function, though it is considerably more complex than a simple Paint Bucket tool.

The Boundary Hatch command lets you add patterns, solid fills, and gradient colors to any closed polygon (see Figure 3.18). The closed polygon can consist of any combination of objects. The only requirement is that the area to be hatched must not have large gaps.

Figure 3.18

Examples of hatch patterns within random shapes formed by a spline, a circle, an arc, and a rectangle

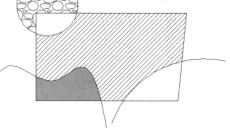

Placing Hatch Patterns: The Basics

A Paint Bucket tool usually just requires you to select a pattern and then click inside an area to be filled. AutoCAD requires you to work through a dialog box to select patterns and areas to fill. This section describes the basic methods for adding hatches and fills.

You can select a hatch pattern from a set of predefined patterns, or if you need just a simple hatch pattern, you can use a user-defined pattern, which consists of just the standard crosshatch lines. This first example describes how to use a user-defined hatch pattern:

1. To open the Hatch and Gradient dialog box, as shown in Figure 3.19, click the Hatch tool in the Draw panel, or enter **H**↵. Hatch is also located in the Draw drop-down list.

2. In the Type drop-down list in the Type and Pattern section, select User Defined. The User Defined option lets you define a simple crosshatch pattern by specifying the line spacing of the hatch and whether it is a single- or double-hatch pattern. The Angle and Spacing input boxes become available so that you can enter values.

3. Enter the spacing between the cross-hatching in the Spacing input box.

4. Enter the angle for the cross-hatching in the Angle input box.

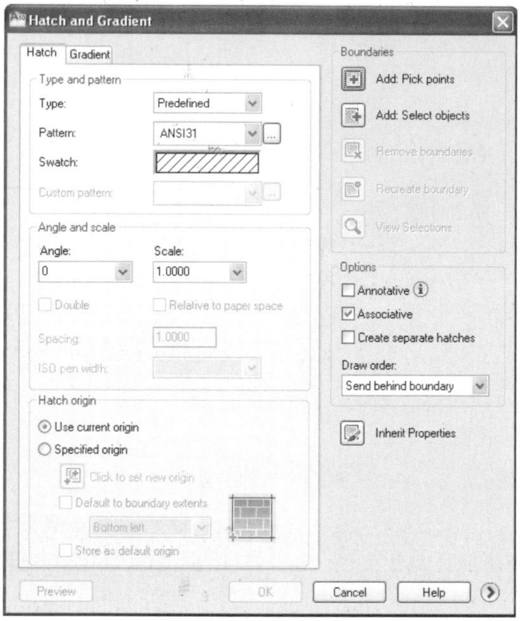

Figure 3.19

The Hatch and
Gradient dialog box

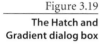

5. Turn on the Double option (just below the Angle input box) if you want a crosshatch hatch pattern. Also notice that the Swatch sample box in the Type and Pattern group displays a sample of your hatch pattern.

6. In the Boundaries section, click the Add Pick Points button. The dialog box momentarily closes, allowing you to select a point inside the area you want hatched.

7. Click a point anywhere inside the area you want hatched. Notice that a highlighted outline appears in the area. This is the boundary AutoCAD has selected to enclose the hatch pattern. You can select additional closed areas at this time.

> If you have text in the hatch boundary, AutoCAD avoids hatching over it, unless the Ignore option is selected in the Island Display Style options. You can find the Island Display Style options in the expanded view of the Hatch and Gradient dialog box. See "Controlling the Behavior of Hatch Patterns and Fills" later in this chapter.

8. Press ↵ to return to the Hatch and Gradient dialog box.

9. Click the Preview button in the lower-left corner of the dialog box. The hatch pattern appears in the area you indicated in step 6. You'll also see the following prompt:

```
Pick or press Esc to return to dialog or <Right-click to accept hatch>:
```

10. Press Esc or the spacebar to return to the dialog box to make further changes, or right-click to apply the hatch pattern. You can also press ↵ to apply the hatch pattern.

In this example, you selected only one area to fill. You can select multiple areas, as indicated in step 7. If after you have previewed the hatch pattern in step 9 you decide you need to select more areas, you can do so by clicking the Add Pick Points button again and selecting more areas.

In step 7, AutoCAD finds the actual boundary for you. Many options give you control over how a hatch boundary is selected. For details, see the section "Understanding the Boundary Hatch Options" later in this chapter.

> Say you want to add a hatch pattern that you previously inserted in another part of the drawing. You might think you have to guess at its scale and rotation angle. But with the Inherit Properties option in the Hatch and Gradient dialog box, you can select a previously inserted hatch pattern as a prototype for the current hatch pattern. However, this feature does not work with exploded hatch patterns.

Using Predefined Patterns

The user-defined hatch pattern is just one type of hatch you can apply to a drawing. AutoCAD also provides sets of predefined patterns. Figure 3.20 shows you all the patterns available. You can also create your own custom patterns, though that process is beyond the scope of this book.

Figure 3.20

The predefined hatch patterns available in AutoCAD

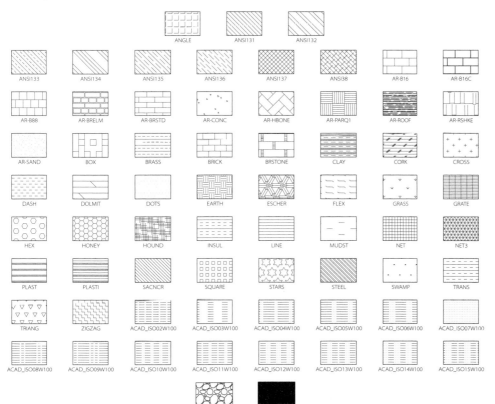

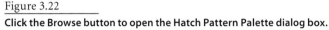

Figure 3.21

Select Predefined from the Type drop-down list.

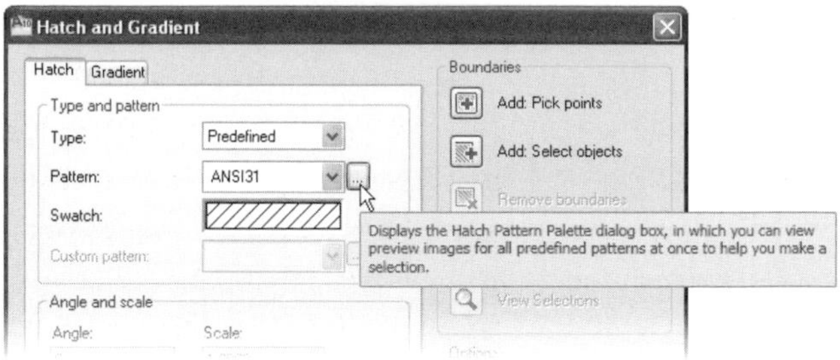

Figure 3.22

Click the Browse button to open the Hatch Pattern Palette dialog box.

To use any of these patterns, select the Predefined option from the Type drop-down list in the Hatch and Gradient dialog box, as shown in Figure 3.21.

You can then select a predefined hatch pattern by clicking the Browse button to the right of the Pattern drop-down list to open the Hatch Pattern Palette dialog box. The Browse button in AutoCAD is indicated by an ellipsis, as shown in Figure 3.22.

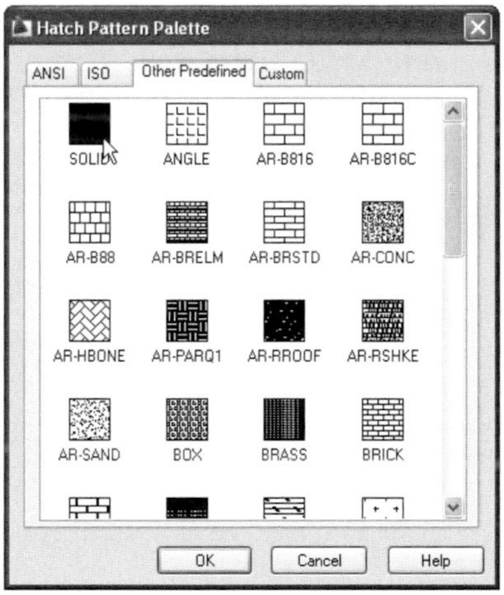

Figure 3.23

The Other Predefined tab in the Hatch Pattern Palette dialog box

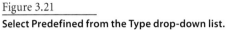

From here you can select a pattern from one of four tabs: ANSI, ISO, Other Predefined, and Custom. The ANSI and ISO patterns are standard patterns used with the ANSI and ISO standards. The Other Predefined patterns are architectural and other patterns you might find useful. The Custom patterns are ones that users have created on their own and placed in a special file.

On the Other Predefined tab, patterns with the AR prefix are architectural patterns that are drawn to full scale, as shown in Figure 3.23. In general, you will want to leave their scale settings at 1. You can adjust the scale after you place the hatch pattern using the Properties palette, as described later in this chapter.

Adding Solid Fills

To add solid fills, you use the same process as adding a predefined hatch pattern, but you use a specific predefined pattern called a *solid*. You can see the solid pattern at the top left of the Other Predefined tab of the Hatch Pattern Palette dialog box.

When you use this pattern, a solid color, initially black, fills the area you select for hatching. You can change the color by altering the Color property of the solid hatch pattern. See Chapter 4 for more about editing the properties of objects.

ANNOTATIVE HATCH PATTERNS

AutoCAD 2010 offers a feature called *annotation scale*. With this feature, you can assign several scales to certain types of objects, and AutoCAD will display the object to the proper scale of the drawing. Hatches can take advantage of this feature to allow hatch patterns to adjust their spacing or pattern size to the scale of your drawing. The Annotative option in the Options group of the Hatch and Gradient dialog box turns on the annotation scale feature for hatch patterns. You'll learn how to use annotation scale in Chapter 8.

Positioning Hatch Patterns Accurately

In the previous example, you placed the hatch pattern without regard for the location of the lines that make up the pattern. In most cases, however, you will want accurate control over where the lines of the pattern are placed. For example, you might want to place a floor tile pattern in a specific location in a floor plan. Or you might want to find the most efficient location for ceiling tiles in a ceiling plan. In the top image in Figure 3.24, a floor tile pattern is placed without regard for the snap origin. The hatch pattern around the perimeter is not evenly spaced. With some careful planning, the hatch pattern's origin is moved to the location shown in the lower image in Figure 3.24. This results in a more evenly spaced tile pattern around the perimeter of the room.

> You can also click the Swatch button to browse through a graphical representation of the predefined hatch patterns.

The Hatch and Gradient dialog box also contains a set of options that let you select an origin for the pattern you are currently placing in the drawing. You can use the Hatch Origin option group in the lower-left corner to determine a point in the drawing to be the hatch origin, as shown in Figure 3.25.

Figure 3.24

Placing a floor tile pattern where you want it using Hatch Origin

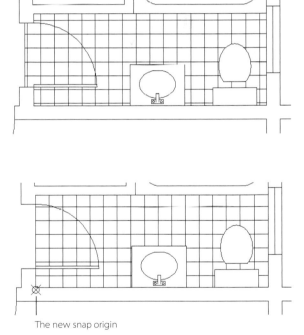

The new snap origin

Figure 3.25

The Hatch Origin option group

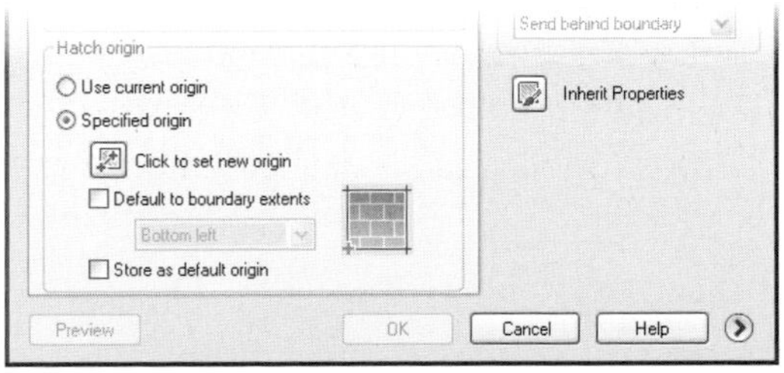

To set a hatch origin, select the Specified Origin option. You can then determine the origin in two ways. You can click the Click to Set New Origin button. The dialog box temporarily closes to let you select an origin in the drawing. The Hatch and Gradient dialog box then returns so that you can apply more options to your hatch pattern.

The other way to set the hatch origin is to use the Default to Boundary Extents option. This option lets you set the origin based on the extents of the hatch boundary rather than on a point you select. The *hatch boundary extents* is an imaginary rectangle that represents the outermost boundary of the pattern. If you are hatching a rectangular area, the hatch boundary extents is the same as your selected boundary, but if the area is an irregular shape, an imaginary rectangular area defines the outermost boundary of the pattern, as shown in Figure 3.26. In this figure, the pattern outside the irregular shape shows you the relationship between the visible pattern and the boundary extents. In reality, only the dark pattern within the irregular shape is drawn.

Figure 3.26

Boundary extents are shown in gray. The hatch pattern appears only within the irregular shape.

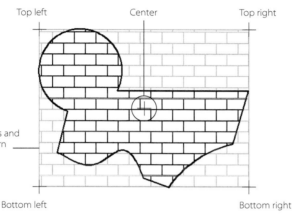

The boundary extents and a sample hatch pattern

When you select this option, you can select options from the drop-down list: Bottom Right, Bottom Left, Top Right, Top Left, and Center. You can select one of these five options to position the hatch origin in relation to the boundary extents. A graphic appears to the right of the list to show the location of the hatch origin. A red cross appears on the graphic telling you where the origin will be when you add the pattern.

The Store as Default Origin option maintains the origin you select as the default hatch origin for later hatch pattern insertions.

Editing the Hatch Area

Figure 3.27

The Associative option in the Hatch and Gradient dialog box

The Hatch command has an option, Associative, that automatically adjusts the shape of a pattern to any changes in the boundary of the hatch pattern. (The Associative option is in the Options section on the Hatch tab in the Hatch and Gradient dialog box, as shown in Figure 3.27.)

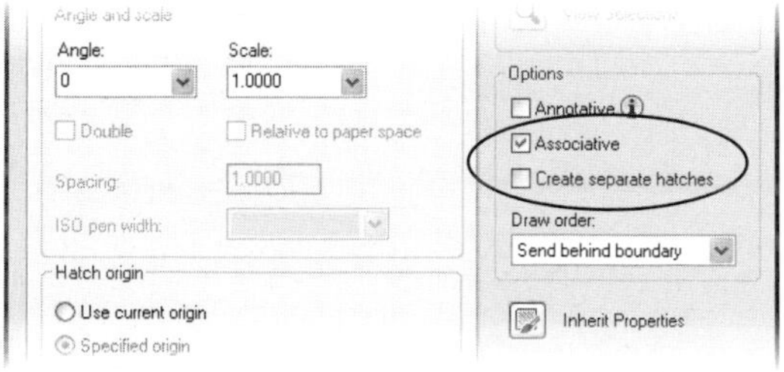

When the Associative option is turned on, the hatch pattern "flows" into any changes you make to the boundary of the pattern. In the right image in Figure 3.28, the diagonal hatch pattern in the center of the rectangle changes when the arc is moved. (The original pattern appears in the left image.)

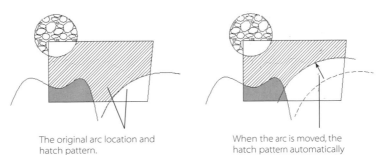

The original arc location and hatch pattern.

When the arc is moved, the hatch pattern automatically adjusts to the new boundary.

Figure 3.28

The Associative hatch option causes hatch patterns to automatically adjust to changes in the pattern's boundary.

The Associative option can save time when you need to modify your drawing, but you need to be aware of its limitations. A hatch pattern can lose its associativity when you do any of the following:

- Erase or explode a hatch boundary
- Erase or explode a block that forms part of the boundary
- Move a hatch pattern away from its boundary

These situations frequently arise when you edit an unfamiliar drawing. Often, boundary objects are placed on a layer that is off or frozen, so the boundary objects are not visible. Or the hatch pattern might be on a layer that is turned off, and you proceed to edit the file, not knowing that a hatch pattern exists. When you encounter such a file, take a moment to check for hatch boundaries so you can deal with them properly. You might need to turn on or thaw all the layers in the drawing so you can make all the hatch patterns visible and selectable (see Chapter 7 for more on layers).

Modifying a Hatch Pattern

Like everything else in a project, a hatch pattern might eventually need changing in some way. Hatch patterns are like blocks in that they act like single objects. You can explode a hatch pattern to edit its individual lines. The Properties palette contains most of the settings you'll need to make changes to your hatch patterns:

1. Double-click the hatch pattern you want to edit. The Hatch Edit dialog box looks the same as the Hatch and Gradient dialog box, as shown in Figure 3.29.

Figure 3.29

The Hatch Edit dialog box

> When you double-click a hatch pattern, you don't display the typical Properties palette. Double-clicking complex objects such as text, blocks, attributes, and hatch patterns opens a dialog box in which you can edit the object in a more direct way. You can still access the Properties palette for any object by selecting the object, right-clicking, and choosing Properties from the context menu.

2. Click the Browse button to the right of the Pattern drop-down list to open the Hatch Pattern Palette dialog box. If the Browse button is not available, make sure that Predefined is selected in the Type drop-down list.

3. Double-click the pattern you want to use, as shown in Figure 3.30.

4. Click OK to accept the change to the hatch pattern. The selected pattern appears in place of the original pattern.

Figure 3.30

Double-click a pattern in the Hatch Pattern Palette to select it.

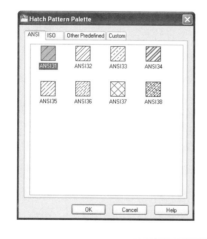

In this example, I used a predefined pattern. You can also replace a pattern with a user-defined pattern if you prefer. Select User Defined from the Type drop-down list, and then specify spacing and angle values.

The other items in the Hatch Edit dialog box duplicate some of the options in the Hatch and Gradient dialog box. They let you modify the individual properties of the selected hatch pattern. The section "Understanding the Boundary Hatch Options" later in this chapter describes these other properties in detail.

> If you create and edit hatch patterns frequently, you will find the Modify II toolbar useful. It contains an Edit Hatch tool that gives you ready access to the Hatch Edit dialog box. To open the Modify II toolbar, right-click an empty area on any toolbar, and then click Modify II in the context menu that opens.

If you prefer, you can modify a hatch pattern using the Properties palette. To open the Properties palette, right-click a pattern and choose Properties from the context menu. The Properties palette displays a Pattern category, which offers a Pattern Name option, as shown in Figure 3.31.

When you click this option, a Browse button appears. Click it to open the Hatch Pattern Palette dialog box. You can then select a new pattern from the dialog box. The Type option in the Properties palette lets you change the type of hatch pattern from Predefined to User Defined or Custom.

Understanding the Boundary Hatch Options

The Hatch and Gradient dialog box contains many other options that you didn't explore in the previous exercises. For example, instead of selecting the area to be hatched by clicking a point, you can select the actual objects that bound the area you want to hatch using the Add: Select Objects button. Clicking the Swatch sample box in the Type and Pattern group opens the Hatch Pattern Palette dialog box, which lets you select a predefined hatch pattern from a graphic window.

Other options in the right column of the Hatch and Gradient dialog box include the following:

Remove Boundaries This lets you remove objects that you do not want to include as part of the boundary. Examples of this are furniture outlines in a floor pattern or some objects that you might have accidentally selected as part of a boundary set.

Recreate Boundary This allows you to re-create a boundary after you've added a polyline or region to an existing hatch pattern boundary.

View Selections This temporarily closes the dialog box and then highlights the objects that have been selected as the hatch boundary by AutoCAD. Press ↵ to return to the dialog box.

Create Separate Hatches You can hatch several separate areas at once in AutoCAD, but by default, even though the hatches are in separate areas, they behave as one object. You can force separate hatch areas to behave as separate hatch objects by turning on this option.

Draw Order This lets you control whether your hatch pattern is drawn over existing objects or whether they are to be placed "underneath" existing objects. Hatch patterns can cover or draw over existing graphics. This is especially true of solid fill or gradient hatch patterns.

Inherit Properties This lets you select a hatch pattern from an existing one in the drawing. This is helpful when you want to apply a hatch pattern that is already used but you do not know its name or its scale, rotation, or other properties.

At the top of the column of options in the Options group is the Associative option. This option lets you determine whether the hatch pattern being inserted is associative or nonassociative. As discussed earlier, an *associative* hatch pattern automatically changes to fill its boundary whenever that boundary is stretched or edited.

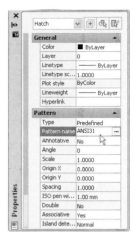

Figure 3.31

Select a hatch pattern from the Properties palette.

Controlling the Behavior of Hatch Patterns and Fills

AutoCAD's Boundary Hatch command has a fair amount of intelligence. It can detect the shape of an area and fill the area accordingly. Boundary Hatch can also detect objects within a closed area, such as an *island*, and hatch around it, as shown in Figure 3.32.

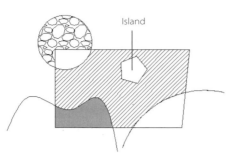

If you prefer, you can control how AutoCAD treats these island conditions and other situations by expanding the Hatch and Gradient dialog box. To do this, click the More Options button in the lower-right corner of the dialog box.

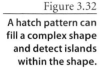

The dialog box expands to the right, showing several more options, as shown in Figure 3.33.

In addition to controlling the island detection feature of hatch patterns, the additional Hatch and Gradient options let you fine-tune other aspects of hatch pattern creation.

ISLANDS

The options in the Islands section control how nested boundaries affect the hatch pattern. The graphics show the effect of the selected option. The Islands options include the following:

Island Detection Detects an island within a boundary.

Normal Causes the hatch pattern to alternate between nested boundaries. The outer boundary is hatched; if a closed object is within the boundary, it is not hatched. If another closed object *is* inside the first closed object, *that* object is hatched. This is the default setting.

Outer Applies the hatch pattern to an area defined by the outermost boundary and by any boundaries nested within the outermost boundary. Any boundaries nested within the nested boundaries are ignored.

Ignore Supplies the hatch pattern to the entire area within the outermost boundary, ignoring any nested boundaries.

BOUNDARY RETENTION

The Boundary Hatch command can also create an outline of the hatch area using one of two objects: 2D regions, which are like 2D planes, or polyline outlines. Boundary Hatch actually creates such a polyline boundary temporarily to establish the hatch area. These boundaries are automatically removed after the hatch pattern is inserted. If you want to retain the boundaries in the drawing, make sure the Retain Boundaries check box is selected. Retaining the boundary can be useful if you know you will be hatching the area more than once or if you are hatching a fairly complex area.

BOUNDARY SET

If the current view contains a lot of graphic data, AutoCAD can have difficulty or be slow in finding a boundary. If you run into this problem or if you want to single out a specific object for a point selection boundary, you can further limit the area that AutoCAD uses to locate hatch boundaries by using the Boundary Set options:

New Lets you select the objects from which you want AutoCAD to determine the hatch boundary, instead of searching the entire view. The screen clears and lets you select objects. This option discards previous boundary sets. It is useful for hatching areas in a drawing that contain many objects that you do not want to include in the hatch boundary.

Current Viewport Tells you that AutoCAD will use the current view to determine the hatch boundary. Once you select a set of objects using the New button, you'll also see Existing Set as an option in this drop-down list. You can then use this drop-down list to choose the entire view or the objects you select for the hatch boundary.

The Boundary Set options are designed to give you more control over the way a point selection boundary is created. These options have no effect when you use the Add: Select Objects button to select specific objects for the hatch boundary.

GAP TOLERANCE

This option lets you hatch an area that is not completely enclosed. The Tolerance value sets the maximum gap size in an area that you want to hatch. You can use a value from 0 to 5000.

INHERIT OPTIONS

If you use the Inherit Properties hatch option to duplicate an existing hatch pattern, the Inherit Options group lets you determine the pattern's origin.

Choosing Colors and Patterns for Gradient Fill Shading

You might have noticed that one of the hatch patterns offered is a solid. The solid hatch pattern lets you apply a solid color to a bounded area instead of a pattern. AutoCAD also offers a set of gradient patterns that let you apply a color gradient to an area.

You can apply a gradient to an area in the same way that you apply a hatch pattern, but instead of using the Hatch tab of the Hatch and Gradient dialog box, you use the Gradient tab to select a gradient pattern, as shown in Figure 3.34.

Instead of hatch patterns, the Gradient tab presents a variety of gradient patterns. It also lets you control the color of the gradient. For example, if you want to set shades of blue, you can select the One Color option and then double-click the blue color swatch, as shown in Figure 3.35.

Figure 3.34

The Gradient tab of the Hatch and Gradient dialog box

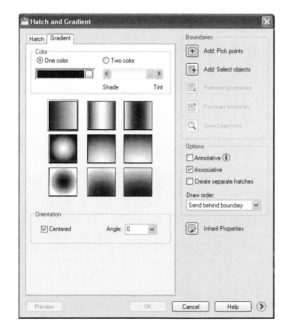

When you double-click the color swatch, the Select Color dialog box opens, displaying a palette of true-color options, as shown in Figure 3.36.

You can then select the color you want for the gradient. The Shade/Tint slider just to the right of the color swatch on the Gradient tab lets you control the shade of the single-color gradient.

If you want the gradient to transition between two colors, click the Two Color radio button. When you click Two Color, the slider below the Two Color option changes to a color swatch. You can double-click the swatch or click the Browse button to the right of the swatch to open the Select Color dialog box.

Just below the One Color and Two Color options are the gradient pattern options. You can choose from nine patterns, and you can select an angle for the pattern from the Angle drop-down list. The Centered option places the center of the gradient at the center of the area selected for the pattern.

To place a gradient pattern, select a set of objects or a point within a bounded area, just as you would for a hatch pattern. You can then click the Preview button to preview your hatch pattern, or you can click OK to apply the gradient to the drawing.

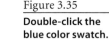

Figure 3.35

Double-click the blue color swatch.

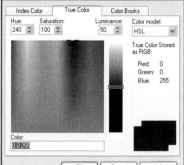

Figure 3.36

The True Color tab of the Select Color dialog box

QUICKLY MATCHING A HATCH PATTERN AND OTHER PROPERTIES

Another tool to help you edit hatch patterns is Match Properties, which is similar to Format Painter in the Microsoft Office suite. This tool lets you change an existing hatch pattern to match another existing hatch pattern. Here's how to use it:

1. Enter **Matchprop**⏎ in the command line.

2. Click the source hatch pattern you want to copy.

3. Click the target hatch pattern you want to change.

The target pattern changes to match the source pattern. The Match Properties tool transfers other properties as well, such as layer, color, and linetype settings. You can select the properties that are transferred by opening the Property Settings dialog box.

To open this dialog box, enter **S**⏎ after selecting the object in step 2, or right-click and choose Settings from the context menu. You can then select the properties you want to transfer from the options shown. All the properties are selected by default. Note that you

continues

QUICKLY MATCHING A HATCH PATTERN AND OTHER PROPERTIES *(continued)*

can also transfer text and dimension style settings. You'll learn more about text and dimension styles in Chapters 9 and 10.

TIPS FOR USING THE BOUNDARY HATCH

Here are a few tips for using the Boundary Hatch feature:

- Watch out for boundary areas that are part of a large block. AutoCAD examines the entire block when defining boundaries. This can take time if the block is quite large. Use the Boundary Set option to "focus in" on the set of objects you want AutoCAD to use for your hatch boundary.

- If the area to be hatched is large yet will require fine detail, first outline the hatch area using a polyline. Then use the Add: Select Objects tool in the Hatch and Gradient dialog box to select the polyline boundary manually, instead of depending on Boundary Hatch to find the boundary for you.

- Consider turning off layers that might interfere with AutoCAD's ability to find a boundary. Boundary Hatch works on nested blocks as long as the nested block entities are parallel to the current UCS.

Drawing Regular Polygons

If you need to draw a regular polygon, such as a hexagon or a pentagon, you can use the Polygon tool in the Draw panel. This tool creates a polyline in the shape of a regular polygon.

The default method for drawing regular polygons is as follows:

1. Click the Polygon tool in the Draw panel, or enter **pol**⏎ at the command prompt.

2. At the `Enter number of sides <4>:` prompt, enter the number of sides you want for your polygon.

3. At the `Specify center of polygon or [Edge]:` prompt, select the center point for the polygon.

4. At the `Enter an option [Inscribed in circle/Circumscribed about circle] <I>:` prompt, press ↵ to specify the distance from the center to a vertex of the polygon. You can also enter **C**↵ if you want to specify the distance from the center to a point tangent to one side of the polygon (see Figure 3.37).

5. At the `Specify radius of circle:` prompt, enter a radius value. This value, in conjunction with the option you select in step 4, determines the size of the polygon. Once you enter a radius, the polygon appears in the drawing.

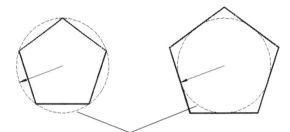

The circle and radius are shown for reference only.

You also have the option to specify the size of the polygon based on the length of one side of the polygon. To do this, enter **E**↵ at the prompt in step 3. You will see the following prompt:

>   Specify first endpoint of edge:

Select a point. You'll then see the following prompt:

>   Specify second endpoint of edge:

You'll also see the polygon follow the cursor with one vertex on the point you selected at the first endpoint prompt:

First endpoint of the edge.

The cursor follows the other endpoint of the edge.

Figure 3.37

The polygon on the left uses the `Inscribed in circle` option in step 4, and the polygon on the right uses the `Circumscribed about circle` option. The radius is the same for both images.

Select a point to place the polygon in the drawing. Remember that you can specify a relative coordinate to specify an exact length for the side of the polygon.

Using Objects to Lay Out Your Drawing

Often when you are sketching with pencil and paper, you draw some lines to help lay out your sketch. You can do the same in AutoCAD using any object. But AutoCAD also provides a few tools specifically designed to help you lay out your drawing.

You can use Divide and Measure to mark off an object at regular intervals. If you are familiar with manual drafting tools, you can think of Measure as analogous to a divider. Measure marks off exact distances along an object. The Divide command is similar to Measure, but instead of marking off a known distance you specify, it marks divisions of an object to exact, equal segments. For example, if you want to mark off a line of unknown length into 12 equal divisions, you use the Divide command.

You can use point objects to mark exact points in a drawing. In fact, the Divide and Measure commands use points as markers. Point objects can be helpful in surveying to mark off datum locations or waypoints, for example.

Ray and Xline are two commands that create lines with special characteristics. Ray creates a line that starts at a selected point and extends into an infinite distance much like the rays of light from the sun. Xline creates a line that has an infinite length in both directions. Unlike rays, xlines do not have a beginning point. You specify a point through which the xline passes and a direction.

Marking Points in a Drawing

Point objects are AutoCAD objects that are commonly used to mark an exact point in a drawing. Point objects are used as markers by commands that mark off equal divisions on objects. You can also create point objects by using the Point command. To place a point in a drawing, choose Multiple Points from the Home tab's expanded Modify panel. Point objects can be difficult to see. Fortunately, you can alter their appearance to make them more visible. To see point objects more clearly, follow these steps:

1. Choose Point Style from the Home tab's expanded Utilities panel to open the Point Style dialog box, as shown in Figure 3.38.

2. Click the *x* point style in the upper-right of the dialog box, click the Set Size Relative to Screen button, and then click OK.

3. If you have already used the Divide or Measure command or have placed points in your drawing, enter **Re↵**. The point objects in the drawing change into *x*'s, as shown in Figure 3.39.

You can change the point style any time, and all the points in a drawing will change to the new style.

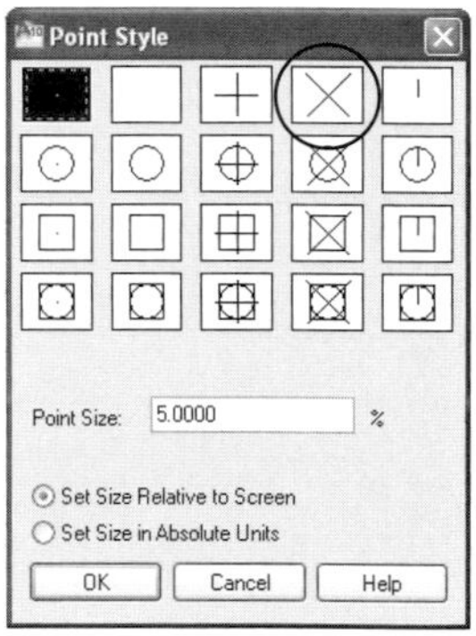

Figure 3.38

The Point Style dialog box

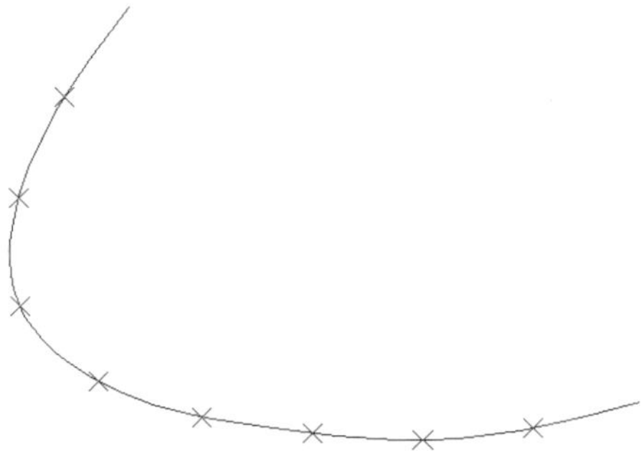

Figure 3.39

An example of point objects, appearing as *x*'s, used to mark divisions on a polyline

If you are using point objects as visual markers only and do not want them to print, you can put them on a layer you create specifically for point objects and then set that layer as a non-printing layer. See Chapter 7 for more about layers.

Marking Off Equal Divisions

You can use the Divide command to divide an object into a specific number of equal segments. The Divide command places a set of point objects on a line, an arc, a circle, a spline, or a polyline, marking off exact divisions. This exercise shows how it works:

1. Click the Divide tool from the Points flyout in the expanded Draw panel, or enter **Div.**↲.

2. At the `Select object to divide:` prompt, select the object you want to mark off.

3. The `Enter number of segments or [Block]:` prompt that appears next asks you for the number of divisions you want on the selected object. Enter the number of divisions you want.

The command prompt now returns, and it might appear that nothing has happened. AutoCAD has placed several point objects on the selected object. These point objects indicate the locations of the divisions you requested. They do not actually cut the object. They just mark the object. You can use the Node osnap to select a point exactly at the point objects' locations.

Dividing Objects into Specified Lengths

The Measure command acts just like Divide; however, instead of dividing an object into equal-length segments, the Measure command marks intervals of a specified distance along an object. For example, suppose you need to mark off segments exactly 4 units long along a curve (see Figure 3.40).

The following steps describe how you use the Measure command to accomplish this task:

1. Click the Measure tool from the Multiple Point flyout of the expanded Draw panel, or enter **Me.**↲.

Figure 3.40

Marking off 4-unit segments on a curve

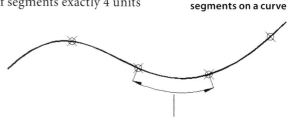

Typical 4-unit segment marked by point objects

2. At the Select object to measure: prompt, click the object closest to the end from which you want the measured divisions to start.

3. At the Specify length of segment or [Block]: prompt, enter the length you want. The point objects appear at the specified distance.

> You can find both Divide and Measure in the Point tool flyout in the expanded view of the Draw panel. Click the title bar of the Draw panel to expand it and view the Point tool.

Using Construction Lines

Many graphics programs include an alignment guide, which is usually a nonprinting line that can be dragged into the work area. AutoCAD offers a similar function in the construction line, otherwise known as the Xline command.

Unlike the alignment guide of other programs, AutoCAD's construction line prints. You can also edit construction lines so that they become a standard line in the AutoCAD drawing, place them with accuracy, and rotate them to any angle you like.

Drawing Multiple Construction Lines through a Point

To draw multiple construction lines through a point, follow these steps:

1. Click the Construction Line tool in the expanded Draw panel, or enter **Xline.⏎** at the command prompt.

2. At the Specify a point or [Hor/Ver/Ang/Bisect/Offset]: prompt, select a point through which the construction line is to pass. If you don't have an exact location, you can always move the construction line later.

3. At the Specify through point: prompt, you'll see a temporary construction line that passes through the point you selected in step 2 and follows the cursor. Select another point to indicate the angle for the construction line.

MARKING OFF INTERVALS USING DRAWING ASSEMBLIES INSTEAD OF POINT OBJECTS

Marking off regular distances isn't the only use for the Divide and Measure commands. You can also place drawing assemblies, such as symbols or parts, at regular intervals along an object. For example, you can use the Block option of Divide or Measure to place a row of sinks equally spaced along a wall or place a row of parking spaces along a curb.

To replace the point objects with assemblies, you use the Block option in the Divide or Measure command. Blocks are an assembly of objects that form an image that can be readily copied, like a rubber stamp. (See Chapter 8 for more about blocks.) The blocks take the place of the point objects as markers.

MARKING OFF INTERVALS USING DRAWING ASSEMBLIES INSTEAD OF POINT OBJECTS (continued)

Here's how to use blocks as markers:

1. Make sure the block you want to use is part of the current drawing file.

2. Start either the Divide command or the Measure command.

3. At the Specify length of segment or [Block]: prompt (or Specify number of segments or [Block]: prompt for the Divide command), enter **B**↵.

4. At the Enter name of block to insert: prompt, enter the name of a block.

5. At the Align block with object? [Yes/No] <Y>: prompt, press ↵ if you want the blocks to follow the alignment of the selected object. (Entering **N**↵ inserts each block at a 0° angle.)

6. At the Enter the number of Segments: prompt, enter the number of segments. The blocks appear at regular intervals on the selected object.

The block's insertion point is placed on the divided or measured object in the location where the point object would usually be placed.

4. You can continue to select points to draw several construction lines through the first point you selected in step 2.

5. Press ↵ to exit the Construction Line tool.

Once you have a construction line in the drawing, you can move, copy, and edit the line as you would other lines.

Drawing Multiple Horizontal, Vertical, or Angled Construction Lines

Using the default method shown in the previous exercise, you can draw multiple construction lines passing through the same point. But what if you want to draw multiple lines that are all vertical or horizontal or all even at an angle? The Construction Line tool offers several options that allow you to add multiple horizontal or vertical lines as well as lines at a specified angle. Here's how these options work:

1. Click Construction Line tool in the expanded Draw panel, or enter **Xline**↵ at the command prompt.

2. At the Specify a point or [Hor/Ver/Ang/Bisect/Offset]: prompt, enter **H**↵ for multiple horizontal lines or **V**↵ for multiple vertical lines.

3. Select points in the drawing to place your construction lines.

4. Press ↵ to exit the Construction Line tool.

For multiple construction lines at the same angle, do the following:

1. Click the Construction Line tool in the expanded Draw panel, or enter **Xline**↵ at the command prompt.

2. At the `Specify a point or [Hor/Ver/Ang/Bisect/Offset]:` prompt, enter **A**↵, and then enter the angle for the lines you want to place in the drawing.

3. Select points in the drawing to place your construction lines.

4. Press ↵ to exit the Construction Line tool.

Optionally, in step 2, you can enter **A**↵ **R**↵ and then select an existing line whose angle you want to match.

Drawing Bisecting Construction Lines

If you need to draw a line that bisects the angle between two other lines, you can do so with the Bisect option of the Construction Line tool. Here's how the Bisect option works:

1. Click the Construction Line tool in the expanded Draw panel, or enter **Xline**↵ at the command prompt.

2. At the `Specify a point or [Hor/Ver/Ang/Bisect/Offset]:` prompt, enter **B**↵.

3. At the `Specify angle vertex point:` prompt, use the Intersection osnap, and select the intersection of the two lines you want to bisect (see Figure 3.41). See "Selecting Exact Locations on Objects" in Chapter 2 if you need a little refresher on using osnaps.

4. At the `Specify angle start point:` prompt, use the Nearest osnap, and select one of the pair of lines you want to bisect.

Figure 3.41

Bisecting a pair of lines with a construction line

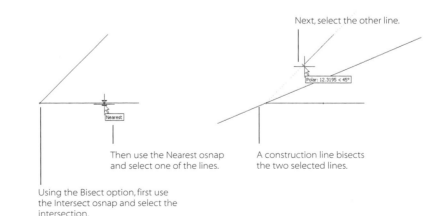

Next, select the other line.

Then use the Nearest osnap and select one of the lines.

A construction line bisects the two selected lines.

Using the Bisect option, first use the Intersect osnap and select the intersection.

5. At the `Specify angle end point:` prompt, use the Nearest osnap, and select the other line. A construction line appears that bisects the pair you selected.

6. You can continue placing bisecting construction lines, or you can press ↵ to exit the command.

Creating Construction Lines Parallel to Existing Lines

The last option of the Construction Line tool lets you create a construction line that is parallel to an existing line. This option works just like the Offset command described earlier in this chapter, but instead of creating a copy of an object, the Offset option creates a straight construction line. Here's how:

1. Click the Construction Line tool in the expanded Draw panel, or enter **Xline**↵ at the command prompt.

2. At the `Specify a point or [Hor/Ver/Ang/Bisect/Offset]:` prompt, enter **O**↵.

3. At the `Specify offset distance or [Through] <Through>:` prompt, indicate a distance by either entering a distance through the keyboard or selecting two points in the drawing area. You can use osnaps to indicate distances based on existing objects in the drawing.

4. At the `Select a line object:` prompt, select the object to which you want to create the construction line parallel.

5. At the `Specify side to offset:` prompt, select the side of the object where you want the copy to appear. AutoCAD creates a parallel construction line at the distance you specified in step 3.

6. Repeat step 4 for more parallel construction lines, or press ↵ to exit the Offset command.

Placing Ray Construction Lines

The construction line is unusual in that it has no endpoint. It extends into a virtual infinity in two directions. If you want a construction line that has a starting point, you can use a ray. A ray can be useful when editing circular objects because it can be easily rotated about an origin point. Here's how to place a ray in a drawing:

1. Click the Ray tool in the expanded Draw panel, or enter **ray**↵ at the command prompt.

2. At the `Specify start point:` prompt, select a point for the beginning of the ray.

3. At the `Specify through point:` prompt, select another point to indicate the direction of the ray.

4. Continue to place more rays by selecting points, or press ↵ to exit the command.

OTHER DRAWING METHODS

You create most 2D drawings in AutoCAD using the commands presented in this chapter, but you can use two other methods: the region and freehand sketching.

The Region object acts more like a paper cutout shape. Regions are always closed outlines of shapes, and you can even convert a closed polyline into a region. You can add and subtract regions to build 2D shapes using what are called Boolean operations. (See Chapter 6 for information about Boolean operations.)

To create a region, first create a closed polyline. You can use the Polyline, Rectangle, or Polygon tool to do this. You can also use the Boundary tool, which will place a closed polyline outline over an enclosed area. You can find the Boundary tool in the expanded Draw panel.

Next, issue the Region command by clicking the Region tool in the expanded Draw panel. Select the closed polylines you want to convert, and then press ↵. You can add and subtract regions using the Boolean operations described in Chapter 6.

The Sketch command lets you draw freehand, though this method of drawing really doesn't make sense unless you are using a drawing tablet. Even then, the Sketch command is rarely used.

If you'd like to find out more about regions and the Sketch command, check the AutoCAD Help system. You'll also find information about these features in *Mastering AutoCAD 2010 and AutoCAD LT 2010* (Sybex, 2009).

Summary

If you like to experiment, you've probably tried to create a few objects on your own before even reading this chapter. And if you've read the first two chapters of this book and have understood the basic way in which AutoCAD operates, drawing objects should be easy to understand.

Things do get tricky, however, when you start to use hatch patterns and gradient shading. If you find you need to draw hatch patterns and gradient fills, you'll want to study the sections that cover those topics more carefully. Also, curved lines can be difficult to master without some practice, so try using spline-fit polylines and splines before you use them in a "serious" drawing.

The layout tools also take a little practice, and you might find that you don't use them that frequently. But when you need them, they are indispensable, so it's a good idea to at least be aware of them and remember where they are in this book for a quick reference.

CHAPTER 4

Editing AutoCAD Objects

This chapter is about editing AutoCAD objects. If you want to know how to make changes to existing objects you've already drawn, this chapter is the place to look.

If you're in a hurry, you might want to skim this chapter to get an idea of what you can do in AutoCAD in terms of editing objects. Or if you are looking for some instruction right now, check the list of chapter topics to see whether the information you need is here.

If you're completely new to AutoCAD, you might want to read the first half of this chapter as a primer, especially since editing in AutoCAD is an integral part of creating new drawings.

The beginning of this chapter covers some basic information that is crucial to just about all the AutoCAD editing commands. Selecting objects, for example, is something you'll be doing a lot, so I explain it in detail. I also explain grip editing, a method of editing that is fairly common in most graphics programs. You'll learn how Dynamic Input provides a way to edit the properties of individual objects. Finally, I'll introduce the Properties palette, an important tool for editing in AutoCAD.

This chapter includes the following topics:

- **Selecting objects**
- **Editing the Windows way**
- **Changing objects with grips and Dynamic Input**
- **Controlling objects using the Properties palette**
- **Using parametric tools to create "smart drawings"**
- **Controlling sizes with dimensional constraint**

Selecting Objects

AutoCAD lets you select objects in a drawing in a variety of ways. Unfortunately, these selection methods aren't always consistent throughout AutoCAD's set of commands. In the following sections, you'll learn about the most common methods for selecting objects.

Using the Standard AutoCAD Selection Method

Many AutoCAD commands prompt you to select objects with the `Select objects:` prompt. Along with this prompt, the cursor changes from a crosshair cursor to a small square.

Whenever you see the `Select objects:` prompt and the square cursor, called the Object Selection cursor, you have a couple of options while making your selection. You can click objects individually or select groups of objects using a rectangular selection area. AutoCAD also provides options to select areas using an irregular polygon boundary.

＋ ———— Standard cursor

＋ ———— Point Selection cursor

▫ ———— Object Selection cursor

AutoCAD's behavior when you are selecting an object is a little different from that of other graphics programs. If you see the `Select objects:` prompt, you are actually in a selection mode, and every action you take is inferred by AutoCAD to be a selection operation. You can continue to add or subtract selections, but AutoCAD won't know you're finished selecting objects until you press ↵.

As already mentioned, you can click objects to select them. Each time you click an object, it is added to the *selection set*, which is the set of objects to be edited by the current command. You can also select objects using a window, commonly called a *marquee* in other programs. To remove a selection, Shift+click the object. This is reversed in most other graphics programs, which require a Shift+click to add objects to a selection.

Practicing Using Selection Options

In this section, you'll learn about the most common selection options in AutoCAD and see what to do when you make the wrong selection.

Before you continue, you'll turn off running osnaps and osnap tracking. Although extremely useful, these features can be confusing to new users.

1. Look at the Object Snap and Object Snap Tracking tools in the status bar at the bottom of the AutoCAD window. If they are turned on, they are highlighted in blue. Click them to turn them off.

Object Snap tool ———— ┘ └ ———— Object Snap Tracking tool

2. You'll want to draw something so you can practice on it. Click the Line tool in the Home tab's Draw panel, and then draw the four sides of a rectangle roughly like the one shown in Figure 4.1. Remember that you can draw the first three sides and then enter **C.⏎** to "close" the rectangle.

3. Click the Arc tool in the Home tab's Draw panel, and select three points to draw an arc roughly where one appears in Figure 4.1. The arc does not have to be exact, but you should place it above the rectangle.

Now you'll see how to select an object in AutoCAD. In the following exercise, you'll practice using a single click to select objects one at a time:

1. Place the cursor over any object, but do not click just yet. As the cursor hovers over an object, notice that the object highlights. This shows you the object AutoCAD will select if you click, and it shows you the extent and shape of the object you are about to select.

2. Click each of the two horizontal lines of the rectangle. As you select the first object, the Quick Properties panel appears. This panel displays some of the properties of the selected object. In addition, the selected object is highlighted, as shown in Figure 4.2. Once you've made a selection, you can deselect objects that you selected accidentally.

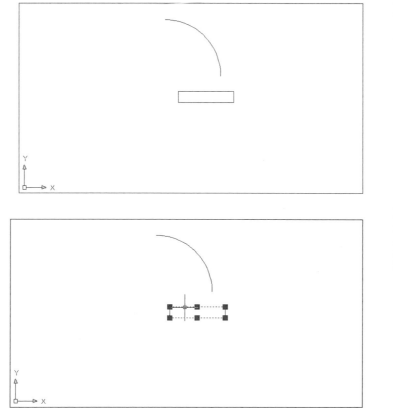

Figure 4.1

A rectangle, drawn using the Line tool, and an arc

Figure 4.2

Selecting the lines of the rectangle and seeing them highlighted

3. Hold down the Shift key, and click one of the highlighted lines. It reverts to a solid line, showing you that it is no longer selected for editing.

4. Shift+click the remaining selected line. Now you're back to having nothing selected.

Clicking objects is perhaps the most intuitive and easiest way to select objects. The additional highlighting helps you determine whether you are about to select the right object. The Quick Properties panel gives you ready access to some of the basic properties of an object. You'll learn more about object properties later in this chapter.

Clicking works fine when you need to be precise about selecting individual objects, but you'll also need a way to select multiple objects efficiently. Next you'll look at the selection window, which lets you quickly select groups of objects.

Selecting Objects with Windows

When you click a blank portion of the drawing area, AutoCAD automatically starts a selection window. A selection window lets you enclose a set of objects to select them. The following exercise demonstrates how it works:

1. Select a point above and to the left of the rectangle shown in the left image of Figure 4.3. Be sure not to select the rectangle itself. Now a window appears that you can drag across the screen as you move the cursor. If you move the cursor to the left, the window appears dotted (see the left image in Figure 4.3) and has a green tint. If you move the cursor to the right, it appears solid with a blue tint (see the right image in Figure 4.3).

2. Select a point below and to the right of the rectangle so that the rectangle is completely enclosed by the window, as shown in the right image in Figure 4.3. The rectangle is highlighted. Notice that the arc is not selected, even though you might have partially included it in the window.

3. Press Esc to clear the entire selection at once.

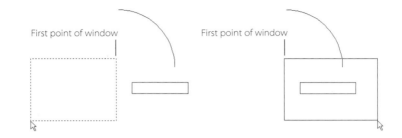

Figure 4.3

The dotted window (left image) indicates a crossing selection; the solid window (right image) indicates a standard selection window.

The two windows you have just seen—the solid, blue tinted one and the dotted, green one—represent a standard window and a crossing window. If you use a standard window, anything that is completely contained within the window is selected. If you use a crossing window, anything that is contained within or that crosses through the window is selected. These two types of windows start automatically when you click any blank portion of the drawing area with either the standard cursor or the Point Selection cursor.

Next, you will select objects with an automatic crossing window:

1. Select a point below and to the right of the rectangle, as shown in Figure 4.4. As you move the cursor left, the crossing (dotted) window appears, and the window area is tinted green.

2. Place the window so it encloses the rectangle and part of the arc (see Figure 4.4), and then click to confirm your selection area. Both the rectangle and arc are highlighted.

Using the selection window and clicking is all you need to do to select objects in AutoCAD. Often you can select a group of objects with either the standard window or the crossing window and then Shift+click to remove anything from the selection set that you don't want to include in the selection. If you are working in a crowded drawing, you can use the scroll wheel of your mouse to zoom in and out while you are selecting objects. It's also a good idea to make sure that the Snap mode in the status bar is turned off while you are making your selections.

Figure 4.4

The rectangle enclosed by a crossing window

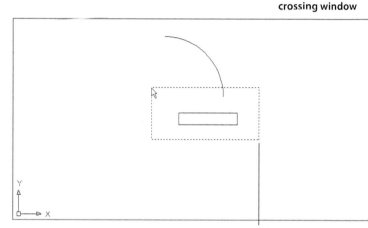

First point of window

Editing the Windows Way

You might have noticed that when you click an object, AutoCAD displays the object's *grips*, which are special square points on the object. These grips most commonly appear on the endpoints of objects, though they can also appear at the midpoint of lines and arcs and at other geometric features of objects. You can use grips to make direct changes to the shape of objects or to quickly move, copy, rotate, or scale the object. The exercise in the following section gives you a feel for how grip-editing works.

In the unlikely event that you do not see grips when you click objects, your version of Auto-CAD might have the grips feature turned off. To turn it on, right-click a blank area of the drawing, and choose Options from the context menu. In the Options dialog box, select the Selection tab. Turn on the Enable Grips option in the Grips section.

Stretching Lines Using Grips

In this exercise, you'll stretch one corner of the rectangle by grabbing the grip points of two lines. First, you'll work with the Dynamic Input option turned off. Later, you'll see how to use Dynamic Input to make detailed changes to objects.

1. Press Esc to make sure you're not in the middle of a command, and then make sure the Dynamic Input tool in the status bar is off. It should be gray.

2. Click a point below and to the right of the rectangle to start a selection window.

3. Click above and to the left of the rectangle to select the rectangle, placing a crossing window around it. Notice that the lines of the rectangle are selected and that the grips appear.

4. Place the cursor on the lower-left corner grip of the rectangle, *but don't click yet*. Notice that the cursor jumps to the grip point and the grip changes color.

5. Move the cursor to another grip point. Notice again how the cursor jumps to it. When placed on a grip, the cursor moves to the exact center of the grip point. This means, for example, that if the cursor is placed on an endpoint grip, it is on the exact endpoint of the object.

6. Move the cursor to the upper-left corner grip of the rectangle, and click. The grip becomes a different color and is now a *hot grip*. The prompt displays the following message:

```
** STRETCH **
Specify stretch point or [Base point/Copy/Undo/eXit]:
```

This prompt tells you that Stretch mode is active. Notice the options in the prompt. As you move the cursor, the corner follows, and the lines of the rectangle stretch (see Figure 4.5).

When you select a grip by clicking it, it turns a solid color (typically red) and is a hot grip. If you want to select more than one grip, you can Shift+click each grip that you want to include in your grip selection.

Shift+click a hot grip again to remove it from the selection.

7. Make sure Osnap mode is turned on, then move the cursor upward toward the top end of the arc, and finally click that point. The rectangle deforms, with the corner placed at your selection point (as shown in Figure 4.5).

Figure 4.5

Stretching lines using hot grips. The left image shows the rectangle's corner being stretched upward. The right image shows the new location of the corner at the top of the arc using the Endpoint osnap.

When you click the corner grip point, AutoCAD selects the overlapping grips of two lines. When you stretch the corner away from its original location, the endpoints of both lines follow.

Here you saw that you can issue an option called Stretch simply by clicking a grip point. A handful of other hot grip options are also available. You'll explore them in the following exercise:

1. Notice that the objects are still selected and the grips are still available. Click the grip point you moved earlier to make it a hot grip again.

2. Right-click to open a context menu that contains a list of grip edit options: Move, Mirror, Rotate, Scale, and Stretch.

    Now try moving and copying the selected objects.

3. Choose Move from the context menu, and then click a point directly to the left of the hot grip, as shown in Figure 4.6. The entire set of objects moves.

4. Click the grip you selected before, right-click, and choose Move again.

5. Right-click again, and choose Copy. You can also enter **C**↵.

6. Select a point below the hot grip. A copy appears.

7. Press ↵, or enter **X**↵ to exit the grip edit. You can also right-click again and choose Exit from the context menu.

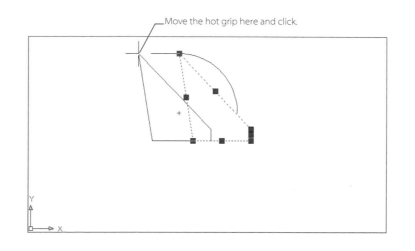

Move the hot grip here and click.

Figure 4.6

Click the location shown to copy the grip.

In this previous set of exercises, you saw how to select a grip and then select grip-edit options from the context menu. You also saw how to stretch grips, move objects, and make a copy.

You can also specify distances and directions using relative Cartesian or polar coordinates. For example, instead of just moving the hot grip and clicking a new location, you can enter a polar coordinate in steps 5 and 6 of the previous exercise. (See Chapter 2 for more about Cartesian and polar coordinates.) The grip will then move or be copied to the exact distance you specify. A third option is to turn on the Dynamic Input feature and use it to specify an exact distance and direction. You'll learn more about the Dynamic Input feature later in this chapter; see the "Changing Objects with Grips and Dynamic Input" section.

Copying, Mirroring, Rotating, Scaling, and Stretching with Grips

The context menu that appears when you right-click a hot grip presents options other than Move. When you select a grip and right-click, you can choose from Mirror, Rotate, Scale, and Stretch. Stretch is the default option, and you've seen how that works with the Move options in the previous exercise. The other options are self-explanatory. You can use the Copy option to make mirrored, rotated, scaled, or stretched copies. Just remember to select the main option first and choose Copy next, since the Copy option affects the current editing mode.

> You can also "cycle" through the Move, Rotate, Scale, and Stretch options by pressing the spacebar while a hot grip is selected.

Another option, Base Point, lets you change the location of the cursor in relation to the current hot grip. By default, the cursor and the hot grip are in the same location and move together. You can right-click, select Base Point, and then select another point to change the location of the cursor in relation to the hot grip, as shown in Figure 4.7.

Figure 4.7

Selecting a base point for the hot grip

The base point is moved away from the grip.

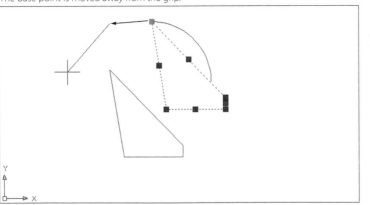

Since you can move the base point, you aren't limited to the actual grip location. This is handy if you want to use other objects as references for your grip edits. For example, you can use the Base Point option to rotate your selection around a point other than a grip point.

You can use the osnaps while grip-editing by Shift+right-clicking to open the Osnap menu.

Using Other Grips Features

Grips let you perform the most common editing tasks you'll encounter as you work with AutoCAD. Along with what you've seen so far, you'll want to be aware of the following grip features:

- You can click endpoint grips to reposition those endpoints.
- Clicking midpoint grips of lines lets you move the entire line. If multiple objects are selected, all the objects also move.
- If two objects meet end to end and you click their overlapping grips, you'll select both grips simultaneously.
- You can select multiple grips by holding down the Shift key and clicking the desired grips. You must hold the Shift key down when you select the first grip.
- When a hot grip is selected, the Stretch, Move, Rotate, Scale, and Mirror options are available from the context menu.
- You can cycle through the Stretch, Move, Rotate, Scale, and Mirror options by pressing ↵ or the spacebar while a hot grip is selected. Watch the command window to see which option is currently active.
- All the hot grip options let you copy the selected objects by either using the Copy option or holding down the Ctrl key while selecting points.
- All the hot grip options let you select a base point other than the originally selected hot grip. Choose Base Point from the context menu.

Changing Objects with Grips and Dynamic Input

So far, you've looked at grip editing with the Dynamic Input feature turned off. This gives you a direct view of the basic grip-editing features that let you perform the more common editing tasks. But once you turn on Dynamic Input, you can begin to edit the actual geometry of the selected objects in a more accurate way. You can alter the length and angle of lines to exact measurements or adjust the radius or length of an arc.

In the following exercise, you'll start with a simple editing task of changing the length of a line. This will show you the basic operation of grip editing with Dynamic Input.

1. Erase all the objects in your drawing, and then draw a line similar to the one in Figure 4.8.

2. Click the Dynamic Input tool in the status bar to turn on the Dynamic Input display. The tool should be blue.

3. Click the line you just drew.

4. Place the cursor over the grip at the right end of the line, but don't click yet. You'll see the length dimension and angle of the line displayed, as shown in Figure 4.9. Make a mental note of the length and angle.

5. Place the cursor over the grip at the left end of the line. Now you'll see the length and angle from a different orientation, as shown in Figure 4.10.

Figure 4.8

A diagonal line to test grips and Dynamic Input

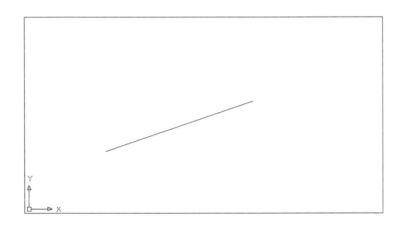

Figure 4.9

Dimensions appear for the line.

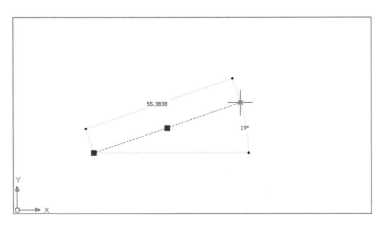

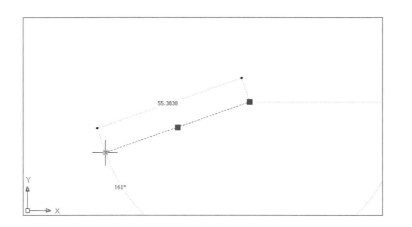

Figure 4.10

The dimensions form a different orientation.

As you can see from this example, you can get immediate information regarding an object just by placing the cursor over its grip points. Next you'll edit the line's length:

1. Click the grip at the right end of the line. You'll now see a highlighted text box near the cursor. If you don't move the cursor, the text box displays the value of 0.000. This value represents the change in the length of the line.

2. Move the cursor around. As the line follows the cursor, the highlighted dimension shows you the change in the length of the line. You'll also see the overall dimension change.

3. Now enter **10**↵. The value in the highlighted text box changes to 10 as you type, and then when you press ↵, the length of the line increases by exactly 10 units. The angle does not change.

In this example, you used the Dimension Input box to increase the length of the line 10 units. You can also enter negative values to reduce the length of the line. But suppose you want to change the line based on the overall length. Here's how you do that:

1. Click the grip on the right end of the line again. Once again you'll see the Dimension Input text box highlighted.

2. Press the Tab key, and move the cursor a bit. Now the overall dimension is highlighted.

3. Enter **22**↵. The line becomes exactly 22 units long.

Finally, you can change the angle of a line without affecting the length:

1. Click the grip on the right end of the line again.

2. Press the Tab key twice until you see the Angle text box highlighted, as shown in Figure 4.11. You might have to move the cursor around to see it.

3. Enter **45**↵ for a 45° angle. The line is reoriented to a 45° angle.

Figure 4.11

**The Angle text box
is highlighted and
ready for input.**

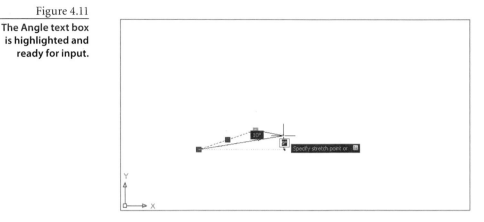

Finally, you can use Dynamic Input as a kind of "heads-up" display while editing. For example, as you enter Cartesian or polar coordinates to move an object, you'll see your input appear at the cursor, so you don't have to look at the command window to make sure you're entering the right values. Try the following exercise to see how this works firsthand:

1. Select the line you've been working on in the previous exercises.

2. Click the right end grip.

3. Right-click, and choose Move. Notice that the cursor changes to show the `Specify move point or` prompt. You'll also see the displacement value highlighted followed by an angle sign (<) and the angle, as shown in Figure 4.12.

4. Enter **10**, and then press the Tab key. Now as you move the cursor, it remains at a fixed distance of 10 units from the endpoint no matter where the cursor is placed, but as you move the cursor, the line "circles" the original grip point, allowing you to specify an angle. Also notice that the angle value is highlighted, showing that you can enter an angle value, as shown in Figure 4.13. If you turn on Polar mode, the cursor will lock on to the cardinal directions of 0°, 90°, 180°, and 270°.

5. Enter **0↵**. The line is moved a distance of 10 units directly to the right of its original location.

Figure 4.12

**The displacement
value is highlighted
and ready for input.**

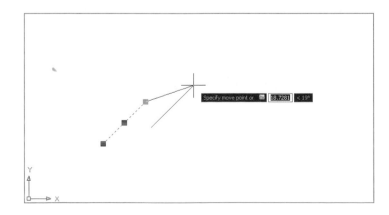

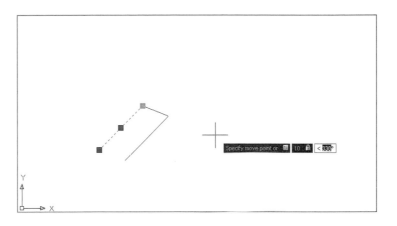

Figure 4.13

The Angle text box is highlighted and ready for input.

In this example, you used a polar coordinate to indicate a distance and an angle for the direction of the move. You can also enter a Cartesian coordinate of **10,0** in step 4 to achieve the same result.

In these examples, you edited only a single line, but the general method is the same for editing all objects: select the object, click a grip, press Tab to move to the property value you want to change, and enter a new value. For circles and arcs, you will see radius and arc lengths. If you select a grip that includes multiple line endpoints, you can press the Tab key repeatedly until you get to the property value of the particular line you want to edit.

Controlling Objects Using the Properties Palette

Besides editing objects directly on the screen, you can also edit them by changing their properties in the Properties palette. You've already seen the Quick Properties panel, which is a simplified version of the Properties palette. The Properties palette and the Quick Properties panel work in the same way, so in this section, I'll focus on the Properties palette, because it contains more options.

The properties of an object include many of the object's geometric values, such as the radius of a circle or the coordinates of the endpoints of a line. Properties also include colors, linetypes, and layer assignments. Many users find the Properties palette so useful that they keep it open all the time. You can gather information at a glance by clicking an object and viewing its properties in the Properties palette. For example, you can find the area of a polyline or region by selecting the object and looking at the area listing in the Properties palette.

You can open the Properties palette (see Figure 4.14) in two ways: by clicking the Properties tool in the View tab's Palettes panel or by right-clicking an object and choosing Properties.

Figure 4.14

AutoCAD's Properties palette showing the properties of a line

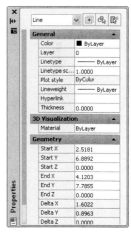

Properties

The information displayed in the Properties palette depends on the object you've selected. Two categories, General and Geometry, appear for nearly every type of object. Table 4.1 describes the General properties.

PROPERTY	MEANING
Color	Specifies the object's color assignment. The default ByLayer means the object inherits the color of the layer to which the object is assigned.
Layer	Specifies the object's layer assignment. All objects have a layer assignment. (See Chapter 7 for more about layers.)
Linetype	Specifies the object's linetype assignment. By default, objects use the ByLayer linetype, which is set according to the object's layer assignment. Typically, this is a continuous linetype. AutoCAD offers a variety of linetypes through the Linetype tools. (See Chapter 7 for more about linetypes.)
Linetype Scale	Controls the appearance of noncontinuous linetypes. This setting lets you set the frequency of line intervals. For example, if you have a dashed line, the Linetype Scale property can set how often the dashes appear within a certain length of the drawing. A global linetype scale is also available that sets scale for all linetypes.
Plot Style	Determines how lines are drawn in the final output of your drawing. You can set up a style to control the color, shading, and corner condition of lines to fine-tune the appearance of your drawing. (See Chapter 12 for more about plot styles.)
Lineweight	Sets the plotted lineweight of an object.
Hyperlink	Sets up or locates a hyperlink from an object to another drawing or file.
Thickness	Specifies the object's extension into the Z coordinate. By giving an object a thickness value greater than or less than 0, it will appear as a 3D object. You can convert objects with thickness to solids and surfaces. (See Chapter 6 for more information about 3D.)

Figure 4.15

The Geometry section (bottom) of the Properties palette

The information in the Geometry section (see Figure 4.15) of the Properties palette depends on the object. A line shows its endpoint coordinates as well as a read-only display of its length and angle. A circle shows its center coordinates and radius as well as circumference and area. A polyline shows its segment widths, area, and vertex coordinates.

You can edit almost all the options listed in the Properties palette. To edit an item, click its name in the left column. The value to the right of the item either turns into a drop-down list from which you can choose an option or turns into a text box that you can edit. Some text boxes also include a Browse button (an ellipsis), as you can see in Figure 4.16.

If an option is not available for editing, it appears in gray. Some items, such as the angle listing for lines, cannot be edited but can be selected for cutting and pasting elsewhere by clicking the QuickCalc icon that appears to the right of the option. The QuickCalc icon looks like a calculator. After you click the icon, you can copy the value for the option from the QuickCalc input box.

If you aren't certain of the function of an option, you can point to the option's name, and a tooltip appears with a brief description of the option.

You can control the display of the Properties palette through a set of options at the top of the title bar. If you click the Auto-hide button near the top of the title bar, the palette is minimized to show just its title bar.

When the palette is "minimized," you can quickly display its contents by placing the cursor on the title bar. This option lets you maximize your drawing area without completely closing the Properties palette.

Figure 4.16

Some boxes in the Properties palette include a Browse button.

Using Parametric Tools to Create "Smart Drawings"

Parametric is a word from mathematics, and in the context of AutoCAD drawings, it means that you can define relationships between different objects in a drawing. For example, you can set up a pair of individual lines to stay parallel or set up two concentric circles to maintain an exact distance between each other no matter how they may be edited.

Parametric drawing is also called *constraint-based modeling*, and you'll see the word *constraint* used in the AutoCAD Ribbon to describe sets of tools. The term *constraint* is a bit more descriptive of the tools you'll use to create parametric drawings because when you use them, you are applying a constraint upon the objects in your drawing.

With careful application of the parametric tools, you can create a drawing that you can quickly modify with just a change of a dimension or two instead of actually editing the lines that make up the drawing. Figure 4.17 shows a drawing that was set up so that the arcs and circles increase in size to an exact proportion when the overall length dimension is increased. This can save a lot of time if you're designing several parts that are similar with only a few dimensional changes.

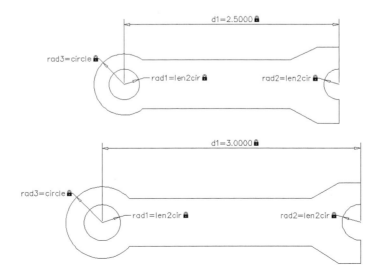

Figure 4.17

The d1 dimension in the top image was edited to change the drawing to look like the one in the lower half.

Adding and Removing a Constraint

You can add constraints to control the way objects behave in relation to each other. For example, you can use constraints to keep lines parallel or circles concentric. The following steps show you how to add a parallel constraint to two lines:

1. Click the Parallel tool in the Parametric tab's Geometric panel.

2. Click the line you want to be parallel to.

3. Click the line that you want to have parallel (left image in Figure 4.18) to the first line. The second line you select changes to be parallel with the first (right image in Figure 4.18).

Figure 4.18

**Using the
Parallel tool**

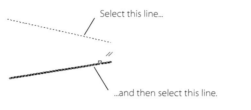

Once you add a constraint, you see a nonprinting icon indicating the constraint that has been applied to the objects. The constraint icon in the drawing matches those you see in the Geometric panel. If you hover your mouse pointer over an icon, you'll see a tooltip that shows the name of the constraint.

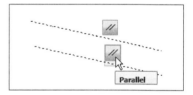

Once the parallel constraint is in place, the two lines will remain parallel when you edit them. If you rotate one line, the other will also rotate, though not around the same axis, to maintain parallelism with the other line.

If you need to remove a constraint, you can right-click the constraint icon and select Delete.

THE ORDER MAKES A DIFFERENCE

When you add constraints, sometimes the order in which you select objects makes an important difference. In the parallel constraint example, the first line selected remains stationary while the second line becomes parallel to the first.

Using Other Geometric Constraints

For the most part, each constraint is fairly easy to understand. The tangent constraint keeps objects tangent to each other. The concentric constraint tool forces arcs and circles to be concentric. The parallel constraint keeps objects parallel.

There are many more geometric constraints you have at your disposal. Table 4.2 gives you a concise listing of the constraints and their purpose. Note that, with the exception of fixed and symmetric, all of the constraints affect pairs of objects.

NAME	USE
Coincident	Keeps point locations of two objects together, such as the endpoint or midpoints of lines. Allowable points vary between objects and are indicated by a red circle marked with an X while points are being selected.
Collinear	Keeps lines collinear. The lines need not be connected.
Concentric	Keeps circles and arcs concentric.
Fixed	Fixes a point on an object to a location in the drawing.
Parallel	Keeps objects parallel.
Perpendicular	Keeps objects perpendicular.
Horizontal	Keeps objects horizontal.
Vertical	Keeps objects vertical.
Tangent	Keeps objects tangent to each other.
Smooth	Maintains a smooth transition between splines and other objects. The first object selected must be a spline. You can think of this constraint as a tangent constraint for splines.
Symmetric	Maintains symmetry between two objects about an axis that is determined by a line. Before using this constraint, draw a line that you will use for the axis of symmetry. You can also use the fixed, horizontal, or vertical constraint to fix the axis to a location or orientation.
Equal	Keeps the length of two lines or polylines equal or the radius of arcs and circles equal.

Table 4.2

The Geometric Constraints

Using Auto Constrain to Automatically Add Constraints

Another way to add constraints is to use the Auto Constrain tool. This tool automatically adds constraints to a set of objects all at once. The following gives an example of how you might use it:

1. Select the Parametric tab, and click the Auto Constrain tool from the Geometric panel, or type **Autoconstrain**↵.

2. Select all the objects that you want to have constrained, and press ↵.

The Auto Constrain tool adds geometric constraints to all of the objects selected. You can see a set of icons that indicate the constraints that have been applied to the objects (see Figure 4.19). The Auto Constrain tool makes a "best guess" at applying constraints.

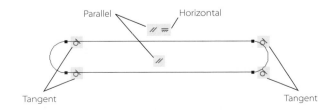

Figure 4.19

A sample drawing with geometric constraints added

The tangent constraint that you see at the ends of the lines keeps the arcs and the lines tangent to each other whenever the arcs are edited. The parallel constraint keeps the two lines parallel, and the horizontal constraint keeps the lines horizontal.

Building Linkages with Coincident Constraints

There is one geometric constraint that is a little different from the rest. The Coincident constraint tool can be used to link two objects together at an endpoint, midpoint, or center of a circle or arc to ensure that the objects do not move away from each other. A simple application of this constraint is to keep the line work together for a set of objects like the diagram of a piston and crank shaft, as shown in Figure 4.20.

In this diagram, the endpoints of the lines are linked using the coincident constraint so that if the line representing the crankshaft is rotated, the piston moves in unison.

The Coincident constraint tool does not display an icon by default. Instead, you see a small blue square where they have been applied. You can hover over the square to view the coincident icon.

Figure 4.20

You can use the Coincident constraint tool to link objects together.

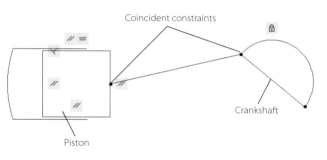

Controlling Sizes with Dimensional Constraint

Dimensional constraints allow you to set and adjust the dimension of an assembly of parts, thereby giving you an easy way to adjust the size and even the shape of a set of objects.

For example, suppose you have a set of parts that you are drafting, each of which is just slightly different in one dimension or another. You can add geometric constraints and then add dimensional constraints, which will let you easily modify your part just by changing the value of a dimension.

Adding and Editing a Dimensional Constraint

Dimensional constraints can be added in a way similar to regular dimensions (see Chapter 10 for more on dimensions). The difference is that dimensional constraints are set up by default so that they do not print. They can also be set up to print if you prefer.

The following describes how you would add a linear dimensional constraint:

1. In the Parametric tab, click the Linear tool in the Dimensional panel.

2. Select two locations for the dimensional constraint (left image in Figure 4.21). If you are dimensioning corners or endpoints of objects, you will see a circular marker indicating the location of the dimensioned location.

3. Click a location to indicate the dimension line location.

4. At the `Dimension text =:` prompt, press ↵ to accept the current value.

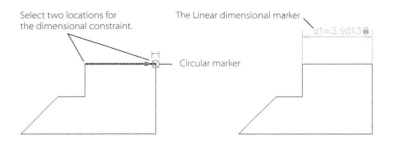

Figure 4.21

Select locations for dimensional constraint.

AutoCAD will show the dimension as dn = length, where n is a number AutoCAD assigns to the constraint (right image in Figure 4.21).

The length of the object you dimension with the dimensional constraint can be changed by changing the dimension value. To do this, double-click on the dimension value and then enter a new value (Figure 4.22).

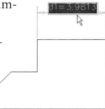

Figure 4.22

Double-click the dimension to change the distance between the dimensioned locations.

Linking Dimensions with the Parameter Manager

Another important feature of the dimensional constraints feature is the ability to link the dimension values. For example, you can set up a dimensional constraint to so that it is always one third the value of another constraint. Figure 4.23 shows a drawing that has two linear dimensional constraints. The following steps describe how those constraints can be linked.

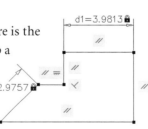

Figure 4.23

A drawing with two dimensional constraints added

1. After adding two dimensional constraints, click the Parameters Manager tool in the Paremetric tab's Manage panel. The Parameters Manager dialog box appears (Figure 4.24). You see a list of the dimensional constraints you've added. These are known as *parameters*.

fx

Parameters Manager

Figure 4.24

The Parameters Manager dialog box

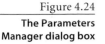

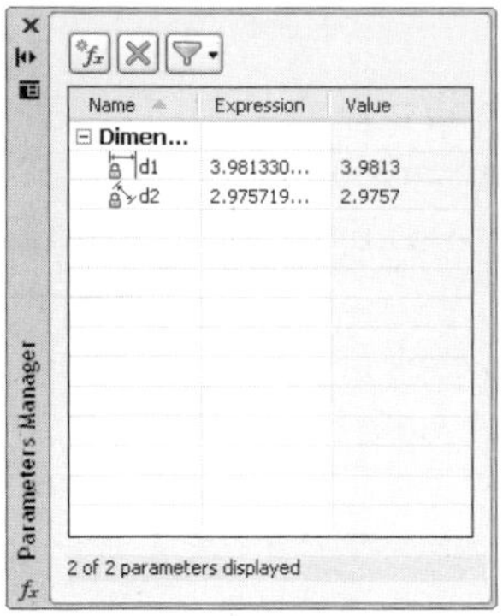

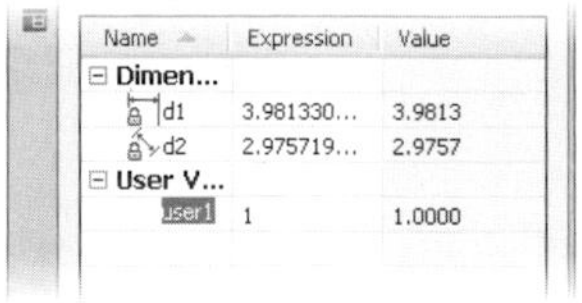

2. Click the Creates New User Parameter tool in the upper-left of the palette. A new parameter called user1 appears under a heading called User Variables.

3. Double-click the Expressions column of the user1 parameter. The expression for the user1 parameter is highlighted.

4. Enter **d1 * 1/3**↵. This tells AutoCAD that your new parameter multiplies the value of the d1 dimensional constraint by ⅓.

5. Next, double-click in the expression column for the d2 parameter and enter **user1**. This gives the d2 dimensional constraint the value of user1, which is the length of d1 times ⅓.

Once a parameter is used in this way, any change in the d1 value will automatically change the d2 value to ⅓ of d1 (see Figure 4.25). You can use any formula you want following the format shown in step 4. Note that the current value of the dimension is shown in the Value column of the Parameters Manager dialog box.

You can rename the parameters by right-clicking the name in the Name column and selecting the name and entering a new name. Instead of d1, d2, and user1, you can change the names to width, height, and ratio to give your parameters a more meaningful name.

Figure 4.25

Change the d1 dimension, and the d2 dimension will follow.

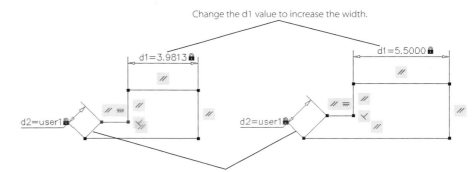

Summary

When you're in a hurry and you are working with an unfamiliar program, you might be tempted to try methods you've used in other programs. You can do that in AutoCAD, and if you're lucky, you might get the results you want. But you might also be a bit confused about some of the behaviors AutoCAD presents.

This chapter described what to expect when you start to click objects in an AutoCAD drawing. Once you've mastered the features presented here, you'll be on your way to gaining control over those mysterious objects in AutoCAD.

CHAPTER 5

Editing with the Modify Panel Tools

The preceding chapter contained information about how to perform the basic editing tasks by clicking objects. In addition to those editing features, you can use editing tools and commands that are unique to CAD drawing.

This chapter provides information about the editing tools in the Home tab's Modify panel. These tools do everything, including joining line endpoints, extending objects to meet other objects, and breaking objects in two. In this chapter, you'll also learn how to edit blocks and external references (xrefs), which are collections of objects that act like a single object. And since polylines are fairly complex, they have their own editing tools, which you'll learn about toward the end of this chapter.

This chapter includes the following topics:

- Selecting objects
- Erasing objects
- Joining objects
- Moving and copying
- Scaling, stretching, and rotating
- Breaking an object into two
- Editing xrefs and blocks
- Editing polylines

Selecting Objects

If you read the preceding chapter, you know that you can select objects by clicking them or by clicking a blank area to start a selection window. Once you have objects selected in this way, you can use grips to make changes to your selection.

But you can also select objects in another way. Many of the tools in the Modify panel present the Select objects: prompt. When you see this prompt, you can use the methods shown in Chapter 4 plus some additional options that give you more flexibility in selecting objects.

When you see the Select objects: prompt, you can use any of the options in the following list to refine your selection. For example, if you enter **all**↵ at the Select objects: prompt, the entire contents of a drawing are selected. Or if you enter **p**↵, the previous set of objects you edited is reselected. After you make a selection, the Select objects: prompt returns, allowing you to continue to select objects. To indicate that you've finished selecting objects, press ↵.

> When single clicks or selection windows aren't powerful enough, you can use these selection options. Some tools in the Draw panel require only that you select a single object, so these options do not apply to them.

All [all↵] Selects all the objects in a drawing except those in frozen or locked layers. (See Chapter 7 for information about layers.)

Crossing [c↵] Is similar to the Window option (see the "Window" entry later in this list) but also selects anything that crosses through the window you define.

Crossing Polygon [cp↵] Lets you select an area by enclosing it with an irregularly shaped polygon boundary. This acts exactly like Window Polygon (see the "Window Polygon" entry later in this list) but, like the Select Crossing option, selects anything that crosses through a polygon boundary.

Fence [f↵] Selects objects that are crossed over by a temporary line called a *fence*. This operation is like crossing out the objects you want to select with a line. When you invoke this option, you can then select points as if you are drawing a series of line segments. When you finish drawing the fence, press ↵ to continue to select more objects by using other selection options, or press ↵ twice to finish your selection.

Last [l↵] Selects the last object you created.

Multiple [m↵] Lets you select several objects before AutoCAD highlights them. In a large file, selecting objects individually can cause AutoCAD to pause after each selection while it finds and highlights each object. The Multiple option can speed things up by letting you first select all the objects quickly and then highlight them all by pressing ↵. This option has no menu equivalent.

Previous [p⏎] Selects the last object or set of objects selected in the previous operation.

Window [w⏎] Forces a standard selection window. Once you enter **w⏎**, you select two points to define a selection window. This option is useful when your drawing area is too crowded to use the autoselect feature to place a window around a set of objects. It prevents you from accidentally selecting an object with a single click when you are placing your window.

Window Polygon [wp⏎] Lets you select objects by enclosing them in an irregularly shaped polygon boundary. When you use this option, you'll see the First polygon point: prompt. You can then select points to define the polygon boundary. As you select points, the Specify endpoint of line or [Undo]: prompt appears. Select as many points as you need in order to define the boundary. You can undo boundary-line segments as you go by pressing the U key. With the boundary defined, press ⏎. The bounded objects are highlighted, and the Select object: prompt returns, allowing you to use more selection options.

Erasing Objects

In AutoCAD, you can erase objects in different ways. You can select an object or a set of objects and press Delete. This works for nearly every type of AutoCAD object. Or you can click the Erase tool in the Home tab's Modify panel (or enter **e⏎** at the command prompt), select an object or set of objects you want to erase, and then press ⏎. Erase works with all AutoCAD objects; so if for some reason you encounter an object you cannot erase by pressing Delete, try the Erase tool.

Some objects will persist either in the current file or as external files, even after being erased. You can reinsert blocks if they are erased from a drawing. Xrefs also remain as external files and are not deleted when erased from a drawing. Image files behave in a way similar to xrefs and are not deleted from your hard drive when you delete them from your AutoCAD drawing.

To delete bitmap images that have been inserted via the Image or Imageattach command, use the Delete key, but you must select the image frame, not the image itself. If the image frame is not visible, enter **imageframe⏎** at the command prompt, and then enter **1⏎** to make it visible.

Finally, if you happen to erase an object by accident, you can usually retrieve it by clicking the Undo tool in the Standard toolbar. AutoCAD lets you undo several steps. (See Chapter 2 for more about Undo.) To restore the last set of deleted objects, use the Oops command. Just enter **oops⏎** at the command prompt. The Oops command is useful if you want to restore objects you deleted several steps back and do not want to undo your work to the point of deletion.

Joining Objects

The whole idea of using AutoCAD is to draw precisely. Not surprisingly, you end up joining objects in exacting ways. One of the most common tasks is joining the endpoints of objects so that they meet exactly end to end.

AutoCAD provides several tools that join the endpoints of objects, particularly arcs, lines, and polylines. In this instance, *joining* means shortening or extending a line, an arc, or a polyline to meet another object, without disturbing the object's orientation.

Figure 5.1

Fillet will join the two lines at the left from end to end (center) or join them with an intermediate arc (right).

Joining End to End with Intermediate Arcs

The Fillet command is one of the more frequently used commands because it is great at doing one thing: it joins lines end to end no matter where the endpoints of those lines are. Optionally, Fillet adds an intermediate arc between the joined lines to form a *bullnose*, or rounded corner, as shown in Figure 5.1.

Fillet also joins two parallel lines with an arc. The following steps describe Fillet's default behavior:

1. From the Home tab's Modify panel, choose Fillet, or enter **F↵** at the command prompt.

2. At the following prompt, click one line:

   ```
   Current settings: Mode = TRIM, Radius = 0.0000
   Select first object or [Undo/Polyline/Radius/Trim/Multiple]:
   ```

3. At the `Select second object or shift-select to apply corner:` prompt, select the other line. The lines will join end to end without disturbing their orientation.

Fillet joins lines, arcs, and polylines. If you join a polyline with a line or an arc, the line or arc becomes part of the polyline.

Rounding Corners

Fillet also lets you round corners by adding an intermediate arc. You might notice several options in step 2, including a Radius option. If you enter **R↵** in step 2, you will see the following prompt:

```
Specify fillet radius <0.0000>:
```

You can enter a radius value and then proceed to select two objects. Instead of joining the objects end to end, AutoCAD adds an arc between the objects.

The Fillet command continues to add arcs until you change the Radius option back to 0.

If you use Fillet to join two parallel lines, AutoCAD automatically uses an arc to join the two lines.

You can also round the corners of a polyline, as shown in Figure 5.2, by using the Radius option in conjunction with the Polyline option.

Start the Fillet command, enter **R↵** and a radius, enter **P↵**, and select the polyline. The vertices of the polyline change into arcs of the specified radius. If you indicate a radius that is too large for the line segments, AutoCAD will report that the radius is too large and will cancel the operation. This happens when the line segments are shorter than the radius.

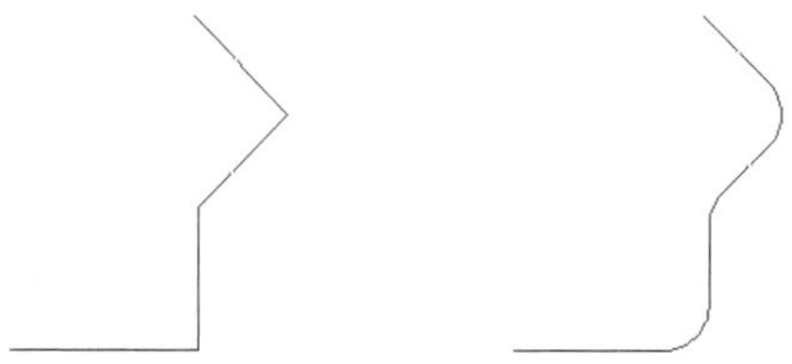

Figure 5.2

The polyline on the right is the result of using the Fillet command on the polyline on the left.

Rounding Without Trimming

If you want to add an arc that is tangent to two objects but you don't want the objects trimmed to join the arc, you can change the Trim setting of the Fillet command. Figure 5.3 shows the effect of Fillet's No Trim option. (Note that the Chamfer command has a similar option that works the same way. See the section "Joining with a Chamfer" later in this chapter.)

To change the way Fillet trims objects, start the Fillet command, and then enter **T↵**. You'll see the following prompt:

```
Enter Trim mode option [Trim/No trim] <Trim>:
```

Enter **N↵**.

Figure 5.3

Fillet with the No Trim setting turned on

The No Trim option becomes the default method that Fillet uses to join lines until you set the option back to Trim.

Controlling Fillet's Behavior

Some additional options are available with the Fillet command that control how Fillet behaves. The following list describes them:

Polyline Applies the Fillet command to all the corners of a polyline composed of straight-line segments. (See Figure 5.2 earlier in this chapter.)

Radius Lets you set the radius of the fillet.

Trim/No trim Allows you to specify whether lines are trimmed when they are filleted. By default, lines are trimmed. You can specify No Trim to leave the lines as they are. Once Trim/No Trim is set, it becomes the default until it is changed.

Multiple Lets you select multiple sets of lines to fillet.

Joining with a Chamfer

Another common editing operation is joining two lines with another intermediate line to form a chamfer, as shown in Figure 5.4. The Chamfer command works much like the Fillet command, with some different options.

Figure 5.4

Chamfer joins the two lines at the left to form the chamfered corner shown at the right.

To join lines with a chamfer, do the following:

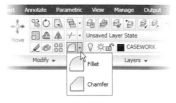

1. In the Home tab's Modify panel, choose Chamfer. If you don't see Chamfer, click the Fillet tool flyout, and then click Chamfer. You can also enter **cha⏎** at the command prompt.

2. You will see the following message:

   `(TRIM mode) Current chamfer Dist1 = 0.0000, Dist2 = 0.0000`

   This tells you the current settings for the chamfer distances.

3. At the `Select first line or [Undo/Polyline/Distance/Angle/Trim/mEthod/Multiple]:` prompt, enter **d⏎** to specify a Chamfer distance.

4. At the `Specify first chamfer distance <1.0000>:` prompt, enter a distance value. The value you enter determines the distance from the intersection of the two lines being chamfered to the beginning of the chamfer, as shown in Figure 5.5.

5. At the `Specify second chamfer distance <2.0000>:` prompt, enter a value for the other chamfer distance. Press ⏎ if you want the first and second chamfer distances to be equal.

6. At the `Select first line or [Polyline/Distance/Angle/Trim/mEthod/Multiple]:` prompt, select one line.

7. At the `Select second line:` prompt, select the other line. The two lines are joined with a chamfer, as shown in Figure 5.6.

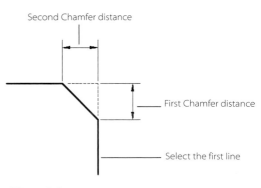

Figure 5.5

The Chamfer distance shown by arrows. The first Chamfer distance is determined by the line that is selected first (at the `Select first line:` prompt).

Once you've set the distances in steps 4 and 5, AutoCAD remembers them for the current drawing. The next time you use Chamfer, you won't have to set the distances. You can immediately select two lines as soon as you invoke the Chamfer command, skipping steps 3, 4, and 5.

Select first line

Figure 5.6

The polyline on the right is the result of using the Chamfer command on the polyline on the left.

Chamfer works on lines and polylines with straight-line segments only. You cannot use the Chamfer command on an arc to a line, for example.

You might notice other options in the previous steps. The following list describes what they do. Remember that to use an option, enter its capitalized letter at the prompt. For example, to use the Trim option in step 5 of the previous example, enter **T**↵. For the mEthod option, enter **E**↵.

Polyline Applies the chamfer to all the corners of a polyline composed of straight-line segments (shown earlier in Figure 5.6).

Distance Lets you specify the distance of the chamfer from the intersection of two lines. The distance can be equal for each line, or lines can have different values. (Also see "mEthod" later in this list.)

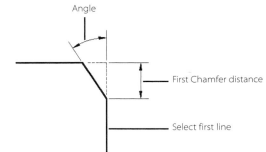

Angle

First Chamfer distance

Select first line

Figure 5.7

Chamfer's Angle option lets you specify the chamfer based on a distance and an angle. The angle is relative to the first line selected at the Select first line: **prompt.**

Angle Lets you specify an angle for the chamfer. You are first asked for a distance value and then asked for the angle (see Figure 5.7). (Also see "mEthod" later in this list.)

Trim Lets you specify whether lines are trimmed when they are chamfered. By default, lines are trimmed. You can specify No Trim to leave the lines as they are (see Figure 5.8). Once you have set Trim/No Trim, it becomes the default until it is changed. This option affects both Chamfer and Fillet.

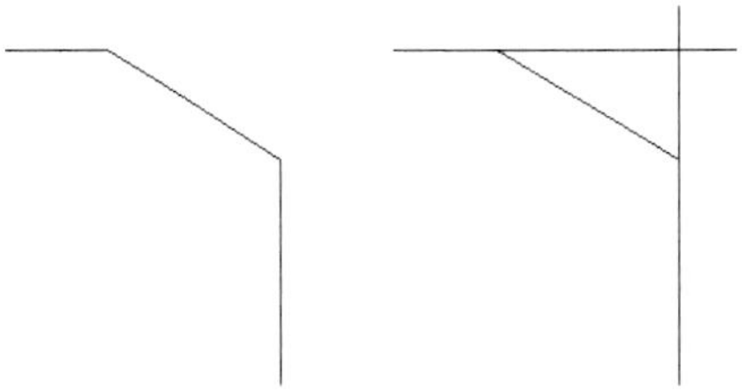

mEthod Lets you choose whether the Chamfer command uses the Distance or Angle setting by default. (See the "Distance" and "Angle" entries in this list.)

Multiple Lets you select multiple sets of lines to chamfer.

Figure 5.8

A chamfer with the default Trim option appears on the left, and the No Trim option appears with the fillet on the right.

Trimming Lines or Extending Them to Other Objects

One fairly common operation in AutoCAD is to extend a line to meet another object or to trim a line or other object back to meet another object. For example, you can quickly trim two rectangles with a circle to form a wrench shape, as shown in Figure 5.9. Or you

can extend a pair of lines to meet another line to form a wall extension, as shown in Figure 5.10.

Trim and Extend work on most AutoCAD objects with the exception of hatch patterns, text, splines, and regions. You can explode hatches and regions to their constituent parts to be trimmed or extended. You can use Trim or Extend on blocks and xrefs by first using the Refedit command. (See Chapter 8 for more about blocks and xrefs.)

Trimming Objects

You can use the Trim command to both trim and extend objects. The following steps show how you might use Trim to truncate a circle, as shown in Figure 5.11.

1. In the Modify panel, click the Trim tool, or enter **tr↵** at the command prompt. You'll see the following message:

       Current settings: Projection=UCS, Edge=None

2. At the following prompt, select the object or set of objects you want to trim to, and then press ↵:

       Select cutting edges ...

       Select objects or <select all>:

In this example, select the circle and line shown in Figure 5.11.

3. At the Select object to trim or shift-select to extend or [Fence/Crossing/
   Project/Edge/eRase/Undo]: prompt, select the part of the object you want to trim.
   In the circle example, select the locations indicated by the dots in the left image in
   Figure 5.11.

4. When you are finished, press ↵.

Extending Objects

To extend an object, start the Trim command as in the first two steps of the previous
example, but instead of clicking the ends you want to trim, Shift+click to select the

objects you want to extend, as
shown in Figure 5.12.

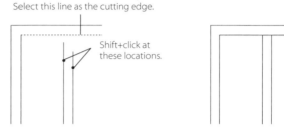

To extend a series of lines to
another object, as in Figure 5.13,
use the Fence Selection option.

Another option is to use
the Extend tool in the Modify
panel. Extend works just like

Figure 5.12

**Shift+click to select
the lines shown on
the left to get the
results on the right.**

Trim, but by default it assumes you want to extend an object to another object rather
than trim objects. You can find the Extend tool on the Trim flyout.

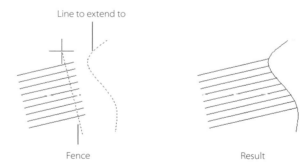

Figure 5.13

**Extending a set of
lines to a curve by
using the Fence
option. Hold down
the Shift key while
placing the fence.**

Using Trim and Extend Options

You can control the way the Trim and Extend commands work through their options.
Six options are available in both commands: Fence, Crossing, Project, Edge, eRase, and
Undo. The following list describes their functions:

Fence This allows you to select objects by using the Fence selection option (see "Selecting
Objects" earlier in this chapter).

Crossing This allows you to select objects by using a crossing window (see "Selecting
Objects" earlier in this chapter).

Project If you are working in 3D, the effects of the Trim or Extend command depend on your viewpoint. Project lets you control whether Trim and Extend are determined by the UCS or the current view. (See Chapter 6 for more about the UCS.)

Edge You might want to extend or trim to an object that does not actually cross the object's path, as shown in Figure 5.14. You can use the Edge option to allow the Trim command to work whether or not objects actually cross.

Figure 5.14

Even though the lines do not cross, as shown in the left image, you can turn on the Edge option to trim to the edge defined by the dotted line in the middle image.

eRase This lets you erase an object while in the middle of a trim or extend operation.

Undo This lets you undo a trim or extend operation.

Moving and Copying

Chapter 4 described how to use grips to move and copy objects. So, why have specific commands for moving and copying when you can use grips? Part of the reason is that grip editing is a feature that was added later in AutoCAD's history, and the Move and Copy commands are the original methods for performing those functions. If you are building macros, you can use the Move and Copy commands but not the grip-editing options. Finally, the Move and Copy commands described in this chapter, along with Rotate, Stretch, and Scale, can take advantage of the selection options described earlier in this chapter. Grip editing cannot. If you have to move or copy a set of objects that cannot be selected easily with single clicks or selection windows, use the Move or Copy command in the Modify panel.

Moving with Accuracy

The Move command is deceptively simple. It's easy enough to move objects in a general way. It gets a little more complicated when you want to move objects with any accuracy. Here are the basic steps for using the Move command:

1. In the Modify panel, click the Move tool, or enter **m⏎** at the command prompt.

2. At the Select objects: prompt, select the objects you want to move.

3. At the Specify base point or [Displacement] <Displacement>: prompt, select a base point. If you want to enter a relative coordinate, you can select any point on the screen, or you can enter @⏎. The @ means "from the last point selected."

4. At the Specify second point or <use first point as displacement>: prompt, you'll see the selected objects move with the cursor. You can select the second point with the cursor or enter an absolute or relative coordinate. (See Chapter 2 for more about coordinates in AutoCAD.)

Using Some Tips for New Users

The trickiest part of the Move command is to understand the base point and the second point in steps 3 and 4 in the preceding exercise. The base point can be anywhere on the drawing. It does not have to be on the object or objects you are trying to move. Once you select a base point, its position stays fixed in relation to the selected objects. This is most obvious when you select a random point for a base point. As you move the cursor, the selected objects move in unison with the cursor, even if the cursor is nowhere near the objects.

Another function that can trip up a new user is the selection process. It is a good idea to become intimately familiar with the many ways you can select objects in AutoCAD. Study the section "Selecting Objects" earlier in this chapter.

Aligning Objects with Osnaps

Finally, you can use osnaps to accurately place the objects you are moving. For example, if you want to move an object so that its corner meets the corner of a second object, do the following. Start the Move command as in step 1 of the preceding exercise; select your object as in step 2; and then in step 3, use the Endpoint osnap to select the corner of the selected object. In step 4, use the Endpoint osnap again to select the corner of the second object. (See the middle image in Figure 5.15.) This is just one example of using osnaps with the Move command. You can use osnaps to join any part of one object to any part of another. For example, you can move the midpoint of a line to the center of a circle using osnaps in steps 3 and 4.

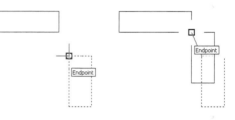
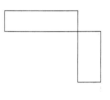

Figure 5.15

Use the Endpoint osnap to select the corner of the object you want to move (left image), and then use it again to select the corner you want to move the object to (center image).

Copying Objects with the Copy Command

The Copy command is virtually identical to the Move command, with the obvious difference that Copy makes copies instead of moving objects. Another difference is that you can place multiple copies in the drawing by repeatedly clicking locations or entering coordinates.

To practice using the Copy command, follow the steps shown in the previous section. The main difference is that after step 4, AutoCAD continues to prompt you with Specify second point or <use first point as displacement>:. You can then continue to make copies by clicking your drawing, or you can press ↵ to exit the Copy command. After the first copy is made, the prompt changes to Specify second point or [Exit/Undo] <Exit>.

To make parallel copies of objects, use the Offset command, as described in Chapter 3.

Making Circular Copies

To make copies in a circular pattern, you use the Array dialog box. You can create patterns such as the tick marks on a clock or the teeth in a gear. You can also set up your circular copies to remain in a fixed orientation, like the numbers on a clock.

PROVIDING BASE POINTS

When you use the Move or Copy command, AutoCAD prompts you for a base point, which can be a difficult concept to grasp. You must tell AutoCAD specifically from where and to where the move occurs. The base point is the exact location from which you determine the distance and direction of the move. Once the base point is determined, you can tell AutoCAD where to move the object in relation to that point.

The base point can come in handy when you want to move or copy an object by using a geometric feature of the object. For example, if you want to move the upper-right corner of a rectangle so that it connects exactly to the endpoint of a line, select the exact corner of the rectangle as the base point for the move. The following steps describe how to do this:

1. Start the Move command, select the rectangle, and press ↵.

2. At the Specify base point or [Displacement] <Displacement>: prompt, Shift+right-click, and select the Endpoint osnap from the context menu.

3. Click the corner of the rectangle you want to connect to the line.

4. At the Specify second point or <use first point as displacement>: prompt, Shift+right-click again, and select Endpoint.

5. Click the endpoint of the line. The corner of the rectangle moves to meet the endpoint of the line.

Here are the basic steps for using the Array dialog box:

1. In the Home tab's expanded Modify panel, click the Array tool, or enter **ar**↵ to open the Array dialog box (see Figure 5.16).

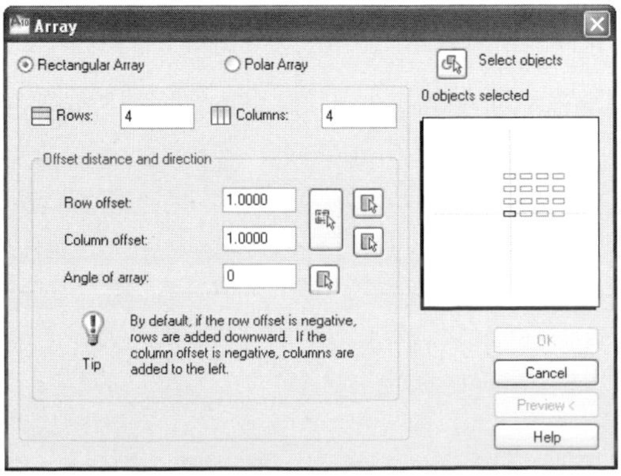

Figure 5.16

The Array dialog box

2. Click the Select Objects button. The dialog box temporarily closes, allowing you to select objects.

3. Select the objects you want to copy, and then press ↵. The Array dialog box reopens.

4. Click the Polar Array radio button at the top of the dialog box to tell AutoCAD you want a circular array. The Array dialog box displays the polar array options, as shown in Figure 5.17.

5. Click the Pick Center Point button. The Array dialog box temporarily closes to allow you to select a center point about which the copies will be made.

6. Select the point that represents the center of the circular array. If you have an object representing the center of the array, you can use an osnap to select the object. Once you've indicated a point, the Array dialog box reopens.

At this point, you've selected an object to array and you've indicated the center location of the array. If you've selected the wrong object or the wrong center point, you can specify these options again.

Now, to complete the process, tell AutoCAD the number of copies in the array and the extent of the array through the circle:

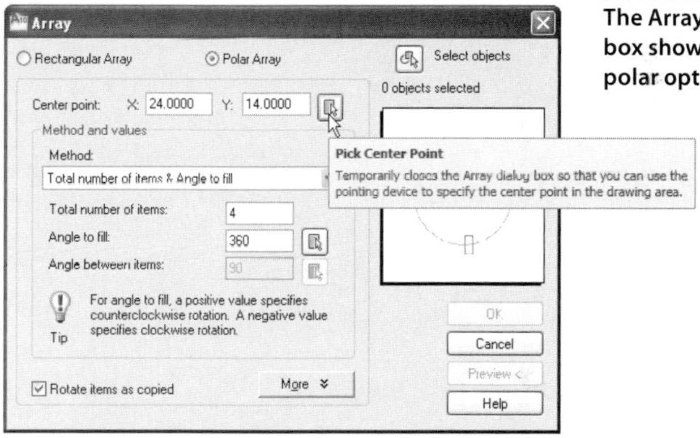

Figure 5.17

The Array dialog box showing the polar options

1. In the Array dialog box, enter the number of copies you want in the Total Number of Items text box. The number you enter should include the original object.

2. In the Angle to Fill text box, enter the angle in degrees that you want your circular copies to fill. For example, if you enter **360**, AutoCAD spreads the copies evenly over the full 360° of the circle. If you enter **180**, the array fills half a circle. You can also click the Pick Angle to Fill button to the right of the Angle to Fill box to graphically select an angle in the drawing.

3. If you want the object to rotate about the array center, turn on the Rotate Items as Copied check box in the lower-left corner of the dialog box. If you turn this option off, the copies are all oriented in the same direction as the original object.

4. Click the Preview button to display the results of your array settings. In addition to the preview, you see the prompt `Pick or press Esc to return to dialog or <Right-click to accept array>:`.

5. If your preview looks correct, right-click. Otherwise, press Esc to return to the Array dialog box.

Copying Rows and Columns

You can use the Array dialog box to copy rows and columns. Here are the steps:

1. In the Home tab's expanded Modify panel, click the Array tool, or enter **ar**↵ to open the Array dialog box.

2. Click the Select Objects tool to temporarily close the Array dialog box.

3. Select the objects you want to copy, and then press ↵ to confirm your selection.

4. In the Array dialog box, click the Rectangular Array radio button (see Figure 5.18).

5. Change the value in the Rows text box to the number of rows you want.

6. Change the value in the Columns text box to the number of columns you want.

7. To set the distance between rows, enter a distance in the Row Offset text box.

8. To set the distance between columns, enter a distance in the Column Offset text box (as shown in Figure 5.18).

9. When you are satisfied with the Array settings, click OK.

Figure 5.18

Copying rows and columns

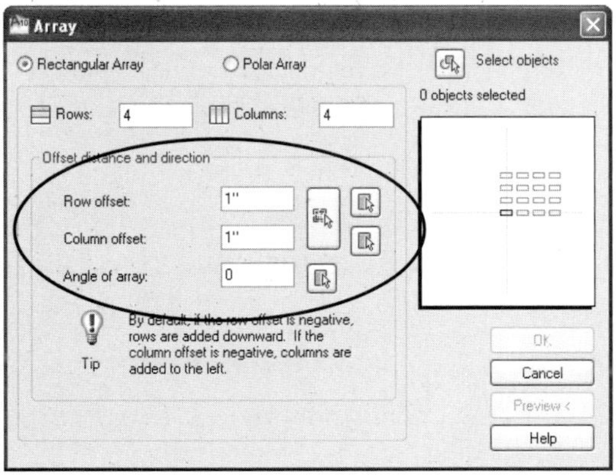

AutoCAD usually draws a rectangular array from bottom to top and from left to right. You can reverse the direction of the array by entering negative values for the distance between columns and rows in steps 7 and 8.

At times, you might want a rectangular array at an angle. To accomplish this, enter the angle in the Angle of Array input box. You can also select the angle graphically by clicking the Pick Angle of Array button just to the right of the Angle of Array input box.

If you prefer, you can graphically indicate the distance between rows and columns by using the options in the Offset Distance and Direction section of the Array dialog box (see the bottom image in Figure 5.19). You might want to use this option when objects are available to use as references from which to determine column and row distances. For example, you might have drawn a crosshatch pattern, as on a calendar, within which you want to array an object. You use the intersections of the hatch lines as references to define the array cell, which is one square in the hatch pattern.

You can also indicate row or column distances individually by using the Pick Row Offset and Pick Column Offset buttons to the right of the Pick Both Offsets button.

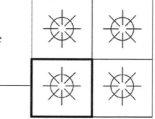

Distance between rows and columns can be indicated with a rectangle.

Scaling, Stretching, and Rotating

You can scale, stretch, and rotate as well as move and copy objects with grips. But as described for the Move and Copy commands, you can also use specific commands for each of these operations. Like the Move and Copy commands, the Scale, Stretch, and Rotate commands give you more flexibility in your selection of objects.

Figure 5.19

You can set the distance between rows and columns graphically by using the Pick Both Offsets option in the Array dialog box.

Scaling to a Specific Scale Factor

To use the Scale command to change the size of an object or a set of objects, do the following:

1. From the Modify panel, choose Scale, or enter **sc**↵ at the command prompt.

2. At the `Select objects:` prompt, select the objects you want to scale, and press ↵.

3. At the `Specify base point:` prompt, select a point around which to scale. If you select a corner of a rectangle, for example, the corner remains in place while the rest of the rectangle expands or contracts around the corner.

4. At the `Specify scale factor or [Copy/Reference]:` prompt, enter a scale value. The selected objects change to the specified scale.

Scaling an Object to Fit Another

A useful feature of the Scale command is the Reference option, which lets you scale an object to match the size of another. The following example shows how to use the Reference option to change the size of a door in a floor plan to fit an enlarged opening:

1. From the Modify panel, choose Scale, or enter **sc**↵ at the command prompt.

2. At the `Select objects:` prompt, select an object or objects.

3. At the `Specify base point:` prompt, use the Endpoint osnap to select the corner of the door, as shown in the left image in Figure 5.20.

Figure 5.20

Scaling a door to
fit an opening

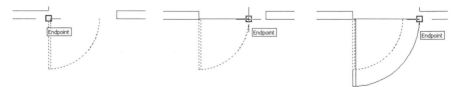

4. At the `Specify scale factor or [Copy/Reference]:` prompt, enter **R↵**.

5. At the `Specify reference length <1>:` prompt, use the Endpoint osnap, and select the same corner of the door you selected in step 3. You can also enter **@↵** since the last point you selected was the point you selected in step 3.

6. At the `Specify second point:` prompt, select the endpoint of the arc that represents the door swing, as shown in the middle image in Figure 5.20.

7. At the `Specify new length or [Points]:` prompt, notice that the door swing endpoint follows the cursor while the corner of the door stays fixed in its corner location. Use the Endpoint osnap again, and select the other corner of the door opening, as shown in the right image in Figure 5.20.

In this example, a door is scaled to fit an opening. This door already had one corner at the same location as one side of the opening. To scale an object to fit another, you need to first align the location you will use as a base point to one end of the object or area to which you want to scale.

Stretching Objects

To move the endpoint of a line or a vertex of a polyline, you can use the Stretch command. Stretch lets you select a single vertex or several vertices and move them to reshape a drawing.

The basic method for using Stretch is as follows:

1. In the Modify panel, click the Stretch tool, or enter **s↵** at the command prompt.

2. At the `Select objects:` prompt, enter **c↵**. This invokes the crossing selection window.

3. Enclose the vertices you want to stretch with the crossing selection window, as shown in the left image in Figure 5.21, and then press ↵. You cannot use a standard window for this operation.

Figure 5.21

Use a crossing win-
dow to select the
vertices you want to
stretch (left image),
and then select a
base point. The ver-
tices will move with
the cursor (right
image).

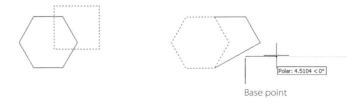

Base point

4. At the `Specify base point or [Displacement] <Displacement>:` prompt, select a base point.

5. At the `Specify second point or <use first point as displacement>:` prompt, you'll see the vertices move as you move the cursor. Select a new location for the vertices, or enter a coordinate.

Although the Stretch command is useful, the grip-editing version of Stretch is just as capable and a bit easier to understand.

See the section "Moving and Copying" earlier in this chapter for tips on selecting base points and objects.

Rotating Objects

In Chapter 4, you learned that you can rotate objects using grips, but in addition you can use the Rotate command to do so. To rotate an object with the Rotate command, do the following:

1. In the Modify panel, click the Rotate tool, or enter **ro↵** at the command prompt. You'll see the following message:

       Current positive angle in UCS: ANGDIR=counterclockwise ANGBASE=0

2. At the `Select objects:` prompt, select the object or objects you want to rotate, and then press ↵.

3. At the `Specify base point:` prompt, select a point around which objects are to be rotated. The objects rotate about the selected point as you move your cursor.

4. At the `Specify rotation angle or [Copy/Reference]:` prompt, enter a rotation angle value, or use the cursor to select a rotation angle.

The message you see in step 1 lets you know the current settings for the angle direction and base angle. This helps you decide whether to enter a positive or negative value for rotation angles.

Aligning the Rotation Cursor with an Object

In step 4 of the preceding example, the selected objects and the cursor rotate around the selected base point. Frequently, the angle indicated by the cursor and the angle of the objects you are rotating do not coincide. This can be a problem, particularly if you want to graphically rotate the selected objects. To align the cursor with the objects you are rotating, you can use the Reference option. This can be helpful if you are trying to rotate one edge of an object to a specific angle or to another object. The following steps describe how you can use the Reference option to align a randomly placed rectangle with the cursor to rotate the rectangle to a specific angle:

1. Click the Rotate tool and select the objects you want to rotate.

2. At the Specify base point: prompt, select a point around which the objects are to be rotated. In the example in Figure 5.22, the cross with the circle represents the base point. Once you select a base point, the objects rotate around the selected point as you move your cursor.

Figure 5.22

Using the Reference option to align the selected objects to the cursor

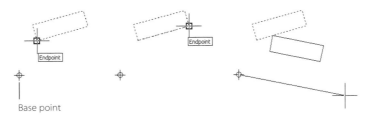

3. At the Specify rotation angle or [Copy/Reference]: prompt, enter **r**↵.

4. At the Specify the reference angle <0>: prompt, use the Endpoint osnap to select the endpoint of the line you want aligned with the cursor, as shown in the left image of Figure 5.22.

5. At the Specify second point: prompt, select the other end of the line you want to align with the cursor, as shown in the middle image of Figure 5.22.

6. At the Specify the new angle or [Points]: prompt, notice that the object is now aligned with the cursor as it rotates about the base point. You can enter an angle value or select a point to finish the command.

You can also use the Reference option to select a specific point on an object as the location being rotated. For example, suppose you want to rotate a set of circles inside a hexagon to align with the corner of the hexagon, as shown in Figure 5.23.

Figure 5.23

The goal is to rotate the circles inside the hexagon (left view) to align with the corners of the hexagon (right view).

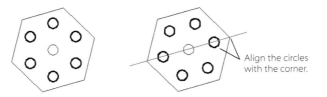

To do this, you can use the Reference option as follows:

1. Start the Rotate command, and select the objects you want to rotate.

2. At the Specify base point: prompt, use the Center osnap to select the center of the hexagon as represented by the central circle (see the left image in Figure 5.24). Once you do this, the objects rotate around the selected point as you move your cursor.

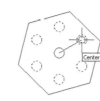 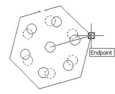

Figure 5.24

Rotating the circles to align with the corners of the hexagon

3. At the `Specify rotation angle or [Copy/Reference]:` prompt, enter **r**↵.

4. At the `Specify the reference angle <0>:` prompt, use the Center osnap to select the center of the hexagon again. You can also enter **@**↵ since the last point you selected was the center.

5. At the `Specify second point:` prompt, use the Center osnap to select the center of one of the circles you are rotating, as shown in the center image of Figure 5.24. Now as you move the cursor, the circle whose center you selected is aligned with the cursor angle.

6. At the `Specify the new angle or [Points]:` prompt, use the Endpoint osnap to select one of the corners of the hexagon, as shown in the right image in Figure 5.24. The circles align with the corners.

To rotate an object around a point that is some distance from your current view, draw a temporary circle whose center is at the location of the rotation center and whose radius intersects with the object you want to rotate. You can then zoom into the object you want to rotate and use the Center osnap to locate the center of the circle as the rotation base point. Delete the circle when you are done, or keep it for future edits. Consider creating a nonprinting layer on which you can keep construction objects such as the circle.

Breaking an Object into Two

If you need to place a gap in a line or an arc or just need to cut a line in half, you'll want to use the Break command. Break is simple to use, but it does have a few quirks. First, it does not work on all types of objects. You can place gaps in lines, polylines (including rectangles, polygons, and clouds), splines, arcs, and circles by using Break. Break allows you to cut an object without actually placing a gap in the object. However, if you use Break on a circle, you must create a gap. You cannot break a circle at a single point.

To use Break to place a gap in an object, do the following:

1. In the expanded Modify panel, click the Break tool, or enter **br**↵ at the command prompt.

2. At the `Select object:` prompt, select the object you want to break at the location where you want the gap to begin.

3. At the `Specify second break point or [First point]:` prompt, select the second point on the object for the opposite side of the gap. The gap appears on the object.

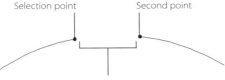

Selection point   Second point

The object breaks between the two points.

Sometimes you want the beginning of the gap at an intersection of two objects, in which case you can't click the object to select the beginning of the gap location. Break lets you select an object independent of the beginning points and endpoints of the gap by using the First Point option. Here's how it works:

1. In the expanded Modify panel, click the Break tool, or enter **br**⏎ at the command prompt.

2. At the `Select object:` prompt, select the object you want to break.

3. At the `Specify second break point or [First point]:` prompt, enter **f**⏎, and then select the beginning location for the gap.

4. At the `Specify second break point:` prompt, select the second point on the object for the opposite side of the gap. The gap appears on the object.

To break an object at a single point without creating a gap, enter **@**⏎ in step 4. This tells AutoCAD that the first and second points of the gap are the same. You can also use the Break at Point tool in the expanded Modify panel to accomplish this.

Editing Xrefs and Blocks

Blocks are AutoCAD objects that are assemblies of other objects. For example, you can draw a chair and then convert the chair into a block named "chair." This block behaves as if it were a single object. All blocks have names to easily identify them during other editing functions. Blocks are useful in creating symbols such as doors and windows in an architectural drawing, chairs and office equipment in a plan layout, or anything that will be repeated frequently in a drawing.

Xrefs are entire drawing files that are imported into other drawing files. When a file has been imported as an xref, it behaves like a single object, just like a block (see Chapter 8). Xrefs can be nested, and they can also contain blocks.

Even though blocks and xrefs behave as single objects, you can still edit the individual components from which they are made, by using the Refedit command. However, for casual or new users, it's much easier to simply open the source xref file and make changes there.

You can also use Refedit to edit blocks, but the Block Editor greatly simplifies block editing.

In Chapter 3, you learned that you can often edit an object just by double-clicking the object. This opens either the Properties palette or a specific dialog box that lets you edit the object. Double-clicking a block opens the Edit Block Definition dialog box (see Figure 5.25).

This dialog box lists all the blocks in the drawing. The block you double-click is automatically selected from the list. To the right is a preview window displaying a thumbnail version of the currently selected block.

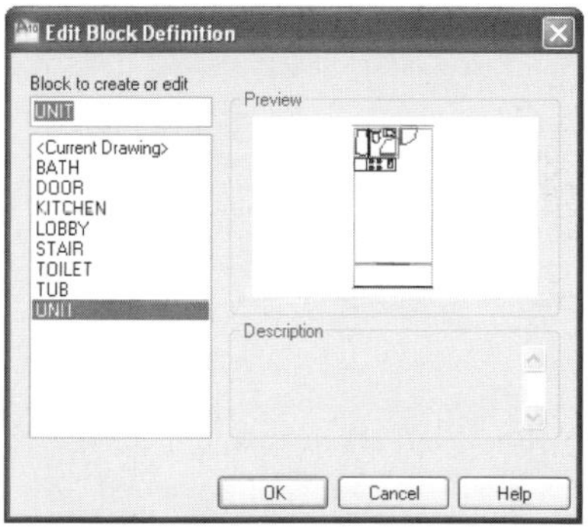

After you select a block name from the list and click OK, you might see a dialog box asking whether you want to see how dynamic blocks are created. Click No, because this is an advanced topic.

Figure 5.25

The Edit Block Definition dialog box

If you feel adventurous, you can take a look at the dynamic block demonstration and try the advanced features on your own.

Once past the dynamic block message, the entire drawing area changes to show just your selected block on a yellow background. This is the Block Editor window (see Figure 5.26). With the Block Editor window open, you will see a different set of Ribbon panels that offer all the tools you'll need for editing blocks, including the advanced geometric and dimensional constraint tools. You won't find a discussion of the Block Authoring palettes or the constraint tools here, because this is for more advanced users. However, you will find that once in the Block Editor window, you can edit the block by using all the usual editing tools described in this and the preceding chapter.

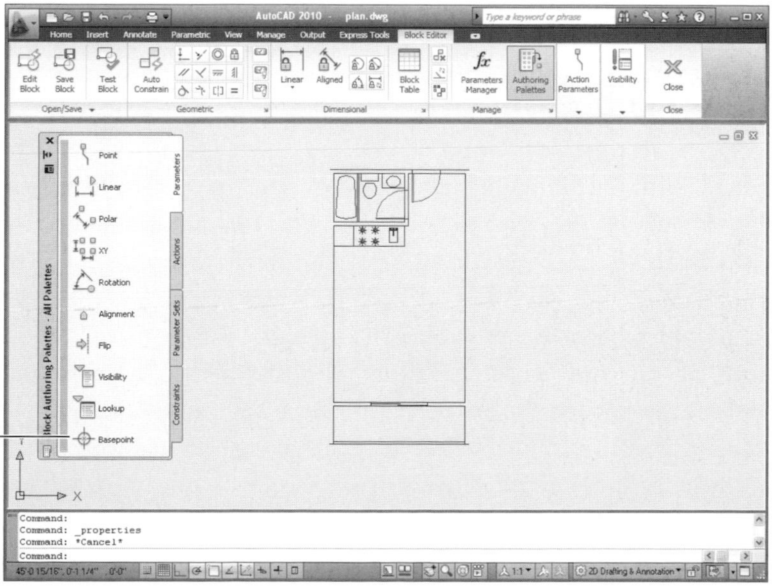

Figure 5.26

The Block Editor window with the Block Editor panels

The Block Authoring palettes offer special tools to create dynamic blocks.

Once you've finished editing your block, you can use the Save tool in the Block Editor's Open/Save panel to save any changes you made to the block. You can then use the Close Block Editor tool in the Close panel to close the Block Editor window and return to the standard AutoCAD window.

Saves block definition

Closes Block Editor and prompts to save changes

If you decide not to save your changes, click the Close tool, and select No when you're asked to save your changes.

If you're editing a block and you encounter a nested block that you want to edit, double-click the nested block. You'll be asked whether you want to save the changes to the current block. Click Yes or No, and then the Edit Block Definition dialog box reopens, this time with the nested block name highlighted. Click OK, and the nested block appears in the Block Editor window. You can then proceed to edit the nested block.

The origin of the drawing in the block editor is the insertion point of the block.

Another way to open another block while in the Block Editor window is to click the Edit Block tool in the Open/Save panel.

You're asked whether you want to save the current block, and then the Edit Block Definition dialog box you saw at the beginning of this section opens. From there, you can select the name of the block you want to edit from the list on the left.

Editing Polylines

Polylines are a great drawing tool because you can use them to perform a number of functions. If you outline an area with a polyline, you can quickly get the area of the outline by checking the properties of the polyline. You can easily convert closed polylines to 3D objects. You can form curves or quickly round the corners of polylines using the Fillet command.

As with other objects, you can edit a polyline by using AutoCAD's grip-editing feature. You can click a polyline to expose its grips and then move the individual grips to reshape the polyline. But an object as versatile as the polyline requires a special tool for editing. The Pedit command lets you fine-tune a polyline's shape. You can add line segments to polylines with Pedit, as well as straighten a polyline or add a new vertex. You can even adjust the overall width of a polyline or taper a polyline to form an arrow.

To use the Pedit command, do the following:

1. Choose the Edit Polyline tool from the expanded Modify panel, or enter **Pe**↵ at the command prompt.

> **REDUCING BLOCKS AND POLYLINES TO SIMPLE LINES AND ARCS WITH EXPLODE**
>
> The Explode command can reduce some of the more complex AutoCAD objects to basic objects. You can reduce polylines, for example, to lines or arcs. You can "unblock" blocks into their constituent objects. You can reduce hatch patterns to lines.
>
> Explode is easy to use. In the Draw panel, click the Explode tool, or enter **x**↵ at the command prompt. At the `Select objects:` prompt, click the object or objects you want to explode, and press ↵.

2. At the `Select polyline or [Multiple]:` prompt, select the polyline you want to edit. If you want to edit multiple polylines, enter **m**↵, and then select them. You'll see the following prompt:

   ```
   Enter an option
   [Close/Join/Width/Edit vertex/Fit/Spline/Decurve/Ltype gen/Reverse/Undo]:
   ```

3. Enter the capitalized letter of the option you want to use, and then follow the prompts to complete the edit.

> If you have Dynamic Input turned on, the prompt options appear as a list by the cursor. You can then select the option you want.

Once you've performed the edit, you are returned to the Pedit prompt. To exit Pedit, press ↵ at the prompt without selecting an option. Table 5.1 describes the functions of the Pedit options.

OPTION	FUNCTION
Close/Open	If the polyline is closed, the Open option appears and allows you to change the polyline from closed to open. If the polyline is open, Close lets you close it.
Join	This lets you join polylines, arcs, and lines to form a single polyline.
Width	This lets you adjust the width of a polyline. You can also use the Properties palette to do this.
Edit Vertex	This opens another set of options that let you edit the vertices of a polyline. You can remove vertices, insert new vertices, and change the width of the polyline at specific vertices, to name a few options. See Table 5.2.
Fit	This changes the polyline to a series of arcs that pass through the vertices. See Chapter 3.
Spline	This changes the polyline into a spline curve. See Chapter 3.
Decurve	This converts a fit or spline polyline into one of straight-line segments.
Ltype Gen	This adjusts the way line types are displayed. With Ltype Gen turned on, line types ignore vertices when generating line patterns.
Reverse	This reverses the direction of a polyline. Reverse is helpful when text appears upside-down in a complex polyline.
Undo	This undoes the last Pedit change of the current Pedit session.

Table 5.1

The Pedit Options

If you select the Edit Vertex option of the Pedit command, you're presented with the following prompt:

[Next/Previous/Break/Insert/Move/Regen/Straighten/Tangent/Width/eXit] <N>:

These options let you manipulate the vertices of a polyline. You'll also see an *x* marker at the beginning of the polyline. The *x* shows you the vertex that is currently available for editing. It indicates which vertex will be affected by the edit options. Table 5.2 explains what these options do.

Table 5.2

The Edit Options of the Pedit Command

OPTION	FUNCTION
Next	Moves the *x* marker to the next vertex for editing.
Previous	Moves the *x* marker to the previous vertex for editing.
Break	Lets you break the polyline from the current vertex marked by the *x* to the next. You'll see the prompt [Next/Previous/Go/eXit] <N>:, which lets you move the *x* marker to the next or previous vertex. The Go option performs the break after you've moved the *x* marker.
Insert	Lets you insert a vertex. The inserted vertex is added in the direction of the next vertex.
Move	Lets you move a vertex.
Regen	Regenerates the polyline after you've made a change using one of the edit options.
Straighten	Lets you straighten a polyline between two vertices. You'll see the prompt [Next/Previous/Go/eXit] <N>:, which lets you move the *x* marker to the next or previous vertex. The Go option straightens the polyline by removing intermediate vertices after you've moved the *x* marker.
Tangent	Lets you change the tangent direction of a vertex.
Width	Lets you change the width of the polyline at the current vertex.
eXit	Exits the Edit option of the Pedit command. You are returned to the Pedit prompt.

RECORD AND PLAY BACK ACTIONS

While not part of the Modify panel, the Action Recorder is one very useful tool that works with other tools in the Modify panel. The Action Recorder enables you to record your activity as an *action macro*. The macro can be played back at any time. This is a great time-saver when you are performing repetitive tasks—something that you may find yourself doing frequently in AutoCAD.

An entire panel is devoted to the Action Recorder in the Manage tab, as shown here:

 — Available action macro drop-down list

To use the Action Recorder, click the Record button. The Record button changes to a Stop button and a red dot appears next to the cursor to remind you that you are recording your activity. You'll also see the Action Tree appear just below the recorder.

RECORD AND PLAY BACK ACTIONS *(Continued)*

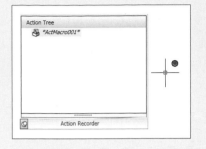

Proceed to work as you normally would in AutoCAD. As you work, your activity is displayed in the Action Tree. When you've completed the activity that you want to record, click the Stop button. The Action Macro dialog box appears, enabling you to give the recorded activity a name and description.

Once you've closed the Action Macro dialog box, you can play back your recorded action macro at any time. From the Action Recorder panel, select the macro name from the Available Action Macro drop-down list and then click Play.

The Action Tree enables you to include some interactivity in your macro. You can right-click on an individual action in the Action Tree to modify its behavior to allow user input. Perhaps the most common modification you'll want to make is to allow different selections or to change coordinate input and point selections. To do this, right-click on an action and select Request User Input.

When you select this option, you will be prompted for input when this particular action comes up in the macro. You can also use the Insert User Message option to have a message display while the macro is running.

Summary

You'll use the editing features discussed in this chapter frequently during typical editing sessions, though you might find you use some more than others. For example, you'll often use Fillet to join two lines to make a corner, and you'll probably use Scale only once in a while to resize objects. Block and xref editing are also features that you might not use all that often, but when you need them, they can be lifesavers.

CHAPTER 6

Creating 3D Drawings

AutoCAD makes it easy to create 3D shapes of any type, from simple boxes and cones to complex curved surfaces. Covering all the 3D modeling features of AutoCAD would require an entire book. This chapter gives you a taste of what can be done, and I hope you'll be able to take some of this information and create your own basic 3D models.

You'll find a mix of tutorials and command descriptions in this chapter. Tutorials walk you through features that you'll use frequently. Other features that are not as important for new users are described with figures and a less detailed discussion of their use.

This chapter includes the following topics:

- Getting to know the 3D modeling workspace
- Drawing in 3D using solids and surfaces
- Changing your point of view
- Creating 3D forms from 2D shapes
- Creating smooth 3D forms with the mesh modeling
- Specifying exact distances in 3D space
- Controlling the appearance of your model

Getting to Know the 3D Modeling Workspace

When it comes to 3D modeling, there really isn't much you can't do with AutoCAD 2010. You can create just about any shape you can imagine in AutoCAD. Of course, the more complex the shape, the more time it will take, but AutoCAD 2010 offers a new level of freedom in 3D modeling that the older versions lacked.

AutoCAD offers some basic shapes known as *solid primitives*. These tools let you quickly create a polysolid, box, wedge, cone, sphere, cylinder, pyramid, or torus (see Figure 6.1). You can edit these primitives to form other, more complex shapes. Other tools allow you to create free-form curves from 2D objects such as lines, arcs, and splines, as shown in Figure 6.2. A Helix tool helps you create spiral shapes such as screw threads or parking garage ramps.

Figure 6.1

The solid primitives available in AutoCAD

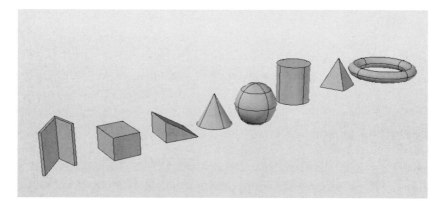

Figure 6.2

Shapes generated from lines, arcs, and splines

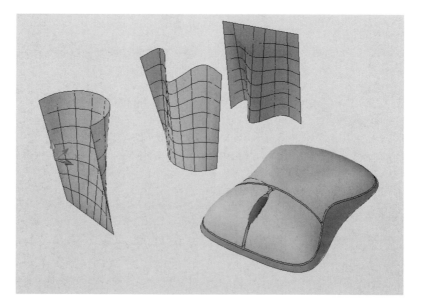

Most of this book is devoted to showing you how to work in what is called the AutoCAD *classic* workspace. This classic workspace is basically a 2D drawing environment, though you can certainly work in 3D as well.

AutoCAD 2010 offers something called the 3D Modeling workspace, which gives you a set of tools to help ease your way into 3D modeling. This 3D Modeling workspace gives AutoCAD a different appearance (see Figure 6.3), but don't worry. It still behaves in the same basic way, and the AutoCAD files produced are just the same.

Figure 6.3

The AutoCAD 3D Modeling workspace

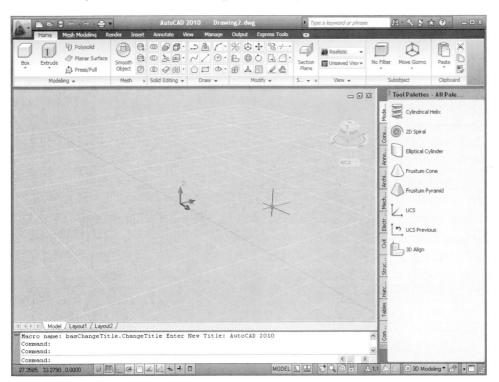

Here's how to switch to AutoCAD's 3D Modeling workspace:

1. Start AutoCAD, click the Workspace Switching icon in the status bar, and then select 3D Modeling. You'll see a new palette appear to the right of the AutoCAD window.

2. To start a new 3D model, click the New tool in the Quick Access Toolbar to open the Select Template dialog box. Select the acad3D.dwt template file, and click Open. Your screen will look similar to Figure 6.3.

3. Point to the tool palettes' title bar to the right, and click the X to close the palettes. The tool palettes are good tools, but as a beginner, you won't be using them.

The 3D Workspace differs from the 2D Drafting & Annotation workspace that you've been working with prior to this chapter. First, the Ribbon offers five panels that are geared toward 3D modeling. In addition, the new drawing, based on the acad3d.dwt template, displays the workspace as a perspective view with a grid. This is really just a typical AutoCAD drawing file with a couple of setting changes. The drawing's view has been set up to be a perspective view by default, and a feature called *visual style* shows 3D objects as solid objects. You'll learn more about the tools that let you adjust the appearance of your workspace later in this chapter. For now, you'll explore the 3D Modeling panels on the Ribbon.

Take a moment to look at the tabs on the Ribbon. You'll see two tabs that you haven't seen before: Mesh Modeling and Render (Figure 6.4). These tabs have been designed to offer ready access to 3D modeling and editing tools you'll need.

In addition, the Draw and Modify panels in the Home tab are slightly different from the Draw and Modify panels you've been working with in prior chapters. Besides some familiar tools, other tools have been added specifically for 3D modeling, as you will see in later sections of this chapter. The Home tab also contains several new 3D-oriented panels: Modeling, Mesh, Solid Editing, Section, and Subobject.

The Ribbon tabs offer some new sets of panels in other tabs. If you select the Render tab, you'll see a set of Ribbon panels that let you create lighting and material effects. The View tab offers some 3D tools to help you navigate your drawing, and the Output tab offers tools that let you create 3D views of your model.

In the next section, you'll gain some firsthand experience creating some 3D shapes and manipulating them. This way, you'll get a feel for how things work in the 3D Modeling workspace.

Figure 6.4

Five tabs of the 3D Modeling workspace's Ribbon

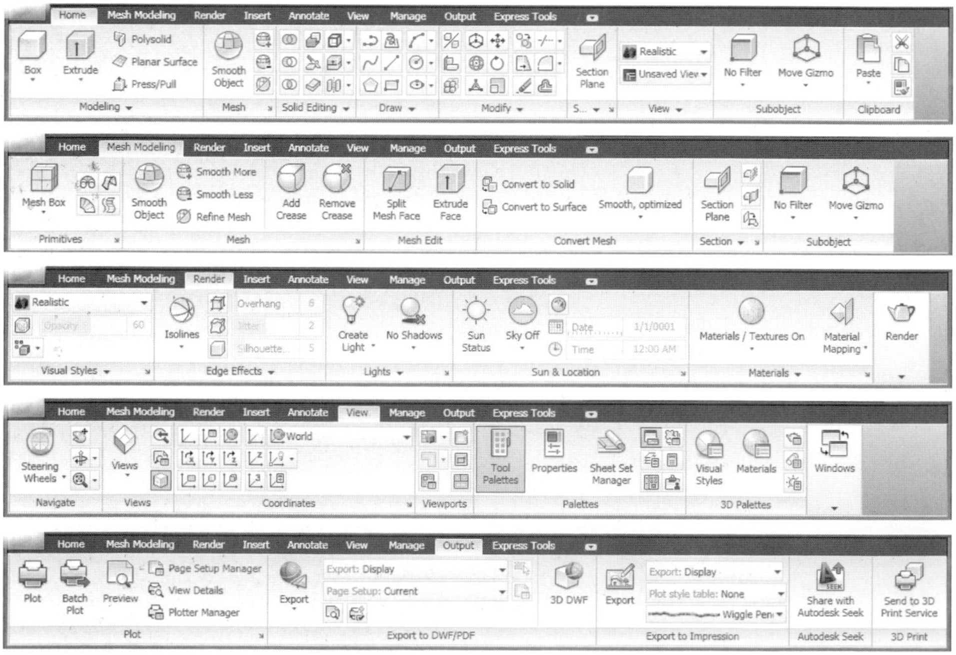

Drawing in 3D Using Solids and Surfaces

You can work with three types of 3D objects in AutoCAD: solids, meshes, and surfaces. You can treat these objects as if they were solid materials. For example, you can create a box and then remove shapes from the box as if you were carving it, as shown in Figure 6.5.

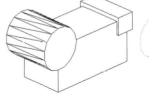

Figure 6.5

Solid modeling lets you remove or add shapes.

With surfaces, you create complex surfaces shapes by building upon lines, arcs, or polylines. For example, you can quickly turn a series of curved polylines, arcs, and lines into a warped surface, as shown in Figure 6.6.

Meshes modeling enables you to form smooth, free-form shapes by editing the faces and edges that appear on the mesh (Figure 6.7). You can control the number of these faces when you create the mesh and add more mesh faces as you work.

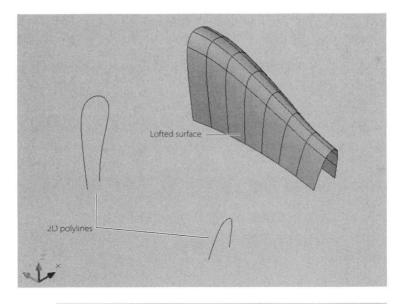

Figure 6.6

Using the Loft tool, you can use 2D objects to define a complex surface.

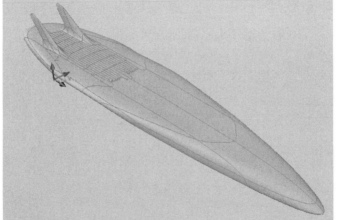

Figure 6.7

Mesh modeling enables you to create smooth shapes.

First, you'll learn how to create a solid box, and at the same time, I'll introduce you to some common modeling features. Next, you'll learn how to create a surface model. You'll get a chance to see how surface modeling differs from solid modeling. Finally, you will be introduced to mesh modeling and you'll learn how to best use each modeling method.

> If you have some experience with AutoCAD 3D (in versions earlier than AutoCAD 2007), you'll notice that the new surface-modeling features are not the same as the surface objects you are accustomed to using, which were created in the older version of AutoCAD. You can edit the new surface objects using Boolean functions, which you'll learn about later in this chapter. Surface objects can also interact with solid primitive objects. You can still create the old-style 3D surface objects, but they are not the same types of objects as those presented in this chapter. You can convert them to the new style surfaces using the Convtosurface command.

Then, the rest of the chapter provides reference material on the individual tools for 3D modeling and editing that you were introduced to earlier. You won't find a comprehensive explanation of all the 3D modeling tools, but I'll provide enough information to get you started. If you're doing a simple study model, you might find all you need in this chapter.

THE PRIMITIVE AND EXTRUDE FLYOUTS

In some of the exercises in this chapter, I'll be asking you to select from the Primitives and Extrude flyouts in the Home tab's Modeling panel. These flyouts typically show the Box and Extrude tools, but since they are flyouts, the default tool can change depending on the last tool used. For this reason, I'll be using the generic names of Primitive and Extrude.

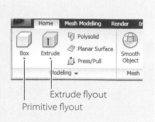

Extrude flyout

Primitive flyout

Creating a 3D Solid

In this section, you'll create a simple box using a 3D solid primitive. You'll then learn how to manipulate the box and how to get around in the 3D workspace.

Start by creating a box using the Box tool in the Home tab's Modeling panel:

1. Click the Box tool in the Home tab's Modeling panel.

2. Click a point near the location shown in Figure 6.8 near coordinate 0,15. You can use the coordinate readout to select a point near 0,15. Once you've clicked, you'll see a rectangle follow the cursor.

3. Click another point near coordinate 20,0, as shown in the left image of Figure 6.8. Now as you move the cursor, the rectangle is fixed, and the height of the 3D box appears.

4. Enter **4**↵ for a height of 4 units for the box. You can also click to fix the height of the box.

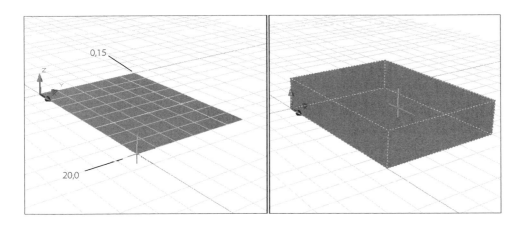

Figure 6.8

Drawing a 3D solid box

You've just created a 3D solid box. By default, the box takes on the current layer color. If you use the acad3D.dwt or acadiso3D.dwt template file to create a new drawing, the default color is a light gray. If you use the acad.dwt or acadiso.dwt template file, the default color is black. If your sample box appears as a black box, do the following:

1. Type **La**↵ at the command prompt.

2. In the Layer Properties Manager dialog box, click the color swatch in the Layer 0 listing, as shown on the left side of Figure 6.9.

3. In the Select Color dialog box, select cyan, as shown on the right side of Figure 6.9.

You used three basic steps to create the box. You first clicked one corner to establish a location for the box, and then you clicked another corner to establish the base size. Finally, you selected a height. You can use a similar set of steps to create any of the other 3D solid primitives found in the Modeling panel. For example, for a cylinder, you select the center, then the radius, and then a height. For a wedge, you select two corners, as you did with the box, and then select the height of the wedge, as shown in Figure 6.10.

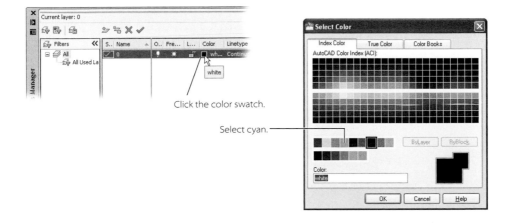

Figure 6.9

Changing the color of the current layer

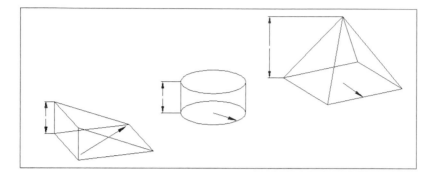

Editing 3D Solids with Grips

Once you've created a solid, you can fine-tune its shape by using grips. If you click the solid to select it, you might see a message alerting you to the new editing options. Dismiss the message, and you will see that grips appear on the 3D solid, as shown in the left image of Figure 6.11.

The square grips at the base of the solid allow you to adjust the location of those grips. The arrow grips allow you to adjust the length of the side to which the arrows are attached. If you click an arrow grip and you have Dynamic Input turned on, a dimension appears at the cursor. You can enter a new dimension for the length associated with the selected grip, or you can drag the arrow to adjust the length. Try the following to get a firsthand feel for how this works:

1. Click the arrow grip toward the front of the box, as shown on the left in Figure 6.11. Now as you move the cursor, the box changes in length.

2. Press the Esc key to clear the grip selection.

   You can also move individual edges by using Ctrl+click:

1. Ctrl+click the top-front edge, as shown on the right in Figure 6.11. You might see a Selecting Subobject dialog box; dismiss it. You'll see that the edge is highlighted, and a grip appears at its midpoint.

2. Click the edge's grip, and move the cursor. The edge follows the grip.

Figure 6.11

Grips appear on a 3D solid.

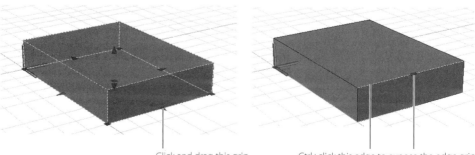

Click and drag this grip.   Ctrl+click this edge to expose the edge grip.

3. Hold down the Shift key, and "pull" the grip forward away from the box's center. The Shift key constrains the motion in the x-, y-, or z-axis.

4. Click a point to fix the edge's new position.

5. Click the Undo button to return the box to its original shape.

As you can see, you have a great deal of flexibility in controlling the shape of the box. The Shift key lets you constrain the motion of the grip.

Constraining Motion with the Gizmo

Another handy tool for grip editing 3D objects is the gizmo. Its icon looks like the UCS icon, and it appears whenever you hover over a grip. Try the next exercise to see how the gizmo works:

1. Ctrl+click the front-top edge of the box again to expose the edge's grip.

2. Place the cursor on the grip, but don't click. The gizmo appears (see Figure 6.12).

3. Place the cursor on the z-axis of the gizmo, but don't click. A blue line appears that extends across the drawing area, and the z-axis of the gizmo changes color.

4. Click the z-axis. Now as you move the cursor, the grip motion is constrained in the z-axis.

5. Click again to fix the location of the grip.

6. Press the Esc key to clear your grip selection.

7. Click the Undo tool to undo the grip edit.

Here you'll see that you can use the gizmo to change the Z location of a grip. You can use the gizmo to modify the location of a single grip or the entire object.

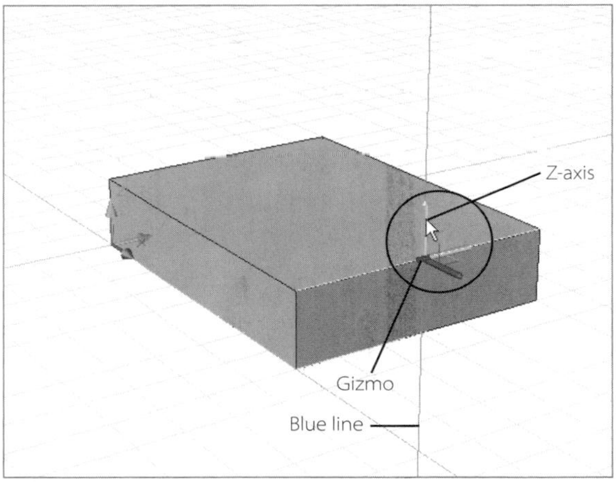

Figure 6.12

Using the gizmo to constrain motion

Rotating Objects in 3D Using Dynamic UCS

Most of the discussion in this book centers on a 2D drawing area. Coordinates in this area reside in what is known as the *world coordinate system* (WCS). This is the default coordinate system that AutoCAD uses in new drawings, but you can also create your own coordinate systems that are subsets of the WCS. A coordinate system that you create is known as a *user coordinate system* (UCS).

UCSs are significant in 3D modeling because they can help you draw in 3D space. You can set up a UCS, for example, that is on a vertical face of the 3D box you created earlier. You could then draw on that vertical face just as you would on the WCS of the drawing. Figure 6.13 shows a cylinder drawn on the side of a box. The vertical grid shows the orientation of the UCS. Also notice that the UCS icon is in the corner of the box.

Figure 6.13

Drawing on the side of a box

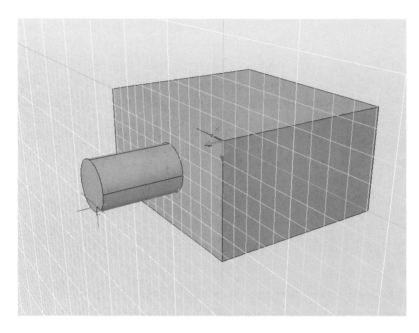

The UCS is a great tool for 3D modeling, but it can be cumbersome to use. A feature called Dynamic UCS automatically changes the orientation of the x-, y-, and z-axes to conform to the flat surface of a 3D object.

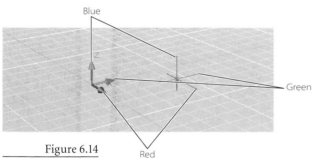

Figure 6.14

The UCS icon at the left and the cursor in 3D to the right are color matched.

If you created the new 3D file by using the acad3D.dwt template, you might have noticed that the cursor looked different. Instead of the usual cross, it has three intersecting lines. If you look carefully, you'll see that each line of the cursor is a different color. In its default configuration, AutoCAD shows a red line for the x-axis, a green line for the y-axis, and a blue line for the z-axis. This color scheme mimics that of the UCS icon, as shown in Figure 6.14.

As you work with Dynamic UCS, you'll see that the orientation of these lines changes when you point at a surface on a 3D object. To see how this works firsthand, try the following exercise. Here you'll use Dynamic UCS to help you rotate the box around the x-axis.

1. Make sure that the Dynamic UCS feature is turned on by checking the Allow/Disallow Dynamic UCS tool at the bottom of the AutoCAD window. It should be a blue color, indicating that it is on. If it isn't, click it to turn it on.

2. Click the Rotate tool in the Home tab's Modify panel.

3. At the Select objects: prompt, click the box, and then press ↵ to finish your selection.

4. At the Specify base point: prompt, don't click anything, but move the cursor from one surface of the box to a side of the box. As you do so, pay attention to the orientation of the cursor. It changes depending on the surface to which you are pointing.

5. Place the cursor on the front side, as shown in Figure 6.15.

6. With the cursor on the front side of the box, Shift+right-click, and select Endpoint from the context menu.

7. Place the osnap cursor on the lower-front corner of the box, as shown in the left image of Figure 6.15. Click this corner. As you move the cursor, the box rotates around the y-axis.

8. Enter **–30** for the rotation angle. Your box should look like the image in the right of Figure 6.15.

Here you'll see that you can hover over a surface to indicate the plane about which the rotation is to occur. You aren't limited to using the surfaces of the object you are rotating. If you have multiple objects in your model, you can use the surface of any object to indicate the rotational plane.

Now, suppose you want to add an object to one of the sides of the rotated box. The next section will show you another essential tool you can use to do just that.

Figure 6.15

Selecting a rotation point and the resulting box orientation

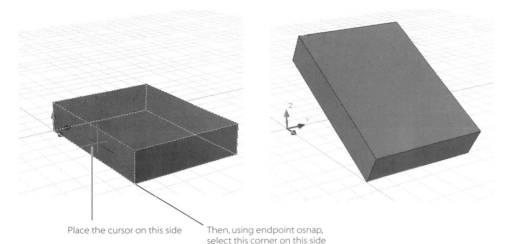

Place the cursor on this side   Then, using endpoint osnap, select this corner on this side

USING OBJECT SNAPS IN 3D SPACE

If you need to place objects in precise locations in 3D, such as endpoints or midpoints of other objects, you can do so using object snaps, just as you would in 2D. But you must be careful when using object snaps as far as Dynamic UCS is concerned.

In the exercise in the "Rotating Objects in 3D Using Dynamic UCS" section, you were asked to make sure that you place the cursor on the side of the box that coincides with the rotational plane before you select the Endpoint osnap. This ensures that the Dynamic UCS feature has selected the proper rotational plane; otherwise, you might find that the box rotates in the wrong direction.

Drawing on a 3D Object's Surface

In the rotation exercise, you saw that you can hover over a surface to indicate the plane of rotation. You can use the same method to indicate the plane on which you want to place an object. Try the following exercise to see how it's done:

1. Click the Primitives flyout in the Modeling panel, and then select Cylinder (Figure 6.16).

2. Place the cursor on the top surface of the rectangle, as indicated in Figure 6.17, and hold it there for a moment. The cursor will align with the angle of the top surface.

3. With the cursor aligned with the top surface of the box, click a point roughly at the center of the box. The base of the cylinder appears on the surface.

Figure 6.16

Select Cylinder from the flyout.

Figure 6.17

Drawing a cylinder on the surface of a 3D solid: place the cursor on the top surface of the box and make sure it is aligned to the top.

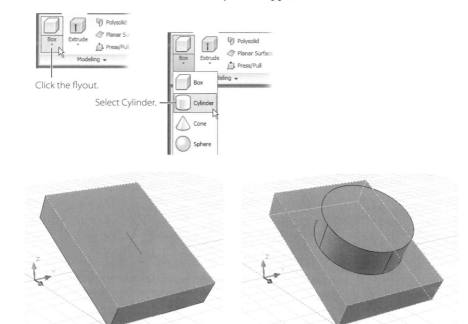

4. Adjust the circle so it is roughly the same 6-unit radius of the one shown in the right of Figure 6.17, and then click to set the radius. You can also enter **6↵**.

5. Enter **4↵** for the height of the cylinder.

This demonstrates that you can use Dynamic UCS to align objects to the surface of an object. Note that the Dynamic UCS works only on flat surfaces. You can't, for example, use Dynamic UCS to place an object on the curved side of the cylinder.

WORKING WITH USER COORDINATE SYSTEMS

Dynamic UCS is a great tool, and it might be all you need to create your 3D models. But at some point, you might find you want a bit more control over the UCS. That's where the standard UCS comes in handy.

A standard UCS is more permanent than Dynamic UCS, and you can use a standard UCS if you need to create an object that is aligned with another object's surface but is not on the object.

In the section "Rotating Objects in 3D Using Dynamic UCS," you learned how to use Dynamic UCS to align your working coordinate system to the side of a box. To create a UCS that remains in place, do the following:

1. From the View tab's Coordinates panel, choose Face, or enter **Ucs↵ F↵**.

2. Click the surface of an object that represents your working plane. You will see the UCS icon move to the surface you select.

3. At the Enter an option [Next/Xflip/Yflip] <accept>: prompt, select Accept from the Dynamic Input display, or press ↵ to accept this location. If it is the wrong location, click Undo and try again. You also have the option to try the Next face, flip the x-axis (Xflip), or flip the y-axis (Yflip).

To return to your previous UCS, type **Ucs↵ P↵** at the command prompt. If you want to return to WCS, choose World from the View tab's Coordinates panel or type **Ucs↵ W↵**.

You can also use three points to define a UCS. To do this, you'll need to use osnaps and a set of objects to which you can snap. You can then take the following steps:

1. From the View tab's Coordinates panel, choose 3-Point, or type **Ucs↵ 3↵**.

2. At the Specify new origin point <0,0,0>: prompt, use an osnap, such as the Endpoint osnap override, and then select an object, such as the corner of a box, as shown here in the left image:

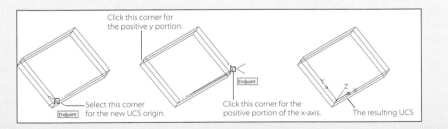

continues

WORKING WITH USER COORDINATE SYSTEMS *(continued)*

3. At the `Specify point on positive portion of the X-axis:` prompt, select another corner along the x-axis, as shown earlier in the middle image. As you do so, notice the rubber-banding line. This visually shows you the x-axis of your newly defined UCS.

4. At the `Specify point on positive-Y portion of the UCS XY plane:` prompt, select another corner along the y-axis from the origin point, as shown in the earlier middle image. Again, notice the rubber-banding line indicating the y-axis of your new UCS.

5. At the `Specify point on positive-Y portion of the UCS XY plane:` prompt, you don't have to select a location exactly on the y-axis of your new UCS. The point you select to define the x-axis will define the UCS's x-axis orientation.

The point you select in step 5, the positive Y location, can be anywhere as long as it defines the general direction of the y-axis.

If you think you'll need to return to this UCS at some future time, you can give the UCS a name by doing the following: click the Named tool in the View tab's UCS Ribbon panel. In the UCS dialog box, right-click the Unnamed option in the list of UCSs, and select Rename to give the current UCS a new name. Click OK to exit the UCS dialog box.

Sculpting Objects with Union and Subtraction

Now suppose you want to create a cylindrical void at the center of the cylinder of the solid you just edited. To do so, you create a 3D solid in the shape of the void and then use the Subtract tool to remove the 3D solid.

Start by combining the cylinder and the box into a single solid object:

1. Click the Union tool in the Home tab's Solid Editing panel.

2. Select the cylinder and the box, and then press ↵.

Although they haven't changed in appearance, both objects are now joined into a single 3D solid. Now create a cylinder that will become the hole in the center of the combined box and cylinder:

1. Click the Cylinder tool in the Home tab's Modeling panel.

2. Place the cursor on the top of the cylinder, and wait until the cursor orients itself to the angle of the cylinder's top surface.

3. Shift+right-click, and choose Center from the context menu.

4. Point to the edge of the cylinder, and when you see the osnap center mark at the center of the cylinder, click. (See the top-left image in Figure 6.18.)

5. Enter **2**↵ for the cylinder radius.

6. Move the cursor downward until you see the cylinder appear below the box, as shown in the top-right image of Figure 6.18, and then click to finish the cylinder.

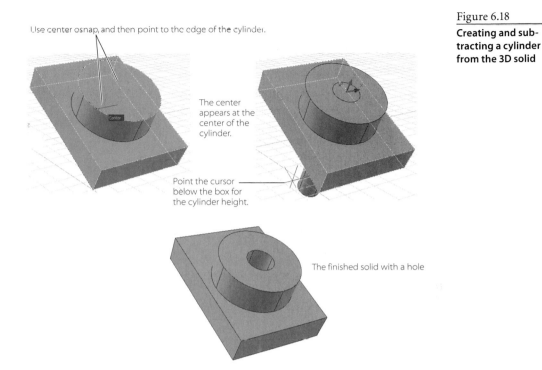

Figure 6.18

Creating and subtracting a cylinder from the 3D solid

You have the void shape in place. To finish this solid, try using the Subtract tool to make a hole in the solid:

1. Click the Subtract tool from the Home tab's Solid Editing panel.

2. At the Select solids, surfaces, and regions to subtract from .. Select Objects: prompt, select the box, and then press ↵.

3. At the Select solids, surfaces, and regions to subtract .. Select Objects: prompt, select the newly created cylinder, and then press ↵. A hole appears in the solid that is centered on the cylinder (see Figure 6.18).

In these exercises, you created a cylinder and subtracted it from the original 3D solid to form a void in the shape of a cylindrical hole. With the tools you've learned how to use so far, you can begin to build nearly any shape you might need.

Making Changes to Your Solid

When you're creating a 3D model, you will hardly ever get the shape right the first time. Suppose you decide that you need to modify the shape you've created so far by moving the hole from the center of the larger cylinder to its edge. This next exercise will show you how you can gain access to the individual components of a 3D solid to make changes.

The model you've been working with is composed of three objects: a box and two cylinders. These individual components of the solid are referred to as *subobjects* of the main solid object. When you use the Union, Subtract, or Intersect tool on a set of objects, the objects merge into a single solid, or at least that is how it seems at first. You can gain access and modify the shape of the subobjects from which the shape is constructed just by holding down the Ctrl key while clicking the solid. Try the following to see how this works:

1. Place the cursor on the solid you've made so far. You'll see that the entire object is highlighted as if it were one object. If you were to click it (but don't do that yet), the entire object would be selected.

2. Hold down the Ctrl key, and move the cursor over the various parts of the solid. First, place the cursor on the hole, then on the cylinder, and finally on the box. As you do this, you will see that the individual parts of the solid are highlighted instead of the whole solid (see Figure 6.19).

3. While still holding the Ctrl key down, click the center of the hole. The grips for the hole appear, as shown on the left side of Figure 6.20. As you might guess, you can use these grips to change the shape and location of the selected solid.

4. Click the center grip of the cylinder and move your cursor. If you find it a bit uncontrollable, turn off Polar mode. As you move the cursor, you'll see that the hole moves with the cursor.

Figure 6.19

Individual objects are highlighted when you use the Ctrl key.

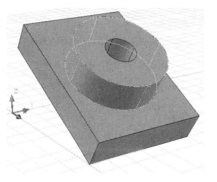
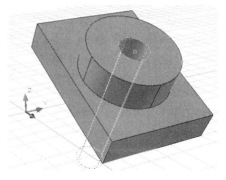

Use Ctrl to select the cylinder, and then click the center grip.

Figure 6.20

You can move the hole-forming cylinder to a new location by using its grip.

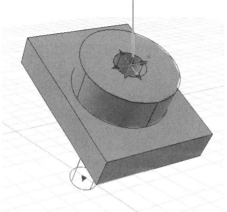
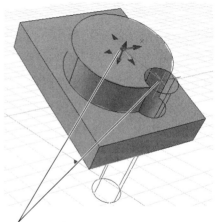

You can move the small cylinder anywhere.

5. Place the hole in the location shown on the right side of Figure 6.20, and click. You've just moved the hole from the center to the edge of the cylinder.

6. Press the Esc key to clear the selection.

This example shows you that the Ctrl key can be an extremely useful tool when you have to edit a solid because it allows you to select the solids that form your model. Once the solid is selected, you can move it, or you can use the arrow grips to change its size.

Changing Your Point of View

Eventually, you'll want to be able to examine your model from different angles. If you are working on a building design, you might even want to see what it's like from inside your design. AutoCAD provides all the tools you'll need to get the view you want. In the following sections, you'll examine the different tools and methods available to see your 3D model from virtually any point of view.

> If you still have the file open from the previous exercise, you can try these tools on the current model. Otherwise, you can open a new file by using the acad3D.dwt template and create a box or other object to use as a practice visual target.

Moving Around Your Model

One of the first tasks you'll want to do with a model is look at it from all angles. The ViewCube is the perfect tool for this purpose. The ViewCube is a device that lets you select a view by using a sample cube. You have already seen the ViewCube in the early part of this chapter. If it is not visible in your drawing, do the following:

1. First make sure Visual Style is set to something other than 2D Wireframe by selecting 3D Wireframe, 3D Hidden, Conceptual, or Realistic from the Visual Styles dropdown list in the Home tab's View panel (Figure 6.21).

2. Click the Toggle ViewCube tool in the View tab's Views panel to reveal the ViewCube (Figure 6.22).

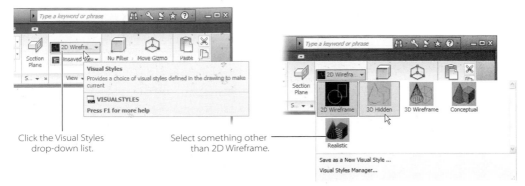

Click the Visual Styles drop-down list.

Select something other than 2D Wireframe.

Figure 6.21

The Visual Styles flyout with 3D Wireframe selected

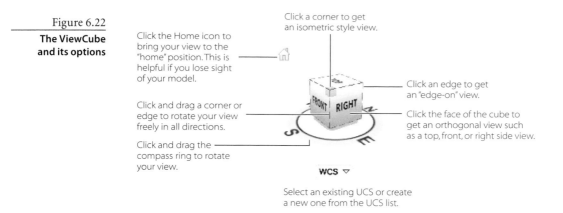

Figure 6.22

The ViewCube and its options

Click the Home icon to bring your view to the "home" position. This is helpful if you lose sight of your model.

Click a corner to get an isometric style view.

Click an edge to get an "edge-on" view.

Click and drag a corner or edge to rotate your view freely in all directions.

Click the face of the cube to get an orthogonal view such as a top, front, or right side view.

Click and drag the compass ring to rotate your view.

WCS ▽

Select an existing UCS or create a new one from the UCS list.

The following list explains what you can do with the ViewCube:

- Click the Home icon to bring your view to the "home" position; this is helpful if you lose sight of your model.

- You can get a top, front, right side, or other orthogonal view just by clicking the word Top, Front, or Right on the ViewCube.

- Click a corner of the cube to get an isometric style view, or click an edge to get an "edge-on" view.

- Click and drag the N, S, E, or W label to rotate the model in the X-Y plane.

- To freely rotate your view of the object in 3D, click and drag the cube.

- From the icon at the bottom, select an existing UCS or create a new one from the UCS list.

You can also change from a perspective view to a parallel projection view by right-clicking the cube and selecting Perspective or Parallel Projection.

Changing Where You Are Looking

AutoCAD uses a camera analogy to help you set up views in your 3D model. With a camera, you have a camera location and a target, and you can fine-tune both in AutoCAD. AutoCAD also offers the Swivel tool to let you adjust your view orientation. The Swivel tool is like keeping the camera stationary while pointing in a different direction. To use the Swivel tool, first you need to be in a visual style other than 2D Wireframe. Next, click Pan on the status bar, right-click, and select Other Navigation Modes → Swivel.

At first, the Swivel tool might seem just like the Pan tool. But in the 3D world, Pan actually moves both the camera and the target in unison. Using Pan is a bit like pointing a camera out the side of a moving car. If you don't keep the view in the camera fixed on an object, you are panning across the scenery. Using the Swivel tool is like standing on the side of the road and turning the camera to take in a panoramic view.

To use the Swivel tool, do the following:

1. Click Pan on the status bar.

2. Right-click in the drawing area, and choose Other Navigation Modes → Swivel. You can also type **3dswivel**↵ at the command prompt.

3. Click and drag in the drawing to swivel your point of view.

4. When you have the view you want, right-click and select Exit.

If you happen to lose your view entirely, you can use the Undo tool in the Quick Access toolbar to return to your previous view and start over.

> Swivel works best when your view is in Perspective mode. See "Changing from Perspective to Parallel Projection" later in this chapter.

Flying Through Your View

Another tool for getting around in your model is the Walk/Fly tool. If you are familiar with computer games, this tool is for you. To start the Walk/Fly tool, first click the Pan tool in the View tab's Navigate panel. Right-click in the drawing area, and choose Other Navigation Modes → Walk. You can also select Fly, which behaves in a slightly different way. When you select one of these options, the Position Locator palette opens (Figure 6.23).

> If your view is not Perspective, you will see a message asking you whether you want to switch to Perspective mode. Click the Change button to proceed.

Figure 6.23
The Position Locator palette

The Position Locator palette gives you a top-down view of your position in relation to your model. You can use the arrow keys to move through your model. Click and drag your mouse to change the direction in which you are looking. A set of crosshairs shows you your target direction.

If you press the F key, Walk changes to Fly mode, and vice versa. The main difference between Walk and Fly is that in Walk, both your position in the model and the point in which you are looking move with the up and down arrow keys. Walk is a bit like Pan. When you are in Fly mode, the arrow keys move you toward the center of your view, which is indicated by the crosshairs.

You can use the Position Locator palette to control your view by clicking and dragging the camera or the view target graphic. If you prefer, you can close the palette and continue to "walk" through your model. When you are finished using Walk, right-click, and choose Exit.

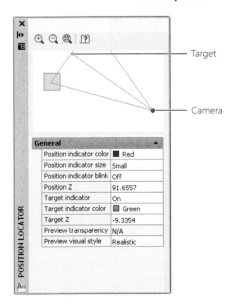

Recording a Fly-Through with ShowMotion

An animated walk-through of a building or model of an object can convey a lot of information about your design. AutoCAD offers the ShowMotion tool that will record a "fly-through" of your 3D model. ShowMotion is actually a set of tools that let you create a fly-through or play an existing fly-through.

To start the ShowMotion feature, click the ShowMotion icon in the status bar. The ShowMotion toolbar appears, as shown in Figure 6.24.

Figure 6.24

The ShowMotion tool and toolbar

Click the New Shot tool in the ShowMotion toolbar to set up a new fly-through. The New View/Shot Properties dialog box appears.

Enter a name for your shot in the View Name text box at the top of the dialog box before you set up your shot. You can then select from a set of predefined movement types from the Movement Type drop-down list.

If you prefer to create your own movement through the model, select Recorded Walk from the View Type drop-down list near the top of the dialog box. Click Start Recording, and the dialog box temporarily disappears to allow you to record your fly-through. Click your mouse button to start your fly-through, and don't let go until you are finished recording. As soon as you click, you see a blue dot, which represents a neutral position. Click and drag your mouse up to move your view forward through your model. Click and drag down below the blue dot to back up. Shift+click and drag to change your view height. To stop your motion, place the cursor on the blue dot, all the while holding down the mouse button. When you are finished, release the mouse button.

You can record a series of named shots and then play them all back to create a complex fly-through of your model.

Saving a View

Figure 6.25

The View Manager option on the 3D Navigation drop-down list

You will eventually arrive at a view that you want to save and return to later. You can use the View Manager dialog box to save the current view under a name that you specify. You can save as many views as you want for study or presentation purposes.

To save a view, click the View Manager option from the 3D Navigation drop-down list in the Home tab's View panel (Figure 6.25), or enter **V↵** at the command prompt. The View Manager dialog box appears, as shown in Figure 6.26.

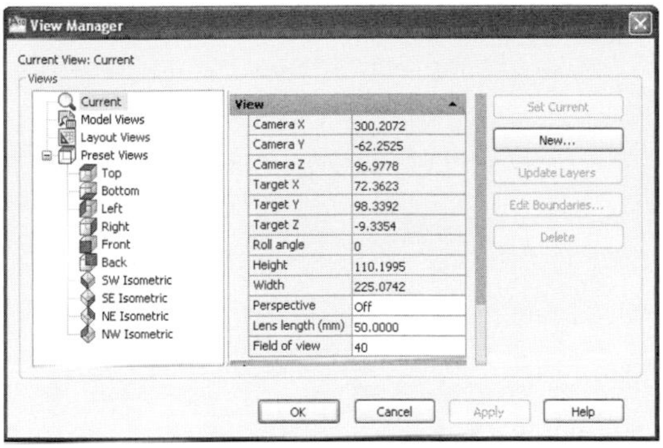

Figure 6.26

The View Manager dialog box and the New View/Shot Properties dialog box

Click the New button, and then enter a name for your view at the top of the New View/Shot Properties dialog box, select Current Display in the Boundary group of the View Properties tab, and then click OK. Click Apply in the View Manager dialog box, and then click OK.

You can then restore your saved view from the same View Manager dialog box. Your saved view's name appears near the top of the Views list box under the Model Views listing.

Creating a Camera

Another way to save views is by using cameras. Cameras provide some additional controls, such as focal length and view angle. You can place as many cameras as you like in your model and then quickly call up the view from each camera. Unlike views saved using the New View/Shot Properties dialog box, you can always make changes to a camera's view once you've created it.

To create a camera, do the following:

1. Type **Camera**↵.

2. At the `Specify camera location:` prompt, you'll see a camera attached to the cursor. Select a location for the camera. The camera appears in the drawing, as shown in Figure 6.27.

3. At the `Specify target location:` prompt, you'll see a rubber-banding line from the camera to the cursor, indicating the direction of the view from the camera. Click a location for the target location.

4. At the `Enter an option [?/Name/LOcation/Height/Target/LEns/Clipping/View/ eXit]<eXit>:` prompt, choose Exit from the Dynamic Input menu, or enter **x**↵.

Figure 6.27

**Placing a camera in
your drawing**

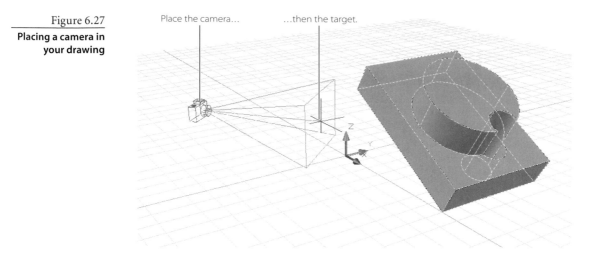

Place the camera...   ...then the target.

Figure 6.28

**The Camera Preview
dialog box**

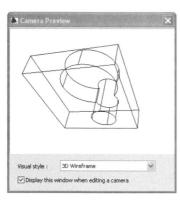

Once you've placed a camera, you can begin to adjust its location by using grips. To do this, click the camera to display its grips. A Camera Preview dialog box also opens to show you roughly what the view from the camera looks like (see Figure 6.28).

You can then click a grip and move it to change the location. Click again to fix the location of the grip. You can hover over the camera or camera target's grip before clicking it to display the gizmo. This will aid you in adjusting the vertical or Z location for the camera.

1. Place the cursor on the camera or target grip, but don't click. After a moment, you will see the gizmo (see Figure 6.29).

2. Move the cursor to the axis within which you want to move the grip. A line appears whose color corresponds to the axis on which your cursor is resting.

3. When you see that line, you can click to move the grip along that line (shown earlier in Figure 6.26). As you move the grip, you can use the camera preview window to help guide your grip location.

4. When you're satisfied with your view, click again to fix the grip's location.

Once you've created a camera, you can open that camera's view in the AutoCAD window through the View Manager dialog box. You can open this dialog box by entering **V**↵ at the command prompt. AutoCAD gives new cameras a default name of Camera1, Camera2, and so on; so to see the view from the first camera you create, click the camera name in the Views list (Figure 6.30).

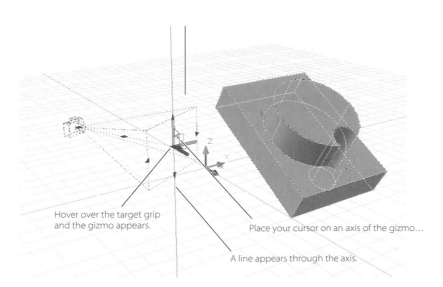

Hover over the target grip and the gizmo appears.

Place your cursor on an axis of the gizmo…

A line appears through the axis.

Changing a Camera's Properties

Just as with any AutoCAD object, cameras have properties. When you click a camera, then right-click, and finally select Properties, the Properties palette for the camera appears. Two properties that you'll want to become familiar with are the camera name and lens length. You might want to change the camera name to something more meaningful to your project. The lens length lets you set the field of view in terms of a camera's focal length (see Figure 6.31).

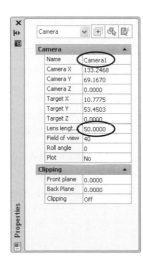

Changing from Perspective to Parallel Projection

When you create a new drawing by using the acad3D.dwt template, you are automatically given a perspective view of the file. If you need a more schematic parallel

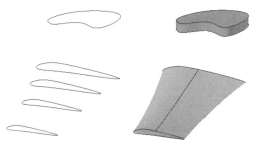

projection style of view, select the Parallel options in the ViewCube context menu. Right-click the ViewCube to view the menu.

You can return to a perspective view by clicking the Perspective option in the same menu, as shown in Figure 6.32.

> You can also click the Pan tool in the status bar, right-click, and select Parallel or Perspective from the context menu.

Creating 3D Forms from 2D Shapes

The 3D solid primitives are great for creating some basic shapes, but in many situations, you will want to create a 3D form from a more complex shape. Fortunately, you can extrude 2D objects into a variety of shapes using additional tools found in the Modeling

panel. For example, you can draw a shape such as a puzzle piece and then extrude it into a third dimension, as shown in the top of Figure 6.33. Or you can use several strategically placed 2D objects that can form a flowing surface such as the wing of an airplane, as shown in the bottom of Figure 6.33.

Extruding a Polyline

You can insert a variety of solid shapes into your drawing. For example, you can create a sphere by choosing Sphere from the Modeling panel. You can then select a center point and a radius, just as you would for a circle, but you end up with a solid sphere.

Another way to create solids is to extrude them from closed polylines. This is a more flexible way to create shapes because you can create a polyline of any shape and extrude it to a fairly complex form.

In the following exercise, you'll start with a pentagon, which is actually a simple closed polyline. From that pentagon, you'll use a variety of tools to form a box.

1. Open a new file in AutoCAD using the acad3D.dwt template.

2. Select Polygon on the Home tab's Draw panel.

3. At the Enter number of sides <4>: prompt, enter **5**↵.

4. At the Specify center of polygon or [Edge]: prompt, enter **0,0**↵.

5. At the `Enter an option [Inscribed in circle/Circumscribed about circle] <I>:` prompt, press ↵.

6. At the `Specify radius of circle:` prompt, enter **17**↵. You now have a 2D polygon similar to the one shown on the left side of Figure 6.34.

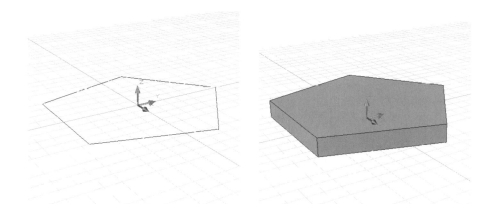

Figure 6.34

Drawing a 3D polygon

> If you extrude an object that is not closed, such as a line or an arc, the Extrude tool will create 3D surfaces.

Now you're ready to change this polygon into a 3D object:

1. Click the Extrude tool in the Home tab's Modeling panel, or enter **Extrude**↵ at the command prompt.

2. At the `Select objects:` prompt, select the polygon, and then press ↵.

3. At the `Specify height of extrusion or [Direction/Path/Taper angle]:` prompt, you will see that the polygon is now a 3D solid whose height follows the cursor. Enter **3**↵ to make the height of the extrusion 3 units. The polygon expands to become a 3D pentagon, as shown on the right side of Figure 6.34.

Figure 6.35

Examples of extruded closed polylines

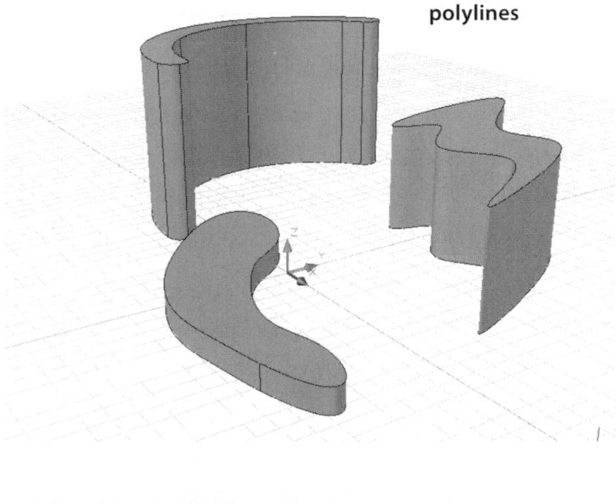

In this exercise, you extruded a simple polygon, but you can extrude any shape you can dream up using open or closed polylines. For example, you can extrude the complex curved shapes, as shown in Figure 6.35.

Extruded shapes created from open polylines instead of closed polylines create 3D surfaces that have no thickness. You can give such an object thickness by using the Thicken tool on the Home tab's Solid Editing panel (see Figure 6.36).

Figure 6.36

The Thicken tool in the Solid Editing panel

Figure 6.36

The Thicken tool in the Solid Editing panel

Click the Thicken tool, and then select the object or 3D surfaces you want to thicken. At the Specify thickness <0.0000>: prompt, enter the desired thickness. Figure 6.37 shows two examples of thickened surfaces.

Figure 6.37

Sample of surfaces before and after using the Thicken Surface tool

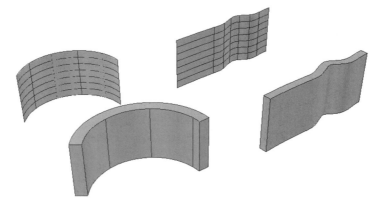

Checking Interference and Finding the Intersection of 3D Shapes

In an earlier exercise, you saw how you can combine solids in various ways to form more complex shapes. Another useful tool for editing solids is the Interfere tool. Interfere lets you find the intersection of two solids. This can be helpful if you need to reproduce a section of a solid or if you want to check to see whether two or more 3D objects come into contact.

Interfere works by creating a third 3D solid that is the shape of the intersection of two other solids. Figure 6.38 shows how you can use an extruded cornice and a simple box to make a copy of a small piece of the cornice.

Figure 6.38

Making a copy of a section of a 3D solid using Interfere: This command makes an intersection of the two, which can be moved to other parts of the drawing.

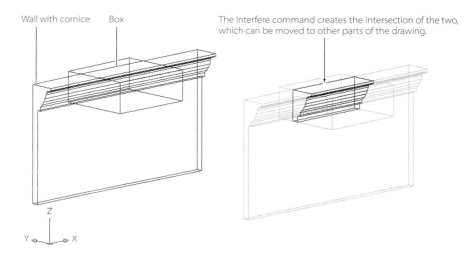

Wall with cornice   Box

The Interfere command creates the intersection of the two, which can be moved to other parts of the drawing.

CONVERTING 3D OBJECTS FROM EARLIER VERSIONS TO 3D SURFACES

Thicken is not the same as the Thickness property of an object. If you have experience with AutoCAD 3D, you know you can change the Thickness property of an object to make it into a 3D object. But an object with a thickness cannot be edited by using the tools described in this chapter. You can convert a simple 2D object with thickness to a full 3D surface object by using the Convert to Surface tool in the expanded Solid Editing panel.

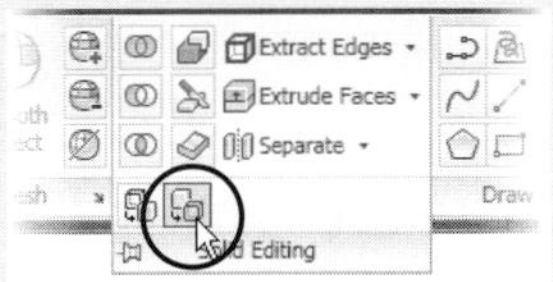

Click the Convert to Surface tool, select the objects you want to convert, and then press ↵. The objects will become true 3D surfaces. Once you've done this, you can use the Thicken Surface tool. In addition, you can convert a closed polyline with a thickness greater than zero to a solid using the Convert to Solid tool, which is also found in the expanded Solid Editing panel.

To work with the Interfere command, follow these steps:

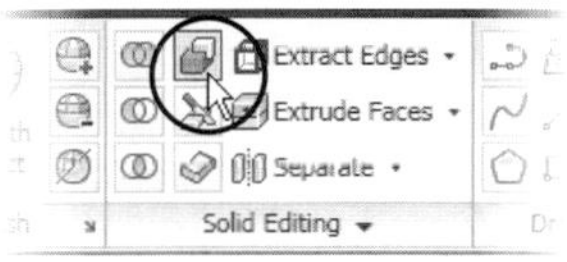

1. Click the Interfere tool in the Home tab's Solid Editing panel, or enter **Interfere**↵ at the command prompt.

2. At the Select first set of objects or [Nested selection/Settings]: prompt, select the cornice and press ↵.

3. At the Select second set of objects or [Nested selection/checK first set] <checK>: prompt, select the box and press ↵. The Interference Checking dialog box appears (see Figure 6.39).

4. In addition, the selected objects will temporarily become transparent, and only the intersection of the selected objects will be visible.

5. Uncheck the Delete Interference Object Created on Close option, and then click Close.

6. Delete the box to reveal the interference object.

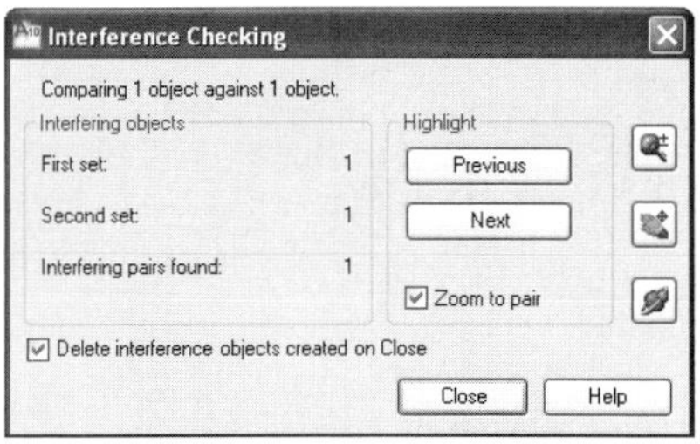

Figure 6.39

The Interference Checking dialog box

As you can tell from the name of the Interfere tool, it is designed to check for interference between 3D solids and surfaces. In this example, you're using it to create a new 3D shape from two existing ones. If you want to check only for interference, you can visually inspect the intersection of the solids in step 3. The Interference Checking dialog box offers the Zoom, Pan, and 3D Orbit tools to let you inspect the interference. The Previous and Next buttons move to the next interference shape when multiple intersections exist. The Zoom to Pair option causes the view to automatically zoom in on the interference shape.

If you just want to create the intersection of two solids and discard the original solids, you can use the Intersect command. Click the Intersect tool in the Home tab's Solid Editing panel, or type **Intersect.↵**, and then select the two or more objects whose intersection you want.

Filleting a Corner

One useful editing command for 3D solids is more commonly used in 2D drawings. If you want to round the corner of a 3D solid, you can do so using the Fillet command. But Fillet behaves in a slightly different way when applied to 3D solids.

Issue the Fillet command by selecting it from the expanded Modify panel, and then select the solid edge you want to fillet (see Figure 6.40). The selected edge is highlighted, and you are prompted for a fillet radius. Once you've entered a radius, you can select other contiguous edges to fillet. Press ↵, and the edges are filleted, as shown in Figure 6.40.

You can also use the Chamfer command to chamfer the corners of 3D solids. Chamfer works like the Fillet command.

Figure 6.40

Selecting the edges to fillet and the result

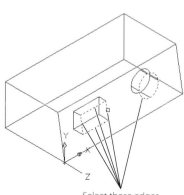

Select these edges.

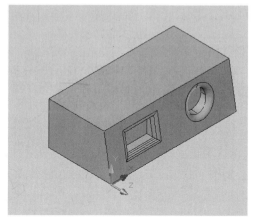

Extruding Along a Path

You've seen how you can extrude a polyline into the third dimension. This method lets you create some basic 3D shapes, but what if you want to create something a bit more complex?

A tool called Sweep allows you to extrude a 2D object along a complex path. You can define the path by using a polyline or a spline.

Figure 6.41 shows how to create the exterior wall of a building using a polyline outline of the wall's profile and a polyline path of the wall's footprint on the ground.

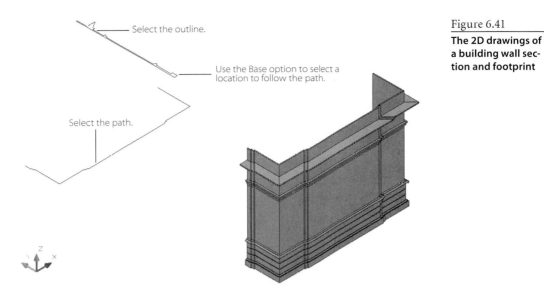

Figure 6.41

The 2D drawings of a building wall section and footprint

To see how the Path option works, draw the outline of the shape you want to extrude, and then draw the path you will use to extrude the outline. Figure 6.41 shows an example of an outline and a path in an isometric view.

The sample outline in Figure 6.41 is a profile or wall section of a building. The path is the building footprint. The footprint has a gap to provide a place to locate the outline, as you will see later.

Once you have both the outline and path drawn, do the following:

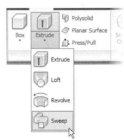

Figure 6.42

The Sweep tool in the Extrude flyout

1. Click the Sweep tool from the Extrude flyout in the Modeling panel (Figure 6.42), or enter **Sweep.⏎** in the command line.

2. At the `Select objects to sweep:` prompt, select the outline.

3. At the `Select sweep path or [Alignment/Base point/Scale/ Twist]:` prompt, enter **b⏎**, and then select the exact location on the outline that is to follow the path. In the wall example, the outer-bottom corner will form the footprint of the building.

4. Select the path for the outline. The outline is extruded along the path. The right side of Figure 6.41 shows the outline and path after using the Sweep tool.

Although you used a building as an example in Figure 6.41, you can use this method to create any number of extruded shapes along a path. The shape can be as simple as a circle extruded along a curve to form a tube or a wall section along a footprint, as in this example. The path doesn't have to be restricted to a plane. You can create a path that goes in any direction in 3D space. AutoCAD also offers the Helix tool, which you can use to create a helix path to draw screw threads or rounded parking garage ramps.

Creating a Helix

Perhaps one of the most frequently asked for 3D tools is one that will allow you to draw a screw thread. AutoCAD offers the Helix tool that you can use to create a spiral path. You can then create a cross section of a screw thread and use the spiral path to create a 3D screw thread. To create a spiral path, do the following:

1. Make sure you are in the 3D Modeling workspace, and then click the Helix tool in the Home tab's expanded Draw panel. You'll see the following prompt:

   ```
   Number of turns = 3.0000     Twist=CCW
   Specify center point of base:
   ```

2. In the drawing area, click a location for the center of the helix. You can also enter a coordinate.

3. At the `Specify base radius or [Diameter] <1.0000>:` prompt, enter a radius for your helix.

4. At the `Specify top radius or [Diameter] <1.0000 >:` prompt, you can enter a different radius value if you want the helix to gradually change its radius from bottom to top.

5. At the `Specify helix height or [Axis endpoint/Turns/turn Height/tWist] <1.0000>:` prompt, you can select the height of the helix. Figure 6.43 shows a helix with the base and top radius set to 9 and the height set to 6.

Once you've created the helix, you can use it with the Sweep tool to create your spiral form. If you decide that you want to alter the dimensions of an existing helix, you can do so by using the Properties palette. Select the helix, then right-click and select Properties, or just double-click the helix. You can edit the radii, height, and number of turns in the helix. Remember that you can also specify the number of turns, the turn height, and the direction that the helix turns at the prompt in step 5. For example, if you want to set the direction of the turns, enter **W** for the Twist option at the prompt in step 2, and then enter **CW** for clockwise or **CCW** for counterclockwise.

Figure 6.43

A helix path and a circle applied to the helix with the Sweep tool

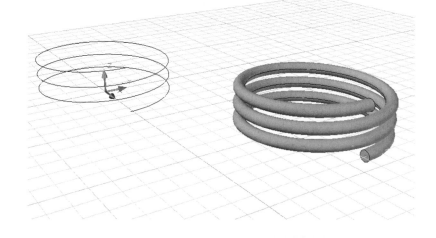

You can find the total length of a helix or the turn slope by looking at the Properties palette for the helix.

Lofting Through Different Shapes

In Figure 6.33 earlier in this chapter, you can see a wing-shaped object that was constructed from a set of 2D cross sections. The tool used to actually create the curved surface is the Loft tool. Loft allows you to create sculpted, free-form shapes such as a wing, a faucet handle, or any number of other sculpted shapes. If you can identify and draw a set of 2D cross sections for a 3D object, Loft will create the 3D shape for you. The object doesn't have to be a solid either. You can loft open polylines, arcs, and lines to form surfaces such as a 3D terrain model from contour lines.

The following example uses a pair of arcs as an example of how the Loft tool works. It also shows you can employ a box to help you quickly lay out an object.

1. Use the Box tool from the Primitives flyout on the Modeling panel to create a box similar to the one shown in Figure 6.44.

    Box

2. Choose Arc from the expanded Draw panel, and then using the Dynamic UCS feature described earlier in this chapter, draw an arc on the side of the box similar to the one in Figure 6.44. Remember that the cursor will change to indicate which surface you are aligned with, and a dashed line will also appear around the surface.

3. Draw another arc, as shown in Figure 6.44.

4. Choose Polyline from the Draw panel, and then draw the three-segment polyline shown in Figure 6.44. Press ↵ when you have drawn the three line segments to exit the Polyline tool.

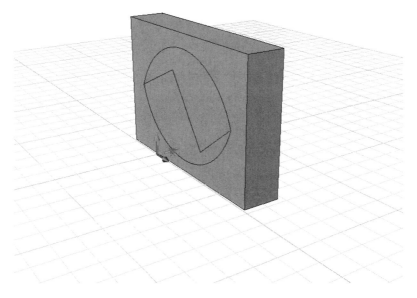

Figure 6.44

Drawing a box with arcs and a polyline on its side

Here you'll see how you can use a box to help you draw an item in 3D space. The box in conjunction with Dynamic UCS lets you orient the arcs in a vertical plane that is perpendicular to the regular WCS.

Now move the arcs apart so you can practice using the Loft tool:

1. Click the box, and press the Delete key to erase it. You used it as an aid to draw the 2D objects on a plane perpendicular to the XY plane only (see Figure 6.45).

2. Click the top arc so that it is the only object selected, and then place the cursor on its center grip. The gizmo appears on the center grip.

3. Place the cursor on the green y-axis of the gizmo. You'll see a green line appear along the axis you are pointing to on the gizmo.

4. With the green line showing, click the gizmo. Now, as you move the cursor, the arc follows and is constrained on the green axis.

5. Place the cursor so that the arc is farther to the right, as shown in Figure 6.46, and then click. You don't have to be exact, since this is just to show generally how drawing in 3D works.

6. Press the Esc key to clear the selection of the arc.

7. Repeat steps 2 through 5, but this time, select the other arc, and move it to the location shown in Figure 6.46.

In this example, you'll see that you can constrain the movement of an object along an axis just by clicking the axis of the gizmo.

Figure 6.45

The 2D objects without the box

Figure 6.46

Moving the arcs

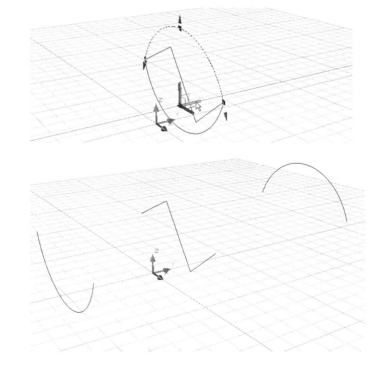

With objects such as the polyline, which has no single grip that controls the location of the entire object, you must use the Move tool to move it. You cannot use the gizmo to move it.

Now that you have the arcs and polyline in place, you can create a surface that flows through them:

Figure 6.47
The Loft tool in the Extrude flyout

1. Click the Loft tool in the Extrude flyout of the Modeling panel (Figure 6.47).

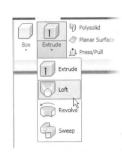

2. At the `Select cross-sections in lofting order:` prompt, select the arcs and polyline in order from left to right. Press ↵ when you've selected all three objects.

3. At the `Enter an option [Guides/Path/Cross-sections only] <Cross-sections only>:` prompt, press ↵, or if you have Dynamic Input turned on, select Cross Section Only from the Dynamic Input display. The Loft Settings dialog box opens (Figure 6.48).

Figure 6.48
The Loft Settings dialog box

4. Make sure Smooth Fit is selected, and click OK. A surface appears that smoothly transitions through the three objects, as shown in Figure 6.49.

Once you've created a lofted 3D object, you can make changes to its shape by adjusting its grips:

1. Click the lofted shape to expose its grips. Although it might not be obvious at first, the grips you see are those of the three objects you used to create the loft.

Figure 6.49
The surface created with the Loft tool

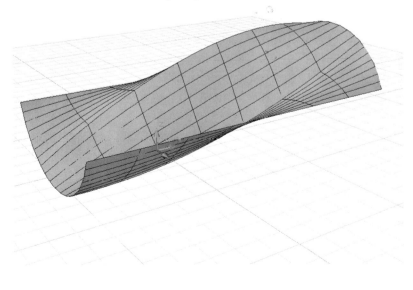

2. Place the cursor on the top grip of the middle polyline, but don't click quite yet (see the left image in Figure 6.50). The gizmo moves to the grip to which you point.

3. Point to the blue Z coordinate on the gizmo. A blue line appears, telling you that you can now click and your motion will be constrained to that axis.

4. Click the Z coordinate of the gizmo, and then move the cursor upward. The loft shape is pulled upward. Click again to fix the grip in a new, higher location. (See the right image in Figure 6.50.)

In this example, you used open objects, but you can use closed polylines, circles, and closed splines as well.

Figure 6.50

Moving a grip with the aid of the gizmo

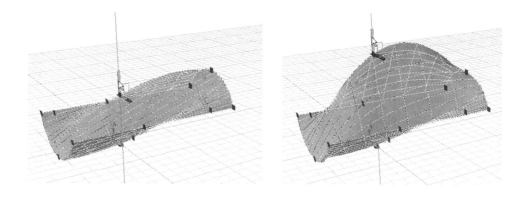

Revolving a Polyline

You've seen how the Extrude and Sweep commands let you create solids in two ways: you can extrude in a straight line or along a path. The Revolve command lets you create a 3D

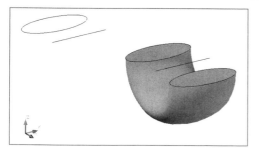

solid by rotating a shape. It extrudes a circle, an ellipse, a closed polyline, or a region along a circular path up to 360°. You can also rotate lines, arcs, or any other open shape to get 3D surfaces. You draw the profile of the shape you want, define an axis of rotation around which the shape will be "rotated," and then use Revolve to turn the shape into a rounded 3D object.

Figure 6.51 shows the progression from 2D objects to revolved 3D solids.

Figure 6.51

An ellipse that has been revolved into a solid (right): Select the shape to revolve (left), and then indicate the axis.

First I drew an ellipse and a line. The ellipse is the shape that is to be revolved, and the line is the axis of revolution.

To revolve the ellipse, follow these steps:

1. Choose the Revolve tool from the Extrude flyout in the Modeling panel (Figure 6.52).

2. At the Select objects to revolve: prompt, select the ellipse, and press ↵.

3. At the `Specify axis start point or define axis by [Object/X/Y/Z] <Object>:` prompt, indicate the axis of revolution by either entering **X**, **Y**, or **Z** or by selecting a line that represents the axis around which the ellipse is to be revolved.

4. At the `Specify angle of revolution or [STart angle] <360>:` prompt, you can press ↵ to revolve the ellipse a full 360°, or you can enter a specific value.

Figure 6.52

The Revolve tool in the Extrude flyout

For the revolved shape in Figure 6.51, I used an angle of 180°. Figure 6.51 shows an ellipse as an example, but you can use any shape you want, such as the cross section of a car wheel or a pulley. Just make sure that when you draw your shape, the outline does not cross over itself, like an 8. AutoCAD will return an error message if you attempt to revolve such a shape.

Creating Smooth 3D Forms with the Mesh Modeling

Mesh modeling enables you to create smooth, curved volumes by manipulating faces and edges that make up an object's surface.

With mesh modeling, you can quickly create curved, free-form shapes that are difficult or even impossible to create by other means. AutoCAD also offers the ability to convert a mesh model into a 3D solid so that you can perform Boolean operations.

Meshes are similar to solids in that they start from a primitive. You may recall that 3D solid primitives are predetermined shapes from which you can form more complex shapes. The mesh primitives are very similar to the 3D solid primitives you learned about earlier. You can see the different mesh primitives that are available by clicking the Mesh flyout in the Primitives panel (Figure 6.53).

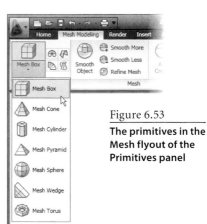

Figure 6.53

The primitives in the Mesh flyout of the Primitives panel

You can place a primitive in your drawing by following these steps:

1. In the Mesh Modeling tab's Primitives panel, click the Mesh tool for the primitive you want. For example, to start your model with a box shape, click the Box mesh, or type **Mesh**↵ **B**↵.

2. At the `Specify first corner or [Center]:` prompt, click a point to start the mesh.

3. At the `Specify other corner or [Cube/Length]:` prompt, click another point or enter a coordinate.

4. At the `Specify height or [2Point]:` prompt, enter the height for your mesh. You now have a basic shape for your mesh.

At this point, you can start to manipulate the faces and edges of the mesh. You can also apply smoothing right away to round off the edges. To smooth a mesh, do the following:

1. Click the Smooth More tool in the Mesh Modeling tab's Mesh panel.

2. Select the mesh you want to smooth and press ↵.

You can select more than one mesh if you like. You can also apply more smoothness to a mesh by repeating these steps. In addition, you can reduce the smoothness by using the Smooth Less tool in the Mesh panel.

Understanding the Parts of a Mesh

Each surface of a mesh is divided into panels. This division of the surface is referred to as a *tessellation* and the individual divisions or tiles of the surface are called *faces* in AutoCAD. You can edit these faces to change the shape and contour of your mesh. You can control the number of faces of a mesh primitive by setting the Tessellation Divisions in the Mesh Primitive Options dialog box (Figure 6.54).

Figure 6.54

The Mesh Primitive Options dialog box

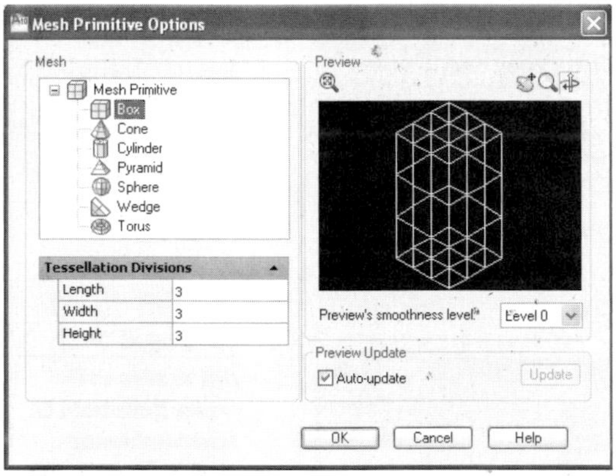

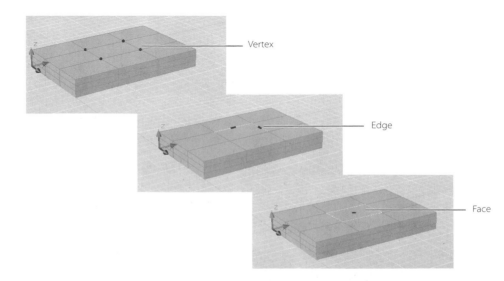

You can open this dialog box by clicking the Mesh Primitive Options tool in the Mesh Modeling tab's Primitives panel title bar.

Figure 6.55 shows the names of the different parts of a mesh: the vertex, the edge, and the face. These three parts are

called subobjects of the mesh, and you can move their position in the mesh to modify a mesh's shape.

Figure 6.55

The subobjects of a mesh

To help you select different subobjects on a mesh, the Subobject panel offers the Filter flyout. If you want to select faces, select Faces from the Filter flyout (Figure 6.56), and then click the face you want to edit.

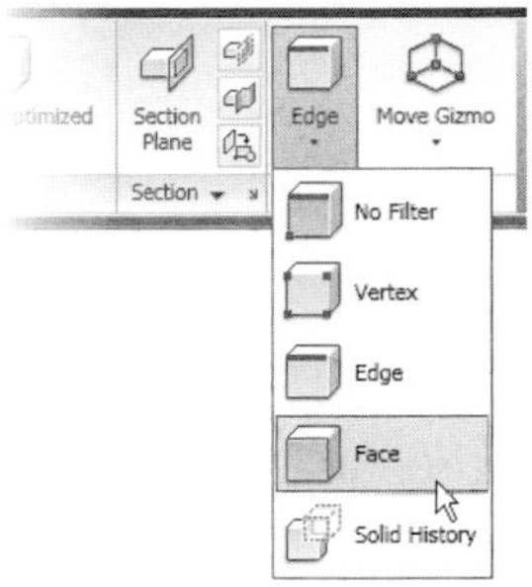

You can select multiple faces by holding down the Ctrl key while clicking on faces. To select edges, use the Edge tool from the Filter flyout.

Once you've selected a subobject, a gizmo appears. You can manipulate the subobject using the gizmo (Figure 6.57).

After you've adjusted the faces and edges, you can apply smoothing to the surface. You can also smooth the mesh before you edit the faces and edges.

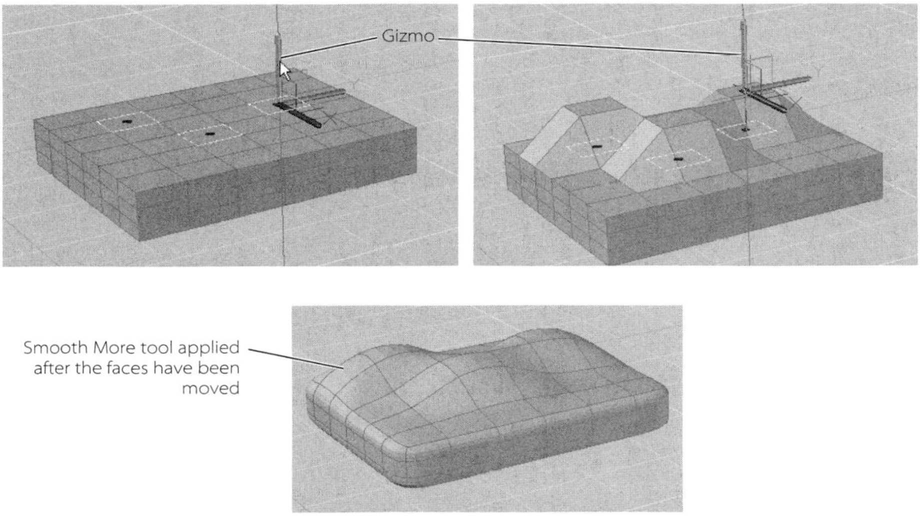

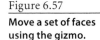

Figure 6.56

Use a filter to select a face.

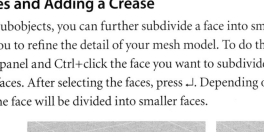

Gizmo

Smooth More tool applied after the faces have been moved

Figure 6.57

Move a set of faces using the gizmo.

Dividing Faces and Adding a Crease

Besides moving subobjects, you can further subdivide a face into smaller faces (Figure 6.58). This will allow you to refine the detail of your mesh model. To do this, click the Refine Mesh tool in the Mesh panel and Ctrl+click the face you want to subdivide. You can select a single face or multiple faces. After selecting the faces, press ↵. Depending on the level of smoothing you've applied, the face will be divided into smaller faces.

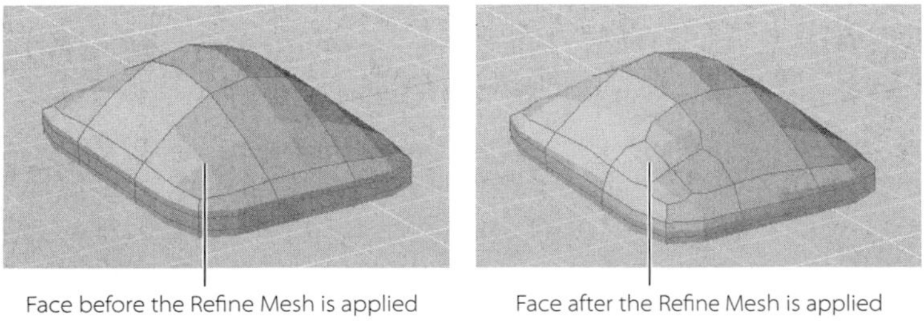

Figure 6.58

Subdividing a face using the Refine Mesh tool

Face before the Refine Mesh is applied   Face after the Refine Mesh is applied

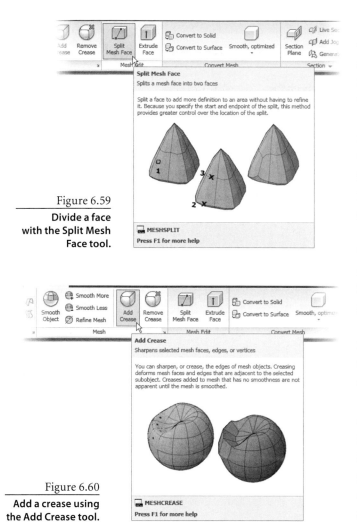

Figure 6.59

Divide a face with the Split Mesh Face tool.

Figure 6.60

Add a crease using the Add Crease tool.

If no smoothing is applied, faces will be divided into four smaller faces. If one level of smoothing is applied, the face will be divided into 16 faces. With each increase in smoothing, the number of faces increases by a factor of 4.

If you want to divide a face into only two faces, you can use the Split Mesh Face tool in the Mesh Edit panel (Figure 6.59). Click the Split Mesh Face tool, and then click the face you want to "split." Indicate the location of the split by clicking two opposing edges of the face.

In some cases, you may want to remove the smoothing of the mesh surface to create a crease. The Add Crease tool enables you to flatten a face or remove the smoothing across a face's edge (Figure 6.60).

For faces, click the Add Crease tool in the Mesh panel, and then click the faces that you want to flatten. You can click multiple faces if you like. Press ↵ twice to finish.

To add a crease along an edge and thereby create a sharp corner, select Edge Filter from the Filter flyout on the Mesh Modeling tab's Subobject panel. Click the Add Crease tool in the Mesh Edit panel and click the edge you want to crease. You can select several edge sub-objects if you like. Press ↵ twice to finish.

Specifying Exact Distances in 3D Space

When you draw in 2D, the z-axis is fairly unimportant. By default, objects you create reside at the 0 (zero) coordinate of the z-axis. In other words, everything you draw is on the plane defined by the x- and y-axes. But just as you can move and copy objects anywhere in the XY coordinate plane, you can also move and copy them along the z-axis.

In the same way that you can specify exact distances in 2D drawings, you can specify locations and distances in 3D space using the @X,Y,Z notation. If you want to move something only within the XY plane, you can omit the Z coordinate in the specification, and AutoCAD assumes you want to maintain the object's current Z coordinate. To specify relative distances in 3D, you can specify the Z coordinate as needed, as shown here:

```
@2,1,1
```

If you enter this at the Specify second point or [Exit/Undo] <Exit>: prompt in the Move or Copy command, your object not only moves 2 units to the right and 1 unit up, but it also moves 1 unit vertically, in the positive direction of the z-axis (see Figure 6.61).

> If you want to move an object only in the z-axis, enter **0** for both the x- and y-axes, as in **@0,0,2↵**. This moves your selected object 2 units in the positive direction of the z-axis.

> You might find it easiest to remember the @X,Y,Z format for specifying distances in 3D, but in typical AutoCAD fashion, you can use two other formats for spatial distances. In the limited space of this book, however, I can't show all the methods for specifying distance in 3D. For future reference, the other methods are the cylindrical format and the spherical format. Both are extensions of the standard AutoCAD polar coordinate format you use in 2D drawing. You can find out more about these formats in *Mastering AutoCAD 2010 and AutoCAD LT 2010* (Sybex, 2009).

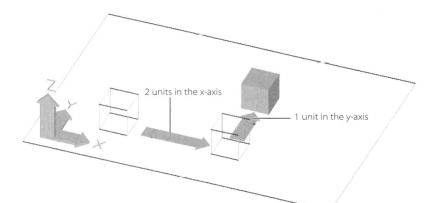

Figure 6.61

The image on the top shows an object moved within the XY plane within the WCS. The image on the bottom shows the same move with an additional Z component.

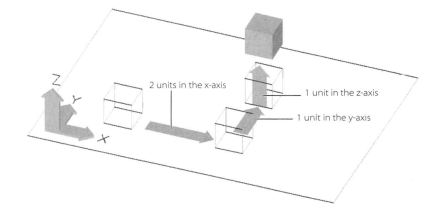

Controlling the Appearance of Your Model

Three-dimensional models are extremely useful in communicating your ideas to others, but sometimes you might find that the default appearance of your model is not exactly what you want. If you're only in a schematic design stage, you might want your model to look more like a sketch instead of a finished product. Conversely, if you're trying to sell someone on a concept, you might want a realistic look that includes materials and even special lighting. AutoCAD offers a variety of tools to help you get every type of view from a simple wireframe to a fully rendered image complete with chrome and wood. In the following sections, you'll get a preview of what is available to control the appearance of your model. I will cover these features only in general terms, but you'll gain an understanding of what is available, and if you're adventurous, you can experiment with the tools presented.

Adding Materials

Having a 3D model of your design can be tremendously useful, but by adding materials, you communicate so much more to the person viewing your model. If you have a model that includes chrome and wood, for example, you can include those materials in your model to see firsthand how it will look, instead of having to imagine those materials.

AutoCAD has had the ability to assign materials to 3D models for some time, but AutoCAD 2010 makes it much easier to do. In this exercise, you'll try your hand at adding material to a box, and then you'll learn about some of the available options:

1. Open a new file by choosing New from the Quick Access toolbar, and then in the Select Template dialog box, select the acad3D.dwt template.

2. Use the Box tool in the Modeling panel to draw a simple box like the one shown here.

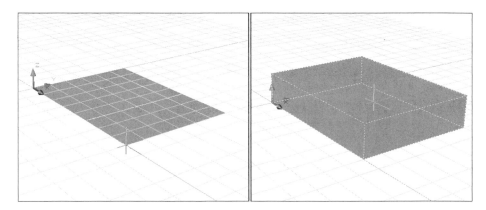

3. Click the Render tab of the Ribbon, and then click the Materials tool in the Materials panel (see the left image in Figure 6.62). The Materials palette appears, as shown on the right side of Figure 6.62.

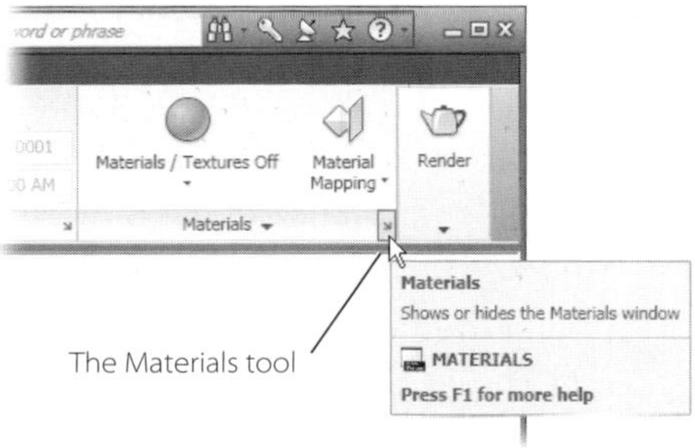

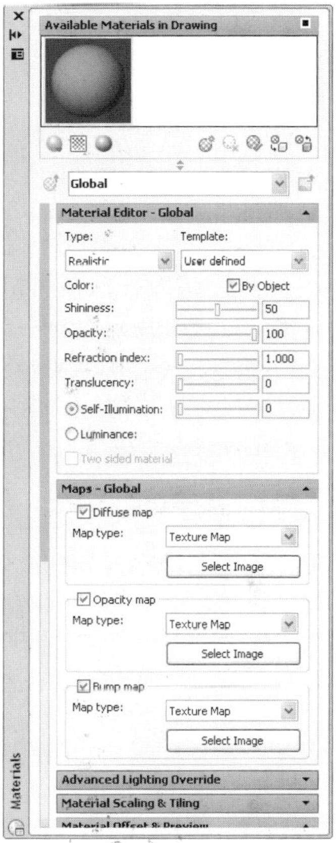

Figure 6.62

The Materials tool in the Materials panel (left) and the Materials palette (right)

The Materials tool

The Materials palette gives you full control over the materials that you assign to your object. You'll see a sample view of the current default material in the upper-left corner of the palette. You can add materials to this area or modify the current material. New objects are automatically assigned the default material.

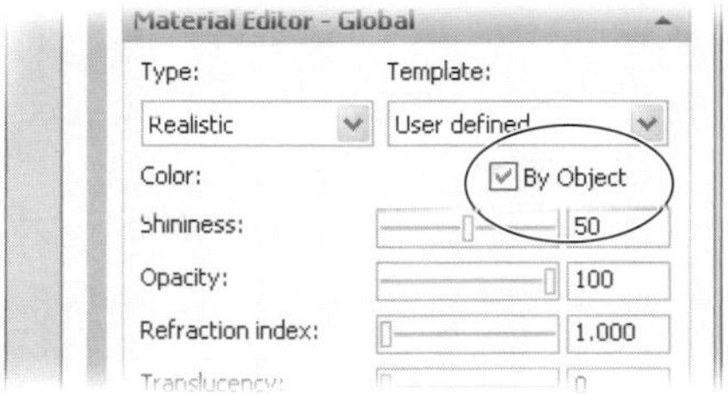

Right now, the default material is rather basic. If you look carefully, you will see that the By Object option is turned on in the Material Editor panel of the Materials palette.

This means that the material uses the object's color, which is currently black or gray. Next, you will turn off this setting and make some modifications to the material's color:

1. Click the By Object option to turn it off. A color swatch appears to the left of the option.

2. Click the color swatch to open the Select Color dialog box (see Figure 6.63).

3. Click the green area in the Select Color dialog box, move the Luminance slider up to about the middle of the setting (as shown in Figure 6.63), and then click OK. The box changes to the color you set.

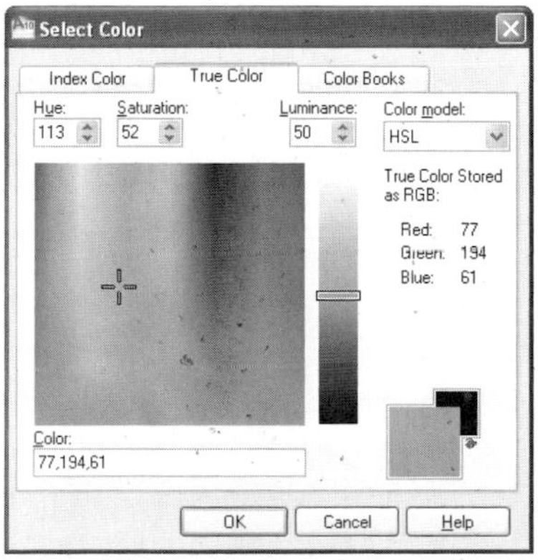

Figure 6.63

The Select Color dialog box with a new color setting for the default material

In this exercise, you altered the default material's color and got immediate feedback from the box in the drawing area. The box changed to the selected color, showing you that the material is assigned to the box.

Color isn't the only thing you can add. Next, try turning your box into a brick box:

1. Click the Select Image button in the Diffuse Map group of the Materials palette.

2. A file dialog box appears showing you a list of bitmap files. If the bitmap files do not appear, browse to the Textures folder in the C:\Documents and Settings\All Users\Application Data\ Autodesk\AutoCAD 2010\R18.0\enu\ folder.

3. Scroll down to the middle of the list, locate the file named Masonry.Unit Masonry.Brick.Modular .Common.jpg, and then click Open. Your box changes in appearance, though it doesn't look quite right.

You've just added a brick bitmap to the default material. Notice that the brick takes over the material color. But the brick pattern might be larger than it should be in relation to the box.

Besides assigning a material, you also have control over the way a material is *mapped* to an object. The material map is the orientation and scale of a material on an object. Right now, in the example given in the previous exercises, the brick pattern is scaled in a way that is too large. In other situations, you might find the material map to be too small. The next exercise shows you how you can control the Material Map scale:

1. Click the Material Mapping flyout arrow tool in the Materials panel (in the Render tab) to open the Mapping flyout menu.

2. Select the Box Mapping option.

3. At the Select faces or objects: prompt, click the box, and then press ↵. The box changes to display the brick pattern more clearly.

You might notice that grips have appeared on the box. These grips allow you to adjust the pattern. The brick pattern is a bit compressed on the box's side. You can make adjustments to the pattern by changing the grips:

1. At the Accept the mapping or [Move/Rotate/reseT/sWitch mapping mode]: prompt, drag the grip at the top of the box upward, as shown in Figure 6.64. As you move the grip, the pattern on the sides of the box scales upward.

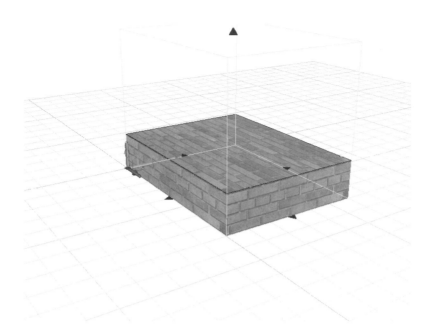

Figure 6.64

Selecting the mapping grip and adjusting it to change the pattern on the side of the box

2. Adjust the pattern to look more like Figure 6.64, and then release the grip.

3. Press ↵ to exit the Mapping tool.

This exercise shows that you can adjust the way the pattern appears on the object.

You might have noticed the options in the prompt in step 1: `Move/Rotate/reseT/sWitch` mapping mode. As you might guess, these options offer further editing capabilities. You can move or rotate the pattern using the Move or Rotate option. Rotate is useful for objects that have been rotated like the box earlier in this chapter. The Reset option resets the mapping to its default size and orientation. This is usually a size that just fits the object being mapped and is parallel to the WCS. The Switch option lets you switch to a different mapping style. You can use four mapping styles: Planar, Box, Cylindrical, and Spherical. Their names describe the way the map is applied to an object (see Figure 6.65).

Figure 6.65

Mapping styles

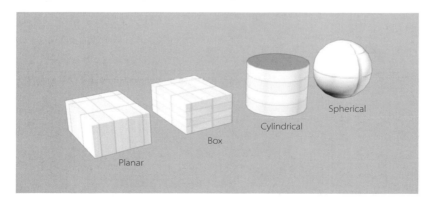

Adding Lights

Besides materials, lighting and shadows can really bring a 3D model to life. With AutoCAD lights, you can control the location and direction of illumination on your model.

AutoCAD offers several types of light, including sunlight. The sunlight option is significant because it allows you to do fairly accurate sun-shadow studies. You can enter a location and time of year, and AutoCAD will generate a light source. Other lights include the following:

- A *point light* behaves like a lightbulb shining in all directions from a single point. Illumination and shadows depend on an object's relationship to a point light.
- You can direct *spotlights* to point in a specific direction or at an object much like a theater spotlight or the headlights of a car. You can also control the spread and falloff of spotlights to produce a focused beam or a soft-edged spot.
- *Distant lights* are similar to spotlights but without controls for spread. Unlike point lights, distant lights illuminate objects and cast shadows from the same direction for all objects in your model.

Placing Lights in a Model

Each light has a slightly different method for placement and control in the model. To get a feel for how lights work, try adding a spotlight to the simple model. The following example describes how you might add a spotlight to the box from the materials exercise. You can try it on any model you have, or you can create a simple box for experimentation.

1. Make sure the Render Ribbon tab is selected, and then click the flyout arrow below the Create Light tool in the Render tab's Lights panel.

Create Light
No Shadows
Lights

Create Light
No Shadows
Point
Spot
Distant

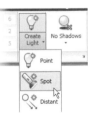

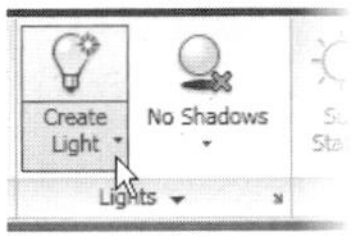

2. Select the Spot tool from the flyout. You might see a message asking you to select from two options. Click the Turn Off the Default Lighting option (see Figure 6.66).

Lighting - Viewport Lighting Mode
Sunlight and light from point lights, spotlights, and distant lights cannot be displayed in a viewport when the default lighting is turned on. What do you want to do?
Turn off the default lighting (recommended)
Keep the default lighting turned on
The default lighting will stay turned on when you add user lights. To see the effect of user lights, turn off the default lights manually.
Always perform my current choice
Cancel

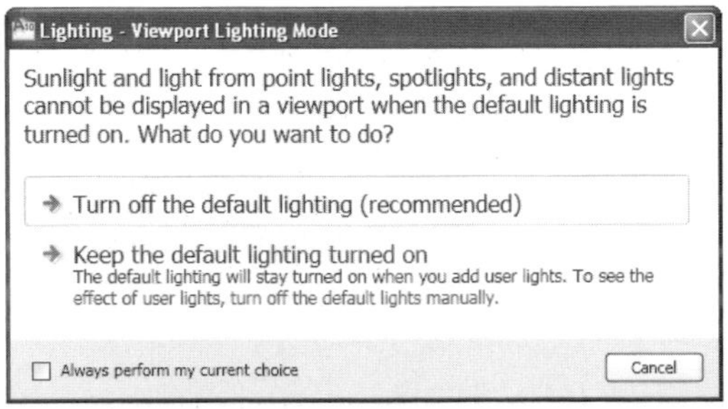

Figure 6.66
Click the Turn Off the Default Lighting option.

By default, AutoCAD places the light on the plane of the current UCS. You can then move it into a different Z coordinate by Shift+clicking and dragging the light's grip.

3. Click a location to the left of the object you want to illuminate. It doesn't matter where you place the spotlight at first, since you can easily move it to another location using grips.

4. Click the location of the spotlight's target location, and then press ↵ to exit the command.

You have the light in place, but you might need to "raise" or "lower" the light source in the z-axis to illuminate part of the top, sides, or bottom of the box. Here's how you do it:

1. Click the light to expose its grips. You'll see not only its grips but also the light cone (Figure 6.67).

2. Hover over the light source grip to display the gizmo, and then click the z-axis of the gizmo (Figure 6.68).

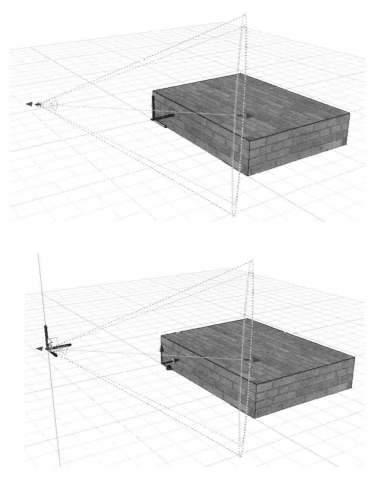

Figure 6.67

The light showing grips and the light cone

Figure 6.68

Displaying the grip tool

3. Move the cursor upward so the light is above the object you are illuminating.

4. When you are satisfied with the light's location, click. You can also adjust the light target's z-axis location using the target grip's gizmo. Although the model doesn't change in appearance, you will see the results of your light when you render your view.

5. Select the Render tab, and then in the Render panel, click the Render tool. You can also enter **Render.↵** at the command prompt.

You will see how the light affects your model in a render window, as shown in Figure 6.69.

Once you've seen the rendered view, you can adjust the light's location. You can also use the light's grips to adjust the spotlight's *hot spot* and *falloff* to spread the light over a greater area or to narrow it down to a "tighter" beam (see Figure 6.70).

The inner cone of light in the selected spotlight represents the hot spot. This is the main area that is illuminated by the spotlight. The falloff is the second outer cone displayed by the selected spotlight. The falloff cone indicates the outer edge of the spotlight that fades from full intensity to no illumination. To get a soft-edge effect on the spotlight, as shown in the upper-right view of Figure 6.70, widen the distance between the hot spot and falloff, as shown in the upper-left view. To get a sharper edge on the spotlight, shorten the distance between the hot spot and falloff, as shown in the bottom views of Figure 6.70.

Figure 6.69

A rendered view of a box

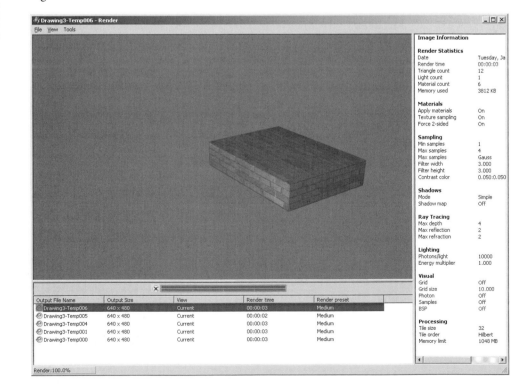

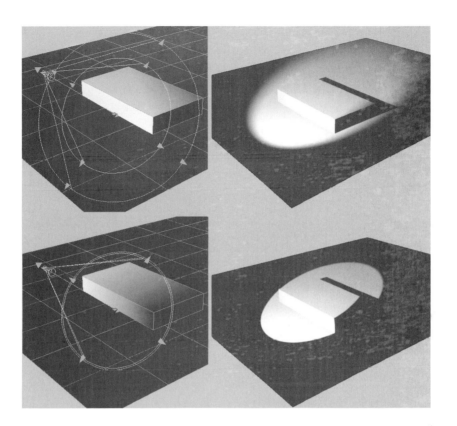

Figure 6.70

Samples of different falloff settings in the left side and the resulting rendered view on the right

If you need to adjust the light's intensity or other characteristics, you can double-click the light to open the Properties palette. There you control whether the light is on or off and its intensity, color, and even attenuation over a distance (see Figure 6.71).

Using Sunlight

The Sunlight tool operates in a different way from the other lights, so it needs some explanation. Unlike the way you use most of the other lights, you don't place the sunlight in the model. Instead, you tell AutoCAD where you are geographically and the time and the date. AutoCAD does the rest.

First, to turn on the sunlight, select the Render tab, and then click the Sun Status tool in the Sun & Location panel so that the button turns blue. This indicates that the sun is turned on.

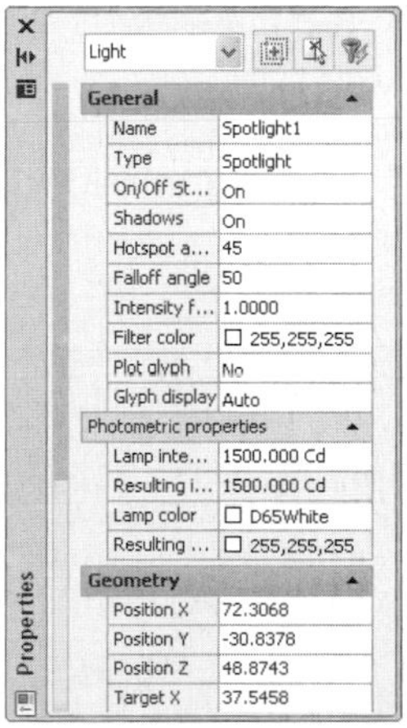

Figure 6.71

The properties of a spotlight

You may see the Lighting – Viewport Lighting Mode dialog box asking you if you want to "Turn off the default lighting (recommended)" or "Keep the default lighting turned on." Select "Turn off the default lighting (recommended)."

To set your geographic location, click the Set Location tool in the Render tab's Sun & Location panel to open the Geographic Location message box (Figure 6.72).

Figure 6.72

Opening the Geo-graphic Location message box

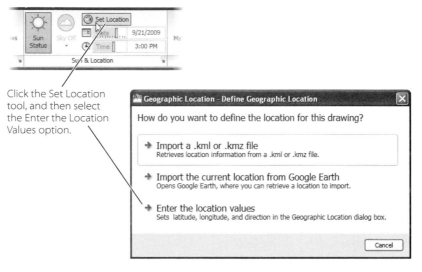

Click the Set Location tool, and then select the Enter the Location Values option.

As you can see from the message, you can set your location using three different methods: by importing a .kml or .kmz file, by importing your location from Google Earth, or by entering the location values. If you select the third option, Enter Location Values, you will see the Geographic Location dialog box (Figure 6.73).

This dialog box lets you select your location by a map by clicking the Use Map button in the upper right. You can also enter your latitude and longitude values.

Figure 6.73

The Geographic Location dialog box

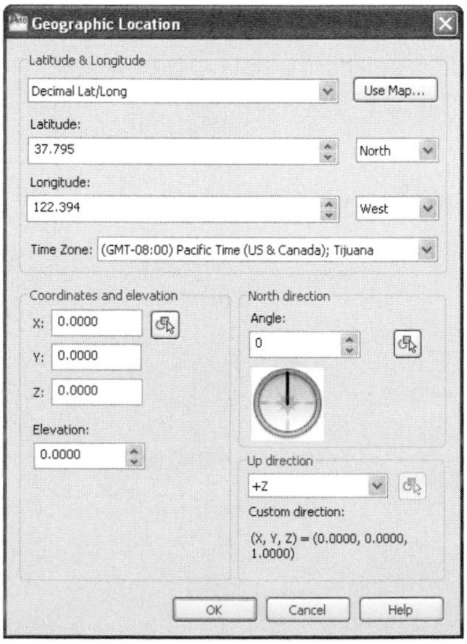

To set the time of day, go to the Render tab, and then click the Sun Properties tool, shown in Figure 6.74, to open the Sun Properties palette. There you'll find the date and time settings. You might have to use the scroll bar to view all of the date and time settings. You can also control the color and intensity of the sunlight as well as the shadow settings from the Sun Properties palette. Or if you prefer, you can set the date and time through the Date and Time sliders in the Sun & Location panel.

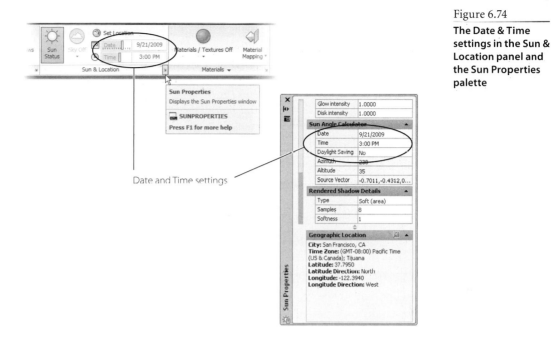

Figure 6.74

The Date & Time settings in the Sun & Location panel and the Sun Properties palette

Getting a Rendered View

In the "Adding Lights" section, you learned how to get a rendered view of your model after adding some lights. You click the Render tool in the Render panel in the Output tab. When you do this, a window appears, and a rendering of your model gradually appears.

You have numerous controls over the rendering output, but most of them are beyond the scope of this book. However, you'll need to know about a few essential items.

Saving Rendered Images

Once the rendering is completed, you can save the rendered view as a 2D image file by choosing File → Save from the Render window. You'll see a typical file dialog box that lets you select the location of the file. You can also select the file format, including TIF and JPEG, from the File of Type drop-down list.

Controlling Resolution

If you want to set the image size in terms of pixels, you can do so before you render the model. Click the Output Size drop-down list in the expanded Render panel to view the size options (Figure 6.75). The list displays several predefined sizes, or you can select Specify Output Size to set a custom size.

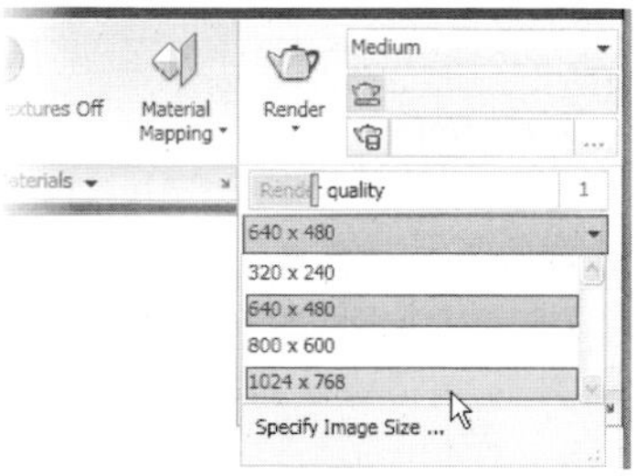

Figure 6.75

The Output Size drop-down list in the expanded Render panel

Adding a Background

If you want to control the color of the background of the rendered image, you can do so through the View command. Select View Manager from the 3D Navigation drop-down list in the Home tab's View panel, or enter **V↵**.

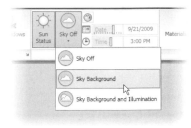

In the View Manager dialog box, click the New button to open the New View/Shot Properties dialog box. In this dialog box, enter a name for your view in the View Name input box, and then select a background option from the drop-down list in the Background group.

The drop-down list on the left side of the Background group offers five options: Default, Solid, Gradient, Image, and Sun and Sky.

The Background dialog box appears if you select Solid, Gradient, or Image (see Figure 6.76). If you select Solid, you can click the Solid Options color box in the Background dialog box to open a Select Color dialog box that allows you to select a color. The Gradient option displays a top, middle, and bottom color sample box. Just as with the Solid Options color box, you can click the sample color boxes to open the Select Color dialog box.

The Image option displays a Browse button so you can browse to an image file on your computer. The image you select appears in the sample box at the bottom.

If you are rendering a building, you also have the option to have a more natural sun and sky background as well as a more realistic lighting effect. To do this, you must first set the Lighting Units system variable to 1 or 2. Type **Lightingunits↵** at the command prompt, and enter **1↵** or **2↵** (this value is already set to 2 in drawings based on the acad3D.dwt template). You will also need to be in a perspective view and not in a 2D Wireframe visual style. You will then be able to select options from the Sky flyout in the Render tab's Sun panel.

Figure 6.76

Three modes of the Background dialog box

You will be able to select the Sun and Sky Background option from the New View/ Shot Properties dialog box to open the Adjust Sun & Sky Background dialog box (see Figure 6.77).

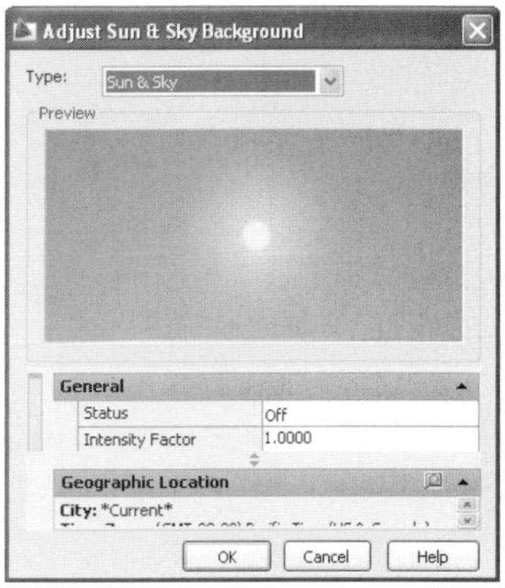

Once you've selected a background, click OK in the Background dialog box, and then click OK in the New View/Shot Properties dialog box. Finally, in the View Manager dialog box, make sure you select your new view from the list box to the left, and click Set Current to make your new view the current one. This is an important step; otherwise, your background will not appear in the drawing. Click OK to exit the View Manager dialog box.

Figure 6.77

The Adjust Sun & Sky Background dialog box

Getting a Wireframe or Shaded View

In the earlier exercises of this chapter, you started to create 3D objects using the default visual style called Realistic. The name of this style might be a little misleading, because it doesn't actually give you a truly realistic view of your model. The Realistic visual style allows you to see curved surfaces more easily, but its main use is to show you material assignments of your object more easily. Sometimes it helps to use a different visual style, depending on your task. For example, a 3D wireframe view of your 3D model can help you visualize and select things that are behind a solid. AutoCAD includes several shaded view options that can bring out different features of your model.

1. Make sure the Render tab is selected, and then click the Visual Styles drop-down list in the Visual Styles panel. Some graphic images appear that give you an idea of what each visual style shows you (see Figure 6.78).

2. Select 3D Wireframe. Your model appears as a transparent wireframe object.

3. To return to the shaded view of your model, choose Realistic from the Visual Styles drop-down list.

Figure 6.78

The Visual Styles drop-down list with 3D Wireframe selected

You might have noticed a few other Visual Styles options. Figure 6.79 shows those options as they are applied to a sphere. 2D Wireframe and 3D Wireframe might appear the same; however, 3D Wireframe uses a perspective view and a background color, while 2D Wireframe uses a parallel projection view and no background color.

Advanced users can control the features of these visual styles and can also create new visual styles. If you'd like to learn more, see *Mastering AutoCAD 2010 and AutoCAD LT 2010*.

Figure 6.79

**Visual styles
applied to a sphere**

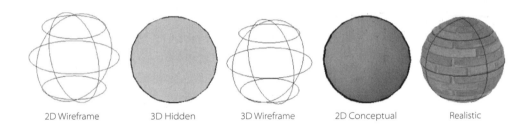

2D Wireframe   3D Hidden   3D Wireframe   2D Conceptual   Realistic

CHANGING 3D VIEWS TO 2D VIEWS AND BACK

Even though the default 2D file looks completely different from the new 3D file you created using the acad3D.dwt template, they are basically the same. They just have different display settings turned on.

You can change the Drawing2.dwg 3D view to a 2D view by doing the following:

1. Choose 2D Wireframe from the Visual Styles drop-down list in the Home tab's View panel.

2. Choose World UCS from the View tab's Coordinates panel.

Your 3D view changes to look like a typical 2D drawing. Likewise, you can convert a 2D view into a 3D one:

1. Choose Realistic from the Visual Styles drop-down list in the Home tab's View panel.

2. Choose SE Isometric 3D Navigation drop-down list in the Home tab's View panel.

3. Enter **Perspective**↵ **1**↵ to turn on the Perspective view.

4. Click the Grid button in the status bar at the bottom of the AutoCAD window.

The file that started out with a 2D view now shows your drawing in 3D.

Summary

In this chapter, you learned about the main tools needed to work in 3D. If you are the adventurous type, you might want to experiment with what you now know. You'll be surprised at how much you can accomplish with your newfound knowledge.

I didn't cover all the tools and options available for 3D modeling. In particular, the Vports command can be helpful to get several simultaneous views of a 3D model while you're editing. Still, armed with the information in this chapter, you will be able to do most of the basic 3D modeling tasks you encounter.

CHAPTER 7

Getting Organized with Layers

The most frequently used tool for getting organized in AutoCAD 2010 is the layering feature. Layers let you sort parts of your drawing into categories. For example, in a typical architectural floor plan, you can have one layer for the walls, another for doors, and yet another for cabinets. You can create other layers for existing conditions if the plan contains renovation work, or you can include electrical and heating diagrams. You can then turn layers on or off so that your drawing displays only the data you need at any given time. You can set layers to have color and lineweights, and objects will inherit those properties. You can even have layers that are visible on your screen but do not print. This feature can be useful if you have a lot of layout information you need to keep with your drawing.

In this chapter, you'll learn how to create and manipulate layers and how objects interact with layers.

This chapter covers the following topics:

- **Creating and assigning layers**
- **Setting the current layer**
- **Controlling layer visibility**
- **Locking layers from printing and editing**
- **Finding the layers you want**
- **Taming an unwieldy list of layers**
- **Saving and recalling layer settings**
- **Using the Layers panel to manage layers**
- **Organizing visual content by using properties**

Creating and Assigning Layers

You use the Layer Properties Manager to create and edit layers. When you're just starting a drawing, especially a complex one, you'll probably spend a lot of time in this tool palette setting up and managing layers. Though it isn't absolutely necessary, setting a color for a new layer is a good step to take right off the bat. Colors are a great way to see at a glance the layer to which an object is assigned.

> If you've recently used the 3D Modeling workspace, make sure you are back in the 2D Drafting & Annotation workspace before beginning any exercises in this chapter. See "Getting to Know the 3D Modeling Workspace" in Chapter 6 for instructions on how to switch to a different workspace.

The following steps introduce you to the Layer Properties Manager and show you how to create a new layer:

1. In the Home tab's Layers panel, click the Layer Properties tool shown in Figure 7.1 or enter **la↵** to open the Layer Properties Manager.

Figure 7.1

The Layer Properties Manager

> The Layer Properties Manager shows you at a glance the status of your layers. Right now, you have only one layer, but as your work expands, so will the number of layers. You will then find this palette indispensable.

2. Click the New Layer tool at the top of the tool palette (see Figure 7.2). A new layer named Layer1 appears in the list box. The name is highlighted, so you can immediately start typing a name for it.

Figure 7.2

Click the New Layer tool toward the top of the Layer Properties Manager.

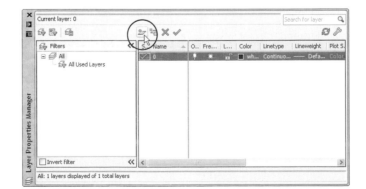

3. As you type, your entry replaces the Layer1 name in the list box. Don't worry if you aren't certain about the name; you can always change it later.

> As a project grows, so does its list of layers. It helps to have a system for naming layers so that you'll be able to find them and sort them easily. For example, you might use a prefix for your layer names such as FP for floor plan and EP for electrical plan. You can also use industry guidelines, such as the American Institute of Architects' layer-naming standards (www.aia.org).

4. With your new layer name highlighted, click the Color icon in that layer's listing, as shown in Figure 7.3. The Color icon is in the Color column and currently shows White as its value.

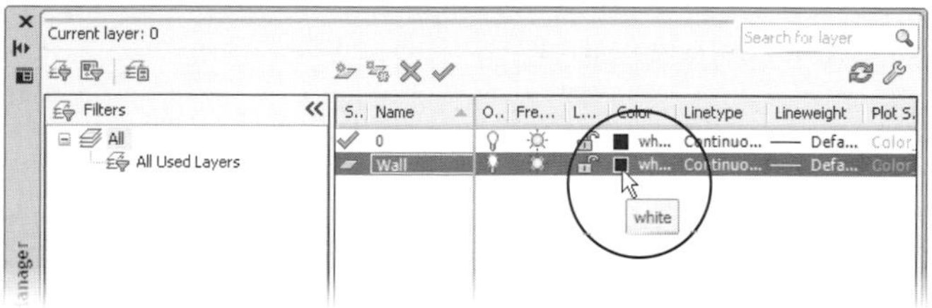

Figure 7.3

The Color icon in the layer listing of the Layer Properties Manager

The Select Color dialog box appears, as shown in Figure 7.4.

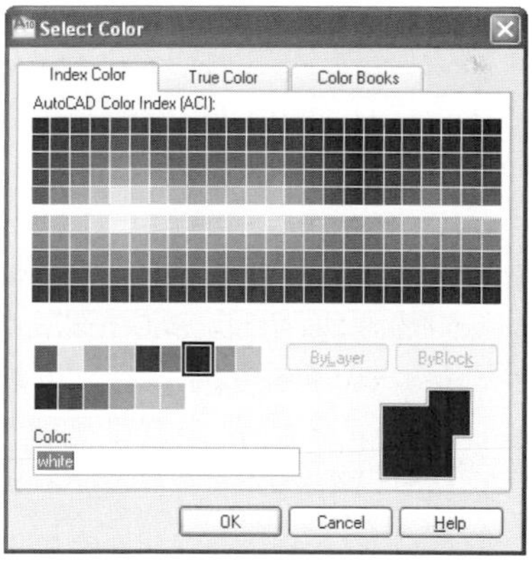

5. In the row of standard colors, click the color you want, and then click OK. Notice that the color swatch in the selected layer is now the color you clicked in the Select Color dialog box.

6. When you return to the Layer Properties Manager, click the X in its title bar to close it.

From this point on, any object assigned to your new layer appears in the color you selected in step 5, unless the object is specifically assigned a different color property.

Figure 7.4

The Select Color dialog box

> The Files tab of the Options dialog box (choose Options from the Application menu) contains the Color Book Locations option, which tells AutoCAD where to look for the Pantone color books. Pantone color books are sets of colors used by the Pantone color system.

Understanding the Layer Properties Manager

The Layer Properties Manager, shown in Figure 7.5, conforms to the Windows interface standard. The most prominent feature of this palette is the layer list box. Notice that the bar at the top of the list of layers includes several buttons for the various layer properties. Just as you can adjust Windows Explorer, you can adjust the width of each column in the list of layers by clicking and dragging either side of the column head buttons. You can also sort the layer list based on a property simply by clicking the property name at the top of the list. You can Shift+click names to select a block of layer names, or you can Ctrl+click individual names to select multiples that do not appear together. These features become helpful as your list of layers enlarges.

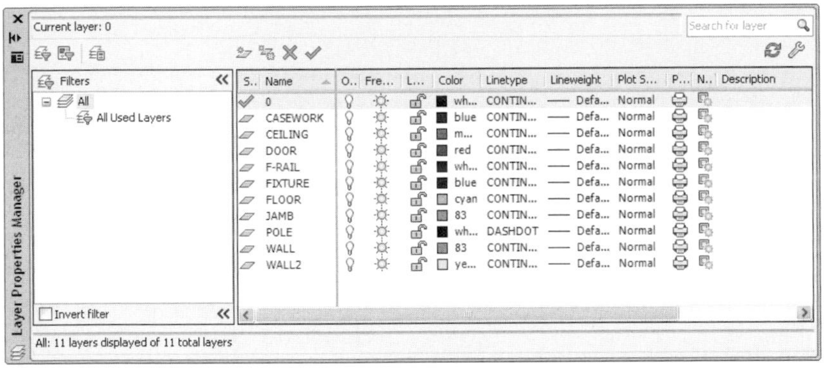

Figure 7.5

The Layer Properties Manager with several layers added

Figure 7.6

The four tool buttons of the Layer Properties Manager let you create a new layer, create a new layer and freeze it in all viewports, delete a layer, and make a selected layer the current one.

Above the layer list, you'll see a box displaying the current layer. Just to the left of the current layer name are four tool buttons, as shown in Figure 7.6.

You've already seen how the New Layer tool works. Another tool that looks similar to the New Layer tool creates a new layer and freezes it in all viewports (see "Controlling Layer Visibility" later in this chapter for more about this tool). The tool with the X icon is the Delete Layer tool. Select a layer or a group of layers, and click this button to delete layers. Be aware that you cannot delete Layer 0, locked layers, or layers that contain objects. The tool with the check mark is the Set Current tool. It allows you to set the current layer on which you want to work. The green check mark under the Status column of the layer list indicates the current layer.

> Another way to create or delete layers is to select a layer or a set of layers from the list box and then right-click to display a menu that includes the same functions as the tools above the layer list.

You'll also notice another set of three tools farther to the left of the Layer Properties Manager. These tools offer features to organize your layers in a meaningful way. You'll get a closer look at these tools a little later in this chapter.

In AutoCAD 2010, the Layer Properties Manager is *nonmodal*, which means it can be kept open and used at any time, even while in the middle of other commands. It behaves like other palettes in AutoCAD, so you can use its auto-hide tool in the title bar to keep it minimized to show just its title bar until you need it. You can also "dock" it to the margins of the AutoCAD window.

Assigning Layers to Objects

When you create an object, that object is automatically assigned to the current layer. In a new drawing, only one layer is called 0 (zero); therefore, when you start to draw in a new drawing, objects are automatically assigned to the 0 layer. When you start to create new layers, you can reassign objects to them using the Properties palette:

1. Select the objects whose layer assignment you want to change.

2. With the cursor in the drawing area, right-click and choose Properties from the context menu to open the Properties palette, as shown in Figure 7.7.

3. Click the Layer option. Notice that a down-pointing arrow appears in the layer name box to the right of the Layer option.

4. Click the down-pointing arrow to display a list of all the available layers.

5. Select the desired layer name from the list. Press Esc to deselect the objects currently selected.

6. Close the Properties palette by clicking the X button in the upper-left corner.

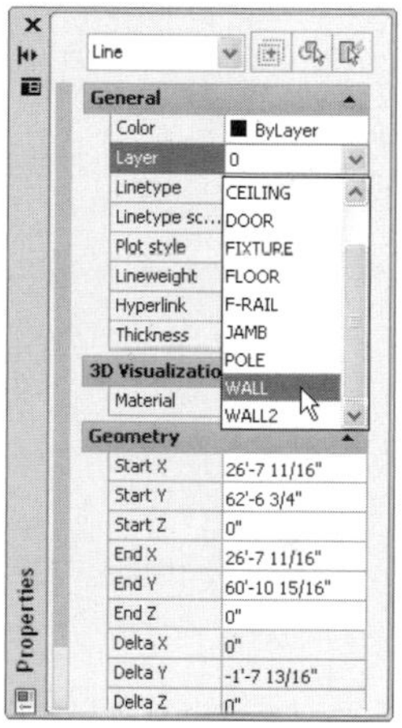

Figure 7.7

The Properties palette with the Layer drop-down list open

If the Color property of the selected objects is set to ByLayer, the objects take on the color of their new layer. The same is true for their linetype and lineweight. On the other hand, if objects have their color property set to a specific color, linetype, or lineweight, their layer assignment will not affect their appearance.

Another way to assign layers to existing objects is to use the layer list in the Home tab's Layers panel (see Figure 7.8).

Ordinarily, this list displays the current layer, and you can set the current layer by selecting it from this list. But when you click an object with no other command active, the list changes to show you the name of the layer to which the selected object is assigned.

Figure 7.8

Selecting a layer from the Layers panel

Once an object is selected, you can easily change its layer assignment by selecting a new name from the layer list.

If you have multiple objects selected and they all have different layer assignments, the list appears blank until you select a new layer from the list. This will give all the selected objects the same layer assignment.

Setting the Current Layer

All objects have a layer assignment, and by default, an object is assigned to the current layer. You can quickly identify the current layer by looking at the layer list in the Layers panel, shown earlier in Figure 7.8.

This list also lets you quickly control some of the layer features, including the current layer. Here's how to change the current layer:

1. Click the arrow button to the right of the layer name on the Layers panel to display a drop-down list that shows you all the layers available in the drawing, as shown earlier in Figure 7.8.

2. Click a layer name. The drop-down list closes, and the selected name appears in the toolbar's layer name box. It is now the current layer.

CONTROLLING COLORS AND LINETYPES OF BLOCKED OBJECTS

Layer 0 has special importance to blocks. (See Chapter 8 for more about blocks.) When objects assigned to Layer 0 are used as parts of a block and that block is inserted on another layer, those objects take on the characteristics of their new layer. On the other hand, if those objects are on a layer other than Layer 0, they maintain their original layer characteristics even if you change that block to another layer. For example, suppose a tub is drawn on the Door layer, instead of on Layer 0. If you turn the tub into a block and insert it on the Fixture layer, the objects that the tub is composed of maintain their assignments to the Door layer, although the Tub block is assigned to the Fixture layer.

It might help to think of the block function as a clear plastic bag that holds together the objects that make up the tub. The objects inside the bag maintain their assignments to the Door layer, even though the bag itself is assigned to the Fixture layer. This might be a bit confusing at first, but it should become clearer after you use blocks for a while.

AutoCAD also allows you to have more than one color or linetype on a layer. For example, you can use the Color and Linetype drop-down lists in the Home tab's expanded Properties panel to alter the color or linetype of an object on Layer 0. That object then maintains its assigned color and linetype, no matter what its layer assignment. Likewise, objects specifically assigned a color or linetype are not affected by their inclusion in blocks.

You might have noticed several icons that appear next to the layer names; these control the status of the layer. You'll learn how to work with these icons later in this chapter. Also notice the box directly to the left of each layer name. This shows you the color of the layer.

Controlling Layer Visibility

AutoCAD offers two methods for controlling layer visibility. The On and Off options turn a layer's visibility on or off. The Freeze and Thaw options not only control layer visibility, but when a layer is frozen, the objects in the frozen layer are ignored. For large drawings, this can improve the speed of object snaps and other operations that search the drawing database.

Freeze and Thaw also have an effect on blocks that is different from the On and Off functions. A block inserted into a layer that has been turned off remains visible if its component objects are on a layer that is still turned on. But a block inserted into a layer that is frozen becomes invisible even though its component objects are on layers that are visible.

The Freeze and Thaw layer options offer a third option, which involves viewports in the layout tabs. You can have multiple viewports in a layout tab (see Chapter 12 for more about viewports in layout tabs), and with the Freeze and Thaw options, you can control the visibility of layers for each viewport. This allows one viewport to display one set of layers, for example, and another viewport to display an entirely different set of layers. Figure 7.9 shows the contents of a layout tab with two viewports, each displaying the same drawing but with different Freeze and Thaw settings.

Figure 7.9

Two layout viewports displaying the same drawing with different layers frozen

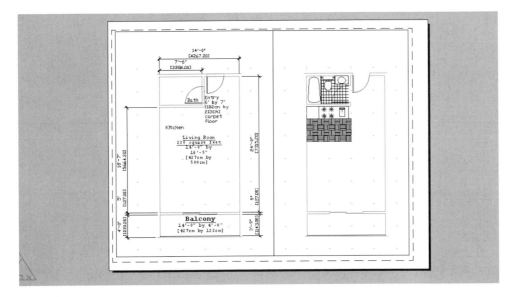

USING TRUE OR PANTONE COLORS

When you choose a color from the Index Color tab of the Select Color dialog box, you'll most often find enough colors to suit your needs. But if you are creating a presentation drawing in which color selection is important, you can choose colors from either the True Color tab or the Color Books tab of the Select Color dialog box.

The True Color tab offers a full range of colors through a color palette similar to one in Adobe Photoshop and other image-editing programs.

You can use the hue, saturation, luminance (HSL) color model, or you can use the red, green, blue (RGB) color model. You can select HSL or RGB from the Color Model drop-down list in the upper-right corner of the dialog box.

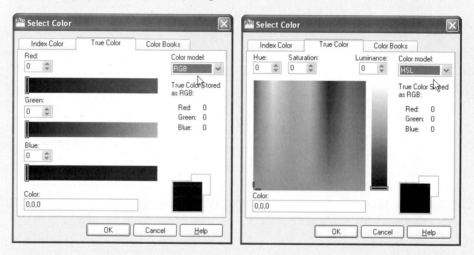

If you installed the Pantone color option when you installed AutoCAD, you can also select from a Pantone color book, using the Color Books tab.

The Color Books tab allows you to match colors to a Pantone color book for offset printing.

Controlling Layer Visibility Using the On/Off Option

You can use the Layer Properties Manager to turn off layers:

1. Open the Layer Properties Manager.

2. In the layer list, click the layer you want to turn off.

3. In the selected layer listing, click the lightbulb icon, as shown in Figure 7.10. The lightbulb icon changes from yellow to gray to indicate that the layer is off. All the objects on the layer you selected in step 2 disappear.

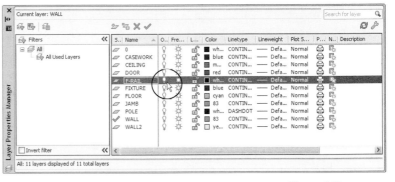

Figure 7.10

The lightbulb icon in the Layer Properties Manager

You can also control layer visibility using the Layer drop-down list on the Layers panel:

1. On the Layers panel, click the Layer drop-down list.

2. Find the layer you want to turn off, and notice that its lightbulb icon is yellow. This tells you that the layer is on and visible.

3. Click the lightbulb icon to make it gray.

4. Now, click the drawing area to close the Layer drop-down list, and the objects on the layer you turned off disappear.

Controlling Layer Visibility with Freeze and Thaw

The Freeze and Thaw options work just like the On and Off options:

1. Open the Layer Properties Manager.

2. In the layer list, click the layer you want to freeze.

3. In the selected layer listing, click the sun icon. The sun turns into a snowflake to indicate that the layer is frozen. All the objects on the layer you selected in step 2 disappear.

Figure 7.11

The Freeze or Thaw in ALL Viewports icon and tooltip in the Layer drop-down list

You can also control layer visibility using the Layer drop-down list on the Layers panel:

1. On the Layers panel, click the Layer drop-down list.

2. Find the layer you want to freeze, and click its sun icon. The tooltip reads Freeze or Thaw in ALL Viewports, as shown in Figure 7.11.

Controlling Layer Visibility in Individual Viewports of a Layout

If you are in a layout view of your drawing and you open the Layer Properties Manager, you'll see several additional columns for each layer: New VP Freeze, VP Freeze, VP Color, VP Linetype, VP Lineweight, and VP Plot Style, as shown in Figure 7.12.

Figure 7.12

The viewport layer options in the Layer Properties Manager

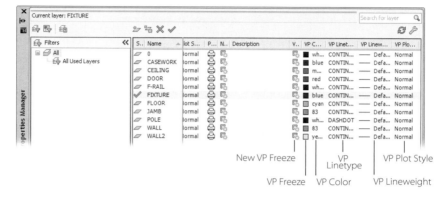

In a layout view, a *viewport* is like a window into your Model tab drawing. A viewport displays the drawing you have created in the model view. You can adjust the view in a viewport to show all of the drawing or just a small portion. You can also control the layer settings in a viewport independently of the layer settings for the model view, and you can have multiple viewports to display different parts of your drawing. To find out more about viewports, see "Setting Up a Drawing for Printing" in Chapter 12.

The VP Freeze option controls the visibility of layers for the currently active viewport. This allows you to control layer visibility in one viewport without affecting the visibility of layers in other viewports on a layout tab. You use it just like the Freeze and Thaw options by clicking the VP Freeze icon to freeze a layer. You must, however, be in the floating model space of the viewport you want to change. Here's how to get to the floating model space for a viewport:

1. If you are in a model view, click the Quick View Layouts tool (see Figure 7.13). You'll see thumbnail views of the model view plus any layout views in the drawing.

2. Click the layout thumbnail you want to use, as shown in Figure 7.14.

Figure 7.13

The Quick View Layouts tool in the status bar

Figure 7.14

The Quick View Layouts thumbnail views and toolbar

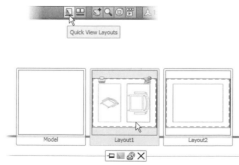

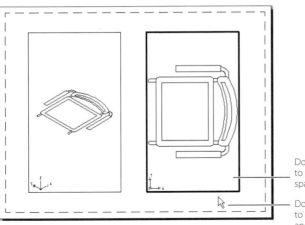

Figure 7.15

The UCS icon appears in each viewport, and the current viewport has a darker border.

Double-click in a viewport to switch to floating model space mode.

Double-click outside the viewports to exit the floating model space mode and get back to paper space.

3. Double-click in the viewport whose layers you want to set. You'll also notice that a UCS icon appears in each viewport and that one viewport has a darker border, as shown in Figure 7.15.

4. Use the scroll bar at the bottom of the Layer Properties Manager to scroll the layer list to the far right.

5. Use the Current VP Freeze option in the Layer Properties Manager to set the visibility of layers for the selected viewport.

6. Exit the floating model space mode by double-clicking outside the viewport.

Figure 7.16

The Freeze or Thaw in Current Viewport icon in the Layer drop-down list

As an alternative, you can use the Layer drop-down list to select the Current VP Freeze option. Click the Freeze or Thaw in Current Viewport icon in the drop-down list to control layer visibility in individual viewports. It is the sun icon with a box behind it, as shown in Figure 7.16.

You've just seen how you can switch between floating model space and paper space by double-clicking inside or outside a viewport. You can also switch between floating model space and paper space by typing **MS↵** for model space or **PS↵** for paper space.

If you want a little more room for your drawing area, you can hide the Model and Layout tabs by right-clicking on them and selecting Hide Layout and Model Tabs. When you do this, you'll see two additional tools in the status bar (Figure 7.17). These tools are the Model and Layout1 tools, and they enable you to switch between the model and layout views of your drawing.

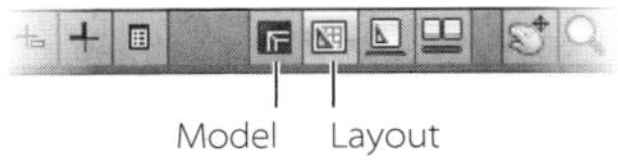

Model   Layout

Figure 7.17

The Model and Layout tools in the status bar

To display the viewport tabs, right-click the Model or Layout tool and select Display Layout and Model Tabs. Turn off the tabs by clicking the Model or Layout tab and selecting Hide Layout and Model Tabs.

Locking Layers from Printing and Editing

You can lock layers so that you don't accidentally change objects assigned to them. This feature is useful when you're working on a crowded drawing and you don't want to accidentally edit portions of it. You can lock all the layers except those you intend to edit and then proceed to work without fear of making accidental changes. The lock option doesn't prevent others from editing the objects on the locked layer. It's just a tool to temporarily lock objects on a layer from editing.

To use the lock option, click the lock icon in the layer listing in the Layer Properties Manager shown in the top half of Figure 7.18.

The lock option also appears in the Layer drop-down list of the Layers panel (see the bottom image in Figure 7.18). The icon changes from an open padlock to a closed one.

Another similar tool is the Plot option. You can click the printer icon (in the Plot column) in the layer list of the Layer Properties Manager to prevent a layer from plotting or printing (see Figure 7.19). The Plot option does not appear in the Layer drop-down list, however.

The layer is still visible, but it just won't print. This is a great option for layers that you use for layouts.

Figure 7.18

The lock icon in the Layer Properties Manager and the Layer drop-down list

The lock icon in the Layer Properties Manager

The lock icon in the Layer drop-down list

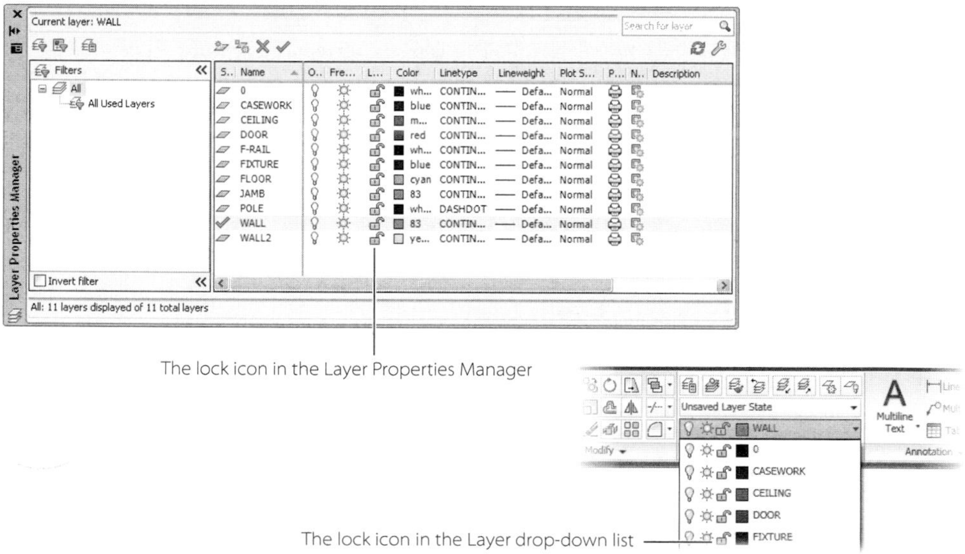

Figure 7.19

The printer icon in the Layer Properties Manager

The plot icon shown as a printer icon

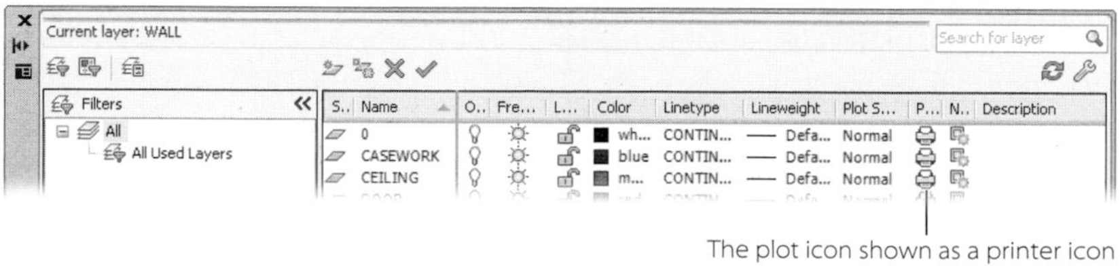

Finding the Layers You Want

With only a handful of layers, it's fairly easy to find the layer you want to turn off. It becomes much more difficult, however, when the number of layers exceeds 20 or 30. The Layer Properties Manager lets you control the list of layers in the same way you can control filenames in Windows Explorer.

Suppose you have several layers whose names begin with C, such as C-lights, C-header, and C-pattern, and you want to find those layers quickly to turn them off. You can click the Name button at the top of the layer list to sort the layer names in alphabetic order. (You can click the Name button again to reverse the order.) To select those layers for processing, click the first layer name that starts with C; then scroll down the list until you find the last layer of the group, and Shift+click it. All the layers between those layers are selected. You can then turn all the selected layers off by clicking one of the lightbulb icons of the selected group of layers.

To deselect some of those selected layers, hold down the Ctrl key while clicking the layer names you don't want to include in your selection. Or Ctrl+click other layer names you do want selected.

The Color and Linetype buttons at the top of the list let you sort the layer list by color or linetype assignments. Other buttons sort the list by virtue of the status: On/Off, Freeze/Thaw, Lock/Unlock, and so forth.

> You can quickly select all the layers in the list by right-clicking the Layer Properties Manager and then choosing Select All. You can also choose Clear All to clear any selections. Select All But Current and Invert Selections do just what they say.

In the previous example, you turned off a set of layers with a single click of a lightbulb icon. You can freeze/thaw, lock/unlock, or change the color of a group of layers in a similar manner by clicking the appropriate layer property. For example, clicking a color swatch of one of the selected layers opens the Select Color dialog box, in which you can set the color for all the selected layers.

Taming an Unwieldy List of Layers

Chances are, you will eventually end up with a fairly long list of layers. Managing such a list can become a nightmare, but AutoCAD provides some tools that help you organize layers so that you can keep track of them more easily. Figure 7.20 shows the tools in the Layer Properties Manager that let you manage your layer lists and settings.

In the upper-left corner of the Layer Properties Manager, you'll see a toolbar

New Group Filter   Layer States Manager

New Property Filter

Figure 7.20

The filter and Layer States Manager options in the Layer Properties Manager

containing three tools that are designed to help with your layer management tasks. From left to right they are as follows:

New Property Filter Lets you filter your list of layers to display only layers with certain properties, such as specific colors or names.

New Group Filter Lets you create named groups of layers that can be quickly recalled at any time. This is helpful if you often work with specific sets of layers. For example, you might have a set of layers in an architectural drawing that pertains to the electrical layout. You can create a group filter called Electrical that filters out all layers except those pertaining to the electrical layout.

Layer States Manager Lets you create sets of layer states. For example, if you want to save the layer settings that have just the Wall and Door layers turned on, use the Layer States Manager tool.

The filters don't affect the layers in any way; they simply specify which layers are displayed in the main layer list.

Filtering Layers by Their Properties

Below the filter tools is the filter list, which is a hierarchical list displaying the sets of layer properties and group filters. Right now, you don't have any filters in place, so you see only All and All Used Layers. The following steps show you how these tools and the filter list box work. You'll start with a look at the New Property Filter tool:

1. Open the Layer Properties Manager.

2. Click the New Property Filter tool in the upper-left corner of the dialog box to open the Layer Filter Properties dialog box, shown in Figure 7.21.

   You'll see two list boxes. The Filter Definition list box at the top is where you enter your filter criteria. The Filter Preview list box underneath the Filter Definition layer box is a preview of your layer list and is based on the filter options. Unless you've already used the Layer Filter Properties tool, there are no filter options, so the Filter Preview list shows all the layers.

Figure 7.21

The Layer Filter Properties dialog box

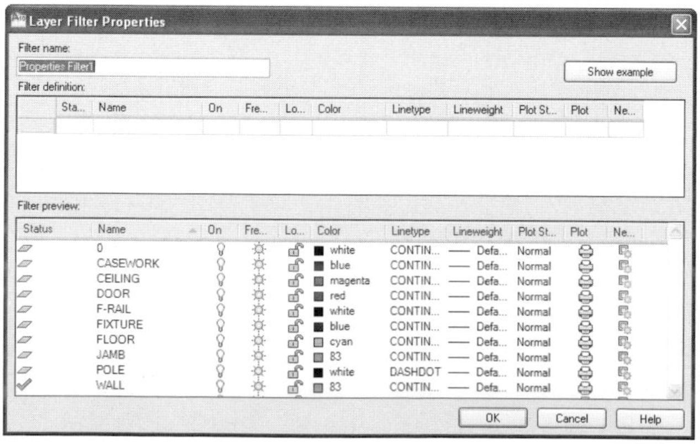

3. In the Filter Definition list box, click the blank box just below the Color label. A Browse button appears in the box (see Figure 7.22).

4. Click in the blank box again, and then enter a color such as **red**↵. The Filter Preview box changes to show only layers that are red. If there are no red layers, the list will be blank.

5. Click twice in the blank box below the one you just edited. Again, you'll see a button appear.

6. Enter another color. Now the layers that are the color you just entered appear in the Filter Preview list.

> You can also select a color from the Select Color dialog box by clicking the button that appears in the box.

7. In the Filter Definition list, click the Name column in the third row down. Notice that a cursor appears followed by an asterisk.

8. Enter the letter for the layer names you want to filter, and then press ↵. You see layers added to the Filter Preview box whose names begin with the letter you entered.

9. In the Filter Name input box at the upper-left corner of the dialog box, change the name Properties Filter1 to something more meaningful for this list, and then click OK. Now you'll see the new filter name in the list box on the left side of the Layer Properties Manager (see Figure 7.23).

You might also notice that the layer list shows only the layers whose properties conform to those you selected in the Layer Filter Properties dialog box.

Once you create a new filter, it will be highlighted in the filter list to the left. This tells you that the new filter is the current layer property filter being applied to the layer list to the right. You can change the layer list display by selecting options in the filter list:

1. Click the All option in the filter list at the left side of the palette, as shown in Figure 7.24.

    The layer list to the right changes to display all the layers in the drawing. You'll also see a brief description of the current layer filter at the bottom of the dialog box.

Figure 7.24

Click the All option in the Layer Proper- ties Manager.

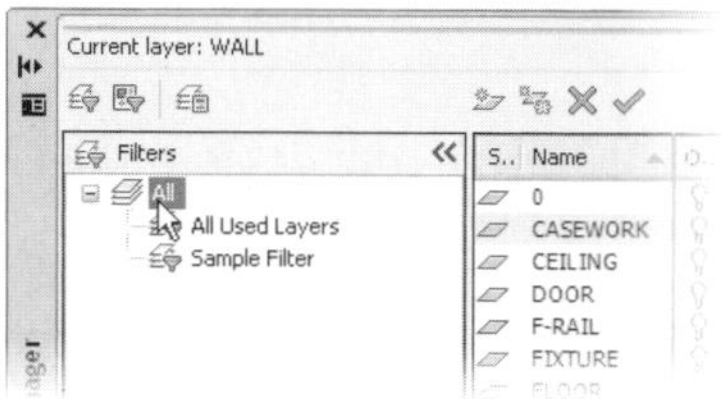

2. Click the All Used Layers option in the filter list. Now, only layers that contain objects appear.

3. Click the name of the new list you created. The layer list changes back to the limited set of layers from your filter list.

4. Double-click the name of your new list. The Layer Filter Properties dialog box opens and displays the list of layer properties you set up earlier for that list. You can edit the criteria for your filter by making modifications in this dialog box.

5. Click Cancel to exit the Layer Filter Properties dialog box.

Creating Layer Groups by Selection

Suppose you want to create a layer filter list by graphically selecting objects on the screen. You can use the New Group Filter tool to do just that:

1. In the upper-left corner of the Layer Properties Manager, click the New Group Filter tool shown in Figure 7.25. You see a new listing appear called Group Filter1.

2. Right-click the Group Filter1 listing, and then choose Select Layers → Add from the context menu.

3. Select the set of objects whose layers you want included in your filter. The layers of the objects you select in step 2 appear in the layer list, filtering out all other layers (see Figure 7.26).

Figure 7.25

The New Group Filter tool in the Layer Properties Manager

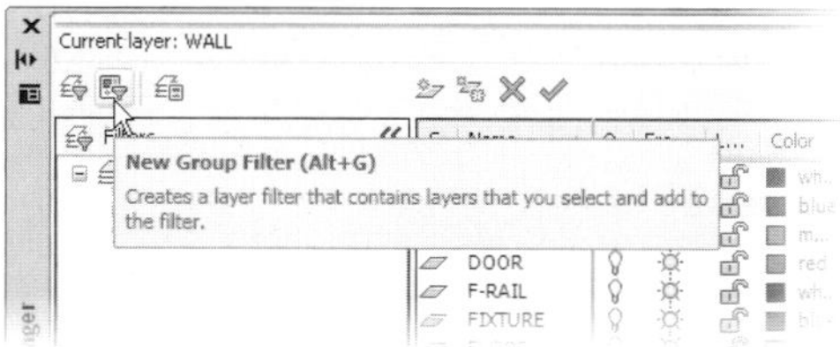

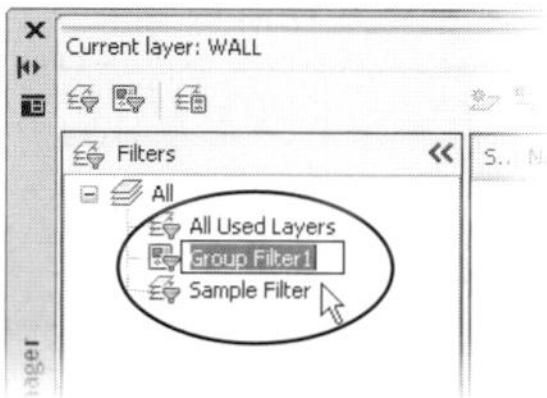

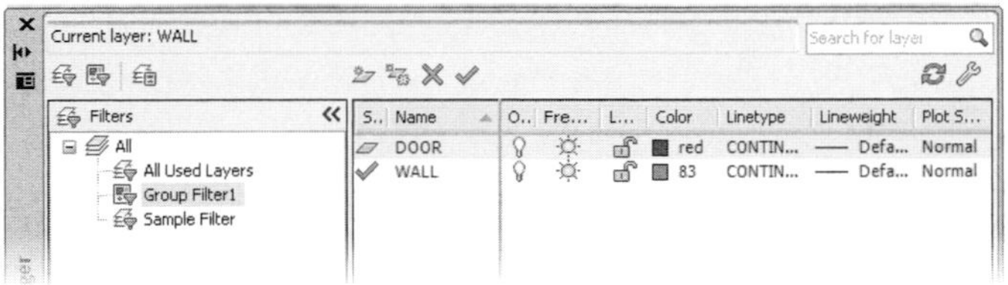

Figure 7.26

The Group Filter1 list after selecting objects

You might have noticed the Select Layers → Replace option in the context menu in step 2. This option lets you completely replace an existing group filter with a new selection set. It works just like choosing Select Layers → Add.

Earlier, you saw how you can double-click a properties filter to edit a properties filter list. But group filters work in a slightly different way. If you want to add layers to your group filter, you can drag them from the layer list to the group filter name. Here's how you do it:

1. In the Layer Properties Manager, click All in the filter list to the left.

2. Click a layer or a set of layers in the layer list to select them. You'll add these layers to the Group Filter1 layer group.

3. Drag selected layers to the Group Filter1 listing in the filter list to the left.

4. To check the addition to the Group Filter1 list, click it in the filter list. This adds the selected layers to the Group Filter1 list.

To delete a layer from a group filter, follow these steps:

1. With Group Filter1 selected, select the layer name you want to delete from the list, and then right-click it.

2. Choose Remove from Group Filter in the context menu. This removes the layer from the Group Filter1 list.

You can also convert a layer properties filter into a group filter. Select the layer properties filter from the filter list, right-click, and then choose Convert to Group Filter. The icon for the layer properties filter changes to a group filter icon, indicating that it is now a group filter.

Applying Filters to the Properties Toolbar Layer List and Other Options

You'll want to know about some additional options just below the filter list (see Figure 7.27). The Invert Filter option changes the list of layers to show all layers *excluding* those in the selected filter. For example, if your new filter contains red layers and you select Invert Filter, the layer list displays all layers *except* those whose

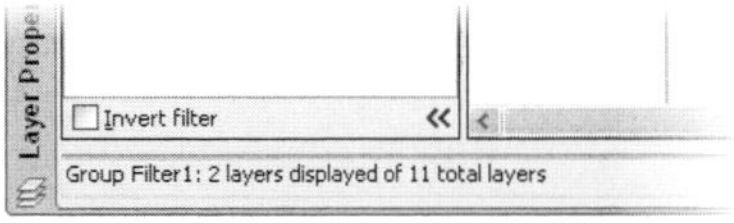

Figure 7.27

The Invert Filter option in the Layer Properties Manger

color is red. The Settings tool in the upper-right side of the Layer Properties Manager (the wrench icon) opens a dialog box that offers additional control over the behavior of layer functions.

Finally, you'll see a text input box in the upper-right corner containing the words *Search for Layer*. You can enter portions of a layer name in this text box to apply additional filters to the layer list currently being displayed. For example, you can enter **G*** in this text input box to display only those layers whose names begin with *G* in the current layer list.

In the next section, I'll give you some tips about how to use layer names with text filters more effectively.

Saving and Recalling Layer Settings

As you start to work with AutoCAD, you'll find you'll want to set up layers in a certain way to edit your drawing. As you progress through your editing session, you'll turn layers on and off. Eventually, you'll want to return to the layer settings you had when you started. You can use the Layer States Manager dialog box to store the way your layers are set up so that you can quickly return to that setup or state when you are done editing.

The ability to save layer states can be crucial when you are editing a file that serves multiple uses, such as a floor plan and a reflected ceiling plan. You can, for example, turn layers on and off to set up the drawing for a reflected ceiling plan view and then save the layer settings. Later, when you need to modify the ceiling information, you can recall the layer setting to view the ceiling data. Let's see how the Layer States Manager dialog box works.

Click the Layer States Manager button in the Layers panel to open the Layer States Manager dialog box, as shown in Figure 7.28.

Take a moment to look at the options in this dialog box. This is where you can also specify which layer settings you want saved with this layer state.

Figure 7.28

The Layer States Manager dialog box

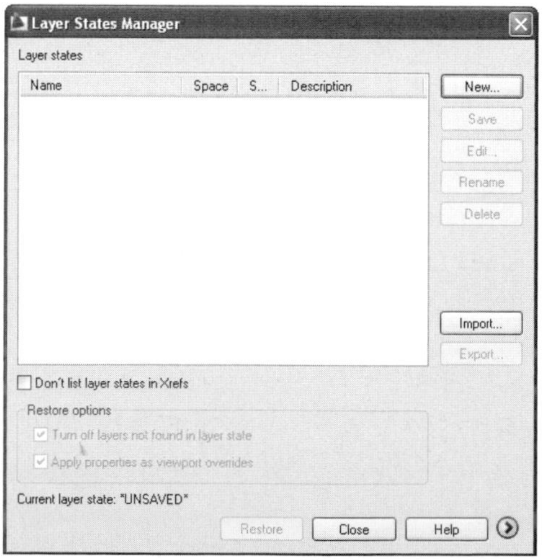

Save the current layer state by following these steps:

1. Click the New button in the Layer States Manager dialog box to open the New Layer State to Save dialog box, shown in Figure 7.29.

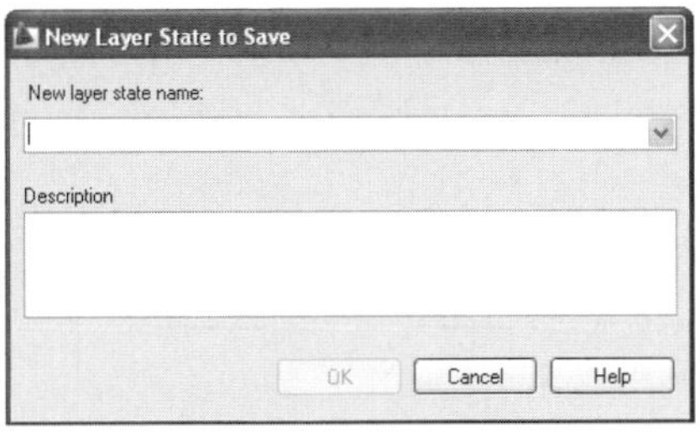

2. Enter a name for the layer state in the New Layer State Name input box. Note that you can also enter a brief description of your layer state. Click OK to return to the Layer States Manager dialog box.

Figure 7.29

The New Layer State To Save dialog box

You've just saved a layer state. The following steps demonstrate how you can restore the saved layer state:

1. Click the Layer States Manager button to open the Layer States Manager dialog box.

2. Select the name of the layer state you want to restore from the list, and then click Restore. When you return to the Layer Properties Manager, you'll notice that the layer settings have returned to the settings you saved.

The layer states are saved with the file so you can retrieve them at a later date. As you can see from the Layer States Manager dialog box, you have a few other options:

Delete Deletes a layer state from the list.

Import Imports a set of layer states that have been exported using the Export option of this dialog box.

Export Saves a set of layer states as a file. By default, the file is given the name of the current layer state with the .las filename extension. You can import the layer state file into other drawing files.

In addition to saving layer states by name, you can quickly revert to the previous layer state by clicking the Layer Previous tool at the top of the Layers panel.

This tool lets you quickly revert to the previous layer settings without affecting other settings in AutoCAD. Note that the Layer Previous mode does not restore the previous state of renamed layers, and it doesn't restore deleted layers or remove new layers.

You'll also want to know about the Select a Layer State drop-down list in the Layers panel. This tool lets you select a layer state quickly without opening the Layer States Manager dialog box.

Once you become familiar with these layer state tools, you'll find yourself using them frequently in your editing sessions.

The Layerpmode command controls the tracking of layer states. It is usually turned on, but if it is turned off, the Layer Previous tool will not work. To turn it on, enter **Layerpmode↵ On↵**.

Using the Layers Panel to Manage Layers

Layers are one of the most frequently used AutoCAD features, so AutoCAD offers some handy shortcuts for controlling layer settings. You can find these shortcuts in the Home tab's Layers panel. If you find yourself having to work with files that other people have created, you might want to review the material in this section.

> All the tools discussed in this section have keyboard command equivalents. Check the status bar when selecting these tools from the toolbar or drop-down list for the keyboard command name.

As you work with AutoCAD, you'll find that you will turn layers on and off frequently and that you will want to make a certain layer active to ensure your drawing stays organized. The Home tab's Layers panel gives you a single-button access to these and other functions (see Figure 7.30). In this section, you'll be introduced to the more commonly used tools in this panel.

Figure 7.30

The Layers panel

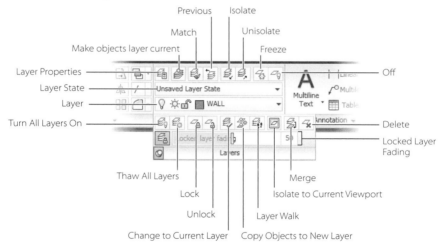

Exploring Layers with Layer Walk

When you work with a file that has been produced by someone else, you usually have to spend some time getting familiar with the way the layers are set up. This can be tedious, but the Layer Walk tool in the expanded Layers panel can help.

As the name implies, the Layer Walk tool lets you "walk through" the layers of a file, visually isolating each layer as you select the layer's name from a list. You can use Layer Walk to select the layers that you want visible, or you can turn layers on and off to explore a drawing without affecting the current layer settings.

To open the LayerWalk dialog box shown in Figure 7.31, click the Layer Walk tool in the expanded Layers panel.

You can click and drag the bottom edge of the dialog box to expand the list so that you can see all the layers in the drawing. You'll see several, if not all, of the layers in the list highlighted. The highlighted layers are currently turned on and visible. Layers that are not selected in the list are off and not visible. The following list describes how you can use the list to explore the layers in a drawing:

- To make a layer temporarily visible without affecting the visibility of the other layers, Ctrl+click the unselected layer in the list.

- To temporarily turn off a layer and make it invisible without affecting the visibility of other layers, Ctrl+click the selected layer in the list.

- To isolate a layer, click the layer name. The selected layer will be the only one visible in the drawing.

- To invert the layer selection, right-click and choose Invert Selection from the context menu. This also inverts the visibility of layers.

- To select layers that do not have objects assigned to them, right-click in the Layer-Walk dialog box, and choose Select Unreferenced from the context menu. If there are any unreferenced layers, they are selected in the list.

- To remove unreferenced layers from the drawing, click the Purge button.

- To select all the layers in the list, right-click in the LayerWalk dialog box again, and choose Select All from the context menu. This makes all the layers of your drawing visible.

- To unselect all the layers, right-click in the LayerWalk dialog box, and then choose Clear All from the context menu.

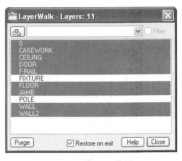

Figure 7.31

The LayerWalk dialog box

You can also lock layers so that they remain visible as you explore the layer in the LayerWalk dialog box. Ctrl+click a set of layers to make them visible, right-click, and then choose Hold Selection from the context menu. Asterisks appear to the left of the selected layer names. Now as you randomly click layer names from the list, the layers with the asterisks remain visible. The Hold Selection option temporarily locks them on so that other selections do not affect their visibility.

Changing the Layer Assignment of Objects

In addition to the Layer Walk tool, the Layers panel includes two tools that change the layer assignments of objects. The Layer Match tool is similar to the Match Properties tool but is streamlined to operate only on layer assignments. Click this tool, select the object or objects you want to change, and then select an object whose layer you want to match.

The Change to Current Layer tool in the expanded Layers panel changes an object's layer assignment to the current layer.

Controlling Layer Settings Through Objects

The remaining tools in the Layers panel let you make layer settings by selecting objects in the drawing. These tools are easy to use: simply click the tool, and then select an object. These tools are so helpful that you might want to consider docking them permanently in your AutoCAD window:

Isolate Turns off all the layers except for the layer of the selected object.

Copy Objects to New Layer Creates a copy of an object and assigns the copy to the layer of an object you select.

Freeze Freezes the layer of the selected object.

Off Turns off the layer of the selected object.

Lock Locks the layer of the selected object. A locked layer is visible but cannot be edited.

Unlock Unlocks the layer of the selected object.

Organizing Visual Content by Using Properties

Part of your work with AutoCAD will involve organizing your drawings visually. You can use color, lineweight, and linetypes, such as dashed and center lines, to help keep your drawing orderly and understandable. Color often helps identify the layer an object is assigned to or helps identify the object's category, such as plumbing or electrical. Color was once the only way to control lineweights in AutoCAD, and you might still see drawings that use color to determine lineweight. Lineweights are also a controllable property, and they can greatly enhance the readability of your drawings. Linetypes have always been used to identify control or datum lines in technical drawings. Centerlines, property lines, fences, and other types of noncontinuous lines are essential to any drawing you'll be doing.

You can assign color, lineweight, and linetypes through layers. You might notice that layers show color, lineweight, and linetypes as part of their attributes. By clicking any one of those attributes in the Layer Properties Manager, you can change its value. You can also set the color, lineweight, and linetype of individual objects.

You've already learned how to set the color of a layer. The following section shows you how to set linetypes and lineweights.

Assigning Linetypes to Layers

You'll often want to use different linetypes to show hidden lines, centerlines, fence lines, or other noncontinuous lines. AutoCAD comes with several linetypes, as shown in Figure 7.32. Included are ISO and complex linetypes, as well as lines that can illustrate gas and water lines in civil work or batt insulation in a wall cavity. ISO linetypes are designed to be used with specific plotted line widths and linetype scales. For example, if you are using a pen width of 0.5mm, set the linetype scale of the drawing to 0.5 as well. The complex linetypes at the bottom of the figure are industry-specific.

Figure 7.32

Standard, ISO, and complex AutoCAD linetypes

Linetype	
BORDER	
BORDER2	
BORDERX2	
CENTER	
CENTER2	
CENTERX2	
DASHDOT	
DASHDOT2	
DASHDOTX2	
DASHED	
DASHED2	
DASHEDX2	
DIVIDE	
DIVIDE2	
DIVIDEX2	
DOT	
DOT2	
DOTX2	
HIDDEN	
HIDDEN2	
HIDDENX2	
PHANTOM	
PHANTOM2	
PHANTOMX2	
ACAD_ISO02W100	
ACAD_ISO03W100	
ACAD_ISO04W100	
ACAD_ISO05W100	
ACAD_ISO06W100	
ACAD_ISO07W100	
ACAD_ISO08W100	
ACAD_ISO09W100	
ACAD_ISO10W100	
ACAD_ISO11W100	
ACAD_ISO12W100	
ACAD_ISO13W100	
ACAD_ISO14W100	
ACAD_ISO15W100	
FENCELINE1	
FENCELINE2	
TRACKS	
BATTING	
HOT_WATER_SUPPLY	HW HW HW
GAS_LINE	GAS GAS GAS
ZIGZAG	

AutoCAD stores linetype descriptions in an external file named Acad.lin or Acadiso.lin (for metric drawings). You can edit this file in a text editor to create new linetypes or to modify existing ones, though customizing linetypes is beyond the scope of this book.

The default linetype in a new drawing is the Continuous linetype. If you want to use a different linetype, you must load it from the linetype file. Here's how you do that:

1. Open the Layer Properties Manager, and then click All in the filter list.

2. Click the word *Continuous* that appears in the layer listing (in the Linetype column) of which you will assign the new linetype. This opens the Select Linetype dialog box, as shown in Figure 7.33. To find the Linetype column, you might need to scroll the list to the right using the scroll bar at the bottom of the list.

   The Select Linetype dialog box displays a list of linetypes from which to choose. In a new file, only one linetype is available by default. You must load any additional linetype you want to use. Once a linetype is loaded, it is available for use at any time.

3. Click the Load button at the bottom of the dialog box to open the Load or Reload Linetypes dialog box, shown in Figure 7.34.

   Notice that the list of linetype names is similar to the Layer drop-down list. You can sort the names alphabetically or by description by clicking the Linetype or Description headings at the top of the list.

4. In the Available Linetypes list, scroll down to locate the Dashdot linetype, click it, and then click OK.

5. Notice that the Dashdot linetype is now added to the linetypes available in the Select Linetype dialog box.

6. Click Dashdot to highlight it; then click OK. Now Dashdot appears in the currently selected layer under the Linetype heading.

7. Click OK to exit the Load or Reload Linetypes dialog box.

Once you've assigned a linetype to a layer, any object assigned to that layer is drawn using that linetype, unless the object is specifically assigned a linetype. You can assign linetypes to objects on an individual basis through the Properties palette, described in Chapter 4.

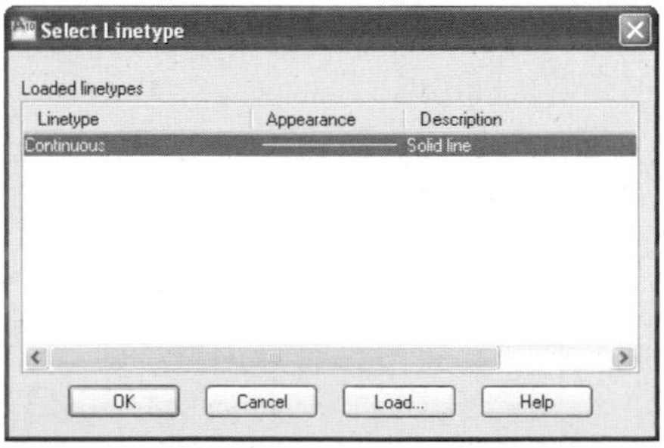

Figure 7.33
The Select Linetype dialog box

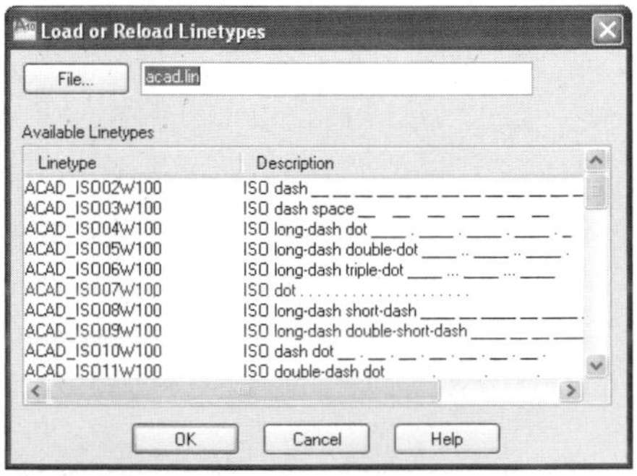

Figure 7.34
The Load or Reload Linetypes dialog box

Controlling Linetype Scale

The appearance of a linetype depends closely on two features in AutoCAD: the Linetype Scale setting and a new feature in AutoCAD 2008 called *annotation scale*. The Linetype Scale setting controls the scale of the dashes or dots in the linetype. The default value is 1, which means the linetype is not scaled. Figure 7.35 shows how the same linetype is affected by two different linetype scale values.

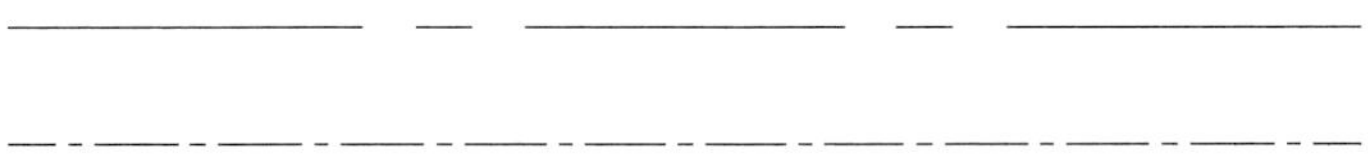

Figure 7.35

The same linetype using two different linetype scales. The upper line uses a scale that is approximately four times the scale of the lower line.

The Annotation Scale value is the scale you want to use for a given layout view.

For example, you can set up a layout view to display the linetype at the correct scale by using the Annotation Scale feature:

1. Make sure you are in Layout view, and then click a viewport border to select it.

2. Click the Annotation Scale drop-down list in the lower-right corner of the AutoCAD window.

3. Select a scale from the list that appears.

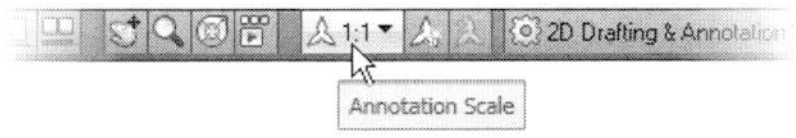

4. Type **Rea⏎** to see the updated scale.

Objects within the viewport that are assigned a noncontinuous linetype will appear at the appropriate scale. Note that you can assign a different annotation scale for each viewport in a layout. The annotation scale for viewports can also be different from the annotation scale set in model view.

> You can fine-tune the appearance of linetypes by using the Ltscale system variable. Enter **Ltscale⏎**, and at the Enter new linetype scale factor <1.0000>: prompt, enter a scale value to change the frequency of the line segments of a linetype.

Figure 7.36

Sample image of different lineweights used in AutoCAD

Setting Lineweights

The Lineweight option in the Layer Properties Manager lets you control the thickness of your lines by adjusting the Lineweight setting. Lineweight settings are designed specifically for printer and plotter output, and you might not see true lineweights in the Model tab. They do appear correctly, however, in the layout tabs when you set up AutoCAD to display lineweights. Figure 7.36 shows a sample view of a drawing from a layout tab.

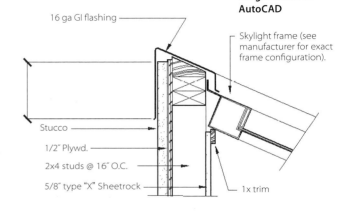

16 ga Gl flashing

Skylight frame (see manufacturer for exact frame configuration).

Stucco

1/2″ Plywd.

2x4 studs @ 16″ O.C.

5/8″ type "X" Sheetrock

1x trim

Turning on Lineweight Visibility

By default, AutoCAD does not display lineweights in either the Model tab or the layout tabs. You can turn on the lineweights by using the Lineweight Settings dialog box shown in Figure 7.37. To open the Lineweight Settings dialog box, click the Lineweight drop-down list in the Home tab's Properties, or enter **Lweight**⏎ at the command prompt.

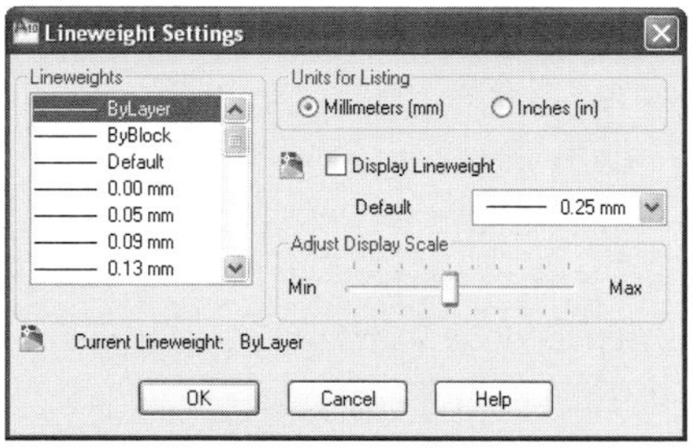

Figure 7.37

**The Lineweight
Settings dialog box**

To turn on the display of lineweights, click the Display Lineweight option. You can also control the degree to which AutoCAD displays lineweights using the Adjust Display Scale slider.

Setting Lineweights by Using the Layer Properties Manager

Just as you can control color and linetypes through layers, you can also control lineweights through layers. The Lineweight option in the Layer Properties Manager controls the lineweight for each layer. When you click the Lineweight column for a layer, the Lineweight dialog box opens (see Figure 7.38), showing you the lineweight options.

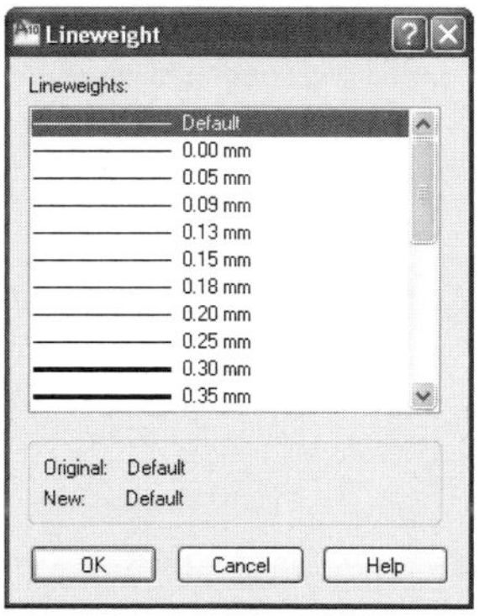

Figure 7.38

**The Lineweight
dialog box**

You can select a lineweight from the list to assign it to the selected layer or layers. Objects assigned to that layer plot will have the assigned lineweights.

SCALE FACTORS IN LEGACY DRAWINGS

With the introduction of annotation scale in the 2008 version, AutoCAD has greatly simpli-fied the way you apply drawing scales to objects. However, it is likely that you will encounter drawings created in earlier versions of AutoCAD. With earlier drawings, users had to under-stand and apply the concept of scale factors to text, blocks, hatch patterns, and linetypes in order to size these features properly for a given scale.

Scale factors are different for metric and imperial (feet and inch) measurement systems. The scale factor for fractional inch scales is derived by multiplying the denominator of the scale by 12 and then dividing by the numerator. For example, the scale factor for ¼″ = 1′0″ is (4 × 12) / 1, or 48 / 1. For ³⁄₁₆″ = 1′0″ scale, the operation is (16 × 12) / 3, or 64. For whole-foot scales, such as 1″ = 10′, multiply the feet side of the equation by 12. Metric scales require simple decimal conversions. For a 10:1 scale, the scale factor is 10. The following table shows

SCALE FACTORS IN LEGACY DRAWINGS *(continued)*

some standard scale conversion factors used in civil and architectural drawings. Once you've determined the scale factor, you can apply it to the linetype scale of your drawing or object.

When you encounter text and dimensions in an older drawing (see Chapter 9), you have to understand how to specify a text height so the text appears in the proper size when it is plotted. The scale factor helps you determine the appropriate text height for a particular drawing scale. For example, you might want your text to appear ⅛″ high in your final plot. But if you draw your text to ⅛″, it appears as a dot when plotted. The text has to be scaled up to a size that, when scaled back down at plot time, appears ⅛″ high. So, for a ¼″ scale drawing, you multiply the ⅛″ text height by a scale factor of 48 to get 6″. Your text should be 6″ high in the CAD drawing in order to appear 1/8″ high in the final plot. Dimensions are also scaled in a similar manner.

SCALE FACTORS FOR ENGINEERING DRAWING SCALES

1″ = n	10′	20′	30′	40′	50′	60′	100′	200′
Scale factor	120	240	360	480	600	720	1200	2400

SCALE FACTORS FOR ARCHITECTURAL DRAWING SCALES

n = 1′0″	¹⁄₁₆″	⅛″	¼″	½″	¾″	1″	1½″	3″
Scale factor	192	96	48	24	16	12	8	4

Setting Lineweights Directly to Objects

You can also assign a lineweight directly to an object in your drawing. The simplest way to do this is to click the object while no command is active and then select a lineweight from the Select a Lineweight drop-down list in the Home tab's Properties panel. You can also use the Properties palette. Select an object, right-click, and choose Properties in the context menu. Select a lineweight from the Lineweight drop-down list (see Figure 7.39).

Yet another way to set lineweights is through the plot-style tables. If you encounter a drawing in which you seem unable to control the plotted lineweights, chances are the lineweight settings are set up in the Plot Style tables for the drawing. See Chapter 12 for more about the Plot Style tables.

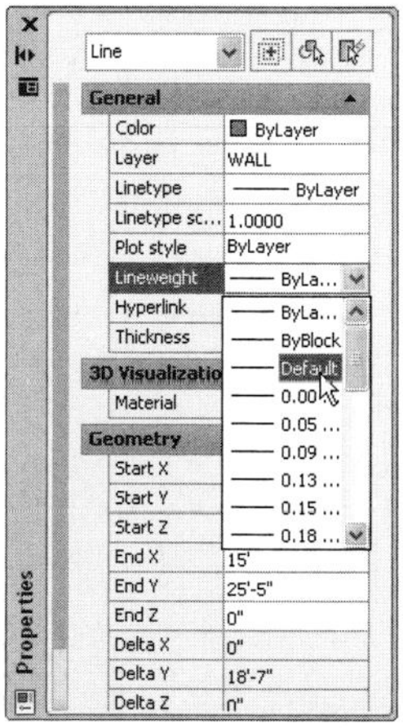

Figure 7.39

The Lineweight drop-down list in the Properties palette

Setting Colors, Linetypes, Linetype Scales, and Lineweights for Individual Objects

If you prefer, you can set up AutoCAD to assign specific colors, linetypes, linetype scales, and lineweights to objects instead of having objects inherit these settings from the layer to which they are assigned. Usually, objects are given default, nongeometric properties called ByLayer, which means each object takes on the color, linetype, linetype scale, and lineweight of its assigned layer. (You've probably noticed the word *ByLayer* in the Properties toolbar and in various dialog boxes.)

Select an object; then right-click and choose Properties to change any property of an existing object. (See Chapter 4 for more information about the Properties palette.) The Properties palette lets you set the properties of individual objects.

You can also open the Home tab's Properties panel, which allows you to control property settings for new and existing objects. For new objects, use the Object Color, Linetype, or Lineweight drop-down list on the Properties panel to set the default values for these properties (see Figure 7.40).

Figure 7.40

The tools and lists options on the expanded Properties panel

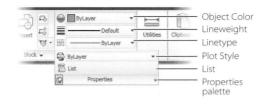

The Object Color drop-down list also contains the Select Colors option (see Figure 7.41). Click it to open the Select Color dialog box.

Figure 7.41

The Select Colors option in the Object Color drop-down list

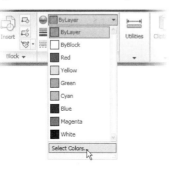

This dialog box lets you select from a broad range of colors. Select a color from the Select Color dialog box, and then everything you draw will be in the selected color, regardless of the current layer color.

For linetypes, you can use the Linetype drop-down list in the Properties panel to select a default linetype for all new objects. The list shows only linetypes that have already been loaded into the drawing, so you must first load the linetype before you can select it. You can load a linetype by selecting the Other option from the drop-down list shown in Figure 7.42.

Figure 7.42

The Other option in the Select a Linetype drop-down list

If you want to set the linetype scale for each individual object, instead of relying on the global linetype scale (the Ltscale system variable), you can use the Properties palette to modify the linetype scale of individual objects. Select the object, right-click, and select Properties. You can then adjust the Linetype scale setting in the Properties palette (see Figure 7.43).

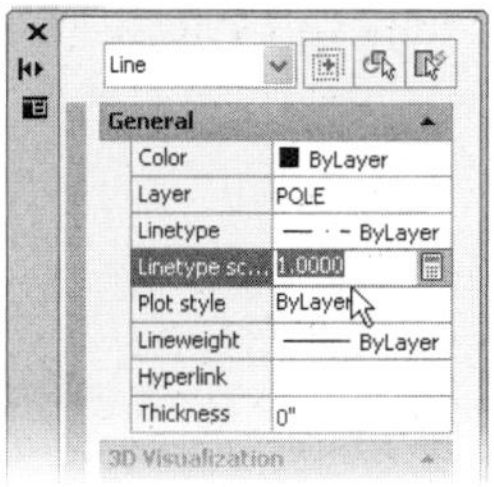

To set the linetype scale to be applied to new objects, set the Celtscale system variable to the linetype scale you want for new objects.

Figure 7.43

The Linetype Scale option in the Properties palette

In the previous section, you saw how to change the global linetype scale setting. This affects all noncontinuous linetypes within the current drawing. You can also change the linetype scale of individual objects by clicking the Properties button on the Standard Annotation toolbar. Or you can set the default linetype scale for all new objects, with the Current Object Scale option in the Linetype Manager dialog box.

When individual objects are assigned a linetype scale, they are still affected by the global linetype scale set by the Ltscale system variable. For example, say you assign a linetype scale of 2 to a dashed line while the Ltscale system variable is set to 12. This assigned scale of 2 is then multiplied by the global linetype scale of 12 for a final linetype scale of 24.

If the objects you draw appear in a different linetype from that of the layer they are on, select Other from the Linetype drop-down list on the Properties panel. Then, in the Linetype Manager dialog box, highlight ByLayer in the Linetype list, and click the Current button. In addition, check the linetype scale of the object itself, using the Properties palette. A different linetype scale can make a line appear to have an assigned linetype that might not be what you expect.

UNDERSTANDING THE BYBLOCK SETTING

As you explore the Layer Properties Manager and the various object properties settings, you'll see a setting called ByBlock. ByBlock makes everything you draw white (or black, depending on the background color), until you turn your drawing into a block and then insert the block on a layer with an assigned color. The objects then take on the color of that layer. This behavior is similar to that of objects drawn on Layer 0. This option is available if you want objects to have a layer assignment other than zero but you want the objects to acquire the color or linetype of the block with which they are combined. The ByBlock linetype works similarly to the ByBlock color.

Summary

AutoCAD's layer system is quite complex and can be daunting to the first-time user. But you don't have to learn everything about layers at one sitting. First, just understand the basics—what layers are used for and that all objects have a layer assignment. Then, learn how layers are created and how objects are assigned to layers. Next, you'll want to know about the ways layers can be turned on and off. After that, you can explore the other layer options as needed.

In conjunction with layers, you'll want to understand how object properties work and how they interact with layers. This is an area you should have at least some familiarity with even as a beginner. Understanding properties will help you understand many of the other ways that AutoCAD can help you organize drawings.

CHAPTER 8

Using Blocks, Groups, Xrefs, and DesignCenter

One of AutoCAD's best qualities is its ability to let you get the most mileage from your drawings. AutoCAD includes several features that help you organize your work so that a single drawing can serve multiple purposes. You can also create sets of objects that can be easily reproduced and modified. To get the most out of AutoCAD, you'll want to be as familiar as possible with these organizational features.

One of the most frequently used features is the *block*, which is a collection of objects that behaves like a single object. Blocks can be duplicated easily, like images from a rubber stamp. And if you need to make a change to several duplicate blocks, you can change one block, and all the copies of that block update to reflect the change.

Groups are similar to blocks in that they are collections of objects that behave like a single object. One difference between blocks and groups is that individual objects within a group are much easier to edit. Copies of groups do not inherit changes from edits made to a group. You can think of the group as a tool to help you keep similar objects together.

Finally, you can import entire drawings if you want to use parts of a drawing as a background. For example, for a large project, one drawing might show the entire floor plan, and several others might show only enlarged portions of that plan. This way, you can get "double duty" from one drawing by using it in several other drawings. Drawings that are imported this way are called *external references*, or *Xrefs* for short.

This chapter includes the following topics:

- **Using blocks to organize objects**
- **Organizing objects by using groups**
- **Getting multiple uses from drawings using external references**
- **Keeping track of drawing components with DesignCenter**
- **Keeping tools on hand with the Tool Palettes window**

If you've recently used the 3D Modeling workspace, make sure you are back in the 2D Drafting & Annotation workspace before beginning any exercises in this chapter.

Using Blocks to Organize Objects

Blocks are one of the oldest methods for grouping objects in AutoCAD. Used properly, they can be a real time-saver. They have the unique ability to be edited globally. For example, you can create a drawing of a chair and then turn it into a block so that the chair behaves as one object. You can then make hundreds of copies of that chair by copying its block form. These copies are referred to as *block references*. If you need to modify the chair later, you can modify one of the block references, and all the other chair blocks update automatically.

Creating a Block

You can easily create blocks from existing objects by following these steps:

1. In the Home tab's Block panel, click the Create tool, or enter **b.⏎** to open the Block Definition dialog box (see Figure 8.1).

2. In the Name text box, enter a name for your block. You need to give the block a name to make it easily identifiable in lists or other dialog boxes.

3. In the Base Point section, click the Pick Point button. This option lets you select a base or an insertion point for the block using your cursor. (The insertion point of a block is like its primary grip point. It is the first point you use to locate the block when it is first inserted into a drawing.) After you select this option, the Block Definition dialog box temporarily closes.

   The Block Definition dialog box gives you the option of specifying the X, Y, and Z coordinates for the base point, instead of selecting a point.

4. Pick a point that will be useful when you insert the symbol, as shown in Figure 8.2. For example, if it is a symbol for a datum point, pick its center. If it's a symbol for a door, pick the door's hinge location.

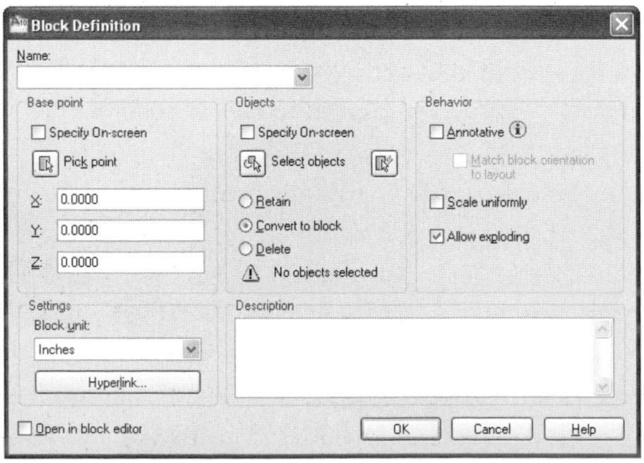

Figure 8.1

The Block Definition dialog box

After you select a point, the Block Definition dialog box reopens. Notice that the X, Y, and Z values in the Base Point section are now the coordinates of the point you picked. For two-dimensional drawings, the Z coordinate should remain at 0.

Next, you need to select the actual objects you want as part of the block.

5. In the Objects section, click the Select Objects button. Once again, the dialog box momentarily closes. You now see the familiar Object Selection prompt in the command line, and the cursor becomes an Object Selection cursor. Select the objects that you want as part of your block.

6. When you've finished your selection, press ↵ to return to the dialog box.

7. From the Block Unit drop-down list, select Inches. Metric users should select the appropriate metric measurement from the list.

8. Click the Description list box, and enter a brief description of your block.

9. Make sure that the Convert to Block radio button in the Objects section is selected. Click OK. The objects you selected in step 5 are now a block with the name you entered in step 2.

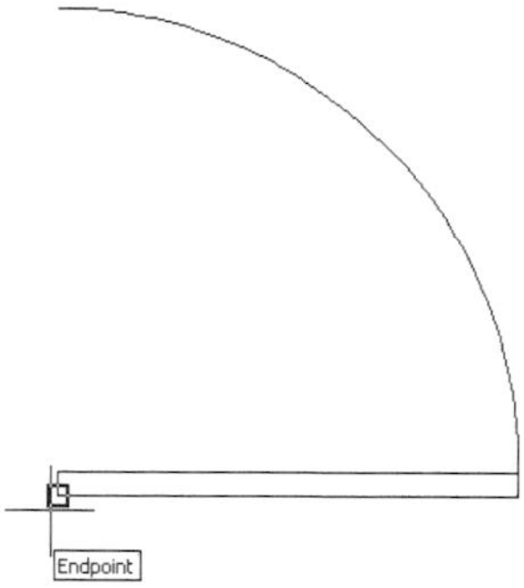

Figure 8.2

Select the insertion point.

> You can press ↵, or right-click and choose Repeat Block from the context menu, to start the Create tool again.

When you turn an object into a block, it is stored within the drawing file as a *block definition*, ready to be inserted into the drawing at any time. The block definition remains part of the drawing file even when you end the editing session. When you open the file again, the block definition is available for your use. In addition, you can access block definitions from other drawings using the AutoCAD DesignCenter and the tool palettes. You'll learn more about these tools later in this chapter.

Understanding the Block Definition Dialog Box

The Block Definition dialog box includes several options that can simplify the use of blocks. If you're interested in these options, take a moment to review the Block Definition dialog box as you read these descriptions.

You've already seen how the Name text box lets you enter a name for your block. AutoCAD does not let you complete the block creation until you enter a name.

You've also seen how to select a base point for your block. The base point is like the handle of the block. It is the reference point you use when you insert the block into the drawing. It is also the primary grip point for the block. In the previous example, you used the Pick Point option to indicate a base point, but you can also enter X, Y, and Z coordinates just below the Pick Point option. In most cases, however, you will want to use the Pick

Point option to indicate a base point that is on or near the set of objects you are converting to a block.

The Objects section lets you select the objects that make up the block. You use the Select Objects button to visually select the objects you want to include in the block you're creating. The QuickSelect button to the right of the Select Objects button lets you filter out objects based on their properties.

Other options in the Objects section let you specify what to do with the objects you're selecting for your block. Table 8.1 lists the Block Definition dialog box options and what they mean.

Table 8.1

Other Block Definition Dialog Box Options

OPTION	PURPOSE
Retain	Keeps the objects you select for your block as they are, unchanged.
Convert to Block	Converts the objects you select into the block you're defining. The block then acts like a single object once you've completed the Block Definition dialog box.
Delete	Deletes the objects you selected for your block. This is what AutoCAD did in earlier versions. You might also notice that a warning message appears at the bottom of the Objects section. This warning tells you whether you've selected objects for the block. Once you've selected objects, this warning changes to tell you how many objects you've selected.
Annotative	Allows you to apply an annotative scale to the block. This feature gives the block the ability to adjust its size to the scale of the drawing. You set the scale through the Annotative Scale setting in model view or the VP Scale setting in a layout viewport.
Match Block Orientation to Layout	Causes the block to always display in "read right" orientation in layout view.
Scale Uniformly	Locks the block's X and Y scales to their original proportions.
Allow Exploding	Allows the block created in the current Block Definition dialog box to be broken down into its component objects using the Explode command.
Block Unit	Lets you determine how the object is to be scaled when it's inserted into the drawing. By default, this value is the same as the current drawing's insertion scale.
Description	Lets you include a brief description or keyword for the block. This option is helpful when you need to find a specific block in a set of drawings.

Inserting a Block

If you delete all the blocks in a drawing, you can still insert a copy of a block at any time, as many times as you want. This is because blocks are stored within the drawing's database as block definitions and are not removed unless you specifically remove them using the Purge command.

To insert a block into the drawing area, do the following:

1. In the Home tab's Block panel, click the Insert tool or enter **i.⏎** to open the Insert dialog box (see Figure 8.3). If there are blocks in the drawing, you will see a preview of the block in the upper-right corner of the dialog box.

2. Click the Name drop-down list to display a list of the available blocks in the current drawing (see Figure 8.4). Once you select a block name, a preview will appear in the upper-right corner of the dialog box.

Figure 8.3

The Insert dialog box

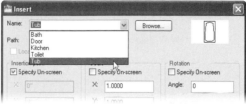

Figure 8.4

The Name drop-down list shows the available blocks in a drawing.

3. Click the name of the block you want to insert.

4. Click OK to display a preview image attached to the cursor. The base point you selected when you created the block is now on the cursor.

5. Click a point to place the block in the drawing. If the Specify On-Screen option is checked in the Insertion Point group of the Insert dialog box, the block will appear on or near the cursor, and you will be prompted for an insertion point.

Scaling and Rotating Blocks

When you insert a block, it appears at the scale and orientation that was used when the block was originally created. In some instances, you might want the block inserted at a rotated angle or at a different size from the original. The Insert dialog box provides two sets of options that let you scale or rotate your block at the time you insert it. If you turn on the Specify On-Screen option in the Rotation section of the dialog box, you are prompted for a rotation angle once you've selected an insertion point. You can specify a rotation angle either by entering an angle value from 0 to 360 or by visually selecting a rotation angle using the cursor. The block rotates with the cursor around the insertion point until you select a rotation angle. You might find that you want the rotation's Specify On-Screen option turned on most of the time so you can adjust the rotation angle of the block while you are placing it in the drawing.

The other options in the Insert dialog box that you did not use are in the Scale section. These options let you scale the block to a different size. You can scale the block uniformly, or you can distort the block by individually changing its X, Y, or Z scale factor. With the Specify On-Screen option unchecked, you can enter specific values in the X, Y, and Z text boxes to stretch the block in any direction. If you turn on the Specify On-Screen option, you'll be able to visually adjust the X, Y, and Z scale factors in real time. Although these options are not used often, they can be useful in special situations if a block needs to be stretched one way or another to fit in a drawing.

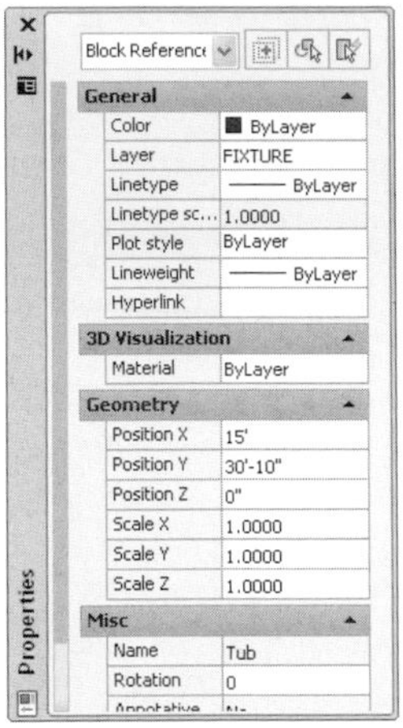

Figure 8.5

**The block
properties**

You aren't limited to scaling or rotating a block when it is being inserted into a drawing. You can always use the Scale or Rotate tool or modify an inserted block's properties to stretch it in one direction or another.

If you select the block and then open the Properties palette, you'll see the properties for the block, including the X, Y, and Z scale values (see Figure 8.5).

Take a moment to study the Properties palette. Under the Geometry heading, you'll see a set of labels that show Position and Scale. These labels might appear as "Pos" and "Sca" if you've adjusted the width of the palette to be too narrow to show the entire label.

Remember that you can drag the left or right edge of the palette to change its width, or drag the vertical separator inside the palette to adjust the width of the columns.

You can change Scale values so that the block is wider or taller than the original block. For example, you can enter **1.5** in the Scale X text box (to the right of the Scale X label) to increase its width by a factor of 1.5.

Once a block has been inserted, you can rotate or uniformly scale it using the Rotate or Scale command.

Understanding the Annotation Scale

One common use for AutoCAD's block feature is to create reference symbols. These are symbols that refer the viewer to other drawings or views in a set of drawings. An example of this would be an elevation symbol on a floor plan that directs the viewer to look at a location on another sheet to see an elevation view of a room. Such a symbol is typically a circle with two numbers, one for the drawing sheet number and the other for the view number on the sheet.

In the past, AutoCAD users had to insert a symbol multiple times to accommodate different scales of the same view. For example, the same floor plan might be used for a ¼″ = 1′-0″ scale view and a ⅛″ = 1′-0″ view. An elevation symbol that works for the ¼″ = 1′-0″ scale view would be too small for the ⅛″ = 1′-0″ view, so two copies of the same symbol would be inserted, one for each scale. The user would then have to place the two symbols on different layers to control their visibility.

The annotation scale feature does away with this need for redundancy. You can now use a single instance of a block even if it must be displayed in different scale views. To do this, you must take some additional steps when creating and inserting the block. Here's how you do it:

1. Draw your symbol at the size it should appear when plotted. For example, if the symbol is supposed to be a ¼″ circle in a printed sheet, draw the symbol as a ¼″ circle.

2. Open the Block Definition dialog box by choosing the Create tool from the Home tab's Block panel.

3. Click the Annotative option in the Behavior section of the Block Definition dialog box. You might also select the Match Block Orientation to Layout option if you want the symbol to always appear in a vertical orientation.

4. Select the objects that make up the block, and indicate an insertion point as usual.

5. Click OK.

After you've followed these steps, you'll need to apply an annotation scale to the newly created block:

1. Click the new block to select it.

2. Right-click, and choose Annotative Object Scale → Add/Delete Scales. The Annotation Object Scale dialog box appears (Figure 8.6).

3. Click the Add button. The Add Scales to Object dialog box appears, as shown in Figure 8.7.

4. Select the scale from the list you'll be using with this block. You can Ctrl+click to select multiple scales. When you have finished selecting scales, click OK. The selected scales appear in the Annotation Object Scale dialog box.

5. Click OK to close the Annotation Object Scale dialog box.

Figure 8.6

The Annotation Object Scale dialog box

Figure 8.7

The Add Scales to Object dialog box

At this point, the block is ready to be used in multiple scale views. You need only to select a scale from the model view's Annotation Scale drop-down list or the Layout view's VP (Viewport) Scale drop-down list, which are both in the lower-right corner of the AutoCAD window.

If you do not see the Annotation Scale drop-down list in the status bar, do the following: at the command prompt, enter **Statusbar⏎ 1⏎**. You can also right-click in the status bar and select Drawing Status Bar, which will display the Annotation Scale drop-down list in a status bar below the drawing area.

The Annotation Scale drop-down list appears in model view, and the VP Scale drop-down list appears in layout view and when a viewport is selected (see Chapter 12 for more about layouts and viewports). In layout view, you can set the VP Scale value for each individual viewport so the same block can appear at the appropriate size of different scale viewports (see Figure 8.8). If you need to use only one annotation scale for the block, set the Annotation Scale drop-down list first and then insert the block. The block will be given the current annotation scale automatically.

Figure 8.8

A single block is used to create different-sized elevation symbols in this layout view. Both views show the same floor plan displayed at different scales (left, ¼″ scale viewport; right, ½″ scale); the block is the same size.

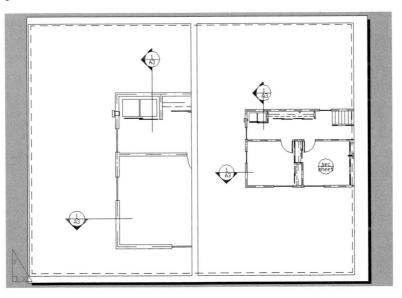

Note that if you want to use several copies of a block that is using annotative scales, you should create the block and assign the annotation scale first and then make copies of the block. If you insert a new instance of the block, you'll have to assign an annotation scale to the new instance of the block. If you are uncertain whether an annotation scale has been assigned to a block, you can click the block, and you will see the different scale versions of the block highlighted. Also, if you hover over a block, you'll see a triangular symbol next to the cursor for blocks that have been assigned annotation scales (Figure 8.9).

Figure 8.9

The Annotation Scale symbol

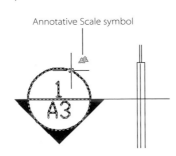

If you find you need to change the position of a block for a particular layout viewport scale, go to model view, select the appropriate scale from the Annotation Scale drop-down list, and then adjust the position of the block.

Importing an Existing Drawing as a Block

Earlier in this chapter, you saw how to create a block from a set of objects in a drawing. You can also treat external drawing files as blocks. For example, you might have drawings of a chair, a table, and other fixtures, each in its own separate file. You can insert those files as if they were blocks in the current drawing. This requires a slightly different way of using the Insert command:

1. In the Home tab's Block panel, click the Insert tool or enter **i.**↵ to open the Insert dialog box.

2. Click the Browse button to the right of the Name drop-down list to open the Select File dialog box, which is a standard AutoCAD file dialog box (see Figure 8.10).

3. Locate and select the drawing you want to insert.

4. Back in the Insert dialog box, click OK to display a preview image of the file attached to the cursor.

5. Click a point to place the block in the drawing.

> You can also use Windows Explorer to drag AutoCAD .dwg files to the AutoCAD window.

When you insert a file in this way, the file becomes a block in the current drawing, and as with any block, if you erase all instances of the inserted file from the drawing, it remains in the file as a block definition ready for you to insert again at a later time if needed. Also, be aware that if such a block is deleted from a drawing, its original source file remains untouched.

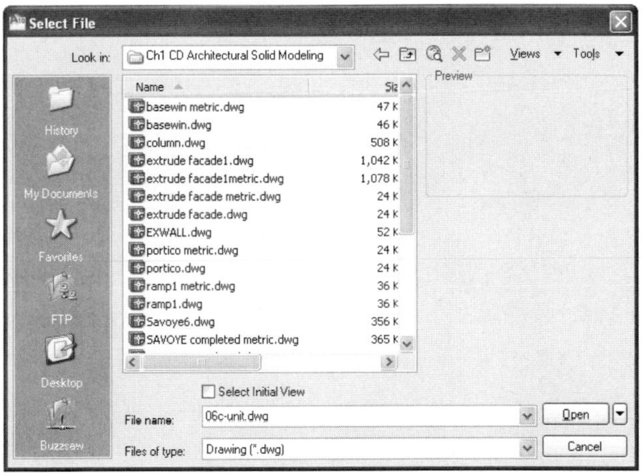

Figure 8.10

The Select File dialog box

> When you insert a drawing file as a block, AutoCAD uses the drawing's origin, 0,0, as the insertion base point. To modify the base point of any drawing, enter **Base.**↵ at the command prompt, and then select the point you want as the drawing's base point.

EDITING A BLOCK

If you need to make changes to a block, you can use the Block Editor described in Chapter 5. Remember that by updating a block definition, all instances of the block that appear in a drawing are also updated. This can help you make quick work of repetitive items in a drawing.

If you need to change only one instance of a block, use the Explode command to reduce a block to its constituent parts. If you are working on a project involving multiple AutoCAD users, make sure exploding a block is okay with your co-workers.

Saving Blocks as AutoCAD Drawing Files

As mentioned earlier, whenever you insert a drawing file using the Insert tool, the inserted drawing automatically becomes a block in the current drawing. When you redefine a block, however, you do not affect the source file you imported. AutoCAD changes the block only within the current file.

You do have the option to save changes to a block back to the original file from which it came using the Write Block feature. The following steps describe the process:

1. Issue the Wblock command by typing **Wblock**↵ or enter **w.**↵ to open the Write Block dialog box, as shown in Figure 8.11.

2. In the Source section, click the Block button.

3. Select the name of the block you want to export from the drop-down list. If the block was originally a file you imported, you'll see the original filename in the File Name and Path input box.

4. Click OK.

5. If you're replacing an existing file, you'll see a warning message telling you that the file already exists. Click Yes to confirm that you want to overwrite the old drawing with the new definition.

Figure 8.11

The Write Block dialog box

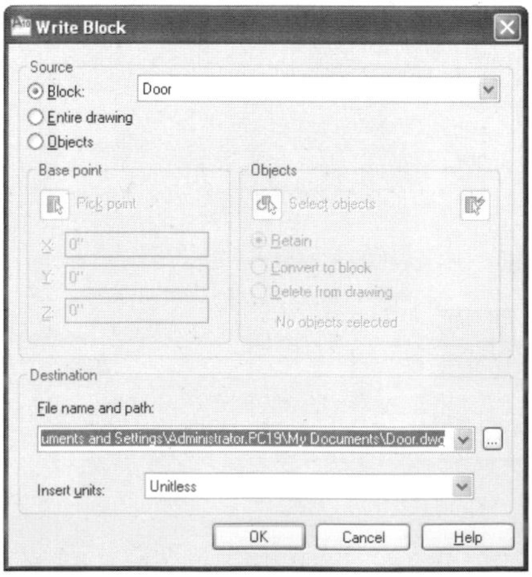

The Write Block dialog box offers a way to save parts of your current drawing as a file. In the previous exercise, you used the Block option in the Source section to select an existing block as the source object to be exported. You can also export a set of objects by clicking the Objects button. If you choose this option, the Base Point and Objects sections become available. These options work the same way as their counterparts in the Block Definition dialog box that you saw earlier.

Selecting the third option in the Source section, Entire Drawing, lets you export the whole drawing to its own file. This might seem to duplicate the Save As option in the Application menu, but saving the entire drawing from the Write Block dialog box actually performs some additional operations, such as stripping out unused blocks or other unused components. This has the effect of reducing file size. You'll learn more about this feature later in this chapter.

Organizing Objects by Using Groups

You might want to group objects so that they are connected yet can still be edited individually. For example, consider a space planner who has to place workstations in a floor plan. Though each workstation is basically the same, some slight variations in each station could make using blocks unwieldy. Using a block, you would need to create a block for one workstation and then for each variation explode the block, edit it, and then create a new block. A better way is to draw a prototype workstation and then turn it into a group. You can copy the group into position and then edit it for each individual situation, without losing its identity as a group.

AutoCAD LT offers a different method for grouping objects. If you are using LT, skip this exercise, and continue with the "Working with the LT Group Manager" section.

To create a group, you use the Object Grouping dialog box as described here:

1. Enter **g**⏎ or **Group**⏎ to open the Object Grouping dialog box, as shown in Figure 8.12.

2. Enter the name for your group in the Group Name text box.

3. Click New in the Create Group section, about midway in the dialog box. The Object Grouping dialog box temporarily closes to allow you to select objects for your new group.

4. At the Select objects: prompt, select the objects you want in your group, and then press ⏎.

5. Click OK. You have just created a group.

Figure 8.12

The Object Grouping dialog box

Now, whenever you want to select the group, you can click any part of it. However, you can still modify individual parts of the group—the desk, the partition, and so on—without losing the grouping of objects.

Toggling Groups On and Off

If you've created a group and now need to edit the individual objects in the group, you can temporarily turn off the group by pressing Shift+Ctrl+A. You'll see a message in the command line indicating whether the groups are on or off. Once they are off, you can edit the individual objects within the group. Press Shift+Ctrl+A again to turn groups back on.

Working with the Object Grouping Dialog Box

Each group has a unique name, and you can also attach a brief description of the group in the Object Grouping dialog box. When you copy a group, AutoCAD assigns an arbitrary name to the newly created group. Copies of groups are considered unnamed, but you can still list them in the Object Grouping dialog box by clicking the Include Unnamed check box. You can click the Rename button in the Object Grouping dialog box to name unnamed groups appropriately.

Objects within a group are not bound solely to that group. One object can be a member of several groups, and you can have nested groups.

> Tables 8.2 through 8.4 show the options available in the Object Grouping dialog box, which you saw in Figure 8.12. AutoCAD LT users have a different set of options. See the "Working with the LT Group Manager" section.

Use the Group Identification section to identify your groups, using unique elements that let you remember what each group's purpose is. Table 8.2 describes the Group Identification options. Table 8.3 shows the Create Group options.

The Change Group options are available only when a group name is highlighted in the Group Name list at the top of the dialog box. Table 8.4 describes those options.

> If a group is selected, you can remove individual items from the selection with a Shift+click. In this way, you can isolate objects within a group for editing or removing without having to temporarily turn off groups.

Table 8.2

The Group Identification Options

OPTION	PURPOSE
Group Name	Lets you create a new group by naming it first.
Description	Lets you include a brief description of the group.
Find Name	Finds the name of a group by temporarily closing the Object Grouping dialog box so you can click a group.
Highlight	Highlights a group that has been selected from the group list. This helps you locate a group in a crowded drawing.
Include Unnamed	Determines whether unnamed groups are included in the Group Name list. Check this box to display the names of copies of groups for processing by this dialog box.

OPTION	PURPOSE
New	Creates a new group. The Object Grouping dialog box closes temporarily so that you can select objects for grouping. To use this button, you must have either entered a group name or checked the Unnamed check box.
Selectable	Lets you control whether the group you create is selectable. See the description of Selectable in Table 8.4.
Unnamed	Lets you create a new group without naming it.

Table 8.3

**The Create
Group Options**

OPTION	PURPOSE
Remove	Lets you remove objects from a group.
Add	Lets you add objects to a group. While using this option, grouping is temporarily turned off to allow you to select objects from other groups.
Rename	Lets you rename a group.
Re-Order	Lets you change the order of objects in a group.
Description	Lets you modify the description of a group.
Explode	Separates a group into its individual components.
Selectable	Turns individual groupings on and off. When a group is selectable, it is selectable only as a group. When a group is not selectable, the individual objects in a group can be selected, but not the group.

Table 8.4

**The Change
Group Options**

Working with the LT Group Manager

If you are using AutoCAD LT, you use the Group Manager to manage groups. Table 8.5 gives a rundown of the tools that are available in the Group Manager dialog box shown in Figure 8.13.

OPTION	PURPOSE
Create Group	Lets you convert a set of objects into a group. Select a set of objects, and then click Create Group.
Ungroup	Removes the grouping of an existing group. Select the group name from the list, and then select Ungroup.
Add to Group	Lets you add an object to a group. You must select at least one group and one additional object for this option to be available.
Remove from Group	Lets you remove one or more objects from a group. To isolate individual objects in a group, first select the group, and then Shift+click to remove individual objects from the selection set. After you isolate the object you want to remove, click Remove from Group.
Details	Lists detailed information about the group, such as the number of objects in the group and whether it is in model space or a layout. Select the group name from the group list, and then click Details.
Select Group	Lets you select a group by name. Highlight the group name in the group list, and then click Select Group.
Deselect Group	Removes a group from the current selection set. Highlight the group name in the group list, and then click Deselect Group.
Help	Opens the AutoCAD LT Help dialog box and shows you information about the group manager.

Table 8.5

**The LT Group
Manager Options**

Figure 8.13

The AutoCAD LT
Group Manager dia-
log box

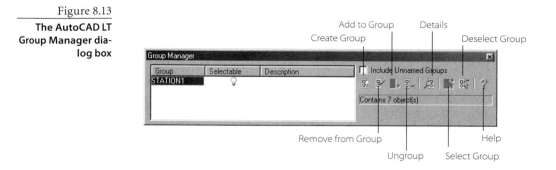

Finding Files on Your Hard Disk

As your library of symbols and files grows, you might begin to have difficulty keeping track of them. Fortunately, AutoCAD includes a utility that lets you quickly locate a file anywhere on your computer. The Find utility searches your hard disk for specific files. You can specify that it search one drive or several, or you can limit the search to one folder. You can limit the search to specific filenames or use wildcard characters to search for files with similar names.

To take a look at the AutoCAD Find dialog box, follow these steps:

1. Click the Open tool in the Quick Access toolbar to open the Select File dialog box, as shown in Figure 8.14.

2. From the Select File dialog box menu, choose Tools → Find to open the Find dialog box, as shown in Figure 8.15.

Figure 8.14

The Select File dialog box

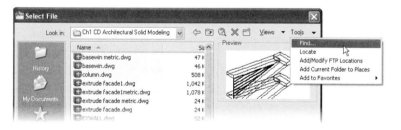

Figure 8.15

The Find dialog box

The Find dialog box has two tabs: Name & Location and Date Modified. The Name & Location tab lets you search for a file based on its location on your computer and the file type. It works in a way that is similar to the Windows Search tool. In the Named text box, enter the name of the file for which you want to search. The default is *.dwg, which in the Type drop-down list causes the Find File utility to search for all AutoCAD drawing files. The Look In drop-down list lets you specify the drive and path to be searched.

1. Click the Date Modified tab. Here you find options that let you search based on the date a file was created (see Figure 8.16).

2. When you're ready, click Cancel to exit the Find dialog box, and then click Cancel to exit the Select File dialog box.

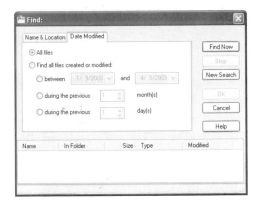

Figure 8.16

The Date Modified tab of the Find dialog box

Getting Multiple Uses from Drawings Using External References

You now know that you can insert a drawing file into the current file as a block. You can also insert a drawing file as an external reference. The difference between an Xref and a block is that an Xref does not actually become part of the drawing's database. Instead, an Xref is "loaded" along with the current file at start-up time. It is as if AutoCAD were opening several drawings at once—the currently active file you specify when you start AutoCAD and any file inserted as an Xref.

The unique feature of an Xref is that any changes you make to the Xref automatically appear in the current file containing the Xref. You don't have to update the Xref file manually as you do blocks. AutoCAD also notifies you if the Xref file has been altered.

Another advantage of Xref files is that since they do not actually become part of a drawing's database, the drawing size is kept to a minimum. This results in more efficient use of your hard disk space.

Xrefs are an excellent way to get multiple uses out of one drawing. You can create a floor plan drawing and then use it as an Xref in another file to place the plan in a site plan. You can then use the file again for enlarged views of kitchen and bath plans and again for a roof plan or overall floor plan. Since you're not duplicating the file, you save on disk and RAM space. And since all these drawings are derived from the same source, you can change the original plan, and all its Xref instances will show the same data. You don't have to update multiple drawings.

When a file is used as an Xref, you can use most of the standard commands and tools on the Xref with the exception of editing individual objects in it. You can modify its layer properties, turn layers on and off, scale, rotate, or move the Xref, and you can use osnaps to locate geometry just like any other object in your drawing. If you need to make changes to the Xref, you can either open it directly or use the Refedit command. You can issue Refedit by double-clicking an Xref. New and casual users should stick to editing Xrefs directly, because the Refedit command is a bit tricky.

You cannot cross-reference a file if the file has the same name as a block in the current drawing. If this situation occurs but you still need to use the file as an Xref, you can rename the block of the same name using the Rename command. You can also use Rename to change the name of various objects and named elements.

Attaching a Drawing as an Xref

You can attach as many files as Xrefs as you want in any drawing. The process is fairly simple, as shown in the following steps.

The Open option in the Xref Manager is not available in LT.

1. Select the Insert tab, and then in the Reference panel, click the External Reference tool in the Reference title bar. You can also enter **xr↵** to open the External References palette (see Figure 8.17).

2. Click the Attach DWG tool in the upper-left corner of the palette to open the Select Reference File dialog box. This is a typical AutoCAD file dialog box, complete with a preview.

3. Locate and select the drawing file you want to insert, and then click Open to open the Attach External Reference dialog box (see Figure 8.18). Notice that this dialog box looks similar to the Insert dialog box. It offers the same options for insertion point, scale, and rotation.

4. Click OK to proceed with the Xref insertion. If the Specify On-Screen option in the Insertion point group is turned on, you will be prompted to specify an insertion point; otherwise, the drawing is inserted in the default location, which is the origin of the current drawing.

Figure 8.17

The External References palette

In this example, you used the simplest default options in the Attach External Reference dialog box. These default settings placed the Xref in the drawing origin and used the default scale of 1:1 and a default rotation angle of 0. These settings place the Xref in the current drawing as it would appear in the original Xref file.

If you prefer, you can turn on the Specify On-Screen option for the Insert Point, Scale, and Rotation features, which in turn lets you set these values, either through the dialog box using the provided X, Y, Z, and Angle text boxes or in the drawing area using your cursor.

Figure 8.18

The Attach External Reference dialog box

If you need to temporarily remove an Xref from the current drawing, you can right-click the name of the Xref in the Xref Manager palette and then select the Unload option. Right-click the name, and use the Reload option to restore an Xref to the drawing.

IMPORTING PDFS

You can import PDF files in a way similar to AutoCAD DWG files as described in the "Attach a Drawing as an Xref" section. Open the External Reference palette as shown in step 1, but instead of clicking the Attach DWG tool, click the flyout arrowhead next to the tool. A menu opens, showing a list of different types of files you can attach. At the bottom of the list you will see Attach PDF.

Select Attach PDF. The Select Reference File dialog box opens, enabling you to locate and select a PDF file. Once you've selected a file and clicked Open, the Attach PDF Underlay dialog box appears. This dialog box allows you to select a page from the PDF if it's a multi-page PDF, and also offers the insertion point and scale options found in the Attach External Reference dialog box. Click OK to insert the file.

Once inserted, you can click on the border of the PDF image to open the PDF Underlay ribbon tab. This tab offers a number of

continues

IMPORTING PDFS *(continued)*

tools similar to those for Xrefs that enable you to control the display and other features of the PDF image.

For example, if the PDF contains layers, you can control their visibility using the Edit Layers tool. The Fade tool in the Adjust panel enables you to fade out the PDF image using a slider.

Updating an Xref While You Draw

Since an Xref is not actually part of the current drawing, other users can edit the source drawing of the Xref even while you are editing the current, referencing drawing. When a file has been modified and saved while you have it open as an Xref, the Manage Xrefs icon in the lower right of the AutoCAD window changes to show a yellow warning icon. This alerts you to make changes in an Xref in the current drawing. You might also see an alert message there.

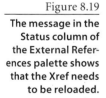

When an Xref is present in the current drawing and it has been modified, you can click the Manage Xref icon to open the External References palette. The Xref that has been changed is indicated by a message and warning symbol in the Status column of the list box, as shown in Figure 8.19.

Figure 8.19

The message in the Status column of the External References palette shows that the Xref needs to be reloaded.

You can then select the Xref that needs to be updated and click the Reload option on the context menu. You can also right-click a blank area of the External References palette and choose the Reload All Xrefs option from the context menu to reload all Xrefs in the drawing.

Differences Between Xrefs and Blocks

Although blocks and Xrefs are quite similar and can be used in similar ways, you'll want to keep in mind a few differences:

- Any new layers, text styles, or linetypes brought in with externally referenced files do not become part of the current file. If you want to import any of these items, use the Xbind command.

- If you make changes to the layers of an externally referenced file, those changes are not retained when the file is saved, unless you check the Retain Changes to Xref Layers option in the Open and Save tab of the Options dialog box. You can find this option in the External References (Xrefs) section. This option instructs AutoCAD to remember any layer color or visibility settings from one editing session to the next. In the standard AutoCAD settings, this option is on by default.

- To segregate layers in Xref files from layers in the current drawing, the Xref file's layers are prefixed with their file's name. A vertical bar separates the filename prefix and the layer name when you view a list of layers in the Layer drop-down list or the Layer Properties Manager dialog box (as in UnitXref | wall).

- You cannot explode Xrefs. You can, however, convert an Xref into a block and then explode it. To do this, select the Xref in the External References palette, right-click, and then choose Bind from the context menu. You then have the option to bind the Xref or insert it. If you choose Bind, the Xref layer names are converted by changing the vertical bar into 0. This keeps layers from the Xref separated from the layers in the current drawing. The Insert option keeps the layer names from the Xref in their original form. If an Xref contains a layer with the same name as the referencing drawing, the two layers are merged.

- If an Xref is renamed or moved to another location on your hard disk, AutoCAD won't be able to find that file when it opens other files to which the Xref is attached. If this happens, you must use the Browse button, next to the Found At option at the bottom of the External References palette, to tell AutoCAD where to find the cross-referenced file. The Browse button appears to the far right of the option when you click the Found At input box.

> Take care when relocating an Xref file with the Found At option's Browse button. The Browse button can assign a file of a different name to an existing Xref as a substitution.

Xref files are especially useful in workgroup environments in which several people are working on the same project. For example, one person might be updating several files that are inserted into a variety of other files. Using blocks, everyone in the workgroup must be notified of the changes and must update all the affected blocks in all the drawings that contained them. With Xref files, however, the updating is automatic, and you avoid confusion about which files need their blocks updated.

NESTING XREFS AND USING OVERLAYS

You can nest Xrefs; however, this can create problems with circular references. A *circular reference* is one in which the referencing drawing is actually referenced in an Xref. To avoid this problem, use the Overlay option in the External Reference dialog box. If you insert an Xref as an overlay, AutoCAD ignores any Xrefs that might be attached to the Xref you are importing into the current file.

You don't have to limit the use of the Overlay option to circular references. You can use it whenever you want Auto-CAD to ignore nested Xrefs.

Keeping Track of Drawing Components with DesignCenter

As you start to build a library of drawings, you'll find that you reuse many components. Most of the time, you'll probably be producing similar types of drawings with some variation, so you'll reuse drawing components such as layer settings, dimension styles, and layouts. Just keeping track of all the projects you've worked on can be a major task. It's especially frustrating when you remember setting up a past drawing in a way that you know would be useful in a current project but you can't remember that file's name or location.

The AutoCAD DesignCenter helps you keep track of the documents you use in your projects. You can think of DesignCenter as a kind of super Windows Explorer that is focused on AutoCAD files. DesignCenter lets you keep track of your favorite files and helps you locate files, blocks, and other drawing components. In addition, you can import blocks and other drawing components from one drawing to another by simply dragging. If you are diligent about setting the Insert Scale value in the Drawing Units dialog box and the Block Scale value in the Block Definition dialog box, you can use DesignCenter to import blocks and drawings of different unit formats into a drawing. The Insert Scale and Block Scale settings will ensure that inserted blocks and drawings will maintain their proper sizes. For example, you can import a 90-centimeter door block from a metric drawing into a drawing that uses imperial units, and DesignCenter translates the 90-centimeter door size to a 2′11.43″ door.

Getting Familiar with DesignCenter

You can adjust the DesignCenter interface in a variety of ways, so it can vary from installation to installation. Try the following steps to get familiar with DesignCenter:

1. Open AutoCAD to a new file, and then select the View tab.

2. Click the DesignCenter tool in the View tab's Palettes panel to open DesignCenter as a floating palette (see Figure 8.20).

Figure 8.20

DesignCenter opens as a floating palette.

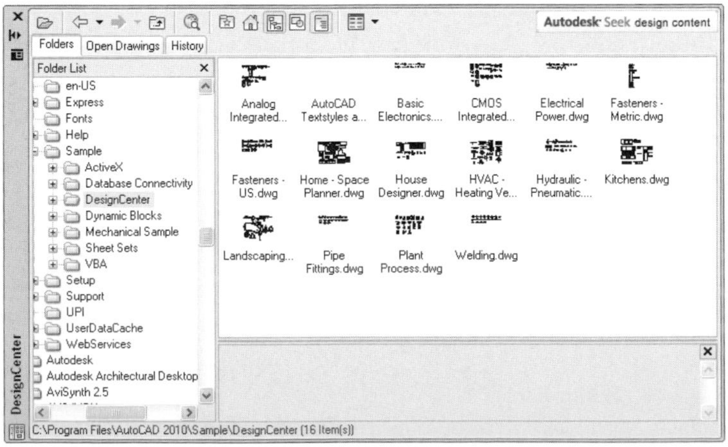

> If your DesignCenter view doesn't look like this, with the DesignCenter window divided into two parts, click the Tree View Toggle tool in the DesignCenter toolbar. The Tree view opens on the left side of the DesignCenter window. Click the Home tool to display the contents of the \Sample\DesignCenter folder.

3. Click the Favorites tool in the DesignCenter toolbar.

    DesignCenter displays a listing of the Autodesk folder. What you are looking at is a view into the C:\Documents and Settings\User Name\Favorites\Autodesk folder, where User Name is your login name. Unless you've already added items to the \Favorites\ Autodesk folder, you'll see a blank view in the panel on the right. You can add contexts to this folder as you work with DesignCenter. You can also see a view showing the tree structure of the files you have open in AutoCAD.

4. Place your cursor on the lower-right corner of the DesignCenter window so that a double-headed diagonal arrow shows; then drag the corner out so you have an enlarged DesignCenter window that looks similar to Figure 8.21. By the way, the view on the right is called the *palette view*, and the view on the left is called the *tree view*.

5. Place your cursor on the border between the tree view and the palette view until you see a double-headed cursor. Then click and drag the border to the right to enlarge the tree view until it covers about one-third of the window.

6. Finally, use the scroll bar at the bottom to adjust the tree view so you can easily read its contents.

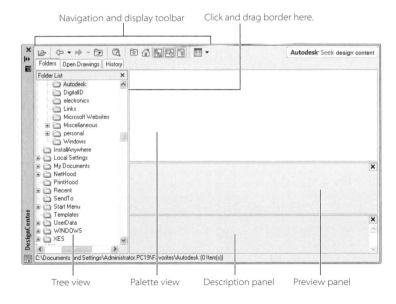

Figure 8.21

The components of the DesignCenter palette

Like the tool palettes and the Properties palette, DesignCenter has an autohide feature. To use it, click the double-headed arrow icon near the bottom of the DesignCenter title bar. DesignCenter closes except for the title bar. You can then quickly open DesignCenter by placing the cursor on the title bar.

Once you have it set up like this, you can see the similarities between DesignCenter and Windows Explorer.

Navigating DesignCenter

You can navigate your computer or network using the tree view, just as you would navigate Windows Explorer. It has a few differences, however, as you'll see in the following exercise:

1. In the DesignCenter toolbar, click the Home tool. The view changes to display the contents of the DesignCenter folder under the \AutoCAD2010\Samples\ folder, as shown in Figure 8.22.

2. Instead of the usual listing of files, you'll see sample images of each file. These are called *preview icons*.

3. Click the Views tool in the DesignCenter toolbar, and then choose Details from the menu. The palette view changes to show a detailed list of the files in the DesignCenter folder.

4. Click the Views tool again, and then choose Large Icon to return to the previous view. The Views tool is similar to the Large Icon, Small Icon, List, and Detail options in Windows Explorer.

If you select a file from the palette view, you'll see a preview of the selected file in the Preview panel of DesignCenter. You can adjust the vertical size of the Preview panel by dragging its top or bottom border.

Figure 8.22

View of the Home location in DesignCenter

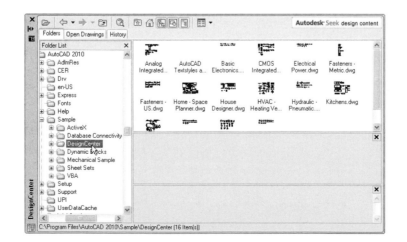

You can also open and close the Preview panel by clicking the Preview tool in the DesignCenter toolbar. The preview can be helpful if you prefer viewing files and drawing components as a list in the main part of the palette view.

Below the Preview panel is the Description panel. This panel displays any text information included with the drawing or drawing element selected in the palette view. To add a description to a drawing, choose Drawing Utilities → Drawing Properties from the Application menu; to add a description to a block, use the Block Definition dialog box.

You can open and close the Description panel by clicking the Description tool in the DesignCenter toolbar. Since the `Basic Electronics.dwg` file doesn't have a description attached, the Description panel shows the message "No description found."

Both the Preview and Description panels can offer help in identifying files. Once you find a file, you can drag it into a folder in the tree view to organize your files into separate folders.

You can also add files to the `Favorites` folder on your PC by right-clicking and then choosing Add to Favorites. The file itself won't be moved to the `Favorites` folder; instead, a context to the file is created in the `Favorites` folder. If you want to organize your `Favorites` folder, open a window to the `Favorites` folder by right-clicking a file in the palette view and choosing Organize Favorites. A window to the `Favorites` folder opens.

Viewing a DWG File's Contents

You can go beyond just looking at file listings. You can look inside files to view their components. To do this, double-click a file in the palette view. The palette view changes to display a list of the file's contents. From here, you can import any of the drawing components from the DesignCenter palette into an open drawing in AutoCAD. In the tree view, the filename is highlighted.

You'll also see Blocks as an option in the palette view. Double-click the Blocks listing, and the palette view changes to list the blocks in the drawing.

> If the block layers are turned off in the drawing you are viewing, you will not see the block previews.

Opening and Inserting Files with DesignCenter

With DesignCenter, you can locate files more easily because you can view thumbnail preview icons. But often that isn't enough. For example, you might want to locate a particular file that contains the name of a manufacturer in an attribute. Once you've found the file, you can load it into AutoCAD by right-clicking the filename in the palette view and then choosing Open in Application Window.

To insert a file into another drawing as a block, drag the file from the DesignCenter palette view into an open drawing window. You are then prompted for insertion point, scale, and rotation angle. If you prefer to use the Insert dialog box, right-click the file-name in the palette view, and choose Insert as Block to open the Insert dialog box, which presents the full set of Insert options, as described earlier in this chapter.

Finally, you can attach a drawing as an Xref by right-clicking a file in the palette view and choosing Attach as Xref. The External Reference dialog box opens, offering the insertion point, scale, and rotation options similar to the Insert dialog box.

Finding and Extracting the Contents of a Drawing

Aside from the convenience of being able to see thumbnail views of your drawing, Design-Center might not seem like much of an improvement over Windows Explorer. But DesignCenter goes beyond Windows Explorer in many ways. One of the main features of DesignCenter is that it lets you locate and extract components of a drawing.

For example, say you want to find a specific block in a drawing. You remember the name of the block, but you don't remember the drawing you put it in. You can search the contents of drawings using DesignCenter's Search dialog box.

In the DesignCenter toolbar, click the Search tool to open the Search dialog box, which looks similar to the Windows Search dialog box but contains a few extra options. For example, you can use the Look For drop-down list to select the drawing component you want to find. Choose Blocks if you are looking for a block, or choose Layers or Linetypes to search for those items (see Figure 8.23).

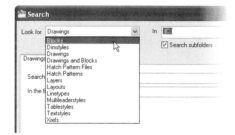

Figure 8.23

Options in the Look For drop-down list of the Search dialog box

Exploring the Search Options

You can use other options in the Search dialog box to narrow your search parameters. You already know that you can specify a particular type of drawing component. You can also specify a location. Table 8.6 describes the search options.

Table 8.6

The Options in the Search Dialog Box

OPTION	PURPOSE
In	Lets you select the drive you want to search.
Look For Options	Lets you select the type of item for which to search. See Figure 8.23 for a list of the options.
Browse	Lets you locate a specific folder to search.
Search Subfolders	Lets you determine whether Search searches subfolders in the drive and folder you specify.
Search Now	Starts the search process.
Stop	Cancels the current search.
New Search	Clears all the settings for the current search so you can start a new search.
Help	Opens the AutoCAD help system to the Search Dialog Box topic.

Finding Additional Hidden Options

When you select Drawings from the Look For drop-down list, the Search dialog box displays additional tabs.

The Drawings tab contains two options:

Search for the Word(s) Lets you specify the text to search for in the Drawing Properties fields.

In the Field(s) Lets you specify the field of the Drawing Properties dialog box to search through, including filename, title, subject, author, and keywords. You'll see these fields when you choose Drawing Utilities → Drawing Properties from the Application menu and click the Summary tab.

The Date Modified tab lets you limit search criteria based on dates.

The Advanced tab contains three options to further limit your search to specific types of drawing data or to a range of dates:

Containing Lets you select from a list of data to search for, including block name, block and drawing description, attribute tag, and attribute value.

Containing Text Lets you specify the text to search for in the types of data you select from the Containing option.

Size Is Lets you restrict the search to files greater than or less than the size you specify.

> **AUTOMATICALLY SCALING DRAWINGS AND BLOCKS AT INSERTION**
>
> When you first set up a drawing, you can specify the type of units in the Units dialog box using the Insertion Scale drop-down list. DesignCenter uses this information to correctly scale a block or drawing drawn in metric to a drawing that is drawn in the imperial format, and vice versa. The same option is offered in the Block Definition dialog box.

Exchanging Data Between Open Files

DesignCenter usually lists files in tree view, but if multiple files are open in AutoCAD, you can set up DesignCenter to display the drawing components of your open files instead. You can change the tree view to show only the drawing files that are currently open, allowing you to exchange drawing components between open files.

To change the tree view, click the Open Drawings tab. The tree view to the left shows only drawings that are currently open. Click the plus sign (+) next to the filename to explore the drawing components of the file. Once you've located a drawing component, you can drag the component from the palette view to the open drawing window. If you prefer to use the Insert dialog box for blocks, right-click the block name in the palette view, and choose Insert Block to open the Insert dialog box, in which you can set the insertion point, scale, and rotation options.

Just as with drawings, you can see a preview and descriptive text for blocks below the palette view. The preview gives you a chance to see what the block looks like when you use DesignCenter to browse through your drawing files.

You can also add the text description at the time you create the block. Before saving the block, enter a description in the Description input box of the Block Definition dialog box. If you're updating older drawing files to be used with DesignCenter, you can add text descriptions to blocks using the Create tool in the Home tab's Block panel. Click the Create tool, and then, in the Block Definition dialog box, select the name of a block from the Name drop-down list. Enter the description you want for this block in the Description input box, and click OK.

Loading Specific Files into DesignCenter

You've seen how you can locate files using the tree view and the palette view. If you already know the name and location of the file you want to work with, you can use a file dialog box to open files in DesignCenter. Instead of using the Open tool in the Quick Launch toolbar, click the Load tool in the left end of the DesignCenter toolbar to open the Load dialog box. This is a standard file dialog box that lets you search for files on your computer or network. If you want to open a file in DesignCenter that you've recently opened, you can use the History tab just above the tree view.

Downloading Symbols from Autodesk Seek

In addition to using DesignCenter to locate files and blocks on your computer or network, you can download content directly from the Autodesk Seek website. This option offers thousands of ready-to-use symbols for a variety of disciplines.

With a connection to the Internet and DesignCenter open, click the Autodesk Seek design content button in the upper-right corner of the DesignCenter palette. The Autodesk Seek website opens, as shown in Figure 8.24.

The list of symbols in Autodesk Seek is extensive and offers content for many Autodesk products besides AutoCAD. Many of the files available for AutoCAD are samples from third-party vendors that offer expanded symbol libraries.

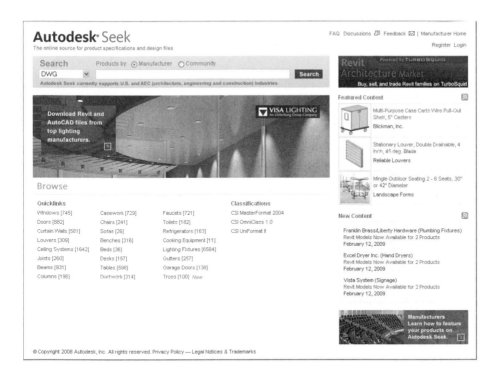

Figure 8.24

The Autodesk Seek website

Keeping Tools on Hand with the Tool Palettes Window

One item that has been fairly conspicuous in the 3D Modeling Workspace is the Tool Palettes window. The main purpose of the Tool Palettes window is to give you easy access to symbols and patterns that you use frequently. It works by giving you ready access to blocks, commands, and other features contained within drawings in your drawing library. In a default AutoCAD setup, the Tool Palettes window offers 3D modeling tools and blocks from drawings in the Samples folder of the AutoCAD installation, but you can add your own tools and blocks just by dragging them to the palette.

The Tool Palettes window provides a simple way to keep a set of blocks ready at any time. At first glance, there is no obvious way to add your own tools to the palettes. Adding tools and palettes to the Tool Palettes window is actually fairly simple. The following exercise shows you how to do it.

First, create a new palette for your custom set of objects:

1. Go to the View tab and click the Tool Palettes tool in the Palettes panel to open the Tool Palettes window.

Tool Palettes

2. Right-click a blank spot in the Tool Palettes window, and choose New Palette from the context menu. A new palette opens along with a text box.

3. Enter a name for your new palette. The new palette appears in the Tool Palettes window with a tab showing the name you just entered.

Now add your custom objects:

1. Open a file containing the block you want to add to the palette.

2. While no command is active, click the block to select it.

3. Click and hold the left mouse button on any part of the block that is not a grip until you see the cursor change to show a small rectangle, as shown in the sample image in Figure 8.25.

4. Drag the block into the tool palette. The block appears in the tool palette.

You can continue to add other blocks in this way. Once you add a block to your new palette, the block is available at any time while you are editing in AutoCAD. Just drag the block from the palette into your drawing.

You do not need the source drawing file open to access the blocks in the palette. AutoCAD remembers which file the block came from and copies the block whenever you drag a copy from the palette.

You aren't limited to blocks. You can also place hatch patterns in a palette. If you copy an object into the palette, such as a line or a text object, the command used to create the object is placed in the palette. For example, if you drag a text object into the palette, you'll see the Mtext command in the palette. If you drag a dimension into the palette, you'll see the dimension symbol that corresponds to the particular type of dimension that you dragged into the palette. For dimensions in particular, you can click the flyout arrow to select a different type of dimension, as shown in Figure 8.26.

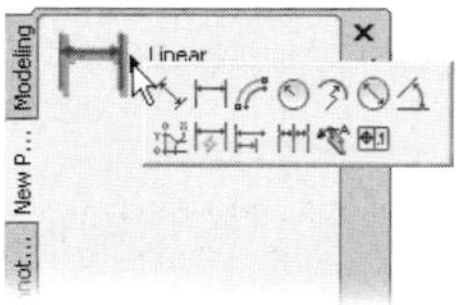

In this way, you can create a custom set of tools and symbols in one place in your AutoCAD workspace.

Figure 8.25

Selecting and clicking a block

Small rectangle below cursor

Figure 8.26

If a dimension is dragged into a palette, the dimension commands appear in the palette.

You can use DesignCenter to add drawing components from multiple files to a tool palette. Using DesignCenter, locate the drawing component you want, and then click and drag it into the tool palette.

Deleting Tools and Palettes

If you find you no longer need a block, a hatch pattern, or a command in the palette, right-click it, and choose Delete from the context menu. To delete an entire palette, right-click a blank portion of the palette, and then choose Delete Palette from the context menu. Click OK to confirm the deletion.

While deleting a palette, you might decide that you want keep one or two items. You can right-click the tool in a palette and choose Copy to copy the item to another palette. Right-click another palette, and choose Paste to paste the copied item to a different palette.

Customizing a Tool

Other context menu options let you rename tools or palettes. You can also edit the properties of symbols in a palette. For example, you can use the context menu options to change the default insertion scale of a block you've stored in a tool palette.

To do this, right-click a block in the tool palette, and then choose Properties to open the Tool Properties dialog box, as shown in Figure 8.27. Click the Scale listing, change its value to whatever scale you want for the block, and then click OK.

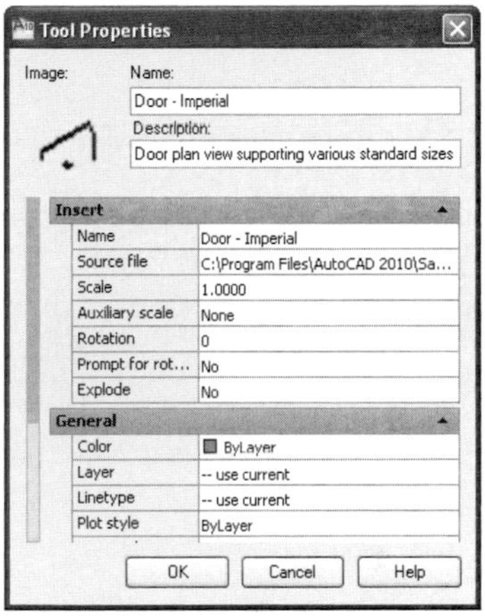

Once you've made this change, it's inserted at the new scale whenever you drag the block into your drawing from the palette.

Using this method, you can have multiple versions of a block tool at different scales. Make copies of the block tool using the right-click Copy option, and then rename the block tool in the palette. Change the scale of the copy (as described in the previous steps) using the right-click Properties option.

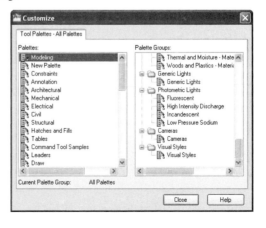

Figure 8.27

The Tool Properties dialog box

Once you've set up your block tools at different scales, you can drag and drop the tool appropriate to the scale of your drawing. And as you can see from the Tool Properties dialog box, you can modify other tool properties, such as color and layer assignments.

You can use this feature to set up sets of tools for drawings at different scales. For example, you can create a palette of architectural wall sections showing different levels of detail depending on the scale of the drawing.

You can also use the Tool Properties dialog box shown in Figure 8.27 to modify solid fills or hatch patterns you've stored in a tool palette. For example, you can add several copies of a solid fill to a tool palette and then use the Tool Properties dialog box to set a different color for each solid fill.

You can perform other types of maintenance operations on tool palettes using the Customize dialog box, which is shown in Figure 8.28. For example, you can change the order of the Tool Palettes window tabs, or you can group tabs into categories that can be turned on or off. To open the Customize dialog box, right-click Tool Palettes window, and choose Customize Palettes from the context menu.

Figure 8.28

The Customize dialog box

To change the order of the tabs, drag the tab names up or down in the left panel. If you select a palette in the left panel and right-click, you can rename, delete, import, or export a palette.

If you use the Export or Import options to move a palette from one computer to another, you must also import or export the drawings that are the source files for the palette tools.

Summary

The features covered in this chapter will help you use your drawings more efficiently. With Xrefs, you can get multiple uses from a single drawing. Blocks let you easily copy sets of objects, and much more. Other features, such as DesignCenter and the tool palettes, help you leverage the work you've done. Once you're comfortable with the basic drawing tools in AutoCAD, make sure you learn about the important features covered in this chapter.

CHAPTER 9

Creating Text

Even though AutoCAD is primarily a drawing program, you may find that you're actually adding more text than graphics to some of your drawings. In fact, annotation can often consume nearly half the time you spend on an AutoCAD drawing.

Fortunately, AutoCAD provides some familiar tools for creating and editing text. AutoCAD's Mtext command lets you place blocks of text in your drawing as short as a single sentence or as long as several paragraphs. Mtext also contains many familiar text-formatting tools, so if you've used a word processor, you should feel at home.

This chapter starts by showing you how to create new text and then discusses text formatting. You'll also learn how to use text styles and what to do when you need to add only a short, single-word note. Since you're drawing to a precise scale most of the time, you'll have to size your text appropriately for your drawing's scale. If you're creating a new drawing, be sure to check out the section on text scaling, "Understanding Text and Scale."

Finally, since tables are a prominent feature in CAD drawings, you'll learn about AutoCAD's Table command, which helps automate table creation. You'll learn how to create a table with spreadsheet-like features and how to import spreadsheets as AutoCAD tables.

This chapter includes the following topics:

- **Adding and formatting text**

- **Understanding text and scale**

- **Using styles to organize your fonts**

- **Adding single words with the single-line text object**

- **Adding tables to your drawing**

If you've recently used the 3D Modeling workspace, make sure you are back in the 2D Drafting & Annotation workspace before beginning any exercises in this chapter. See "Getting to Know the 3D Modeling Workspace" in Chapter 6 for instructions on how to switch to a different workspace.

Adding and Formatting Text

To add text in AutoCAD, you use the Mtext command, otherwise known as the Multiline Text tool. When you start the command, you must first draw a window indicating the area where your text will appear. Once that's done, the Text Editor tab appears, allowing you to enter the text you want. Here's how this works:

1. Select the Multiline Text tool from the Annotate tab's Text panel.

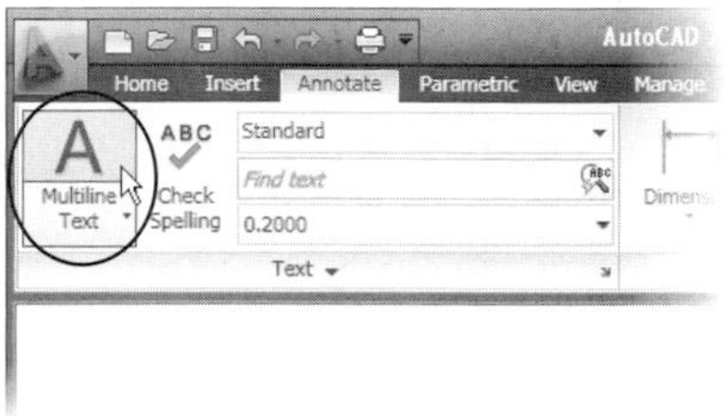

2. Click the first point indicated in Figure 9.1 to start the Text Boundary window. You don't have to be too precise about where you select the points for the boundary, because you can adjust the location and size later.

3. Click the second point to indicate the size of the text boundary. The Ribbon changes to show the Text Editor tab, and the Text window appears over the area you just selected (see Figure 9.2).

4. Start typing, and the text appears within the Text window. The size and formatting of the text is as it will appear in the drawing. The default font is a native AutoCAD font called Txt. You can also use TrueType fonts and PostScript fonts, but be aware that such fonts can slow down your work in AutoCAD, especially if you have lots of text.

5. Click the Close Text Editor panel in the Text Editor tab. The text appears in the drawing.

Figure 9.1

Indicating the text location with the text boundary

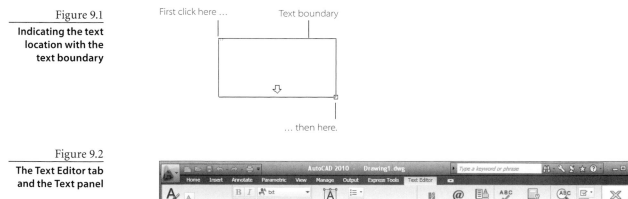

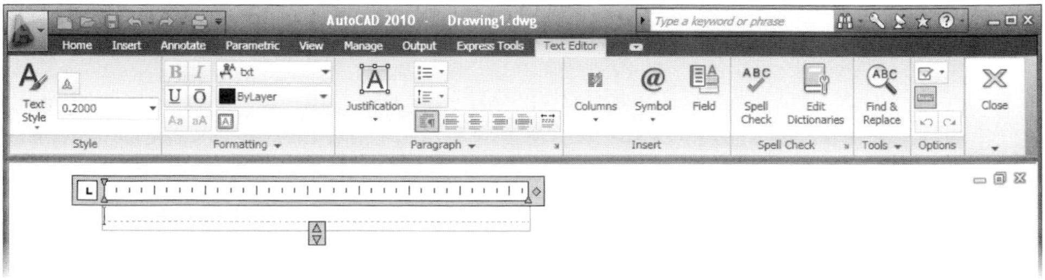

Figure 9.2

The Text Editor tab and the Text panel

The Text Editor tab and text panel work like any text editor, so if you make a typing error, you can highlight the error and then reenter the letter or word. You can also perform other word processing functions such as font and format changes. AutoCAD also automatically wraps text as you type.

AutoCAD offers many of the same tools you expect to see in a word processor. You can format the text for height and font, or you can add bold, italic, or underline with the click of a button.

Adjusting the Text Height and Font

The most common text-editing features you'll want to know about are the text height and font controls. The following example describes how to change an existing Multiline Text object:

1. Double-click an existing Mtext object to display the Text Editor tab and the text in a Text panel, as shown in Figure 9.3.

2. Select the text you want to reformat in the Text panel.

3. In the Text Editor tab, click the Text Height drop-down list, and select a text height in drawing units. Or, instead of selecting a value, click the current height value, and enter a new value. The highlighted text changes to a different size.

4. Click Close Text Editor in the Text Editor tab. The text appears in the new height.

To change the font, repeat these steps, but instead of using the Text Height drop-down list, select a font from the Font drop-down list shown in Figure 9.4.

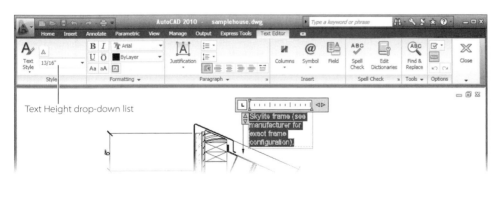

Figure 9.3

The Text Editor tab and Text panel with selected text

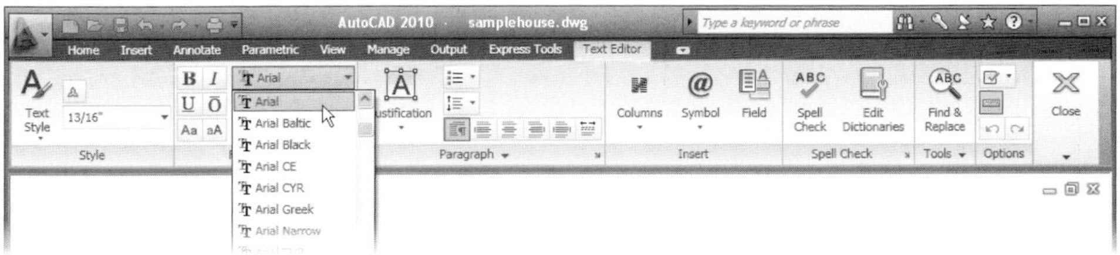

Figure 9.4

The Font drop-down list in the Text Editor tab

Using Color, Columns, Alignment, Lists, and Special Symbols

A variety of additional formatting tools are available in the Text Editor tab. Figure 9.5 shows where these tools are, and Table 9.1 describes their uses. They're fairly straightforward, and if you've used other word processing programs, you should find them easy to use. Most are common to most word processors; a few, such as Text Style and Annotative, are unique to AutoCAD.

Table 9.1

Text Formatting Tools

TOOL	USE
Bold/Italic/Underline/Overline	Select text, and then select one of these options to add bold, italic, underline or overline (line over text) to the text.
Undo/Redo	Click to undo or redo current edits.
Color	Select text, and then choose a color from this drop-down list.
Ruler	Click to turn the ruler at the top of the Text panel on or off.
Columns	Indicate the number of columns and how the columns are set up.
Paragraph/Justify/Distribute	Set up the paragraph formatting including tabs, indents, and paragraph spacing.
Line Spacing	Set the line spacing within paragraphs.
Left/Center/Right	Click the appropriate tool to align the text to the left, center, or right side of the text boundary.
Numbering	Select a list of text, click this tool, and then select Letter, Number, or Bullet to add letters, numbers, or bullets to the list.
Insert Field	Opens the Fields dialog box, allowing you to add a field text. See "Adding Formulas to Cells" later in this chapter for more about fields.
Symbol	Place the cursor at a location for the symbol, and then click the Symbol tool to find and add a symbol. (See Figure 9.6 for the available symbols.)
Oblique Angle (in expanded Formatting panel)	Select text, and then enter an Oblique Angle value. The effect is to skew the text characters in a way similar to an italic formatting.
Tracking (in expanded Formatting panel)	Select text, and then enter a tracking value in the Tracking text box. A value greater than 1 increases the spacing between letters, and a value less than 1 decreases the spacing.
Width Factor (in expanded Formatting panel)	Select text, and enter a width value in the Width text box. A value greater than 1 stretches the text, including individual letters, horizontally. A value less than 1 compresses the text, including the letters.

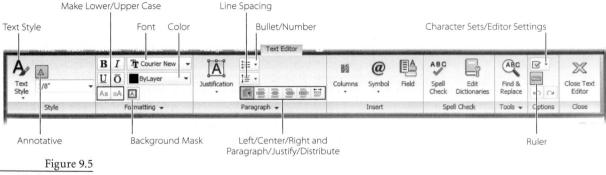

Figure 9.5

Additional features of the Text Editor tab

Degree	x°	Flow Line	℻
Plus/Minus	±	Identity	≡
Diameter	⌀	Monument Line	ℳ
Almost Equal	≈	Not Equal	≠
Angle	∠	Ohm	Ω
Boundary Line	℔	Omega	Ω
Center Line	℄	Property Line	℗
Delta	Δ	Subscript 2	x_2
Electrical Phase	φ	Superscript 2	x^2

Figure 9.6

Symbols offered by the Symbol option. See "Symbol" in Table 9.1 for information about how to use these symbols.

Adjusting the Text Boundary

Once you've placed the text in the drawing, you might find that you need to adjust the text boundary or the area that it takes up in the drawing. For example, the text might occupy a space that is too tall, and you may want to widen the Text *boundary window* so that it takes up less vertical space. The boundary window is the area within which the text is made to fit. To adjust the boundary, click the text you want to adjust. The grips appear indicating the corners of the boundary window, though you don't actually see the boundary window outline. Click a grip, and then drag to reposition the grip.

AutoCAD's word-wrap feature automatically adjusts the text formatting to fit the text boundary. This feature is especially useful to AutoCAD users, because other drawing objects often affect the placement of text. As your drawing changes, you'll need to adjust the location and boundary of your notes and labels.

Setting Indents and Tabs

When you're editing text, you'll notice the ruler at the top of the Text panel. Figure 9.7 shows that ruler, including tabs and indent markers.

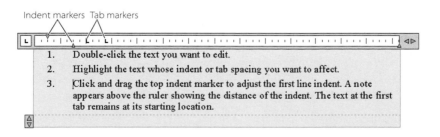

Figure 9.7

The ruler at the top of the text editor lets you quickly set tabs and indents for text.

If you need to set indents, do the following:

1. Double-click the text you want to edit to open the Text Editor tab.

2. Highlight the text whose indent or tab spacing you want to adjust.

3. Drag the top indent marker to adjust the first line indent. A note appears above the ruler showing the distance of the indent. The text at the first tab remains at its starting location.

4. Drag the bottom indent marker to adjust the indent of the body of the paragraph. The paragraph moves with the marker. You see a message at the ruler showing the distance of the indent for the body of the text.

5. Click the ruler to place tab locations. You can drag on existing tab locations to adjust them. Remove tabs by dragging them out of the ruler.

6. Click Close Text Editor in the Text Editor tab to accept your changes.

You can set paragraphs of a single Mtext object differently, giving you a wide range of indent-formatting possibilities. Just select the text you want to set, and then adjust the indent markers. You can also change the Tab Setting option to left, right, center, or decimal tabs. To select a Tab Setting option, click the tab symbol to the far left of the ruler. The symbol will change to indicate which type of tab will be placed in the ruler.

Click here to change the tab setting option.

1.   Double-click the text you want to edit to open the Text Formatting toolbar.

To set tabs, all you have to do is click the Text panel's Formatting bar (see Figure 9.7). An L-shaped marker appears in the Text panel ruler, indicating a tab position. You can add as many tab markers as you like. Once they are placed, you can move them by dragging them.

Adding a Background Mask to Text

At times you'll need to add text over other graphic elements in your drawing. For example, you might need to place a label over line work or a hatch pattern. In this situation, you'll want to add a mask behind your text to make it more readable. You can do this using AutoCAD's Background Mask feature. To use this feature, double-click the text to which you want to add a background, and then when the Text Editor tab appears, right-click the Text panel, and choose Background Mask from the context menu to open the Background Mask dialog box, shown in Figure 9.8.

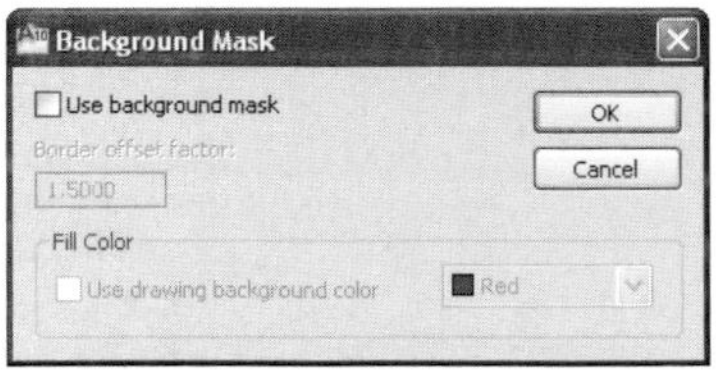

Figure 9.8

The Background Mask dialog box for text

Turn on the Use Background Mask option, and then click OK. The mask will appear in the color shown in the Color drop-down list. Optionally, you can select a different color from the list or turn on the Use Drawing Background Color option if you want the mask to take on the current background color of the drawing. The Border Offset Factor option lets you control the distance beyond the text that the mask covers. The Background Mask option is also available while you are creating and editing Multiline text. With the Text Editor tab and Text window open, highlight the text, right-click, and select Background Mask to open the Background Mask dialog box.

Making Changes to Multiple Text Objects

If you want to make changes to the text, you must focus on the specific Mtext object you want to edit. You can't open one Mtext object and expect to be able to edit any text string in the drawing. This can make global changes to text a bit trickier than usual, but you can use a few tools to make global changes easier.

Scaling Multiple Text Objects

You can quickly change the size of text by using the Scaletext command. Select the Annotate tab, and then select Scale from the expanded Text panel; or enter **Scaletext** at the command prompt. Next, select the text you want to scale. Press ↵ when you've completed your selection. You'll see the following prompt:

```
[Existing/Left/Center/Middle/Right/TL/TC/TR/ML/MC/MR/BL/BC/BR]<Existing>:
```

Enter the letters that correspond to the base point location around which the text will be scaled. You can enter **TL** for top left, **TC** for top center, **TR** for top right, and so on. Once you've entered an option, you'll see the next prompt:

```
Specify new model height or
[Paper height/Match object/Scale factor] <Current height>:
```

At this prompt you have three options. You can enter a new height; you can enter **p**↵, enter a different text height, enter **m**↵, and then select another text object whose height you want to match; or you can enter **s**↵ and then enter a scale factor to scale the text to a specific ratio.

Changing Justification of Multiple Text Objects

You've seen how you can change the justification of an individual text object. You'll often find that you need to change the justification of several text objects at one time. AutoCAD offers the Justifytext command for this purpose. To use it, open the Annotate tab and select Justify from the expanded Text panel, or enter **Justifytext**↵

at the command prompt. At the `Select object:` prompt, select the text you want to change, and then press ↲ to confirm your selection. You'll see the following prompt:

```
Enter a justification option
[Left/Align/Fit/Center/Middle/Right/TL/TC/TR/ML/MC/MR/BL/BC/BR]
<current justification >:
```

Enter the letters corresponding to the type of justification you want to use for the text. Once you've entered an option, the selected text changes to conform to the selected justification option.

Using AutoCAD's Spelling Checker

Although AutoCAD is primarily a drawing program, you will likely be including quite a bit of text in your drawings. If you're like me, you can make frequent spelling mistakes as you rush to finish a drawing. Fortunately, AutoCAD provides a spelling checker. If you've ever used the spelling checker in a typical word processor, such as Microsoft Word, the AutoCAD spelling checker's operation will be familiar to you.

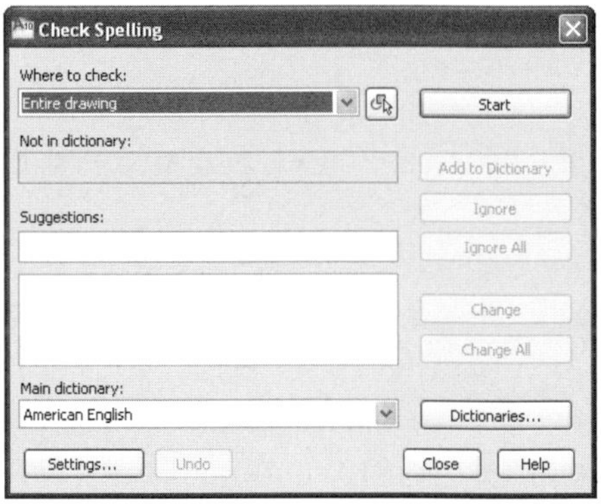

Figure 9.9

The Check Spelling dialog box

1. From the Annotate tab, select Check Spelling from the Text panel, or enter **sp**↲. The Check Spelling dialog box opens, as shown in Figure 9.9.

2. Click the Start button to check the spelling in your drawing.

3. If you want to limit the spell check to the current model or layout space, you can do so by selecting Current Space/Layout from the Where to Check drop-down list. You can further limit the spelling check to a single text object or a set of text objects.

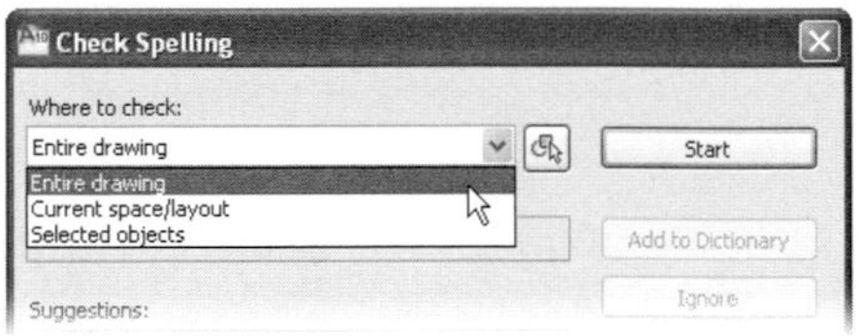

> You can choose Quick Select from the Utilities panel to select all the text in the drawing at once. Quick Select lets you select objects based on their properties or the object type, such as Line or Mtext.

In the Check Spelling dialog box, you'll see the word in question, along with the spelling checker's suggested alternative in the Suggestions input box. If the spelling checker finds more than one suggestion, a list of suggested alternative words appears below the input box, just like a in typical spelling checker. You can then highlight the desired replacement and click the Change button to change the misspelled word, or you can click Change All to change all occurrences of the word in the selected text. If the suggested word is inappropriate, choose another word from the replacement list (if any), or enter your own spelling in the Suggestions input box. Then choose Change or Change All.

Table 9.2 describes the Spelling Checker options.

OPTION	PURPOSE	
Add to Dictionary	Adds the word in question to the current dictionary.	Table 9.2
Ignore	Skips the word.	**The Spelling Checker Options**
Ignore All	Skips all occurrences of the word in the selected text.	
Change	Changes the word in question to the word you have selected (or entered) from the Suggestions input box.	
Change All	Changes all occurrences of the current word when there are multiple instances of the misspelling.	
Dictionaries	Lets you use a different dictionary to check spelling. This option opens the Change Dictionaries dialog box, described in the upcoming section.	

The dictionary in the spelling checker includes types of notation that are more likely to be found in technical drawings. It will also check the spelling of text that is included in block definitions.

Using AutoCAD's Find-and-Replace Text Feature

Just as the spelling checker plays an important role in CAD drawings, the find-and-replace function found in most word processors is also a welcome tool. AutoCAD's find-and-replace function is similar to the same tool in other word processors. A few options, however, are unique to AutoCAD. Here's how it works:

1. In the Annotate tab's Text panel, enter the text you want to locate in the Find text input box.

2. Click the Find text icon to the right of the input box. The Find and Replace dialog box appears (see Figure 9.10).

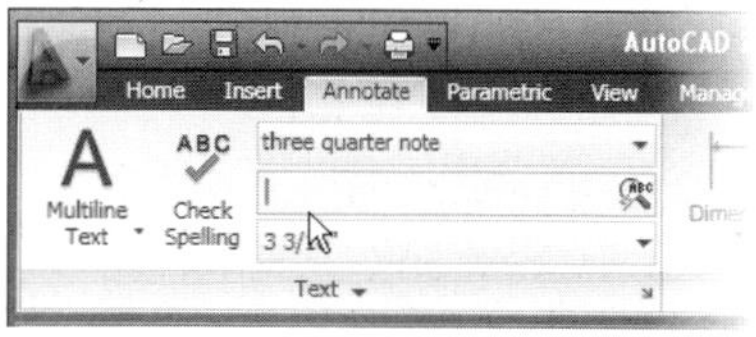

3. If you want to replace the found text with another text string, enter the replacement text in the Replace With input box, and click the Replace button.

4. Click Find Next to find the next occurrence of your text.

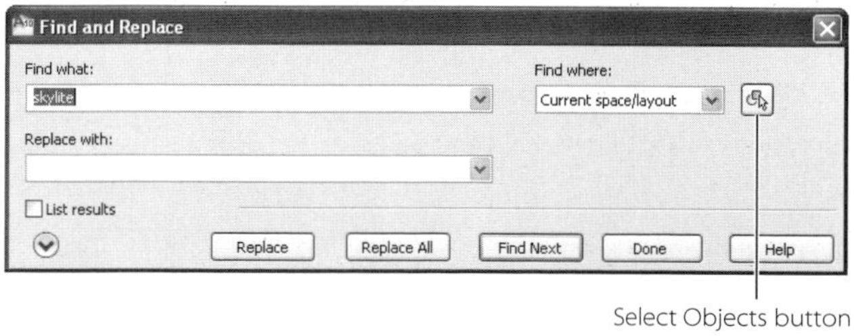

Figure 9.10

The Find and Replace dialog box

Select Objects button

If you want to replace all occurrences of a word in the drawing, click Replace All. You can also limit your find-and-replace operation to a specific area of your drawing by clicking the Select Objects button in the upper-right corner of the Find and Replace dialog box (see Figure 9.10).

When you click the Select Objects button, the Find and Replace dialog box closes temporarily to allow you to select a set of objects or a region of your drawing. The find-and-replace function then limits its search to those objects or the region you select.

You can further control the types of objects that the find-and-replace feature looks for by clicking the More Options button in the lower-left corner of the Find and Replace dialog box to expand the dialog box (see Figure 9.11). With these additional options, you can refine your search by limiting it to blocks, dimension text, standard text, or hyperlink text. You can also specify whether to match case or find whole words only.

Figure 9.11

The expanded Find and Replace Options dialog box

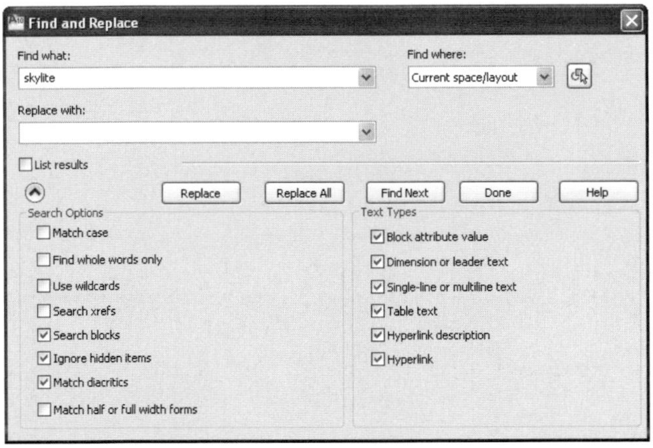

Importing Text Files from Other Programs

With multiline text objects, AutoCAD allows you to import ASCII text or rich text format (RTF) files. RTF files can be exported from Microsoft Word and most other word processing programs and retain their formatting in AutoCAD.

To import text, first select the text from your document, and then choose Edit → Copy or press Ctrl+C to copy the text to the Windows Clipboard. In AutoCAD, choose Paste Special from the Paste flyout on the Home tab's Clipboard panel to open the Paste Special dialog box. Click the Paste button, and then select AutoCAD Entities from the As list box. Click OK. You'll see the text drag into the drawing area as a bounding box. Click a location to place your text. The inserted text will use the current text-style formatting.

You can also import entire text files by doing the following: start the Mtext command, then right-click in the Text window, and finally select Import Text. The Select File dialog box opens and allows you to locate and select a text file. You can import plain-text files (.txt) or RTF files (.rtf).

Understanding Text and Scale

AutoCAD allows you to draw at full scale, that is, to represent distances as values equivalent to the actual size of the object. When you later plot the drawing, you tell AutoCAD at what scale you want to plot, and the program reduces the drawing accordingly. This gives you the freedom to enter measurements at full scale and not worry about converting them to various scales every time you enter a distance.

On the other hand, text and dimensions that annotate a drawing don't follow the same rules when it comes to drawing scale. Since text size and dimension size are determined by their final print size, you need a way to include them in a drawing at the size you want for the scale of the drawing. For example, the typical size of text in a technical drawing is about ⅛″ high. If you draw text at that size in your full-scale drawing, the text will appear very small. Fortunately, AutoCAD offers the annotation scale feature that automatically adjusts the size of text and dimensions to fit the scale of the drawing.

Using Annotative Scale

To use the annotation scale feature, you must use text and dimensions that have their Annotative Scale property turned on. You can do this to existing text and dimensions by following these steps:

1. Select the Text or Dimension object.

2. Right-click, and select Properties.

3. In the Properties palette, find the Annotative setting in the Misc panel, and make sure it's set to Yes.

   If you're creating new text, you can use the Annotative text style that already has the Annotative setting turned on. You can select the Annotative text style by selecting it from the Text Style drop-down list in the expanded Annotation panel. You can also create a custom text style (see "Using Styles to Organize Your Fonts" later in this chapter). For dimensions, you can use the Annotative dimension style, which you can select from the Dimension Style drop-down list in the Annotation panel (see "Using Dimensions" in Chapter 10).

Adding Scales to Your Text

Once you have the Annotative setting turned on for your text, you need to add the scale you intend to use. Here's how to do this:

1. Select the text you want to set up for a particular scale.

2. Right-click, and then choose Annotative Object Scale → Add/Delete Scale. The Annotation Object Scale dialog box appears.

3. Click the Add button. The Add Scale to Object dialog box appears.

4. Select the scales you intend to use for the drawing from the list. You can use Ctrl+click to select multiple options from the list.

5. Click OK, and then click OK again in the Annotation Object Scale dialog box.

Once you've done this, you can set the size of your text by selecting a scale from the Annotation Scale drop-down list at the lower-right corner of the AutoCAD window.

Or if you're in a layout view, you can set the VP Scale setting or Annotation Scale drop-down list, but you won't see these lists unless a viewport is selected.

> If you encounter an older AutoCAD file, the text will not have the Annotative feature but will be set to a fixed size, which is usually quite large. If you need to add text, you can set up any new text to use the Annotative feature, or you can copy existing text and edit it to keep the text size and font consistent.

Using Styles to Organize Your Fonts

As you start to use AutoCAD, you'll notice a lot of styles—styles for dimensions, styles for plotting, and styles for text. If your drawing is fairly simple, you might not need to worry about text styles. But if you are working with a large drawing project, you'll want to set up a few text styles. If you are working with others on a large project, you'll almost certainly encounter text styles, so it will help to know about them.

You can think of text styles as a way to store your most common text formatting. Styles store text height and font information, so you don't have to reset these options every time you enter text. You might have a style for notes, another for larger drawing labels, and yet another for title block information. And styles also include some settings not available in the Text Editor tab.

Creating and Setting a Style

Even if you don't set up a style on your own, the moment you add text to a drawing, you're using a text style. In AutoCAD, the Standard text style is the default. It uses the AutoCAD Txt font and numerous other settings that you'll learn about in this section. These other settings include Width Factor, Oblique Angle, and Default Height.

If you've followed the instructions in the previous sections of this chapter to create text, you know that you can modify the formatting of a string of text as you enter the text. But for the most part, once you've set up a few styles, you won't need to adjust settings such as fonts and text height each time you enter text. You can select from a list of styles you've previously created and just start typing.

The following exercise shows you how to create a style:

1. In the Annotate tab, click the Text Style tool in the title bar of the Text panel, or enter **st⏎** to open the Text Style dialog box (see Figure 9.12).

2. Click the New button to open the New Text Style dialog box.

3. Enter a name for your new style; then click OK.

4. To select a font for your style, click the Font Name drop-down list in the Font group.

5. In the Height input box, enter the text height you want for your style, or leave it as 0 if you want more flexibility in determining the text height when you create text.

6. Click Apply, and then click Close.

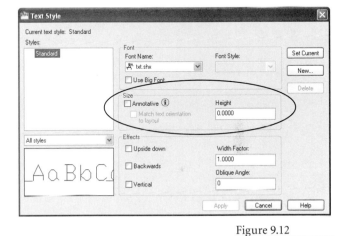

Figure 9.12

The Text Style dialog box

Your new style becomes the default style whenever you use the Mtext or Text command.

To rename a text style, select the style name in the Styles list box, right-click, and then select Rename. The name will be highlighted, allowing you to enter a new name.

Using a Text Style

As you add text to your drawing, you can easily switch between text styles. To change the default text style, do the following: in the Annotate tab's Text panel, select the text style from the Selects a Text Style drop-down list, as shown in Figure 9.13.

The selected style becomes the current, default style.

You can also change the style of existing text by using the Multiline Text editor. Double-click a text object, and then, in the Text panel, select the text whose style you want to change. Next, select the style from the Style drop-down list on the Text Editor tab (see Figure 9.14).

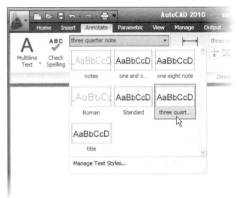

Figure 9.13

The Text Style drop-down list in the Text panel

Figure 9.14

The Style drop-down list on the Text Editor tab

Now you know how to create and use a new style. Other settings are available in the Text Style dialog box. Table 9.3 describes those settings and their purposes. Some of them, such as the Width Factor, can be quite useful. Others, such as the Backwards and Vertical options, are rarely used.

Table 9.3

The Text Style Settings

SECTION	OPTIONS	PURPOSE
Buttons	Set Current	Sets the current text style. Select a style from the Styles list, and click the Set Current button.
	New	Lets you create a new Text style.
	Delete	Deletes a style. This option is not available for the Standard style.
	Help	Opens the Help window and displays information about the Text Style dialog box.
Font	Font Name	Lets you select a font from a list of available fonts. The list is derived from the font resources available to Windows, plus the standard AutoCAD fonts.
	Font Style	Offers variations of a font, such as italic or bold, when they are available.
	Use Big Font	Allows the use of Asian-language big font files.
Style	Annotative	Controls whether the text uses the Annotative feature for automatic scaling of text.
	Match Text Orientation to Layout	Controls whether annotative text is "read right" regardless of view orientation.
	Paper Text Height	Lets you enter a height for text. For Annotative text, you can set the height of text in the printed output.
Effects	Upside Down	Prints the text upside down.
	Backwards	Prints the text backward.
	Vertical	Prints the text vertically.
	Width Factor	Adjusts the width and spacing of the characters in the text. A value of 1 keeps the text at its regular width. Values greater than 1 expand the text, and values less than 1 compress the text.
	Oblique Angle	Skews the text at an angle. When this option is set to a value greater than 0, the text appears italicized. A value of less than 0 (–12, for example) causes the text to "lean" to the left.

Adding Single Words with the Single-Line Text Object

You may find that you're entering a lot of single words or simple labels that don't require all the bells and whistles of the Multiline Text editor. AutoCAD offers the *single-line text object*, which is simpler to use and can speed text entry if you're adding only small pieces of text.

1. Click the Single Line Text tool in the Text flyout on the Home tab's Annotation panel, or enter **dt**↵ to issue the Dtext command.

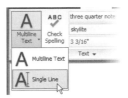

2. At the `Specify start point of text or [Justify/Style]:` prompt, select the starting point for the text. Notice that the prompt offers the Justify and Style options.

3. If the current text style has a height of zero, the `Specify height:` prompt appears. You can enter a height value or indicate a height by clicking two points in the drawing area. You can also just press ↵ to accept the default height.

4. At the `Specify rotation angle of text <current rotation angle>:` prompt, enter a rotation angle, or press ↵ to accept the default, 0. You can specify any angle other than horizontal (for example, if you want your text aligned with a rotated object). Once you've entered an angle, you'll see a text I-beam cursor at the point you selected in step 2.

5. At the `Enter text:` prompt, enter the text you want. As you type, the word appears in the drawing as well as in the command window.

6. Press ↵ to move the cursor down to start a new line, or click a location in the drawing area to move to an entirely different location to continue your text.

7. Press ↵ without entering text to exit the Dtext command.

You can add single lines of text in different parts of your drawing fairly quickly. Dtext uses the current default text style setting.

If you make a typing error while using Dtext, you can select the text in the drawing with your cursor and make the appropriate changes just as you would in a word processor. You can also paste text from the Clipboard into the cursor location by using the Ctrl+V keyboard combination or by right-clicking the command line to access the context menu.

Even if you don't create Dtext objects, you may encounter them as you edit drawings created from other sources. Fortunately, they are easy to edit.

When you double-click a Dtext object, the text highlights and a box appears around the text. You can then either start typing to replace the entire text or click a location to add or delete text, just as you would in any text editor.

If you need to change other properties of single-line text, you can use the Properties palette. Select the Dtext object, and then right-click and choose Properties from the context menu. You can then edit the text-related properties such as style, height, rotation angle, and width factor. (See Chapter 4 for more about the Properties palette.)

Adding Tables to Your Drawing

One of the most common text items in a drawing is the table (or *schedule* as it is often called in architectural drawings). Tables are often used for lists of parts that include specifications and part numbers, as shown in Figure 9.15. Tables provide vital information about a design that cannot be conveyed by drawings alone.

		Room Finish Schedule					
No.	Room	Finish				Ceiling Ht.	Area	Remarks
		Floor	Base	Walls	Ceiling			
110	Lobby	B	1	A	1	10'-0"	200sf	
111	Office	A	1	B	2	8'-0"	96sf	
112	Office	A	1	B	2	8'-0"	96sf	
113	Office	A	1	B	2	8'-0"	96sf	
114	Meeting	C	1	B	2	8'-0"	150sf	
115	Breakout	C	1	B	2	8'-0"	150sf	
116	Womens	D	2	C	3	8'-0"	50sf	
117	Mens	D	2	C	3	8'-0"	50sf	

Figure 9.15

A sample schedule created with the Table tool

Frequently, tables are generated in a spreadsheet since the tabular format of spreadsheets fits with the table format. The AutoCAD table feature gives you an easy way to include tables with your drawing, either by creating them directly in AutoCAD or by importing them from spreadsheet files.

Creating a Table

Before you create your table, you need to know the number of rows and columns you'll want. Don't worry if you're not certain of the exact number; you can add or subtract them at any time. For practice, you can create a table that contains four rows and five columns.

Start by creating the basic table layout:

1. In the Home tab's Annotation panel, click the Table tool or enter **Tb↵** to open the Insert Table dialog box (see Figure 9.16).

2. In the Column & Row Settings group, enter **4** for Columns and **5** for Data Rows.

3. Click OK. The dialog box closes, and you see the outline of a table follow your cursor.

Figure 9.16

The Insert Table dialog box

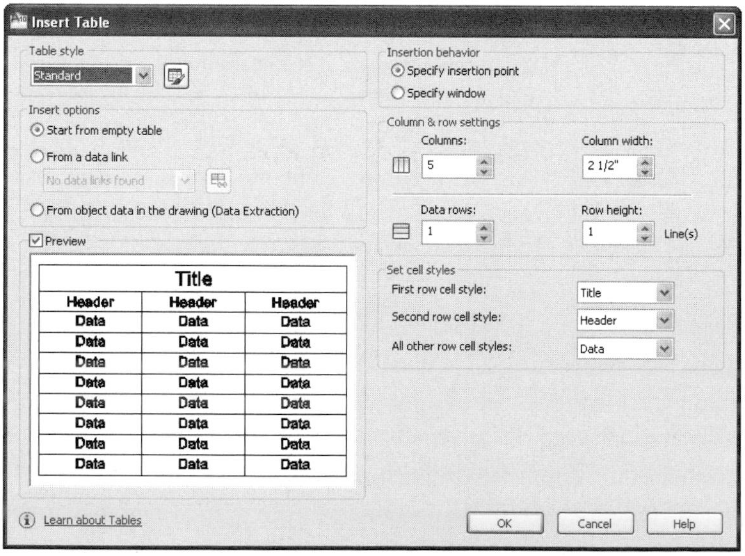

4. Position the table in the center of your drawing area, and click to place the table. The table appears with a cursor in the top cell. You also see the Text Editor tab appear in the Ribbon panel area.

5. Enter a title for your table, and then press ↵. Notice that the cursor moves to the next cell.

6. When you have finished entering text in the table, click Close Text Editor in the Text Editor tab, or just click outside the table.

Once you've finished, you'll have a table with two additional rows besides the five data rows you indicated in step 2—the title row at the top, which has only one column, and a row for the column heads.

Adding Cell Text

Once you have the table in place, you can easily add text to the individual cells. Just double-click inside a cell to open the Text Editor tab (see Figure 9.17). A text cursor appears inside the cell, allowing you to type the text you want. The Text Editor tab lets you format the text.

Double-click inside a cell to add text.

Figure 9.17
A table cell ready for editing

Combining Cells

When formatting your table, you might want to merge adjacent cells to create larger cells for headings or for other purposes. Here are the steps to follow to merge cells:

1. Click the first cell you want to merge. The Table Cell tab appears, and the cell displays its grips (see Figure 9.18).

2. Shift+click the cell at the other end of the group of cells you want to merge (see Figure 9.19). The group of cells is selected.

3. Right-click the selected cells, and then choose Merge → All from the context menu. The selected cells merge into a single cell. You can also click the Merge Cell tool on the Merge panel of the Table Cell tab.

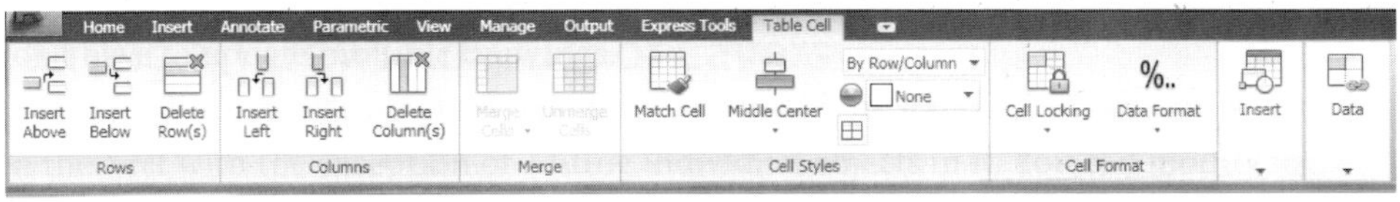

Figure 9.18
The Table Cell tab appears when you click a table cell. This tab offers typical spreadsheet tools for formatting cells or adding formulas to cells.

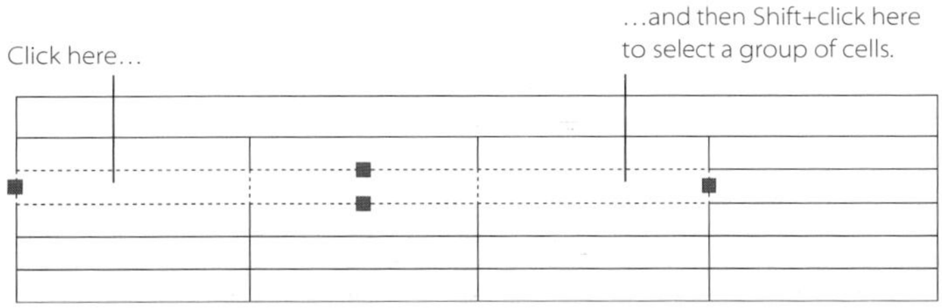

Click here…

…and then Shift+click here to select a group of cells.

Figure 9.19
Selecting a group of cells in a table

You have the option to restrict the merging of cells to rows (choose Merge → By Row) or to columns (choose Merge → By Column) in the context menu in step 3.

> You saw how the Table Cell tab appears when you click a cell. If you click a cell and then start typing, the Table Cell tab is replaced by the Text Editor tab to allow you to make formatting changes to the cell text.

Adjusting Table Cell Text Orientation

You can adjust the orientation of the text in cells to accommodate different table styles. For example, to use space more efficiently, a table frequently has column headings that are oriented vertically. The following exercise shows you how to change the text orientation from horizontal to vertical. Before you start, it will help to have text already placed in the cells you're editing so you can adjust the cell size as you work.

1. Click the cell to select it. You should see the cell grips. If not, press Esc, and click the cell again.

2. Shift+click another cell to select a group of cells.

3. Click the grip at the bottom of the selected group, and move it down. The entire row becomes taller, as shown in Figure 9.20. This provides room for the text when you rotate it.

Figure 9.20

A group of cells selected and made taller

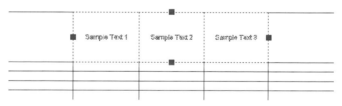

4. Right-click the selected cells, and then choose Properties from the context menu to open the Properties palette.

5. Click the Text Rotation option in the Content group.

6. Change the text rotation value to 90 (see Figure 9.21). The text rotates into a vertical orientation.

   With the text in this orientation, the columns are too wide, so you'll want to change the cell width for the selected cells.

7. With the Properties palette still open, click the Cell Width option near the top of the palette, and then enter an appropriate value for the cell width. You

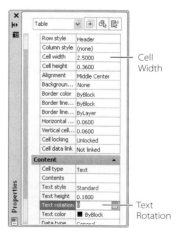

Figure 9.21

The Text Rotation option in the Properties palette

might need to experiment with this value until you get something that looks appropriate. The cells change to their new width.

You can also adjust the width of multiple cells by adjusting the grip location, as shown in Figure 9.22. For example, instead of changing the cell width value in step 7, you can move the left or right grip of the selected group of cells.

Adjusting Table Cell Text Justification

Besides text orientation, you can change the justification of text within the cells. Here's how:

1. Select a cell or click a cell, and Shift+click another cell to select a group.

2. Right-click the selected cells, and choose Alignment → Middle Center. The text is centered in the cells. You can also click the alignment flyout arrow in the Table Cell tab's Cell Styles panel, and select Middle Center from the list that appears.

You can also control the margin between the text and the cell border for the entire table by using the Cell Margin options in the Properties palette. Select the entire table, right-click, and choose Properties. In the Properties palette, click the Vertical Cell Margin option or the Horizontal Cell Margin option in the Table group (see Figure 9.23).

Adding or Deleting Rows and Columns of Cells

Now suppose you want to delete a row of cells in a table. Here's what to do:

1. Click a cell in the row you want to delete.

2. Right-click, and then choose Rows → Delete.

To add a row, do the following:

1. Select a cell adjacent to the location where you want a new row.

2. Right-click, and choose Rows → Insert Above or Rows → Insert Below, depending on where you want the new row.

You might notice a Columns option in the context menu. The Columns option works in a similar way to the Rows option, letting you insert a column to the left or right of a selected cell.

All of these options are also available on the Table Cell tab. See Figure 9.18 earlier in the chapter for their locations.

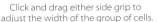
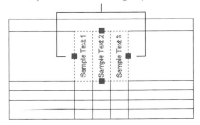
Click and drag either side grip to adjust the width of the group of cells.

Figure 9.22

Adjusting the width of a group of cells

Figure 9.23

The Vertical Cell Margin option in the Properties palette

Adding Formulas to Cells

One of the greatest benefits of using spreadsheets is that you can apply formulas to the values in a cell. AutoCAD's table feature lets you include formulas in cells so you don't have to rely on an external spreadsheet program when generating tables.

1. Click the cell where you want to place your formula. The Table Cell tab appears.

2. Click the Formula flyout in the Table Cell tab's Insert panel, and select Sum, as shown in Figure 9.24. You may have to expand the Insert panel to see the Formula flyout.

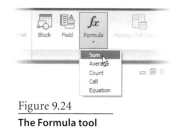

Figure 9.24

The Formula tool

3. Select the cells that bracket the value you want to add by placing a selection window inside the cells. For example, to get the sum of the top four cells in Figure 9.25, click inside the first cell A2, and then complete the selection window by clicking in cell B3. The formula appears in the cell you selected in step 1 (see Figure 9.26). In addition, the Text Editor tab appears in place of the Table Cell tab. This enables you to modify the formula if you need to do so.

4. Click OK, and you'll see the Sum value in the cell you selected in step 1.

You'll notice that the cell with the formula shows a gray background. This background indicates that the cell contains a formula, which is actually a special type of text called a *field*. This background does not print; it is there to help differentiate fields from other types of text.

Figure 9.25

Selecting a cell range for the Sum function

	A	B	C	D
1				
2	100	150		
3	200	250		
4	300	350		
5	400	450		
6	500	550		
7				

Click on cell A2...   ...then click in cell B3.

Figure 9.26

The cell with the new formula

	A	B	C	D
1				
2	100	150	=Sum(A2:B3)]	
3	200	250		
4	300	350		
5	400	450		
6	500	550		
7				

Using Other Math Operations

In the previous example, you saw how you can use the Sum option in the Formula drop-down menu. If you look again at the options in that menu (shown in Figure 9.24), you'll see the Equation option. If you select that option, you can enter your own formula directly in the cell. The Equation option simply adds the equal sign to the cell before you start typing.

Once you select the Equation option, you can string several cell addresses together to add multiple cells, as follows:

```
=A2+A3+A4...
```

You can also subtract, multiply, or divide by using the – (subtract or minus), * (multiply or asterisk), or / (divide or hash) keys. To perform multiple operations on several cells, you can group operations with parentheses. For example, if you want to add two cells together and then multiply their sum by another cell, you can use the following format:

```
=(A2+A3)*A4
```

You might have noticed the Average and Count buttons that appear in the Formula drop-down list. Average gives the average value of a range of cells, and Count returns the number of cells you select. Once you've selected a set of cells, you'll see a formula appear in the cell that automatically applies the operation to the selected cells. For example, clicking the Average button produces a formula similar to the following:

```
=Average(A1:B5)
```

A range of cells is indicated using a colon as in A1:B5. You can use this format when entering formulas manually. You can also include a single cell with a range by using a comma, as follows:

```
=Average(A1:B5,C6)
```

Adding Formulas Directly to Cells

If you're in a hurry, you can add a formula directly to a cell without using the Formula tool. To do this, double-click the cell, and then when the Text Editor tab appears, enter the formula with the addition of an = (equal sign) at the beginning, as in the following:

```
=A2+A3
```

The cell automatically converts to a formula field with the appropriate value. The only drawback to this method is that you have to decipher the cell address on your own. If you click a cell, the cell row and column labels appear to help you find the appropriate address.

Editing Formulas

Finally, if you want to change a formula, you can double-click the Formula cell to open the Text Editor tab. You can edit the formula directly in the cell or use the Formula tool to create a new formula.

Exporting Tables

In some situations, you'll want to export your AutoCAD table to a spreadsheet program or a database. You can do this through a somewhat hidden option in a context menu. Take the following steps:

1. Select the entire table by clicking the table border.

2. Right-click anywhere outside the table, and then choose Export from the context menu to open the Export Data dialog box. This is a typical file dialog box.

3. Specify a name and location for your exported table data, and click Save.

Notice that the file is saved with a .csv filename extension. This is a common spreadsheet file format known as a *comma-delimited file* and can be read by most spreadsheet programs, including Microsoft Excel. To open the exported file in Excel, choose the Open tool to open the Open dialog box, and then select Text File (*.prn, *.txt, *.csv). You can then locate the exported table and open it.

Tables exported to Excel lose their formulas. Formula cells are converted to simple values.

Importing Tables

It's not unusual for a table to be generated in an Excel spreadsheet by someone other than the person drawing plans in AutoCAD. You can easily import Excel spreadsheets into AutoCAD and convert them to AutoCAD tables.

You can import Excel files in two ways: you can copy and paste data directly from Excel to AutoCAD, or you can create a data link. With the cut-and-paste method, you'll get a simple copy of the imported data, but if you use a data link, the imported data is updated whenever the source Excel file changes.

To perform a simple copy-and-paste operation, do the following:

1. In Excel, select the cells you want to export, and then press Ctrl+C.

2. In AutoCAD, click the Paste flyout on the Home tab's Clipboard panel and select Paste Special to open the Paste Special dialog box (see Figure 9.27).

3. Select AutoCAD Entities from the list box, and then click OK. The imported spreadsheet appears at the cursor.

4. Click to place the spreadsheet in the drawing.

Once the spreadsheet is placed, you can use any of the table-editing methods described in this chapter to adjust its appearance.

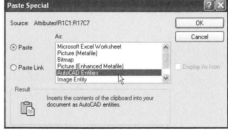

Figure 9.27
The Paste Special dialog box

If you'd like to import a table that is linked to the source Excel spreadsheet, make sure the Paste Link radio button is selected in the Paste Special dialog box shown in Figure 9.27.

Besides importing entire Excel spreadsheet cells, you can also import parts of a spreadsheet into an existing table by doing the following:

1. Select a cell or set of cells, and click the Link Cell tool in the Table Cell tab's Data panel. You may need to expand the Data panel to find the Link Cell tool. The Select a Data Link dialog box appears, as shown in Figure 9.28.

2. Click the Create a New Excel Data Link listing in the list box. The Enter Data Link Name dialog box appears.

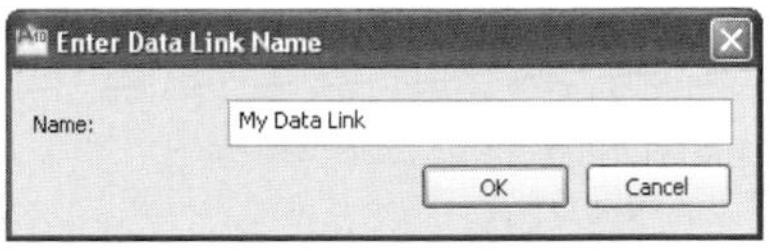

3. Enter a name for your data link, and then click OK. The New Excel Data Link dialog box appears, as shown in Figure 9.29.

4. Click the Browse button in the upper-right corner of the dialog box next to the drop-down list and browse to the Excel file you want to import. Once you've made your selection, a preview of your table appears in the dialog box, as shown in Figure 9.30. You also see some additional options that allow you to select the elements of the spreadsheet to import.

5. Select Link Entire Sheet or use the Link to Range option to select a range of cells.

6. Click OK in the New Excel Data Link dialog box and again in the Select a Data Link dialog box.

Once you've taken these steps, you'll be notified of changes made to the original spreadsheet and will be given the option to update the imported table with the new data in the source spreadsheet.

> If the spreadsheet is large, AutoCAD may pause a moment while importing the data in step 5.

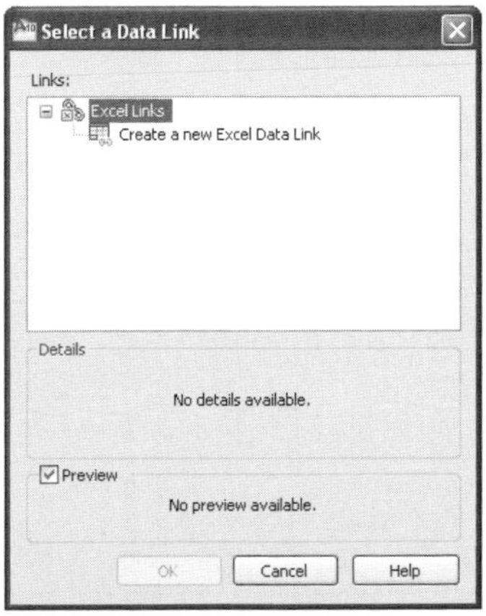

Figure 9.28
The Select Data Link dialog box

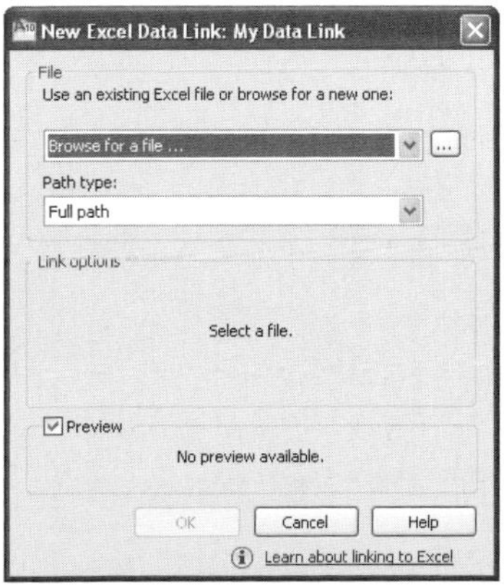

Figure 9.29
The New Excel Data Link dialog box

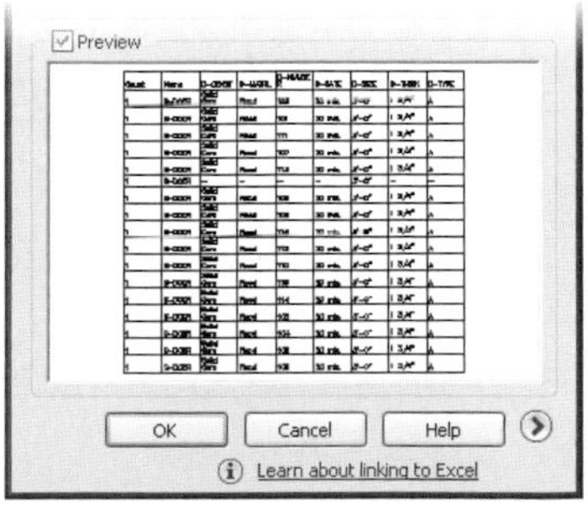

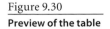

Figure 9.30
Preview of the table

Editing Table Lineweights

The text in a table is not the only part that you may want to control. The line work within the table is also important. You can emphasize parts of a table by making the lineweight bolder for certain groups of cells, for example.

> Before you can see the effects of the lineweight settings for cell borders, you need to turn on the display of lineweights. From the Home tab's Properties panel, click the Lineweight drop-down list, select Lineweight Settings, and then turn on the Display Lineweight setting in the Lineweight Settings dialog box. Click OK to close the dialog box.

You can control the lineweight of cell borders by doing the following:

1. Select a single cell by clicking it, or select a group of cells by clicking one cell to select it and then Shift+clicking another cell.

2. From the Table Cell tab's Cell Styles panel, choose Cell Borders to open the Cell Border Properties dialog box (see Figure 9.31). You can use this dialog box to fine-tune the appearance of the line work of the table.

3. Click the Lineweight drop-down list, and select a lineweight.

4. Select the line you want to change by clicking one of the line tools that surround the sample graphic (shown in Figure 9.31.) For example, you can click the Outside Borders button to change the lineweight of the outermost borders of the cell or group of cells.

5. Click OK to apply the changes to the cell borders (see Figure 9.32).

The Cell Border Properties dialog box also lets you set the line colors by choosing a color from the Color drop-down list before selecting an Apply To option.

Figure 9.31

The Cell Border Properties dialog box

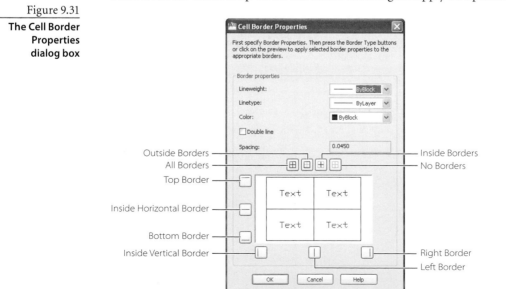

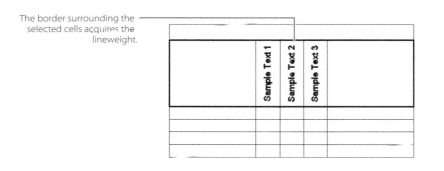

The border surrounding the selected cells acquires the lineweight.

In the example, you use the Outside Borders option. Table 9.4 describes all the border options.

If you want to select only the vertical or horizontal inside borders, first click the No Borders button, and then click the desired border in the graphic of the Cell Border Properties dialog box. As you click lines in the sample image, they lighten or darken to indicate their selection.

OPTION	PURPOSE
All Borders	Applies the changes to the borders of all the selected cells
Outside Borders	Applies the changes to only the outside borders of a group of cells
Inside Borders	Applies the changes to only the inside borders of a group of cells
No Borders	Lets you select which border you want to affect by clicking the graphic in the Apply To group

Changing Cell Background Colors

In addition to the table borders, you can change the background color for the cells of the table through the Background Fill tool in the Table Cell tab's Cell Styles panel or the Properties palette for selected cells. Select a group of cells in the table that you want to affect (but don't select the entire table), right-click, and choose Properties to open the Properties palette. Click the Background Fill option in the Cell group.

Adding Graphics to Table Cells

One of the more interesting features of the Table tool is its ability to include blocks in a cell. This can be useful if you want to include graphic elements in your table. Adding a block to a cell is easy:

1. Click a cell to select it.

2. Click the Block tool in the Table Cell tab's Insert panel to open the Insert a Block in a Table Cell dialog box (see Figure 9.33).

Figure 9.33

The Insert a Block in a Table Cell dialog box

3. Select a block name from the Name drop-down list. You can also click the Browse button to the right of the list to open a file dialog box that allows you to select a drawing file for import to the cell.

4. Once you've selected a block and specified the settings in the Properties group of the dialog box, click OK. The block appears in the cell you've selected.

The Properties group in the dialog box allows you to specify the alignment and size of the inserted block. By default, the AutoFit option is turned on. This option adjusts the size of the block to make it fit in the current cell size.

Creating Table Styles

Most users will have a set of table formats they use frequently. Door and window schedules in architectural plans will be fairly similar from project to project, for example.

For this reason, AutoCAD offers custom table styles. You can create a table style that matches some of the formatting you usually use for your projects. Then when you need a table, you can use your custom style and save yourself some table-formatting work.

Table styles allow you to set up the properties of the title, column heads, and data in advance so you don't have to set up those features each time you create a table. When you're ready, you can select your custom table style and specify the number of columns and rows.

To create a table style, take the following steps:

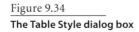

1. From the Annotate tab's Tables panel title bar, click the Table Style tool or enter **ts↵** to open the Table Style dialog box.

You can see the Standard table style in the list box shown in Figure 9.34.

2. Click New to open the Create New Table Style dialog box, as shown in Figure 9.35. This is where you give your new table style a name.

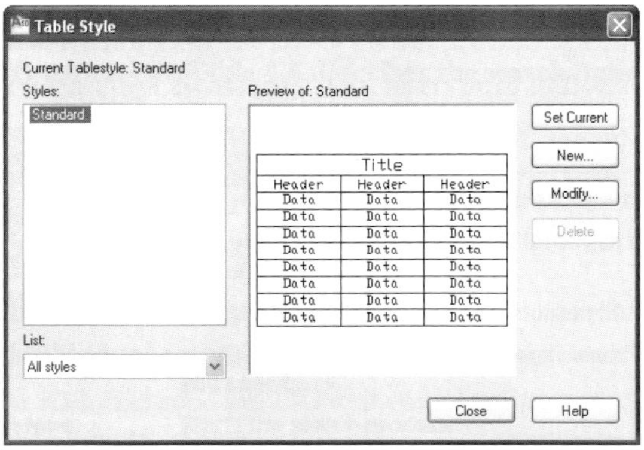

Figure 9.34
The Table Style dialog box

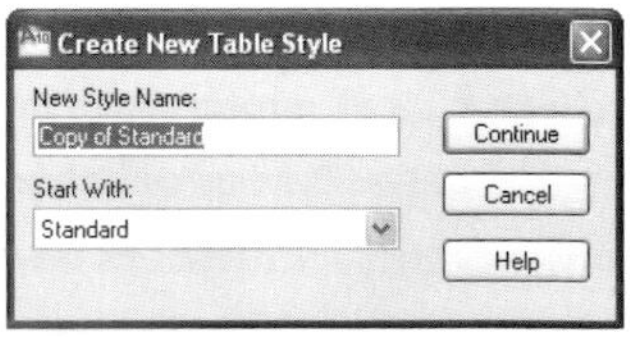

Figure 9.35
The Create New Table Style dialog box

3. Enter a name for your table style—for example, My Table Style—and click Continue to open the New Table Style dialog box (see Figure 9.36).

4. Set up your table style by using the options in this dialog box, and then click OK to close the dialog box.

5. Click Close to exit the Table Style dialog box.

Figure 9.36

The New Table Style dialog box

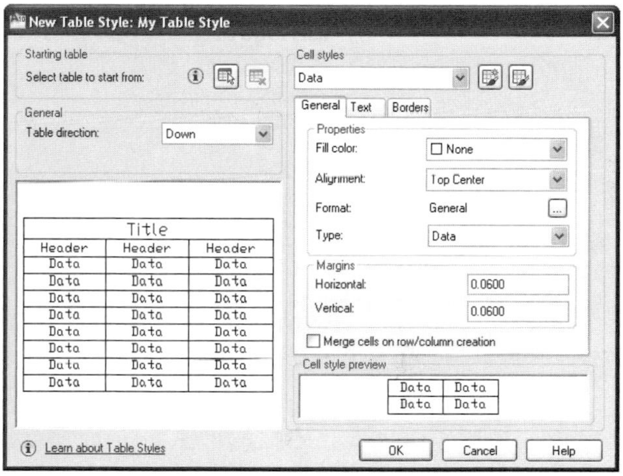

You'll see that your new table style appears in the Styles list of the Table Style dialog box and in the Table Style drop-down list of the Tables control panel. If you want to edit an existing table style, open the Table Style dialog box again, select the style you want to edit from the list, and click the Modify button. This opens the Modify Table Style dialog box, which allows you to edit the existing style. The Modify Table Style dialog box is identical to the New Table Style dialog box shown in Figure 9.36.

Once you've created a style, you can select it from the Table Style group of the Insert Table dialog box (see Figure 9.37).

You can also get to the New Table Style dialog box by clicking the Launch the Table Styles Dialog button just to the right of the Table Style Name drop-down list in the Insert Table dialog box. This opens the Table Styles dialog box. You can then click the New button to open the New Table Style dialog box.

Let's take a closer look at the New Table Style dialog box in Figure 9.36. You saw in step 4 of the previous exercise that the three tabs at the top of the dialog box all contain the same set of options. This dialog box allows you to specify the text-formatting options for each of these three table elements: data, column headers, and title.

Figure 9.37

The Table Style group in the Insert Table dialog box

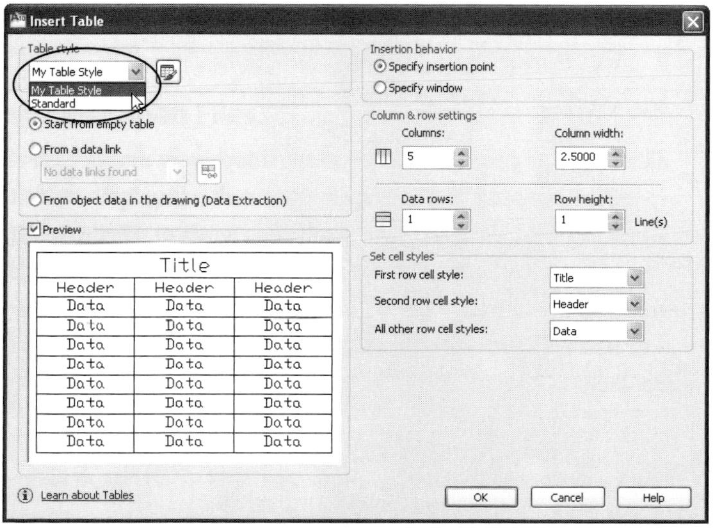

The Starting Table group lets you select an existing table as the starting point for your new table style. The General group lets you determine whether the Title and Header rows appear at the top or the bottom of the table.

You can select the table element you want to set up by selecting it from the Cell Styles drop-down list in the upper-right side of the dialog box. As you make changes, the graphic to the left shows how your changes affect your table style.

The Cell Styles group also offers three tabs: General, Text, and Borders. The General tab offers options for the formatting of the type of cell you have selected in the Cell Styles drop-down list. The Text tab lets you set up the text style, angle height, and color of the cell text. The Borders tab lets you control the color and lineweight of the table line work. The options on this tab work just like the options in the Cell Border Properties dialog box you saw in an earlier exercise.

Summary

Creating and editing text are tasks that nearly everyone has to tackle at some point. If your job is to just update the text in a drawing, all you have to do is double-click the text and make your changes in the Text panel that appears. Format changes are a little more involved, but if you're familiar with most text editors, you'll find that AutoCAD's text-editing features follow methods used in most other word processors. Creating text requires some familiarity with methods for scaling your text properly to make it the correct size. Also, placing the text in the Model tab or a layout tab affects how you deal with text scaling.

Another type of annotation you'll want to know about is dimensioning. In the next chapter, you'll learn about the tools for creating dimensions in AutoCAD and how you can change dimensions as your drawings change.

CHAPTER 10

Using Dimensions

Dimensions are a key part of technical drawing and drafting. You could almost say that dimensions are the reason we produce CAD drawings in the first place, since they convey critical information about our designs. Before the days of AutoCAD, we used dimensions to communicate specific proportions of a design. Now we can use temporary dimensions to help keep track of critical measurements in a drawing.

Adding dimensions to your drawing is fairly easy. In this chapter, I'll discuss the types of dimensions available and how to apply them to your drawing. One of the trickier aspects of dimensioning in AutoCAD is to understand scale factors. Just as with text, you have to apply a scale factor to your dimensions before they appear properly in the Model tab of your drawing.

Finally, since many standards and styles of dimensioning exist, AutoCAD provides many options that let you set up dimensions in just the way you want. But with so many settings, you might feel just a bit lost when you want to fine-tune the appearance of your dimensions. This chapter will help you.

This chapter includes the following topics:

- **Understanding the parts of an AutoCAD dimension**
- **Dimensioning in the model or layout view**
- **Drawing linear dimensions**
- **Dimensioning nonorthogonal objects**
- **Adding a note with an arrow using the Leader tool**
- **Using ordinate dimensions**
- **Adding tolerance notation**
- **Editing dimensions**
- **Setting up the dimension's appearance**

If you've recently used the 3D Modeling workspace, make sure you are back in the 2D Drafting & Annotation workspace before beginning any exercises in this chapter. See "Getting to Know the 3D Modeling Workspace" in Chapter 6 for instructions on how to switch to a different workspace.

Understanding the Parts of an AutoCAD Dimension

If you were drawing dimensions by hand, you would not need to know the names of the dimension's components. Now that you're using CAD and reading this book, it will help to know these names so you can better understand the discussions that follow in this chapter.

Figure 10.1 shows a typical dimension along with the names of its parts. Not all these parts appear in all styles of dimensions. For example, the dimension line extension is used only in architectural drawings. Also, architectural drawings do not use arrows when dimensioning straight lengths. Instead, a "tick" mark is used, which looks like a diagonal line.

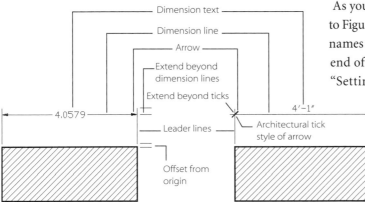

As you read this chapter, you might want to refer to Figure 10.1 when you need clarification about the names of the dimension components. Toward the end of this chapter, you'll find a section called "Setting Up the Dimension's Appearance" that describes how to change the appearance of your dimensions to suit your style of drawing. You'll learn more about the dimension components in that section.

Figure 10.1

The components of a dimension for two common styles

DIMENSIONING STANDARDS

Besides the components of a dimension, you'll want to know about the standards that govern the placement and style of dimensions in a drawing. Each industry has a different set of standards for text size, text style, arrow style, dimension placement, and general dimensioning methods. These issues are beyond the scope of this book; however, I urge you to become familiar with the standards associated with your industry. Many resources are available to you if you want to find out more about dimension standards. Here are just a few resources on the subject:

- For mechanical drafting in the United States, check the American Society of Mechanical Engineers (ASME) website at www.asme.org.

- For European standards, see the International Organization for Standardization website at www.iso.org.

- For architectural standards in the United States, see the American Institute of Architects (AIA) website at www.aia.org.

Dimensioning in the Model or Layout View

The first big question new users ask regarding dimensioning is which view to use for dimensioning. Just as with text, you can add dimensions in either the model view or a layout view. This is an important choice because it affects the way you set up your dimensions. Here are some points to remember when deciding which view to use:

- You can add your dimensions in a layout view, which has the advantage of letting you specify sizes of text, arrows, and other dimension features at their full size without having to add annotative scales. The drawback is that you cannot see or edit the dimensions while you work on your drawing in the model view. You have to be either in the layout view known as *paper space* or in the model view space, also known as *floating model space*. However, dimensions do have a feature called *associative dimensioning* that allows them to automatically adjust to changes in the objects they are dimensioning, no matter which view you use to add dimensions.

- You can add your dimensions directly in the model view. This has the advantage of allowing you to see and edit text and graphics at the same time without switching between model and paper space. The disadvantage is that you have to make sure you're using the annotative scale feature and that you have assigned the proper annotative scale values to your dimensions. This ensures that the arrows and text appear at the correct size when you plot your drawing. (See the Scale for Dimension Features Group item in Table 10.6 later in this chapter.)

Even if you choose to do all your dimensioning in a layout view, you'll want to know how to work with dimensions that have been drawn in the model view. Countless older AutoCAD drawings are dimensioned in the model view. If you work with AutoCAD professionally, one of those drawings will eventually cross your computer screen.

CONTROLLING THE SIZE OF DIMENSION FEATURES

As you begin to use dimensions in AutoCAD and you're working in the model view, you might find that the arrows and text are way too small for your drawing. This usually happens when new users try to dimension a drawing in the model view.

If this happens, you'll need to change the way AutoCAD scales dimension components. Just as with text, dimension components such as arrows and text need to be scaled up to appear correctly in the model view (see Chapter 9). You can use the annotative scale feature of AutoCAD to set the scale for dimensions. The procedure for using annotative scales for dimensions is the same as it is for text. See "Understanding Text and Scale" in Chapter 9 to learn more about annotative scale.

Drawing Linear Dimensions

The most common type of dimension you'll be using is the *linear dimension*, an orthogonal dimension measuring the width and length of an object. AutoCAD provides three dimensioning tools for this purpose: Linear, Continue, and Baseline. These tools are readily accessible from the Annotate tab's Dimension panel.

You can also find dimension tools in the Home tab's Annotation panel. This chapter will focus on the Annotate tab.

Placing Horizontal and Vertical Dimensions

Linear dimensions are those that are aligned either vertically or horizontally. They constitute the bulk of dimensions in most projects. The following steps describe how to apply linear dimensions.

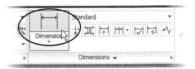

Using osnaps is crucial in producing accurate results in all dimensioning tasks.

1. Click the Dimension Linear tool from the Annotate tab's Dimensions panel, or enter **dli** ↵ at the command prompt.

2. At the `Specify first extension line origin or <select object>:` prompt, Shift+right-click, and use an osnap to select the exact location on an object, such as an endpoint or an intersection of two lines on the drawing you're dimensioning (see Figure 10.2).

The prompt in step 2 gives you the option of pressing ↵ to select an object. If you do this, you're prompted to select the object you want to dimension, rather than the actual distance to be dimensioned.

3. At the `Specify second extension line origin:` prompt, use an osnap to select the other end of the object you're dimensioning, as shown in Figure 10.2.

Figure 10.2

Using a linear dimension

Use osnaps to select endpoints or other features of the object being dimensioned.

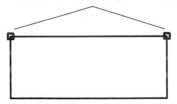

Select a location for the dimension line.

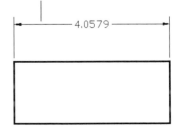

4. In the next prompt, `Specify dimension line location or [Mtext/Text/Angle/`
`Horizontal/Vertical/Rotated]:`, you'll see a temporary dimension at the cursor
location. Position the temporary dimension where you want the dimension to
appear, and then click.

If you prefer to be more precise about the dimension line location, in step 4 you can
enter a relative distance from the last point selected.

Continuing a Dimension

You'll often want to enter a group of dimensions strung together in a line. You can use
the Continue option in the Dimension menu to do this. This option assumes you've
already placed one linear or aligned dimension and are ready to continue with a string of
dimensions from the last dimension (see "Dimensioning Nonorthogonal Objects" later in
this chapter for information about aligned dimensions).

1. Choose Continue from the Annotate tab's
   Dimensions panel, or enter **dco**↵.

2. At the `Specify a second extension line`
   `origin or [Undo/Select] <Select>:` prompt,
   select the next location you want to dimension (see the left image in Figure 10.3).
   You can continue to add more dimensions until you press ↵.

If you find that you've selected the wrong location for a continued dimension, click the
Undo tool, or enter **u**↵.

The Continue Dimension option continues from the last dimension you added to the
drawing. The last-drawn extension line is used as the first extension line for the continued dimension. If you need to continue a string of dimensions from a dimension other
than the last one you placed in the drawing, press ↵ at the `Specify a second extension`
`line origin or[Undo/Select]:` prompt in step 2 of the previous example. When you see
the `Select continued dimension:` prompt, click the extension line from which you want to
continue. You can then proceed to add dimensions.

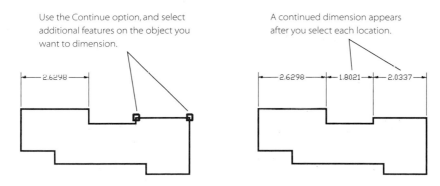

Use the Continue option, and select
additional features on the object you
want to dimension.

A continued dimension appears
after you select each location.

Figure 10.3

**A continued string
of dimensions**

Drawing Dimensions from a Common Base Extension Line

Frequently, you need to dimension from a single datum point, as shown in Figure 10.4. This means you need several dimensions starting from the same location. To accommodate this, AutoCAD provides the Baseline option.

Figure 10.4

A baseline dimension

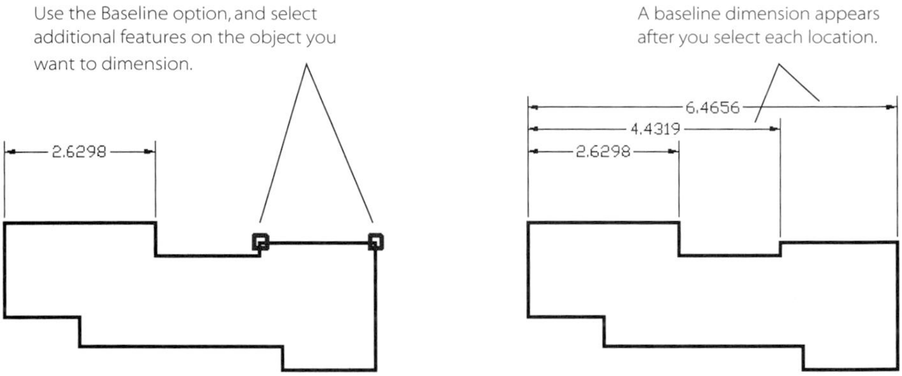

Use the Baseline option, and select additional features on the object you want to dimension.

A baseline dimension appears after you select each location.

As with the Continue option, Baseline assumes you have already placed at least one other linear or aligned dimension in the drawing.

Since you usually select exact locations on your drawing as you dimension, you might want to turn on running osnaps to avoid the extra step of selecting osnaps from the Osnap context menu.

1. From the Annotate tab's Dimensions panel, click the Continue tool's flyout and select Baseline or enter **dba**↵ to start a baseline dimension.

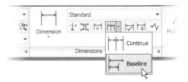

2. At the Specify a second extension line origin or [Undo/Select] <Select>: prompt, use an osnap to select another feature you want to dimension in your drawing.

3. Press ↵ twice to exit the Baseline Dimension command.

The Baseline Dimension option works in a similar way to the Continue Dimension, except that Baseline Dimension allows you to use the first extension line of the previous dimension as the base for a second dimension.

The distance between the two parallel dimension lines is controlled by the Baseline Spacing setting in the Lines tabs of the New Dimension Style and Modify Dimension Style dialog boxes.

Just as with the Continue Dimension option, the Baseline Dimension option continues from the last dimension you added to the drawing by default. If you need to add more baseline dimensions from a dimension other than the last one you placed in the drawing, press ↵ at the Specify a second extension line origin or [Undo/Select] <Select>: prompt in step 2 of the previous example. Then click the extension line from which you want to continue. You can then proceed to add dimensions.

Adding a String of Dimensions with a Single Operation

AutoCAD provides a method for creating a string of dimensions using a single operation *while in the Model tab.* The Qdim command lets you select a set of objects instead of having to select points. The following exercise demonstrates how the Qdim command works.

To use Qdim, click the Quick Dimension tool in the Annotate tab's Dimensions panel, or enter **Qdim.**↵. Next, place a crossing selection window (start your window to the left

of the selection area) around the area you want to dimension, and then press ↵. You'll see a string of dimensions at the cursor. Click to place the dimension string in the drawing.

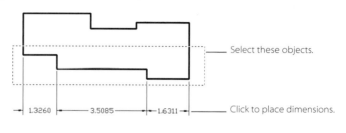

The Qdim command can be a time-saver when you want to quickly dimension a wall in an architectural drawing, for example, or any set of contiguous lines in a drawing. It might not work in all situations, but if the object you're dimensioning is fairly simple, it can be all you need.

> This example uses a simple crossing window to select the wall. For more complex shapes, try using a crossing polygon selection window (see "Selecting Objects" in Chapter 5 for more about the Crossing Polygons selection).

Dimensioning Nonorthogonal Objects

Most of your dimensions will be horizontal or vertical, which are handled easily with the linear dimension. But eventually you'll need to apply many other types of nonorthogonal dimensions. For example, you might need to dimension a hexagonal shape whose sides are at 30° angles. In the following sections, you'll find out how to add dimensions to objects that are turned at an angle. You'll also learn about dimensioning arcs and circles.

Adding Nonorthogonal Linear Dimensions

You can add a linear dimension to an object that is not in a horizontal or vertical orientation using the aligned dimension. This type of dimension aligns the dimension line with the two points you select for dimensioning, as described in the following steps:

WHAT IS THE "MAIN FLYOUT" IN THE DIMENSIONS PANEL?

Throughout this chapter, you'll use the flyout from the large icon on the left side of the

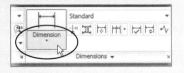

Dimensions panel. In a newly opened drawing, this is the Linear tool flyout. Since the icon changes depending on the last tool used in the flyout, I'll refer to this icon as the *main flyout*.

1. Choose Aligned from the main flyout in the Annotate tab's Dimensions panel, or enter **dal↵** to start the aligned dimension.

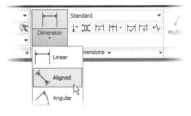

2. At the Specify first extension line origin or <select object>: prompt, use an osnap to select the first end of the object being dimensioned.

USING OSNAPS WHILE DIMENSIONING

Dimensions can adjust themselves to changes in the objects they are measuring. To take advantage of this feature, make sure you use osnaps while adding dimensions. The osnaps ensure that you're selecting exact points on objects so that AutoCAD can keep track of what it is you're dimensioning. If you don't know how to use osnaps, see Chapter 2.

In addition, you can dimension an object by selecting it instead of pointing to locations on the object. This also enables the dimension to "follow" the changes made to the dimensioned object.

3. At the Specify second extension line origin: prompt, use an osnap again to select the other end of the object being dimensioned.

4. At the Specify dimension line location or [Mtext/Text/Angle]: prompt, you'll see a dimension follow the cursor. Click a point to place the dimension. The dimension appears in the drawing, as shown in Figure 10.5.

Just as with linear dimensions, you can enter **t↵** in step 4 to enter alternative text for the dimension.

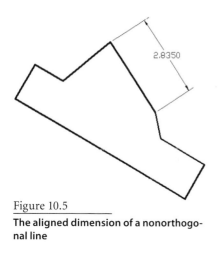

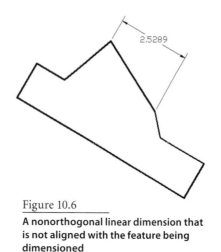

Figure 10.5

The aligned dimension of a nonorthogonal line

Figure 10.6

A nonorthogonal linear dimension that is not aligned with the feature being dimensioned

You might also need to place a dimension at an angle that is not necessarily aligned with the drawing feature being dimensioned, as shown in Figure 10.6.

Here's how to draw this type of dimension:

1. Click Linear from the main flyout on the Dimensions panel.

2. At the `Specify first extension line origin or <select> object:` prompt, use an osnap to select an appropriate location on the object being dimensioned.

3. At the `Specify second extension line origin:` prompt, use an osnap again to select the other end of the object being dimensioned.

4. At the `Specify dimension line location or [Mtext/Text/Angle/Horizontal/Vertical/Rotated]:` prompt, enter **r↵** to use the Rotated option.

5. At the `Specify angle of dimension line <0>:` prompt, specify the angle at which the dimension line is to be placed. The angle value you enter is in relation to the x-axis of the drawing, so if you enter **0**, for example, the dimension line will be horizontal.

6. At the `Specify dimension line location or [Mtext/Text/Angle/Horizontal/Vertical/Rotated]:` prompt, you'll see the dimension line follow your cursor. Select a point to place the dimension line.

Dimensioning Arcs and Circles

Dimensioning diameters of arcs or circles is fairly simple:

1. Choose Diameter from the main flyout in the Dimensions panel, or enter **ddi↵**.

2. At the `Select arc or circle:` prompt, select the circle or arc you want to dimension.

3. At the `Specify dimension line location or [Mtext/Text/Angle]:` prompt, you'll see the Diameter dimension drag along the circle as you move the cursor. If you move

the cursor outside the circle, the dimension changes to display the dimension on the outside. (See the right image in Figure 10.7.)

4. Place the dimension where you want it, and then click.

Figure 10.7

Dimension showing the diameter of a circle

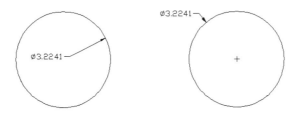

AutoCAD gives you the option to place the dimension text inside or outside the circle as you drag the temporary dimension over the circle. Be aware that, although AutoCAD gives you a great deal of flexibility in the placement of dimensions, certain dimensioning standards define specific rules for dimensioning circles.

The Radius tool on the Dimensions tab gives you a radius dimension just as the diameter dimension provides a circle's diameter. Figure 10.8 shows a radius dimension on the

Figure 10.8

A radius dimension shown on the outside of the circle

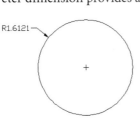

outside of the circle, but you can place it inside in a manner similar to the diameter dimension. The Center Mark tool on the Dimensions tab just places a cross in the center of the selected arc or circle.

If you're dimensioning a large arc radius and you can't show the center of the arc within the area of your drawing, you can use a jogged radius dimension (choose Jogged from the Dimension flyout in the Annotate tab's Dimensions flyout) instead of the usual Dimension → Radius option. The Jogged option places a jog in the dimension line to indicate that the center is not shown in the drawing (Figure 10.9).

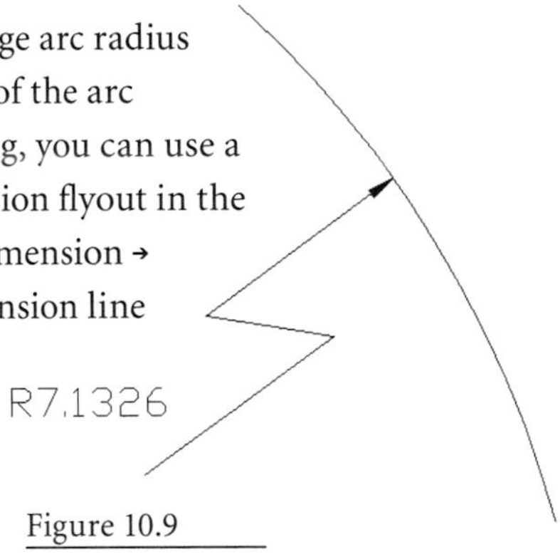

R7.1326

Dimensioning Angles and Arc Lengths

Figure 10.9

The jogged radius dimension

Dimensions aren't always used to show distances. You can use the angular dimension to indicate the angle between features in your drawing. Here's how:

1. Choose Angular from the main flyout of the Dimensions panel or enter **dan**↵ to start the angular dimension.

2. At the Select arc, circle, line, or <specify vertex>: prompt, select the first line whose angle you want to dimension.

3. At the Select second line: prompt, select the other line whose angle you want to dimension.

4. At the `Specify dimension arc line location or [Mtext/Text/Angle]:` prompt, the dimension moves to different locations as you move the cursor. This allows you to select the angle to dimension, as shown in Figure 10.10.

5. When the dimension appears in the location you want, click that point to fix the dimension in place.

In addition to the angle of an arc, you can also dimension the length of an arc. Choose Dimension → Arc Length, and then select the arc whose length you want to dimension. The dimension appears and drags with the cursor. You can then click to place the Arc Length dimension.

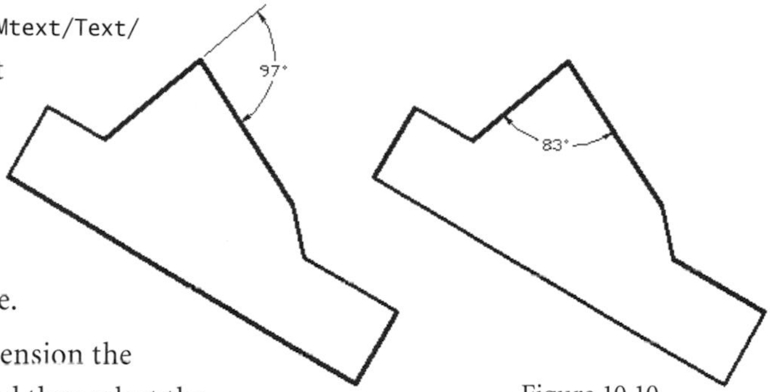

Figure 10.10

Two examples of an angular dimension

WHY DO MY ANGULAR DIMENSIONS SHOW ONLY WHOLE DEGREES?

By default, AutoCAD's dimensioning feature rounds off angular dimensions to the nearest degree. Follow these steps to show angles less than a whole degree:

1. Select the angular dimension, then right-click, and finally select Precision.

2. Click the Precision option, and select the value you want for the dimension.

    You can also change the Angle Precision setting for the current dimension style using the Modify Dimension Style dialog box, which is the same as the New Dimension Style dialog box. See "Setting Up the Dimension's Appearance" later in this chapter.

Adding a Note with an Arrow Using the Leader Tool

After dimensions, notes are the most common notation feature found in AutoCAD drawings. Choosing Multileader from the Annotate tab's Leaders panel lets you add a note with an arrow pointing to the object the note describes. Here's how it works:

1. Choose Multileader from the Annotate tab's Leaders panel (see Figure 10.11), or enter **mld.↵**.

2. At the `Specify leader arrowhead location or [leader Landing first/Content first/Options] <Options>:` prompt, select a point to indicate the location for the arrow.

3. At the `Specify leader landing location:` prompt, click another point to indicate the other end of the arrow. You'll see the Text Editor tab appear along with the text cursor at the note location.

4. Enter the note you want, and then click the Close Text Editor panel. The note appears at the end of the leader, as shown in Figure 10.12.

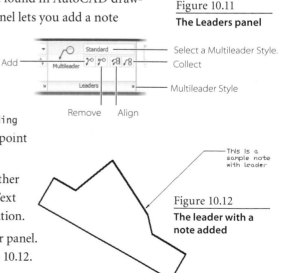

Figure 10.11

The Leaders panel

Figure 10.12

The leader with a note added

The text in the note will be in the current text style, unless you specify another style in the Text tab of the New Dimension Style or Modify Dimension Style dialog box. (See the "Setting Up the Dimension's Appearance" section later in this chapter.)

The Multileader tool offers a lot of options that are not obviously presented when you're using it. In step 2 of the previous example, after choosing Multileader, you can press ↵ to modify the behavior of the Multileader tool. You'll see the following prompt:

```
Enter an option [Leader type/leader lAnding
/Content type/Maxpoints/First angle/Second angle
/eXit options] <eXit options>:
```

Table 10.1 gives you a rundown of these options and their function.

Table 10.1

The Multileader Options

OPTION	FUNCTION
Leader type	Allows you to choose between straight line arrows and curved arrows.
Leader lAnding	Determines whether a leader landing is used. The leader landing is the short line that connects the arrow to the note.
Content type	Lets you select between text or a block for the leader note. You also have the option to choose none.
Maxpoints	Lets you set the number of points you select for the arrow. The default is 2.
First angle	Lets you constrain the angle of the leader arrow to a fixed value.
Second angle	Lets you constrain the angle of the second line segment of the arrow if you're using more than two points for the Maxpoints option.
eXit options	Lets you return to the main part of the Leader command to draw the leader.

Creating Multileader Styles

Besides the options shown in Table 10.1, you can create multileader styles to control the appearance of multileaders. Multileader styles are similar in concept to text and dimension styles. They allow you to set up the appearance of the leader under a name that you can call up any time. For example, you might want to have one type of leader that uses a block instead of text for the note and another leader that uses a dot in place of an arrow. Or you might want to set up a style that uses curved lines instead of straight ones for the leader line. You can create a multileader style for each of these types of leader features and then switch between each leader style depending on the requirements of your leader note.

To set up or modify a multileader style, click the Multileader Style tool in the Leaders panel title bar (shown earlier in Figure 10.11). You can also enter **Mleaderstyle**↵ at the command prompt. This opens the Multileader Style Manager dialog box shown in Figure 10.13. From here, you can select an existing style from the list at the left and click Modify to edit it, or you can just click New to create a new one. If you click New, you're asked to select an existing style as a basis for your new one. You also have the option to give your new style the annotative scale feature. See Chapter 9 for more about annotative scale.

You can turn the annotative scale feature on or off for existing Multileader styles using the Modify Multileader Style dialog box shown in Figure 10.14.

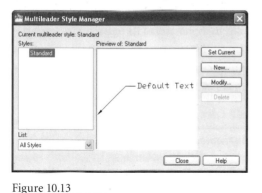

Figure 10.13

The Multileader Style Manager dialog box

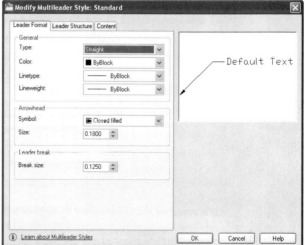

Once you've selected Modify or New, you'll see the Modify Multileader Style dialog box (see Figure 10.14).

Table 10.2 describes the options in each of the tabs of the Multileader Style dialog box. Some of these options are the same as those for the Multileader command.

Once you've set up a multileader style, you can make it the default style by selecting the style from the Multileader Style drop-down list in the Leaders panel.

Figure 10.14

The Modify Multileader Style dialog box

TAB AND PANEL	FUNCTION
Leader Format Tab	
General	Lets you set the leader line to straight or curved. You can also set the color, lineweight, and linetype for the leader line.
Arrowhead	Controls the arrowheads.
Leader Break	Controls the size of the gap in a leader line when the Leaderbreak command is applied. Leaderbreak places a break on a leader line where two leader lines cross.
Leader Structure Tab	
Constraints	Determines the number of line segments in the leader line. You can also apply angle constraints to the leader line segments.
Landing Settings	Controls the leader line landing segment. This is the last line segment that points to the note.
Scale	Lets you control the scale of the leader components. You can either apply a fixed scale or use the Annotative option to have the drawing's annotative scale apply to the leader.
Content Tab	
Multileader Type	Lets you select the type of object that will be used for the leader note. The options are Mtext, Block, and None.
Text Options	Gives you control over the way the leader note appears. You can control color, text style, size, justification, and orientation.
Leader Connection	Determines the position between the leader line and the note.

Table 10.2

The Multileader Style Dialog Box Options

The selected style will be applied to any new multileader you add to your drawing. You can also change the style of an existing multileader. To do this, click the multileader to select it, and then select the multileader style you want from the Multileaders Style drop-down list, which can be found in the Annotate tab's Multileader panel.

Editing Multileader Notes

If you need to make changes to the note portion of a multileader, you can do so by double-clicking the note. This opens the Text Editor tab, allowing you to make changes as if you were editing in a word processor.

At other times, you might want to make changes to the leader line, arrows, or other graphic features of the multileader. For example, you might want to have all the notes aligned vertically for a neater appearance. Or you might want to add more leader arrows so the note points to several objects in the drawing instead of just one.

The Leaders panel offers several tools that let you make these types of changes to your leader notes (see Figure 10.11). The Add and Remove tools let you add or remove leaders from a multileader. The Add tool is handy for single notes that point to several objects. The Align tool lets you align the note portion of several multileaders. Finally, the Collect tool lets you collect several multileaders that use blocks for notes into a single note.

Using Ordinate Dimensions

You use ordinate dimensions when a dimension in a part is measured from a critical feature. For example, the holes in a machine part might all have to be precisely located in relation to the center of a machine hole in the part, as shown in Figure 10.15. In ordinate dimensions, the dimension labels are shown as X coordinates or Y coordinates from the critical feature.

Before you apply ordinate dimensions, you need to establish the origin of the drawing at the location of the critical feature. You use the UCS to do so.

Figure 10.15

An example of ordinate dimensions

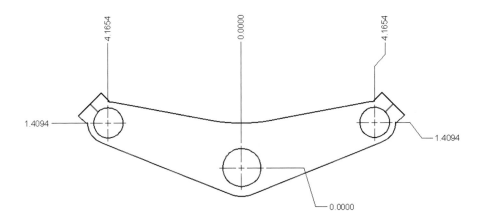

To use an AutoCAD ordinate dimension, follow these steps:

1. In the View tab's Coordinates panel, choose the Origin tool, or enter **ucs.↵ or.↵**.

2. At the `Specify new origin point <0,0,0>:` prompt, click the exact location of the origin of your part.

3. Toggle on Ortho mode.

4. From the Annotate tab's Dimensions panel, select Ordinate from the main flyout, or enter **dor.↵** to start the ordinate dimension.

5. At the `Specify feature location:` prompt, click the item you want to dimension.

> The direction of the leader determines whether the dimension will be of the Xdatum or the Ydatum.

6. At the `Specify leader endpoint or [Xdatum/Ydatum/Mtext/Text/Angle]:` prompt, position the rubber-banding leader that appears at the cursor perpendicular to the coordinate direction you want to dimension. When you have the leader where you want it, click.

In steps 1 and 2, you used the UCS feature to establish a second origin in the drawing. The Ordinate Dimension tool then uses that origin to determine the ordinate dimensions.

You might have noticed options in the command window for ordinate dimensions. The Xdatum and Ydatum options force the dimension to be of the X or Y coordinate, no matter what direction the leader takes. The Mtext option opens the Text Editor tab, allowing you to append or replace the ordinate dimension text. The Text option lets you enter a replacement text directly through the command window.

> As with all other dimensions, you can use grips to adjust the location of ordinate dimensions.

If you turn Ortho mode off, AutoCAD draws the dimension leader with a jog to maintain the orthogonal placement orientation of the leader. (Refer to Figure 10.15.)

Adding Tolerance Notation

If you're drawing a part that must be machined within a certain range of dimensions, you can use a tolerance dimension. Tolerance lets you specify a tolerance range for features in your drawing. It produces a note that uses industry-standard notation, as shown in Figure 10.16.

To use the Tolerance command, enter **tol.↵** at the command prompt or choose the Tolerance tool from the expanded Dimensions panel to open the Geometric Tolerance dialog box (see Figure 10.17).

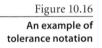

Figure 10.16

An example of tolerance notation

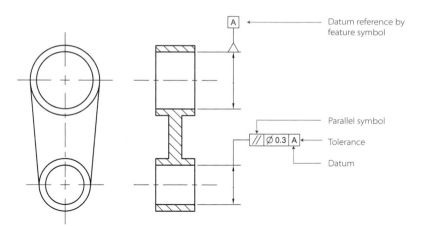

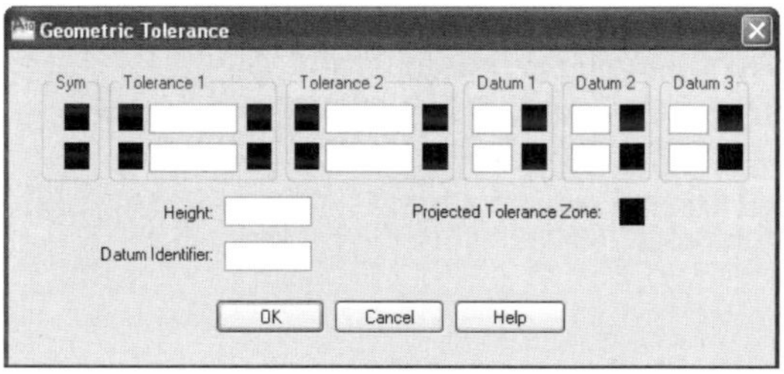

Figure 10.17

The Geometric Tolerance dialog box

This dialog box lets you enter tolerance and datum values for the feature control symbol, which indicates the type of tolerance asked for in a tolerance dimension. You can enter two tolerance values and three datum values. In addition, you can stack values in a two-tiered fashion (vertically).

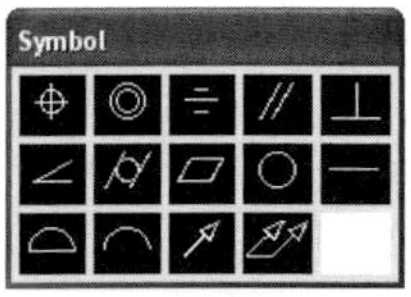

Click a box in the Sym group to open the Symbol dialog box (see Figure 10.18).

Figure 10.18

The Symbol dialog box

Figure 10.19 shows what each symbol in the Symbol dialog box represents. The bottom image shows a sample drawing with a feature symbol used on a cylindrical object.

In the Geometric Tolerance dialog box, you can click a box in any of the Datum groups or a box in the right side of the Tolerance groups to open the Material Condition dialog box (see Figure 10.20). This dialog box lets you add a material condition symbol.

Figure 10.19

The Tolerance symbols

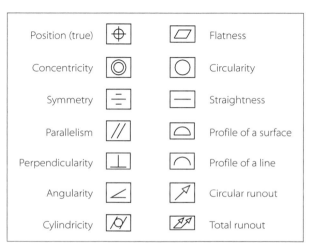

Figure 10.20

The Material Condition dialog box

Editing Dimensions

As you begin to add more dimensions to your drawings, you'll find that AutoCAD occasionally places dimension text or a line in an inappropriate location or that you need to modify the dimension text. In the following sections, you'll look at how you can modify dimensions to suit those special circumstances.

Although the instructions in the following sections describe methods for editing specific parts of dimensions, you can adjust dimensions through the Properties palette.

Appending Data to Dimension Text

Most of the time, you'll accept the dimension value that AutoCAD provides, but you might want to append text to a dimension value or even change it entirely. While you're adding dimensions and you see the temporary dimension dragging with your cursor, you can enter **t**↵ to change the dimension text. You can then enter an entirely different text at the command prompt. You can also use the less-than (<) and greater-than (>) signs to add text either before or after the default dimension. For example, if you enter <> **Verify**, after entering the t↵ option, the word *Verify* appears after the dimension value. You can click the Contents option in the Properties palette to modify the existing dimension text in a similar way.

You can also append text to a dimension that has already been placed in your drawing. Here is an example of how to do this:

1. Enter **ed**↵. This is the alias for the Ddedit command.

2. Click the dimension whose value you want to edit. The Text Editor tab (see Figure 10.21) appears with the current dimension value highlighted in the Text panel.

3. Click the location for either in front of or after the dimension text, and then enter the text you want to add.

4. Click Close Text Editor in the Text Editor tab. The dimension changes to include the text you just added.

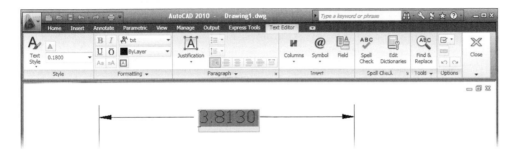

Figure 10.21

A dimension with the Text Editor tab

In addition to appending to the dimension value, you can do any of the following while editing the dimension text:

- You can replace the dimension text entirely by deleting the dimension value in the Text panel.

- You can restore a dimension text value that has been modified by entering <>.

- You can completely remove the dimension text by replacing the dimension value with a space.

You can also have AutoCAD automatically add a dimension suffix or prefix to all dimensions, instead of just a chosen few, by using the Suffix or Prefix option in the Primary Units tab of the New Dimension Style or Modify Dimension Style dialog box (see "Setting Up the Dimension's Appearance" later in this chapter for more about the Modify Dimension Style dialog box).

> Instead of using the Ddedit command described in the previous exercise, you can select a dimension, right-click, and then choose Properties from the context menu. You can then edit the dimension value by entering a value in the Text Override setting. You can use the <> brackets as described earlier in this section to append text in the Text Override settings.

Making Changes to Multiple Dimensions

You can use the Dimension Edit tool to quickly edit existing dimensions and change more than one dimension's text at a time. For example, you can use the Dimension Edit tool to change a string of dimensions to say *Equal* instead of showing the actual dimensioned distance. The following steps show an alternative to using the Properties palette for appending text to a dimension:

1. Enter **ded**↵ at the command prompt.

2. At the `Enter type of dimension editing [Home/New/Rotate/Oblique]<Home>:` prompt, enter **n**↵ to use the New option. The Text Editor tab appears with a new dimension value of 0.0000. The 0.0000 is a placeholder indicating where the actual dimension text will appear.

3. Enter the text you want to append to the dimension. If you want, you can delete the 0 dimension to replace the dimension value entirely.

4. Click Close Text Editor.

5. At the `Select objects:` prompt, select the dimensions you want to edit. The `Select objects:` prompt remains, allowing you to select several dimensions.

6. Press ↵ to finish your selection. The dimension changes to include your new text or to replace the existing dimension text.

The Dimension Edit tool is useful in editing dimension text, but you can also use this command to make graphical changes to the text. Here are the other Dimension Edit tool options:

Home Moves the dimension text to its standard default position and angle.

Rotate Rotates the dimension text to a new angle.

Oblique Skews the dimension extension lines to a new angle. See the "Skewing Dimension Lines" section later in this chapter for more information.

Detaching Dimension Text from the Dimension Line

If you try to move the dimension text away from a dimension using the dimension text's grip, you'll find that the entire dimension line follows the text. You can separate the dimension from the text by changing one of the settings for the dimension's properties:

1. Click the dimension text to expose its grip.

2. Right-click and choose Properties from the context menu to open the Properties palette.

3. Scroll down the list of properties until you see the Fit options. If you do not see a list of options under Fit, click the down-pointing arrow to the right to display a new set of options, as shown in Figure 10.22.

4. Scroll down the list until you see the Text Movement option, and click this option.

5. Click the arrow that appears next to the Keep Dim Line with Text listing to open the drop-down list; then select the Move Text, Add Leader option shown in Figure 10.23.

6. Close the Properties palette.

Figure 10.22

The Fit options in the Properties palette

You can now move the text independently of the dimension line. As you do, AutoCAD draws a leader from the dimension line to the dimension text.

If you prefer that the leader not appear, you can select Move Text, No Leader in step 5 of the previous example.

Figure 10.23

The Move Text, Add Leader option in the Fit options group

Rotating Dimension Text

You might find that you need to rotate the text of a dimension in conjunction with moving the dimension text. Follow these steps:

1. Choose the Text Angle tool from the Annotate tab's expanded Dimension panel.

2. At the `Select dimension:` prompt, select the dimension whose text you want to rotate.

3. At the `Specify angle for dimension text:` prompt, enter an angle, or select two points to indicate an angle visually.

You can also use the Dimension Text Edit tool (Dimtedit command) to align the dimension text to either the left or right side of the dimension line. This is similar to the Alignment option in the Multiline Text Editor that controls text justification.

As you've seen in this section, grips are especially well suited to editing dimensions. With grips, you can stretch, move, copy, rotate, mirror, and scale dimensions.

Skewing Dimension Lines

If you're adding dimensions to an isometric or other axonometric drawing, you'll want to skew the dimension lines in relation to the dimension extension lines. You can do this using the Oblique option:

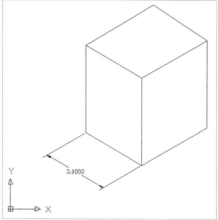

1. Choose the Oblique tool from the Annotate tab's expanded Dimension panel, or enter **ded↵ o↵**. You can also select the Dimension Edit tool from the Dimension toolbar and then enter **o↵**.

2. At the Select objects: prompt, select the dimension you want to skew, and press ↵ to confirm your selection.

3. At the Enter obliquing angle (Press ENTER for none): prompt, enter an angle value appropriate to your drawing. The dimension skews so that the extension lines are at the angle you entered (see Figure 10.24).

Figure 10.24

A dimension on a 2D isometric drawing using the Oblique option

Setting Up the Dimension's Appearance

The default dimensions created by AutoCAD are generic and do not conform to any particular drafting standard. They work fine in a pinch if you just need to create a descriptive, technical drawing. If you're an architect or mechanical drafter, you'll want to change the style to follow the standards of the industry in which you are working. Or perhaps you just want to change the style a little to conform to your particular office's way of doing things.

You can add dimensions using the default settings and then change each dimension so that it appears correctly for your application, but that is extremely time-consuming. Instead, you can use *dimension styles* to set up the appearance of your dimensions beforehand. Once you create a style, you merely have to make the style the default and then start dimensioning.

Creating a Dimension Style

Dimension styles are like text styles. They determine the font, size of dimension arrows, and configuration of your dimensions. You might set up a dimension style for special types of arrows or to position the dimension text above the dimension line as in an architectural drawing. You can set up multiple dimension styles for different situations. Here's how to set them up:

1. Choose the Dimension Style tool from the title bar of the Annotate tab's Dimension panel, or enter **d**↵ at the command prompt to open the Dimension Style Manager dialog box.

2. Select Standard from the Styles list (see Figure 10.25). Metric users should select ISO-25.

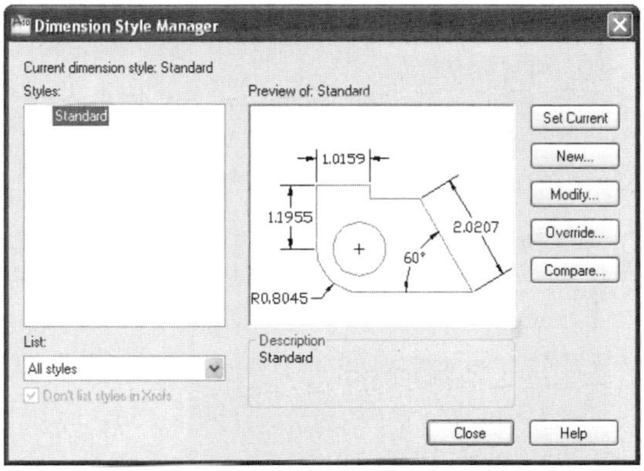

3. Click New to open the Create New Dimension Style dialog box (see Figure 10.26).

4. With the Copy of Standard or ISO-25 name highlighted in the New Style Name input box, enter a new name for your style. You might also simply leave the name as Copy of Standard or ISO-25 if that works for you. If you are working with others on a project, check to make sure your dimension style name conforms to any standards that other members of the team might be using.

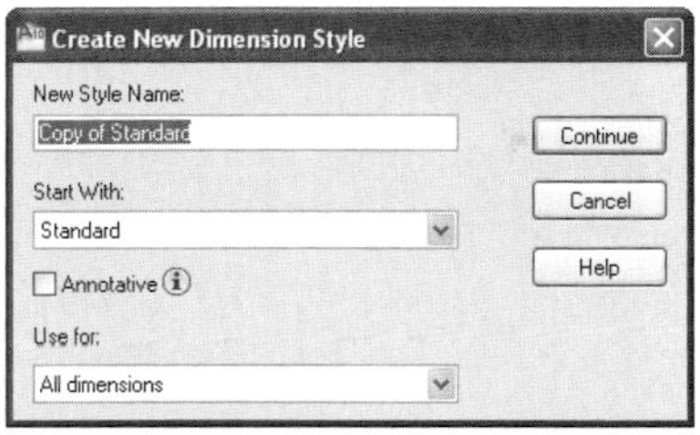

5. Click Continue to open the New Dimension Style dialog box, as shown in Figure 10.27.

You're now ready to set up your style's appearance. The New Dimension Style dialog box has several tabs, each of which controls a different aspect of the dimension's appearance.

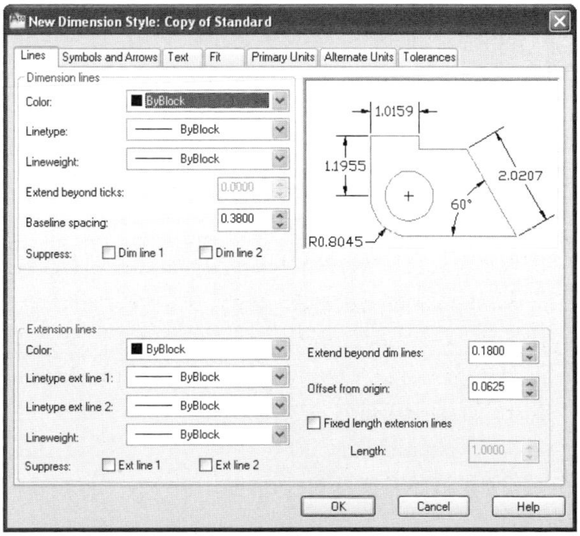

Figure 10.25

The Dimension Style Manager dialog box with the Standard style selected

Figure 10.26

The Create New Dimension Style dialog box

Figure 10.27

The New Dimension Style dialog box

Since dimensions have so many variables, you might find the number of settings overwhelming. Before you jump in and try to set up a dimension style, skim the introductory paragraph for each tab description given next. You might find that you need to change only a few settings for your style.

Setting Up the Dimension Graphics

The options in the Lines tab (refer to Figure 10.27 in the previous section) and the Symbols and Arrows tab (see Figure 10.28) give you control over the appearance of dimension and extension lines, arrowheads, and center marks. Figure 10.29 shows an example of some of the dimension components that are affected by these options. Table 10.3 describes the options in the Lines tab, and Table 10.4 describes the options for the Symbols and Arrows tab. Whenever you change any of these settings, you get immediate feedback on their effect on the dimension's appearance in the graphic that appears in the upper right of the dialog box.

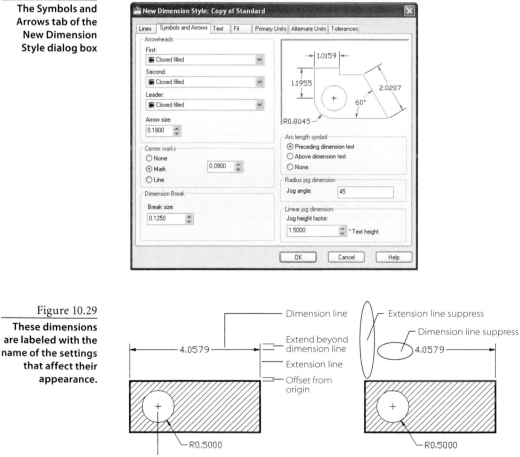

Figure 10.28

The Symbols and Arrows tab of the New Dimension Style dialog box

Figure 10.29

These dimensions are labeled with the name of the settings that affect their appearance.

The value you enter for the sizes of the dimension-line components, such as arrow size and offset from origin, should be the size you want when the drawing is printed. If you're adding dimensions in model space and you need to apply a scale factor, you must enter a scale factor value in the Use Overall Scale Of option in the Fit tab. All other dimension settings are scaled to the value you enter there.

OPTION	FUNCTION
The Dimension Lines Group	
Color	Sets the color of the dimension line.
Linetype	Sets the linetype for the dimension line.
Lineweight	Sets the lineweight for dimension lines.
Extend Beyond Ticks	Sets the distance that the dimension line extends beyond the extension lines. This option is not available when arrows are used.
Baseline Spacing	Specifies the distance between dimensions that use a common baseline.
Suppress	These check boxes let you suppress the dimension line on either side of the dimension text.
The Extension Lines Group	
Color	Sets the color for extension lines.
Linetype Ext Line 1	Sets the linetype for the first extension line.
Linetype Ext Line 2	Sets the linetype for the second extension line.
Lineweight	Sets the lineweight for extension lines.
Extend Beyond Dim Lines	Sets the distance that extension lines extend beyond dimension lines.
Offset from Origin	Sets the distance from the extension line to the object being dimensioned.
Fixed Length Extension Lines	Forces the extension lines to be a fixed length set by the Length text box.
Length	Sets the length for extension lines when the Fixed Length Extension Lines option is turned on.
Suppress	Suppresses extension lines indicated by the checked item.

Table 10.3

The Lines Tab Settings

OPTION	FUNCTION
The Arrowheads Group	
First	Sets the type of arrowhead to use on dimension lines. By default, the second arrowhead automatically changes to match the arrowhead you specify for this setting.
Second	Sets a different arrowhead from the one set for the first option.
Leader	Sets an arrowhead for leader notes.
Arrow Size	Sets the size for the arrowheads. Enter a value for the final printed size of your arrows.
The Center Marks Group	
None/Mark/Line	Sets the type of center mark used in Radius and Diameter dimensions.
Size	Sets the size of the center mark.
The Arc Length Symbol Group	
Preceding/Above/None	Sets the location of the arc length symbol for arc length dimensions.
The Radius Dimension Jog Group	
Jog Angle	Sets the angle for the Radius Dimension Jog symbol.

Table 10.4

The Symbols and Arrows Tab Settings

Setting the Appearance of the Dimension Text

You can adjust the appearance of the dimension text on the Text tab of the New Dimension Style dialog box. Text style, color, and height are a few of the features you can adjust here. You can also specify the default location of the dimension text in relation to the dimension line and extension lines. Figure 10.30 shows the Text tab, and Table 10.5 describes the options on this tab.

Figure 10.30

The Text tab of the New Dimension Style dialog box

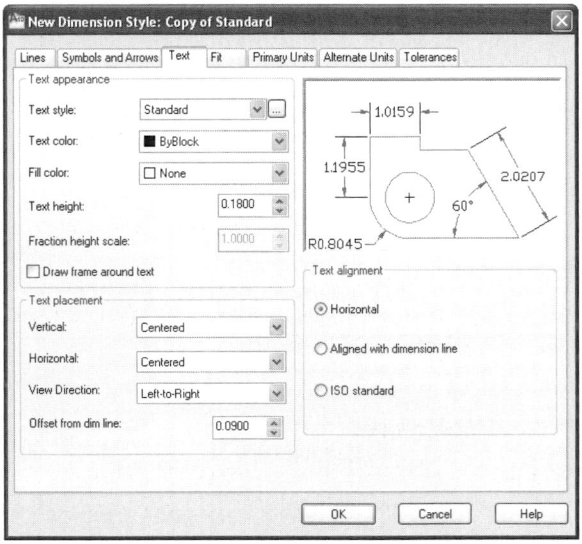

Table 10.5

The Text Tab Settings

OPTION	FUNCTION
The Text Appearance Group	
Text Style	Sets the text style for your dimension text. You need to first create a text style using the Text Style dialog box (choose Format → Text Style). You can use an Annotative text style to keep the dimension text at the proper size for the drawing scale. See "Understanding Text and Scale" in Chapter 9 for more about Annotative text styles.
Text Color	Sets the color for your dimension text.
Fill Color	Sets the color for dimension text background.
Text Height	Sets the height for dimension text. This option is valid only for text styles with their Height value set to 0 (zero).
Fraction Height Scale	Sets a scale factor for the height of fractional text. This option is meaningful only when Architectural or Fractional is selected on the Primary Units tab.
Draw Frame Around Text	When turned on, draws a rectangle around the dimension text.
The Text Placement Group	
Vertical	Sets the vertical position of the text in relation to the dimension line. Centered places the text in line with the dimension line, and the dimension line is broken to accommodate the text. Above places the text above the dimension line, leaving the dimension line unbroken. Outside places the text away from the dimension line at a location farthest from the object being dimensioned. JIS places the text in conformance with the Japanese Industrial Standards.

OPTION	FUNCTION
Horizontal	Sets the location of the text in relation to the extension lines. Centered places the text between the two extension lines. At Extension Line 1 places the text next to the first extension line and between the two extension lines. At Extension Line 2 places the text next to the second extension line and between the two extension lines. Over Extension Line 1 places the text above the first extension line. Over Extension Line 2 places the text above the second extension line.
View Direction	Specifies the reading direction of dimension text. Options are Left-to-Right and Right-to-Left.
Offset from Dim Line	Sets the distance from the baseline of text to the dimension line when text is placed above the dimension line. Also sets the size of the gap between the dimension text and the endpoint of the dimension line when the text is in line with the dimension line. You can use this to set the margin around the text when the dimension text is in a centered position that breaks the dimension line.
The Text Alignment Group	
Horizontal	Forces the text in a horizontal orientation, regardless of the dimension line orientation.
Aligned with Dimension Line	Aligns the text with the dimension line.
ISO Standard	Aligns the text with the dimension line when it is between the extension lines; otherwise, the text is oriented horizontally.

Specifying Text and Arrow Placement in Tight Spaces

Quite often, you must place dimensions in such a location that arrows and text will not fit between the extension lines. You can use the options on the Fit tab to specify what AutoCAD should do when the dimension runs out of room. You can also use the Fit tab to specify the overall scale factor for your dimensions, which is especially critical if you add dimensions in the Model tab. Figure 10.31 shows the Fit tab, and Table 10.6 describes the options on this tab.

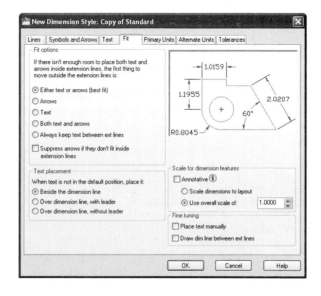

Figure 10.31

The Fit tab of the New Dimension Style dialog box

SETTING UP DIMENSIONS FOR U.S. ARCHITECTURAL DRAWINGS

If you need to set up an architectural drawing, follow these steps in the New Dimension Style dialog box.

On the Primary Units tab (see Figure 10.32 later in this chapter), follow these steps:

1. In the Linear Dimensions group, open the Unit Format drop-down list and choose Architectural.

2. Select 0′0¼″ from the Precision drop-down list, just below the Unit Format list. The Precision option allows you to set the amount that the dimension text will be rounded off. It doesn't actually limit the precision of the drawing.

3. Select Diagonal from the Fraction Format drop-down list.

4. Turn off the 0 Inches option in the Zero Suppression group.

On the Text tab (see Figure 10.30 earlier in this chapter), follow these steps:

1. In the Text Alignment group, click the Aligned with Dimension Line radio button.

2. In the Text Placement group, open the Vertical drop-down list and select Above.

3. In the Text Placement group, change the Offset from Dim Line value to ¹⁄₁₆. The value changes to its decimal equivalent of 0.625. This setting controls the size of the gap between the dimension line and the dimension text.

On the Symbols and Arrows tab (see Figure 10.28 earlier in this chapter), follow these steps:

1. In the Arrowheads group, open the first drop-down list and choose Architectural Tick.

2. In the Arrowheads group, change the Arrow Size setting to ¹⁄₈.

3. On the Lines tab (see Figure 10.27 earlier in this chapter), follow these steps:

   • In the Dimension Lines group, highlight the value in the Extend beyond Ticks input box, and then enter ¹⁄₁₆ ↵.

   • In the Extension Lines group, change the Extend Beyond Dim Lines setting to ¹⁄₈ ↵.

   • In the Extension Lines group, change the Offset from Origin setting to ¹⁄₈.

On the Fit tab (see Figure 10.31 earlier in this chapter), follow these steps:

1. In the Scale for Dimension Features group, click the Use Overall Scale Of radio button.

2. Double-click the list box just to the right of the Use Overall Scale Of radio button, and then enter the desired scale factor. See Chapter 9 for more about scale factors and text size.

	OPTION	FUNCTION
Table 10.6		
The Fit Tab Settings	**The Fit Options Group**	
	Either Text or Arrows (Best Fit)	Fits either text or arrows between the extension lines, depending on which of the two items fits best.
	Arrows	Moves arrows outside the extension line first and then text.
	Text	Moves text outside the extension line first and then arrows.

OPTION	FUNCTION
Both Text and Arrows	Moves both the text and the arrows outside the extension line.
Always Keep Text Between Ext Lines	Forces the arrows and text to remain between the extension lines.
Suppress Arrows if They Don't Fit Inside Extension Lines	Completely suppresses arrows if they do not fit between the extension lines.
The Text Placement Group	
Beside The Dimension Line	Keeps the text and dimension line together.
Over Dimension Line, With Leader	Allows independent movement of the text and the dimension line. A leader is added if the text is moved from the dimension line.
Over Dimension Line, Without Leader	Allows independent movement of the text and the dimension line.
The Scale for Dimension Features Group	
Annotative	Determines whether the dimension style uses annotative scale. See "Understanding Text and Scale" in Chapter 9 for more about annotative scale.
Use Overall Scale Of	This combined radio button and input box sets the overall scale of the dimension components, including text and arrows.
Scale Dimensions to Layout	Scales the dimension components to the scale factor assigned to the paper space viewport in which the drawing appears.
The Fine Tuning Group	
Place Text Manually	Lets you manually place dimension text when the text does not fit between extension lines.
Always Draw Dim Line Between Ext Lines	Forces AutoCAD to draw a dimension line regardless of the width between extension lines.

Specifying the Unit Style Settings for Dimensions

The options on the Primary Units tab let you set the format and content of the dimension text, including the unit style for linear and angular dimensions. Figure 10.32 shows the Primary Units tab, and Table 10.7 describes the options on this tab.

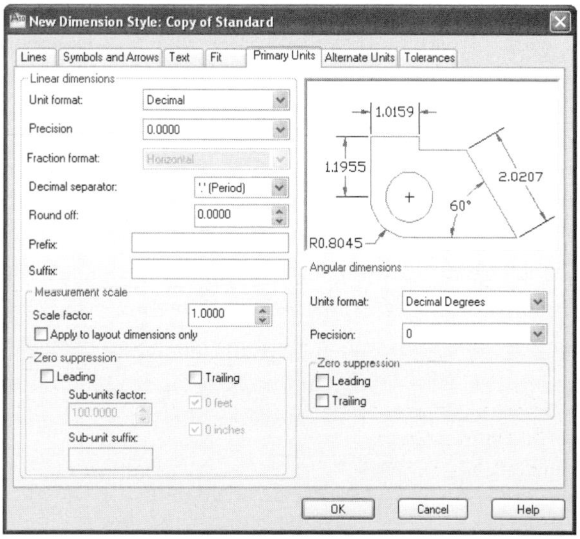

Figure 10.32

The Primary Units tab of the New Dimension Style dialog box

Table 10.7

**Primary Units
Tab Settings**

OPTION	FUNCTION
The Linear Dimensions Group	
Unit Format	Sets the unit style of the dimension text. The options are Scientific, Decimal, Engineering, Architectural, Fractional, and Windows Desktop.
Precision	Sets the precision of the dimension text. This option rounds off the dimension text to the nearest precision value you set. It does not affect the actual precision of the drawing.
Fraction Format	Specifies how fractions are displayed. The choices are Horizontal, Vertical, and Not Stacked. These options apply only to architectural and fractional unit formats.
Decimal Separator	Sets the decimal separator for dimension unit formats that display decimals. You can choose a period, a comma, or a space.
Round Off	Sets the degree of rounding applied to dimension text. For example, you can set this option to 0.25 to round off dimensions to the nearest 0.25, or ¼, of a unit.
Prefix	Sets a prefix for all linear and aligned dimension text. The prefix is added to the beginning of all linear dimension text.
Suffix	Sets a suffix for all linear and aligned dimension text. The suffix is added to the end of all linear dimension text.
Measurement Scale Group	
Scale Factor	Multiplies the dimension value by a scale factor. You can set this value to 25.4, for example, to show dimension values in millimeters for drawings created in Imperial units.
Apply to Layout Dimensions Only	Applies the measurement scale factor to paper space layouts only.
Zero Suppression Group	
Leading, Trailing	Suppresses zeros so they do not appear in the dimension text. For example, with the Leading option selected, 0.50 will be shown as .50 (point five zero). With Trailing selected, it is shown as 0.5.
Sub-Units Factor	Enables you to set the number of decimal places for values less than 1. A value of 100 will allow two decimal places.
Sub-Unit Suffix	Enables you to apply a suffix such as cm for centimeters or mm for millimeters.
The Angular Dimensions Group	
Units Format	Sets a format for angular dimensions. The options are Decimal Degrees, Degrees Minutes Seconds, Gradians, and Radians.
Precision	Sets the precision for the angular dimension text.
Zero Suppression: Leading, Trailing	Suppresses leading or trailing zeros in angular dimensions.

Using the Alternate Units Tab

The Alternate Units tab lets you apply a second set of dimension text for linear dimensions. You can use this set for alternate dimension styles or units. For example, you can use alternate units to display alternate metric dimension values in addition to the main dimension values in feet and inches. Figure 10.33 shows the Alternate Units tab, and Table 10.8 describes the options on this tab.

To turn on Alternate Units, click the Display Alternate Units check box. AutoCAD then includes an additional dimension text in the format you specify on this tab.

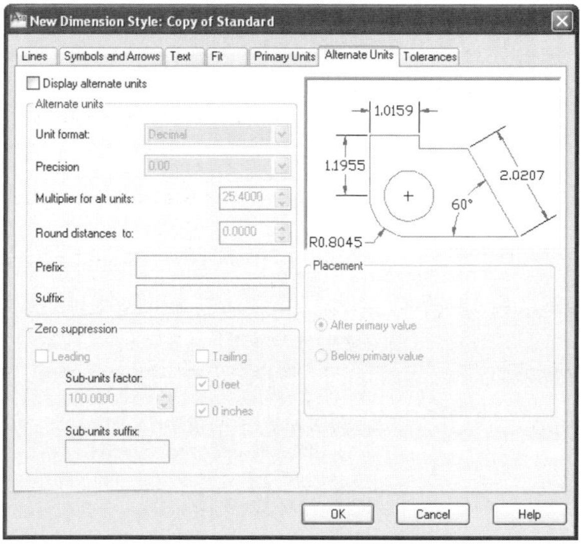

Figure 10.33

The Alternate Units tab of the New Dimension Style dialog box

OPTION	FUNCTION
The Alternate Units Group	
Unit Format	Sets the unit style of the dimension text. The options are Scientific, Decimal, Engineering, Architectural Stacked, Fractional Stacked, Architectural, Fractional, and Windows Desktop.
Precision	Sets the precision of the dimension text. This option rounds off the dimension text to the nearest precision value you set. It does not affect the actual precision of the drawing.
Multiplier for Alt Units	Sets a multiplier value for the dimension text. This option multiplies the dimension text value by the multiplier value. For example, if you want alternate dimensions to display distances in centimeters even though the drawing was created in inches, you can enter 2.54 for this option.
Round Distances To	Sets the value rounding applied to alternate dimensions.
Prefix	Adds a prefix for all linear and aligned alternate dimension text.
Suffix	Adds a suffix for all linear and aligned alternate dimension text.
The Zero Suppression Group	
Leading, Trailing, Feet, Inches	Suppresses zeros so they do not appear in the dimension text. For example, with the Leading option selected, 0.50 is shown as .50 (point five zero). With Trailing selected, it is shown as 0.5.
Sub-Units Factor	Enables you to set the number of decimal places for values less than 1. A value of 100 will allow two decimal places.
Sub-Units Suffix	Enables you to apply a suffix such as cm for centimeters or mm for millimeters.
The Placement Group	
After Primary Value	Sets the alternate dimension text to appear behind and aligned with the primary dimension text.
Below Primary Value	Sets the alternate dimension text to appear below the primary dimension text and above the dimension line.

Table 10.8

The Alternate Units Tab Settings

Using the Tolerances Tab

The options on the Tolerances tab let you add tolerance dimension text and include options for tolerance dimension text formatting. Figure 10.34 shows the Tolerances tab, and Table 10.9 describes the options on this tab.

Figure 10.34

The Tolerances tab of the New Dimension Style dialog box

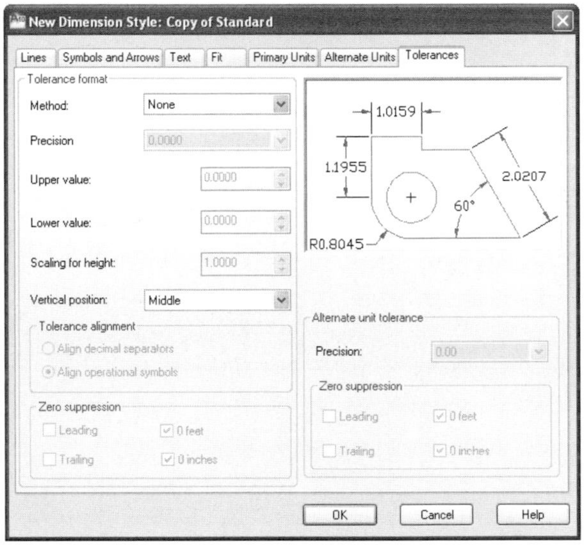

Table 10.9

The Tolerances Tab Settings

OPTION	FUNCTION
The Tolerance Format Group	
Method	Sets the format for the tolerance dimension text. The options are None, Symmetrical, Deviation, Limits, and Basic. None turns off the tolerance dimension text. Symmetrical adds a plus/minus tolerance dimension. This is a single dimension preceded by a plus/minus sign. Deviation adds a stacked tolerance dimension showing separate upper and lower tolerance values. The Limits option replaces the primary dimension with a stacked dimension showing maximum and minimum dimension values. The Basic option draws a box around the primary dimension value. If an alternate dimension is used, the box encloses both primary and alternate dimension text.
Precision	Sets the precision of the tolerance dimension text. This option rounds off the dimension text to the nearest precision value you set. It does not affect the actual precision of the drawing.
Upper Value	Sets the upper tolerance value for the Symmetrical, Deviation, and Limits tolerance methods.
Lower Value	Lets you set the lower tolerance value for the Deviation and Limits tolerance methods (Dimtm).
Scaling for Height	Sets the size for the tolerance dimension text as a proportion of the primary dimension text height.
Vertical Position	Sets the vertical position of the tolerance text. The options are Top, Middle, and Bottom. The Top option aligns the top tolerance value of a stacked pair of values with the primary dimension text. Middle aligns the gap between stacked tolerance values with the primary dimension text. Bottom aligns the bottom value of two stacked tolerance values with the primary dimension text.
Zero Suppression: Leading, Trailing, Feet, Inches	Suppresses zeros so they do not appear in the tolerance dimension text. For example, with the Leading option selected, 0.50 is shown as .50 (point five zero). With Trailing selected, it is shown as 0.5.

OPTION	FUNCTION

The Alternate Unit Tolerance Group

Precision	Sets the precision of the alternate tolerance dimension text. This option rounds off the dimension text to the nearest precision value you set. It does not affect the actual precision of the drawing.
Zero Suppression: Leading, Trailing, Feet, Inches	Suppresses zeros in alternate unit tolerance dimensions so they do not appear in the dimension text.

Setting the Current Dimension Style

Before you can begin to use your new dimension style, you must make it the current default:

1. In the Styles list in the Dimension Style Manager dialog box, click the name of style you want to be current.

2. Click the Set Current button at the far right of the dialog box.

3. Click Close to exit the Dimension Style Manager dialog box.

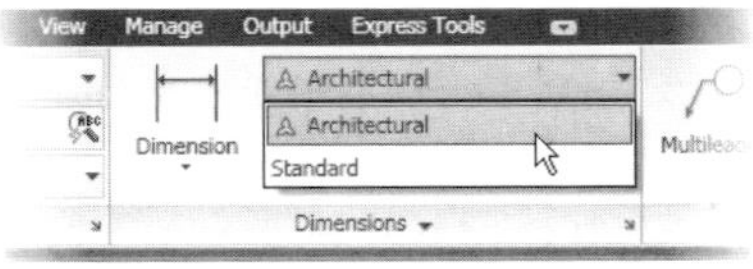

Figure 10.35

The Dimension Style drop-down list in the Dimensions panel

You're now ready to use your new dimension style. You can also select a dimension style from the Dimensions panel's Select a Dimension Style drop-down list (see Figure 10.35).

Editing a Dimension Style

Once you've created a dimension style, you can always change it. To do so, you use the Modify option in the Dimension Style Manager dialog box:

1. In the Dimensions panel, click the Dimension Style tool or enter **d**↵ to open the Dimension Style Manager dialog box.

2. Select the name of the dimension style you want to edit in the list box at the left of the dialog box.

3. Click Modify to open the Modify Dimension Style dialog box.

Use the steps in the previous section as a guide to adjust your dimension styles.

Summary

As you work with dimensions, you might find that you'll make adjustments to the dimension style little by little, until you set up a style just the way you want. Once you've reached that point, you probably won't change your dimension styles often. You can then save your dimension style to a file using Express Tools, a set of optional plug-in tools that you can add to AutoCAD 2010 (not available in 2010 LT), or you can add them to your most frequently used template file so the styles are available at all times.

CHAPTER 11

Gathering Information

AutoCAD drawings can contain a great deal of information. You can store text-based information both as labels in the drawing and as hidden written information, and you can also query graphic elements to find distance and area measurements.

This chapter provides information about how you can store and retrieve information about the drawing. You'll find out how to gather information from your drawing when you're measuring an area or looking for a lost file. You'll also find information about how to add textual data to help you when you're doing file searches with DesignCenter.

This chapter includes the following topics:

- Measuring areas
- Finding the coordinate of a point
- Measuring distances
- Measuring angles
- Getting the general status of the drawing
- Finding the time spent on a drawing
- Adding nondrawing data to store with your drawing
- Finding text in a drawing
- Locating and selecting named components
- Finding missing support files

If you've recently used the 3D Modeling workspace, make sure you are back in the 2D Drafting & Annotation workspace before beginning any exercises in this chapter. See "Getting to Know the 3D Modeling Workspace" in Chapter 6 for instructions on how to switch to a different workspace.

Measuring Areas

One of the first measurement tasks you're likely to need to perform is measuring the area in a drawing. It might be the area of a site plan or the floor space of a commercial building. Before AutoCAD came along, finding the area in a drawing was a tedious and error-ridden job. Now that you're using AutoCAD, you can quickly find areas of all shapes and sizes, and you'll be certain that you have an accurate area calculation.

You can measure an area in several ways. It's easiest to measure an area that is completely bounded by objects. The boundary can consist of individual objects, or it can be a single, closed polyline or spline. You can also find an area by selecting a set of points that defines the corners of a boundary. This method is useful for areas that have straight sides, such as a typical property line in a city grid.

Measuring the Area of a Polygonal Shape

If you're trying to find the area of a polygonal shape, you can use the Measuregeom command, which appears in the Measure flyout in the Home tab's Utilities panel. The following steps describe the process:

1. In the Home tab's Utilities panel, click the Measure flyout and then click the Area tool, or enter **Measuregeom**↵ **Ar**↵ at the command prompt.

2. Following the boundary edge, select the corners of your polygon. Use osnaps to make accurate point selections (see Figure 11.1). As you select points, you'll see a green area showing you the area that AutoCAD is measuring.

3. When you have selected all the corners, press ↵. You'll see a message in the command line that gives the area and perimeter you just selected.

4. Type **X**↵ to exit the Measuregeom command or select eXit from the Dynamic Input menu.

The shape can be as simple as a box or as complex as the one shown in Figure 11.1. You'll get an accurate reading as long as all the sides of the polygon are straight.

Besides the Area tool, the Measure flyout and Measuregeom command offer several other measuring tools: Distance, Radius, Angle, Area, and Volume. Table 11.1 gives you a rundown of these options.

Figure 11.1

Select points sequentially on a polygonal shape, as shown by the numbers, to find its area.

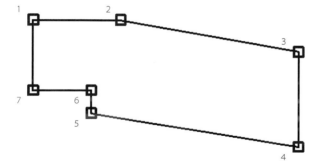

OPTION	USE	
Distance	Returns the distance between two points. Type **D**↵ and select two points. You can also measure cumulative distances by typing **M**↵ after selecting the first point.	
Radius	Returns the radius of an arc or circle. Type **R**↵ and select an arc or circle.	
Angle	Returns the angle of an arc or the angle between two lines. Type **A**↵ and select the arc or two nonparallel lines.	
ARea	Returns the area of a set of points or boundary. Type **AR**↵ to use this option.	
Volume	Returns the volume of an area. Type **V**↵, then select an area. Once an area has been selected, indicate a height.	
eXit	Exits the current option or the Measuregeom command. You can also press the Esc key.	

Table 11.1

The Measuregeom Command Options

Measuring the Area of Complex or Curved Shapes

If the area you want to measure has curves in its boundary or if it's just too complex to use the previous method, the best step to take is to place a hatch pattern within the boundary. You can then use the Properties palette to find the area. The advantage to this method is that you'll always have a way to quickly get an area measurement. At any time, you can look at the properties of the hatch pattern that fills the boundary.

Using the Hatch Command to Create a Polyline Outline

Although the main purpose of the Hatch command is to place a hatch pattern in your drawing, hatch patterns can also tell you the area they occupy. Before you begin, however, you must be sure that the area you're trying to define has a continuous border.

> If you're measuring a room with an open doorway, draw a temporary line across the doorway before using the Hatch command. Or if your drawing contains a door header layer, turn it on to display the door header. Also turn off the layer of any door blocks that might interfere with the creation of a hatch pattern of the entire room.

1. Click the Hatch tool in the Home tab's Draw panel or type **H**↵ to open the Hatch and Gradient dialog box, as shown in Figure 11.2.

2. Click the Add: Pick Points button. The Hatch and Gradient dialog box closes.

3. At the `Select internal point or [Select objects/remove Boundaries]:` prompt, click the interior of the area you want to measure. You'll see the area outlined with a dashed line.

4. Press ↵, and then in the Hatch and Gradient dialog box, click OK. Hatch draws a hatch pattern on the current layer. You can always change the layer assignment of the hatch pattern later.

Figure 11.2

**The Hatch and
Gradient dialog box**

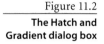

Figure 11.3

**The Area listing in the
Geometry group of the
Properties palette**

5. Select the newly created hatch pattern, right-click, and choose Properties.

6. In the Properties palette, scroll down to the Geometry group to find the Area listing, as shown in Figure 11.3.

If you want to copy the area value from the Properties palette, click the QuickCalc icon to the right of the area value and highlight the text from the QuickCalc display.

You can use any hatch pattern you want because they'll all report the same area. Once you've obtained the area measurement of the hatch pattern, you can delete it. If you want to keep the hatch pattern for future reference, you can put it on a separate layer and turn off that layer.

If you put the hatch pattern you're using for area calculations on a different layer for future reference, make sure you turn off plotting for that layer. This will prevent you from accidentally including those hatch patterns in your plotted output. See Chapter 7 for more about layer settings.

If there is a gap anywhere in the area you're trying to measure, you might get an error message that says the area you're trying to select is not closed. You can use the Gap Tolerance setting to tell AutoCAD to ignore gaps of a certain size. You can also have the Hatch command place a polyline outline of the hatch area by turning on the Retain Boundaries option in the Hatch and Gradient dialog box. By including a polyline outline, you can delete the hatch pattern and still obtain the area of the polyline outline from the

Properties palette just as you would for a hatch pattern. (See steps 5 and 6 of the previous example.) See Chapter 3 for more information about the Gap Tolerance and Retain Boundaries options.

Measuring Areas That Contain Islands

You might need to measure an area that contains other shapes such as circles or polygons, as shown in Figure 11.4. The Hatch command offers the ability to ignore these "islands" within a boundary. If your measurement must exclude these other shapes, make sure that the Island Detection option in the Hatch and Gradient dialog box is turned on and set to either Normal or Outer. Island Detection is turned on by default.

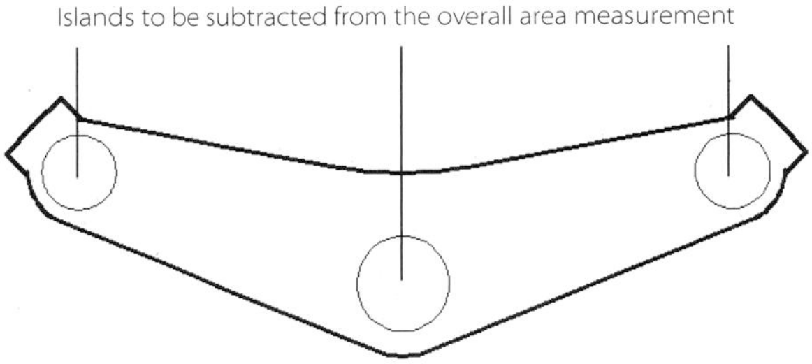

Finding Cumulative Area Values

If you need to find the cumulative area of several spaces, you can place individual hatch patterns in those spaces, select all the hatch patterns, and then open the Properties palette. You'll see a Cumulative Area listing in the Geometry group that reports the total area of all the selected hatch patterns. (See the bottom of Figure 11.3 earlier in this chapter.)

Another tool you can employ is the QuickCalc calculator (Figure 11.5). You might have noticed a small calculator icon to the far right of the Area listing in the Properties palette. If you click that icon, the QuickCalc calculator opens with the area value already displayed.

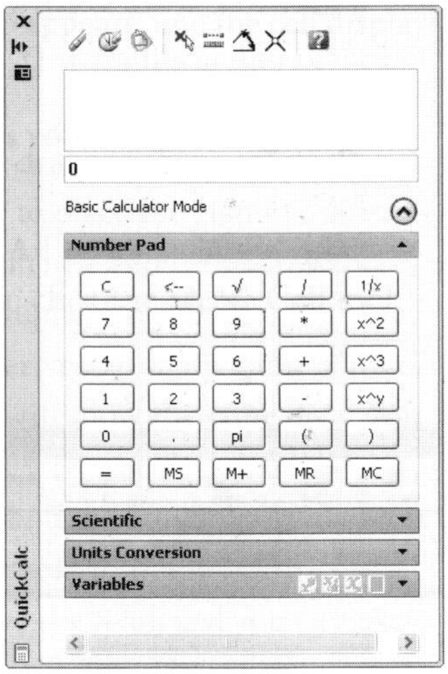

You can use the Memory functions of the calculator to store and add area values, perform conversions, or do any other operation you require. You can also open the QuickCalc calculator by right-clicking and selecting QuickCalc from the context menu.

Finding the Coordinate of a Point

If you need to find the coordinates of several points in reference to a datum point, you must first set up a UCS with its origin at the datum point. You can then use the ID command to quickly find the coordinates.

1. In the View tab's Coordinates panel, click the Origin tool, or enter **ucs.⏎ Origin.⏎** at the command prompt.

2. At the Specify new origin point <0,0,0>: prompt, use an osnap to select the datum point.

Figure 11.4

An area containing other shapes, or "islands," that you do not want in your area measurement

Islands to be subtracted from the overall area measurement

Figure 11.5

QuickCalc calculator

3. In the Home tab's expanded Utilities panel, click the ID Point tool.

4. At the `Specify point:` prompt, use an osnap to select the exact point in your drawing. The coordinates are displayed in the command line.

If a reference datum point is not important, you can skip steps 1 and 2 and start at step 3.

If the coordinate system you're measuring from is at an angle in relation to AutoCAD's default or WCS, you can rotate the UCS around the z-axis before using the ID command:

1. In the View tab's Coordinates panel, click the Z tool.

2. At the `Specify rotation angle about Z axis <90>:` prompt, enter an angle or select two points to indicate an angle graphically. The UCS rotates to the new angle.

3. Go to step 3 of the previous example to obtain the coordinates of the point you want.

If you'd like to learn more about the UCS, see Chapter 6.

Measuring Distances

Measuring distances is simple:

1. In the Home tab's Utilities panel, click the Distance tool from the Measure flyout, or enter **Measuregeom.**↲↲ at the command prompt.

2. At the `Specify first point:` prompt, use an osnap, and select the start point of the distance you want to measure.

3. At the `Specify second point:` prompt, use an osnap to select the endpoint of the distance. You'll see temporary dimensions showing you the direct distance plus the x- and y-axis distances. The distance is also displayed in the command line in the following format:

```
Distance = x.xxxx,  Angle in XY Plane = xx,  Angle from XY Plane = x
Delta X = x.xxxx,  Delta Y = x.xxxx,   Delta Z = x.xxxx
```

4. Type **X**↲ to exit the Measuregeom command or click the eXit option from the Dynamic Input menu.

Measuring Angles

You can use the Distance command described in the previous section to find the angle represented by two points. But what if you want to find the angle between two lines, as in Figure 11.6?

Figure 11.6

Using angular dimension to find the angle between two lines

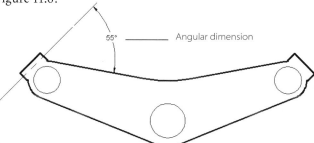

The Measuregeom command in the form of the Measure flyout offers a way to find angles such as the one shown in Figure 11.6.

1. In the Home tab's Utilities panel, click Angle from the Measure flyout, or enter **Measuregeom**↵ **A**↵ at the command prompt.
2. At the `Select arc, circle, line, or <specify vertex>:` prompt, select the first line.
3. At the `Select second line:` prompt, select the second line. You'll see a temporary dimension displaying the angle between the lines.
4. Type **X**↵ or select eXit from the Dynamic Input menu to exit the Measuregeom command.

By default, AutoCAD's dimensioning feature rounds off angular dimensions to the nearest degree. You can adjust the Precision value for dimension styles to show angular values that are less than a whole degree. For more information, see "Using Other Drawing Unit Options" in Chapter 2.

Getting the General Status of the Drawing

You can quickly get the status of many drawings settings using the Status command. This command displays the current settings for limits, snaps, grids, the display area, and other features. This information can help you understand a drawing or help troubleshoot a problem. Here's how it works:

1. From the Application menu, choose Drawing Utilities → Status, or enter **Status**↵ at the command prompt.
2. The Text window displays a listing of the current status of the drawing, as shown in Figure 11.7.

Table 11.2 describes the options shown by the Status command.

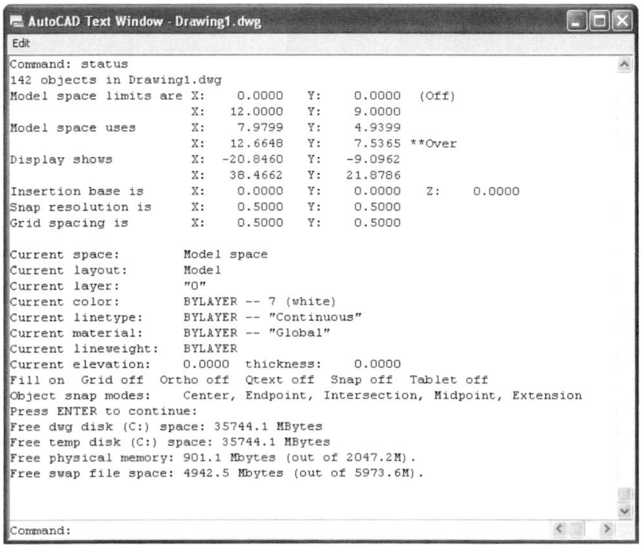

```
AutoCAD Text Window - Drawing1.dwg
Edit
Command: status
142 objects in Drawing1.dwg
Model space limits are X:     0.0000   Y:     0.0000  (Off)
                       X:    12.0000   Y:     9.0000
Model space uses       X:     7.9799   Y:     4.9399
                       X:    12.6648   Y:     7.5365 **Over
Display shows          X:   -20.8460   Y:    -9.0962
                       X:    38.4662   Y:    21.8786
Insertion base is      X:     0.0000   Y:     0.0000   Z:     0.0000
Snap resolution is     X:     0.5000   Y:     0.5000
Grid spacing is        X:     0.5000   Y:     0.5000

Current space:        Model space
Current layout:       Model
Current layer:        "0"
Current color:        BYLAYER -- 7 (white)
Current linetype:     BYLAYER -- "Continuous"
Current material:     BYLAYER -- "Global"
Current lineweight:   BYLAYER
Current elevation:    0.0000  thickness:    0.0000
Fill on  Grid off  Ortho off  Qtext off  Snap off  Tablet off
Object snap modes:    Center, Endpoint, Intersection, Midpoint, Extension
Press ENTER to continue:
Free dwg disk (C:) space: 35744.1 MBytes
Free temp disk (C:) space: 35744.1 MBytes
Free physical memory: 901.1 Mbytes (out of 2047.2M).
Free swap file space: 4942.5 Mbytes (out of 5973.6M).

Command:
```

Figure 11.7

The AutoCAD Text window showing the drawing status

Table 11.2

The Status Items and Their Meanings

ITEM	MEANING
(Number) Objects In D:\Folder\Subfolder	The number of AutoCAD objects in the drawing.
Model Space Limits Are	The coordinates of the Model tab limits. (See Chapter 2 for more details about limits.)
Model Space Uses	The area the drawing occupies; equivalent to Zoom extents.
**Over:	If present, this item means that part of the drawing is outside the area defined by the drawing limits.
Display Shows	The area shown by the current view.
Insertion Base Is, Snap Resolution Is, and Grid Spacing Is	The current default values for these settings.
Current Space	Model (model space) or Layout (paper space) tab.
Current Layout	The current tab.
Current Layer	The current layer.
Current Color	The current color.
Current Linetype	The current linetype.
Current Material	The current 3D modeling material.
Current Lineweight	The current lineweight setting.
Current Elevation/Thickness	The current default Z coordinate and the current thickness of objects. These are both 3D-related settings.
Fill, Grid, Ortho, Qtext, Snap, and Tablet	The status of these settings.
Object Snap Modes	The current default osnap setting.
Free Dwg Disk (Drive:) Space	The amount of space available to store drawing-specific temporary files.
Free Temp Disk (Drive:) Space	The amount of space left on your hard drive for AutoCAD's resource temporary files.
Free Physical Memory	The amount of free RAM available.
Free Swap File Space	The amount of Windows swap file space available.

Finding the Time Spent on a Drawing

You might want to find out how much time you actually spent on a drawing for billing purposes, or you might just want to keep track of how long a drawing takes. Using the Time command is a quick way to get this information:

1. Enter **Time**↵ at the command prompt.

2. The Text window displays the time information, as shown in Figure 11.8.

3. At the Enter option [Display/ON/OFF/Reset]: prompt, press ↵ to exit the Time command.

As you can see in Figure 11.8, the information is self-explanatory. You can also turn the timer off by entering **Off** ↵ at the prompt in step 3, or you can reset the timer to clear the current values by entering **R**↵.

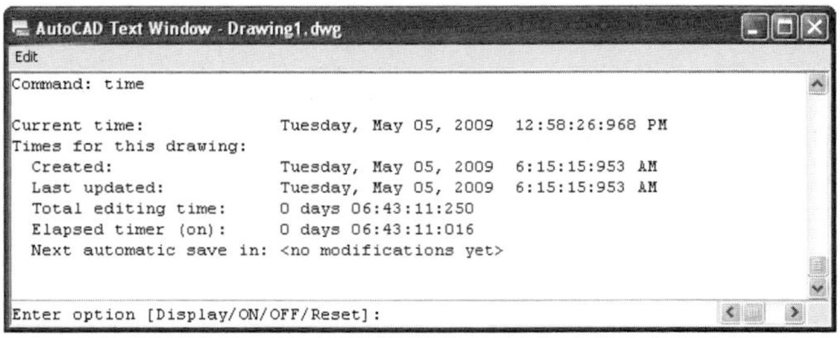

Figure 11.8

The time information in the AutoCAD Text window

```
AutoCAD Text Window - Drawing1.dwg
Edit
Command: time

Current time:            Tuesday, May 05, 2009  12:58:26:968 PM
Times for this drawing:
  Created:               Tuesday, May 05, 2009  6:15:15:953 AM
  Last updated:          Tuesday, May 05, 2009  6:15:15:953 AM
  Total editing time:    0 days 06:43:11:250
  Elapsed timer (on):    0 days 06:43:11:016
  Next automatic save in: <no modifications yet>

Enter option [Display/ON/OFF/Reset]:
```

Adding Nondrawing Data to Store with Your Drawing

The drawing's Properties dialog box lets you store nondrawing data with your drawing file. This can be textual information such as the project name, people involved in creating the drawing, or comments regarding the drawing. You can even add a keyword in the event that you'll need to search for this file using the AutoCAD DesignCenter or the Windows Search tool.

To get to the drawing's Properties dialog box, choose Drawing Utilities → Drawing Properties from the Application menu. The General tab contains information such as the file size and when the drawing was created (see Figure 11.9).

The Summary tab contains the Title, Subject, Author, Keywords, and Comments text boxes in which you can enter data (see Figure 11.10).

The Statistics tab offers editing dates and times. The Custom tab (see Figure 11.11) lets you enter further textual data to be stored with the drawing.

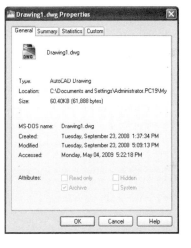

Figure 11.9

The General tab of the drawing's Properties dialog box

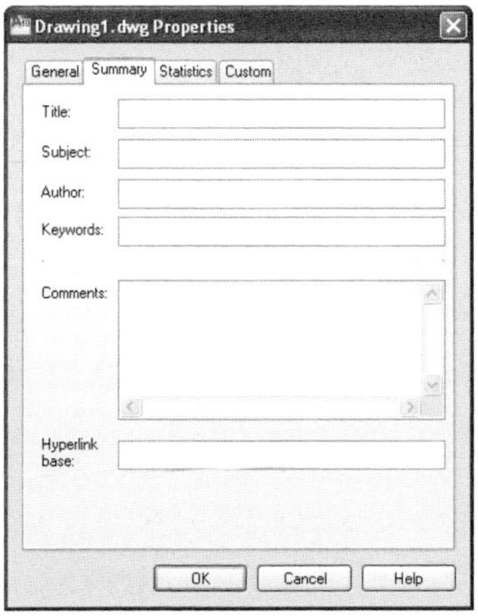

Figure 11.10

The Summary tab of the drawing's Properties dialog box

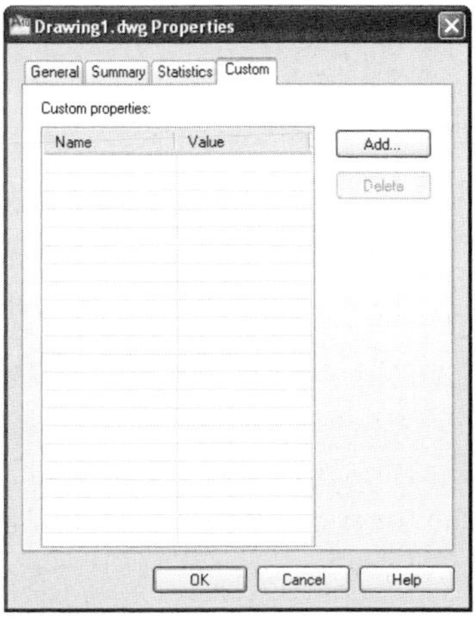

Figure 11.11

The Custom tab of the drawing's Properties dialog box

Finding Text in a Drawing

You often have to find a string of text to replace it or to simply locate a part of a drawing indicated by the text. AutoCAD offers the Find command to help you locate specific text in a drawing, including attribute values and dimension text. Here's how it works:

1. Go to the Annotate tab's Text panel to the Find Text input box, as shown in Figure 11.12.

2. In the Find Text input box, enter the text you want to find.

3. Click the Find text tool to the right of the input box. The Find and Replace dialog box appears.

4. If the text exists in the drawing, your view will change to display the found text.

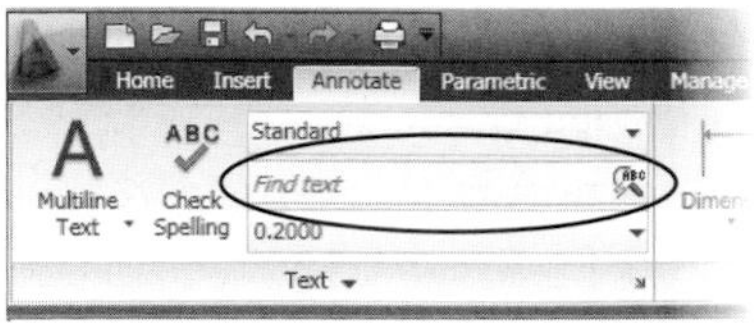

Figure 11.12

The Find Text input box in the expanded Text panel

You can use the Find command to search for attribute text, table text, dimension text, and hyperlinks. If you click the More Options button in the Find and Replace dialog box, the dialog box expands to display additional options (see Figure 11.13). This is where you can specify whether the search is case sensitive, search for whole words, or use other search criteria.

Figure 11.13

The Find and Replace dialog box with the options displayed

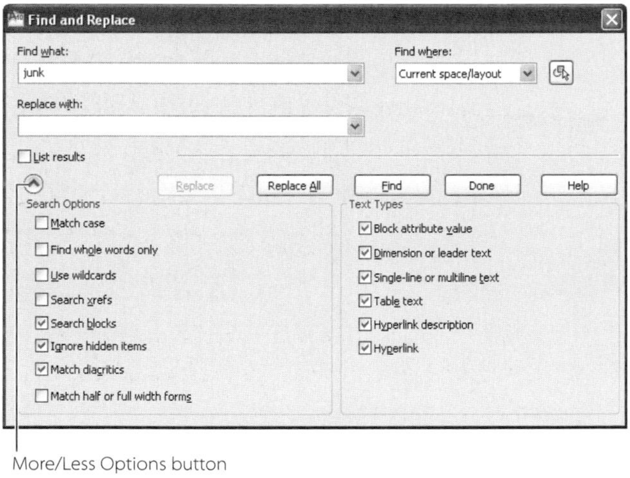

More/Less Options button

Locating and Selecting Named Components

As your drawings become more complex, you'll have a harder time finding specific items you need to edit. For example, you might need to replace the text style of some notes that have been set improperly. You have a couple of tools that can help you find items in your drawing based on their name or the name of a property they possess. You can use the Quick Select feature, which is actually intended to select objects based on their properties. You can also use DesignCenter, which can show you graphic representations of named components in your drawing.

Searching Using Quick Select

You can locate objects based on the type of object or a property using the Quick Select tool. If the object has a name, such as a *block*, for example, you can also locate it with this tool. Although Quick Select is intended as a selection tool, since it highlights the objects in your drawing, you can see where the selected objects are in the drawing and then use the Zoom feature to zoom in on their locations.

The following example shows how you can find a block in a drawing:

1. In the Home tab's Utilities panel, click the Quick Select tool to open the Quick Select dialog box.

2. Select Entire Drawing from the Apply To drop-down list.

3. Select Block Reference from the Object Type drop-down list.

4. In the Properties list, select Name.

5. In the Operator list, select = Equals, as shown in Figure 11.14.

6. Locate the name of the block you want in the Value drop-down list.

7. Click OK. You'll see the selected objects highlighted in the drawing.

Figure 11.14

The Quick Select dialog box with = Equals selected in the Operator list

One feature you'll want to be aware of is the Operator list. By default, it shows = Equals, which lets you find an object whose property equals the one shown in the Value list, but you can also base your selection on properties that are not equal to the settings you select. If the selection criteria involve a numeric value, you can also use greater-than or less-than operators.

You can also use DesignCenter to locate named items such as blocks, linetypes, text styles, and dimension styles.

Viewing a List of Named Components

If you don't necessarily need to find a named element in a drawing but just want to see a listing of them, you can use DesignCenter. DesignCenter shows you not only the named components in open drawings but also the named components in other drawing files. You can even search folders containing drawing files to locate a particular named component. You can find a detailed discussion of DesignCenter in Chapter 8.

Finding Missing Support Files

Sometimes a drawing appears incomplete or incorrect because of missing support files. If font files are missing, AutoCAD attempts to substitute another font, but your text will not appear as it was intended. Or if a custom linetype was used for parts of the drawing, they will not appear correctly. Whole parts of a drawing will be missing if AutoCAD can't find Xrefs.

If you open an AutoCAD drawing and find that you're missing support files such as these, it might be that you need to direct AutoCAD to the proper location for these files.

Locating Xrefs

If you open a drawing and most of it appears to be missing, chances are an Xref has been misplaced. You'll know an Xref is missing because you'll see a text string that starts with the word *Xref* and is followed by a search path, as shown in Figure 11.15.

Another clue that you're missing an Xref is an exclamation point in the lower-right corner of the AutoCAD window (see Figure 11.16).

Figure 11.15

Text shown in place of a missing Xref

Figure 11.16

The lower-right corner of the AutoCAD window shows an exclamation point with a paper clip icon.

If this happens to you, do the following:

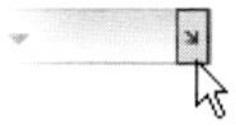

1. In the Insert tab's Reference panel, click the External References tool on the Reference title bar or enter **Xref↵** at the command prompt to open the External References palette, as shown in Figure 11.17. You can also click the exclamation point in the lower-right corner of the AutoCAD window.

2. You'll see the name of the missing Xref in the list box. Make note of the filename, and then use the Windows Search utility (choose Start → Search → For Files or Folders) to find the missing file.

3. Back in AutoCAD, select the missing external reference from the External References palette list box.

4. Locate the Found At text box near the bottom of the External References palette, and click the text box. If you don't see the Found At text box, right-click in the External Reference palette's list box, and select Preview/Details Pane.

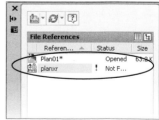

Figure 11.17

The External References palette

5. Click the Browse button (the one that shows an ellipsis) to the right of the Found At text box (Figure 11.18) to open the Select New Path dialog box.

6. Browse to the location of the missing file, and select it.

7. Back in the External References palette, you should see that the exclamation point has disappeared and the file is listed as Loaded, as shown in Figure 11.19.

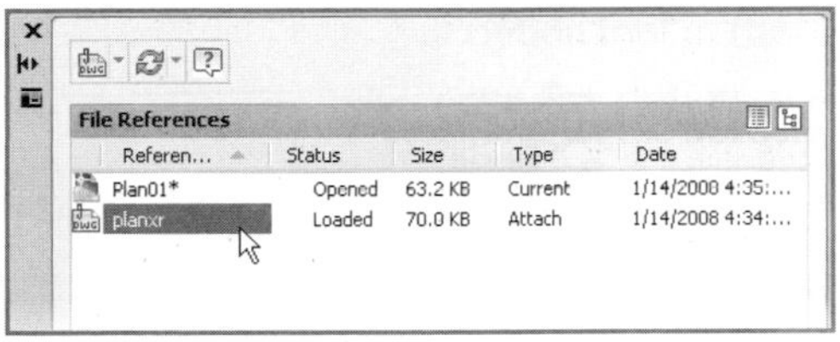

Another option is to first look at the name of the search path shown in the drawing or in the Saved Path text box of the External References palette, as shown in Figure 11.20.

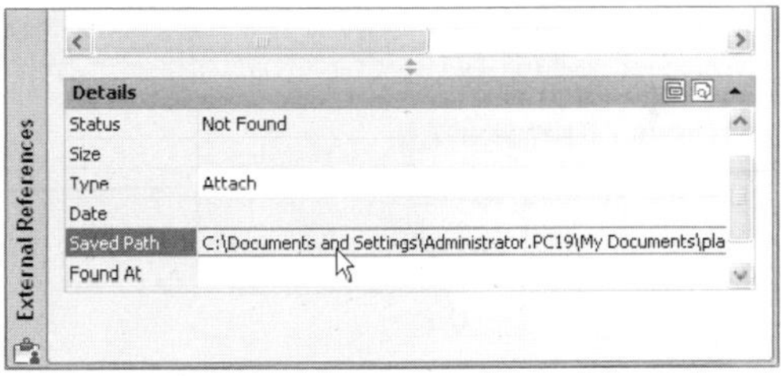

This tells you where AutoCAD expects to find the file. Use the Windows Search utility to find the missing Xref, and then place the files drive and folder location in the text box labeled Found At near the bottom of the External References palette. You can also place the file in the same folder as the current drawing.

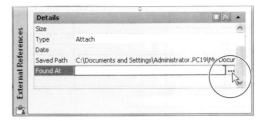

Figure 11.18

Click the Browse button to open the Select New Path dialog box.

Figure 11.19

The External References palette showing Loaded in the Status column

Figure 11.20

Locate the Saved Path text box in the External References palette to display the search path for the Xref.

Locating Fonts, Linetypes, and Hatch Patterns

AutoCAD relies on external files for fonts, linetypes, and hatch patterns. Occasionally, you'll encounter a drawing that cannot find one or all these external files, in which case the drawing produces the wrong display for these items. This might happen when you receive files from another source, such as a consultant or a client.

If the support files are in the same folder as the drawing that uses them, you shouldn't have a problem, but you might find that, for whatever reason, you have to maintain the folder structure from the original source location. In this case, the support files might not be where AutoCAD expects to find them.

Using the Options dialog box, you can tell AutoCAD to look in a specific location for these support files:

1. Right-click in the drawing area and select Options from the context menu, or enter **Options.↵** in the command line, to open the Options dialog box.

2. Make sure the Files tab is selected, as shown in Figure 11.21.

Figure 11.21

The Files tab in the Options dialog box

3. Click the plus sign to the left of the Support File Search Path option. The option expands to show a list of the current search paths.

4. Click the Add button, and then click the Browse button to open the Browse for Folder dialog box (see Figure 11.22).

5. Find the location of your support files, and then click OK. The new location appears in the Support File Search Path list box.

6. Click OK to exit the Options dialog box.

Figure 11.22

The Browse for Folder dialog box

Summary

In this short chapter, you saw some of the most important features in AutoCAD. Finding measurements is perhaps the simplest, yet most useful, AutoCAD tool. Other information, such as the time spent editing or getting the overall settings in one view, can save time and guesswork if you're managing a project.

Other features discussed in this chapter can help you troubleshoot a problem. Locating missing files is a fairly common task, especially if you're sharing files with another office, and the Status command is often the first step in diagnosing other file-related problems.

CHAPTER 12

Laying Out and Printing Your Drawings

Printing in AutoCAD is a bit more complicated than in other applications—for a good reason. You'll often be required to print a drawing multiple times over the course of a project, and you'll want your drawings to be consistent from one print to the next. And since AutoCAD is a graphics program, you'll spend a greater amount of time laying out your drawings on a sheet in order to visually organize your work.

This chapter covers two aspects of printing: preparing your drawing's final appearance in a layout view and printing your drawing. With a layout view, you can get an idea of how your drawing will look before you commit it to paper.

With AutoCAD's print features you can store your printer settings so you can easily and accurately reproduce prints. Since AutoCAD offers some advanced 3D capabilities, you can combine 3D views with 2D drawings. You can even include information about the file to easily identify the source for the printed drawing.

If you're new to AutoCAD and you need to get started with printing, you'll want to read the first section of this chapter carefully. It provides an overview of the layout and print features in a tutorial format. The sections that follow give you more detailed information about layout views and how to use them. After that, you'll find more detailed information about how to print your drawing and the settings associated with printing.

This chapter includes the following topics:

- Setting up a drawing for printing
- Printing your drawing
- Storing your printer settings
- Controlling color, lines, and fills through plot styles
- Assigning named plot styles directly to layers and objects
- Converting a drawing from color plot styles to named plot styles

If you've recently used the 3D Modeling workspace, make sure you are back in the 2D Drafting & Annotation workspace before beginning any exercises in this chapter. See "Getting to Know the 3D Modeling Workspace" in Chapter 6 for instructions on how to switch to a different workspace.

Setting Up a Drawing for Printing

In most programs, you choose Print and send your drawing to the printer. Although you can do this in AutoCAD, the best way to control your print results is to set up how your drawing will look in a layout view.

In the following sections, you'll learn how you can set up the scale and location of your drawing on the printed page exactly as you want it. To help you get familiar with the process, the first part of this chapter is a tutorial showing you the parts of the layout views and how they behave. You'll then learn how to set the scale and location of your drawing on the printer media before you actually send the drawing to the printer.

Exploring the Layout Views

When you're ready to print your drawing, you'll need to do a little setup first. The layout views help you set up your drawing precisely the way you want it to appear before you print. The following steps introduce the layout views:

1. Open a new drawing and add a few objects, such as rectangles and circles. You'll use these to see how the layout views work.

2. Click the Layout1 tab in the lower-left corner of the drawing area. This opens a layout view of your drawing. You'll see your objects appear within a rectangle, which itself is inside a white rectangular area, as shown in Figure 12.1.

Figure 12.1

A view of your drawing in the Layout1 tab

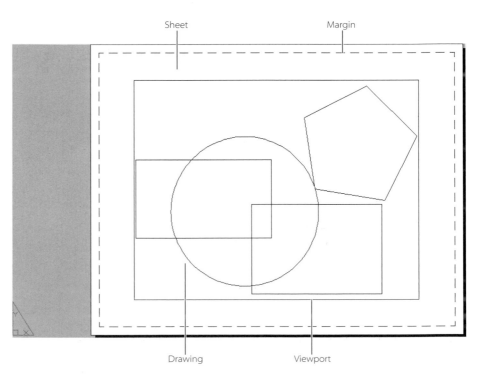

The white area represents the paper onto which your drawing will be plotted. It appears over a gray area, and you'll see a drop shadow behind the white area. The dashed line indicates the nonprintable border of your printer. Finally, the solid rectangle that frames your drawing is a viewport, which is like a window into your Model tab drawing. This viewport behaves like any other AutoCAD object in that it has properties that you can edit through the Properties palette. You can set the viewport's layer, linetype, and color assignment, and you can change its width and height using grips. You can even hide the viewport outline by turning off its layer.

Exploring the Viewport

The viewport has a few properties that are quite unusual. First, it displays the drawing you created in the Model tab. Second, it has properties that control the exact scale of the view it displays. You can also pan and zoom the view, so you're not fixed to any one view within the viewport. The following steps will get you familiar with the viewport:

1. Try selecting part of your drawing by clicking inside the viewport. Nothing is selected. This is because you're currently in the layout space, otherwise known as *paper space*. Later, you'll see how you can reach into the viewport to edit your view while still in a layout view.

2. Click the viewport border, right-click, and choose Properties from the context menu. You can see from the Properties palette that the viewport is just like any other Auto-CAD object. You can even hide the viewport outline by turning off its layer.

3. Close the Properties palette, and then with the viewport still selected, press Delete, or click the Erase tool in the Home tab's Modify panel. The view of your drawing disappears.

This shows you that the viewport is like a window into the drawing you created in the Model tab. Once the viewport is erased, the drawing view goes with it. Here's how to restore the viewport:

1. Click the Undo tool from the Quick Access toolbar or enter **U**↵ to restore the viewport.

2. Double-click in the viewport (see Figure 12.2).

You'll notice that the viewport border becomes thicker. By double-clicking in the viewport, you changed to *floating model space*. Floating model space allows you to edit the drawing within the viewport as if you were in the Model tab.

Figure 12.2

Double-click anywhere in the viewport.

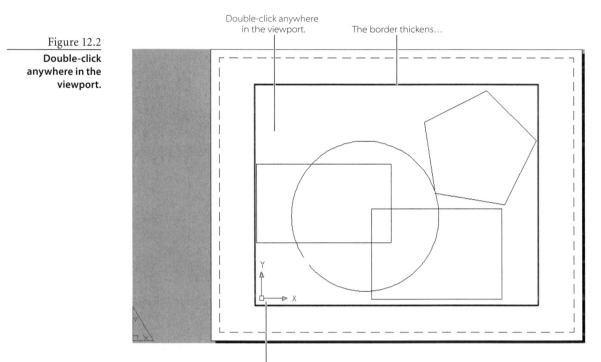

Double-click anywhere in the viewport.

The border thickens…

…and you see the model space UCS icon in the lower-left corner of the viewport.

Take a closer look at the viewport, and you'll see that the UCS icon appears within the viewport. The viewport looks as if it were a miniature version of the Model tab. In fact, that's exactly how floating model space behaves. You can think of floating model space as a shortcut to the contents of the Model tab. Follow these steps to experiment further with the viewport:

1. Click any of the objects you drew at the beginning of this exercise. You can now select objects within the viewport.

2. Try zooming and panning your view. Changes in your view take place only within the boundary of the viewport.

3. Choose All from the Zoom flyout in the View tab's Navigate panel or enter **Z↵ A↵** to display the entire drawing in the viewport once again.

4. Double-click anywhere outside the viewport to return to paper space. The viewport border returns to its original thickness, and the UCS icon disappears from within the viewport.

This exercise showed you the unique characteristics of the layout views. The objects within the viewport are inaccessible until you enter floating model space by clicking the Paper button in the status bar.

The layout views can contain as many viewports as you like, and each viewport can hold a different view of your drawing. You can size and arrange each viewport in any way you like, which gives you the freedom to lay out your drawing as your needs dictate.

> Nothing prevents you from drawing in a layout view around and on top of a viewport. In fact, some users find it convenient to draw dimensions and notes in a layout view to help keep drawing notation consistent when multiple viewports are present. Another common practice is to add title blocks and borders in a layout view to frame your drawing. Items you draw in a layout view will not appear in the model view.

Selecting a Paper Size and Orientation

In a new AutoCAD setup and with a new drawing, AutoCAD assumes you want to print your drawing on an 8.5″ × 11″ sheet of paper, so that is the size of the default paper area shown in a layout view. If you have a printer capable of printing larger formats, you can set up the layout to show larger sizes and different drawing orientations. The following introduces the Page Setup Manager and the Page Setup dialog boxes:

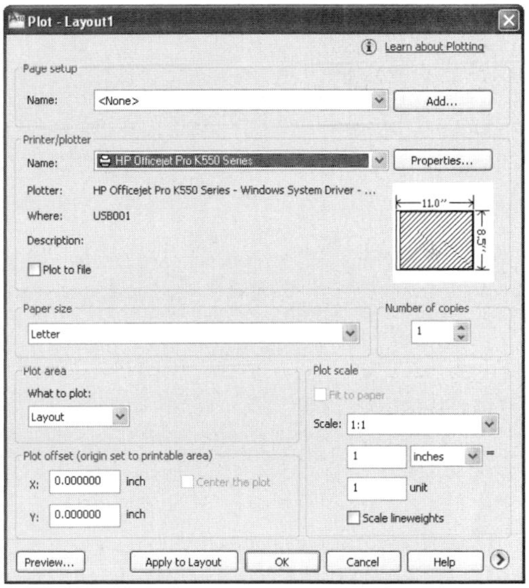

Figure 12.3

The Plot dialog box

1. Choose the Plot tool from the Quick Access toolbar to open the Plot dialog box, as shown in Figure 12.3. You can also choose Plot in the Output tab's Plot panel.

2. Click the Name drop-down list in the Printer/Plotter group, and select the printer you want to use.

3. Click the More Options button in the lower-right corner of the dialog box. It's the round button with the right-pointing arrow (see Figure 12.4).

Figure 12.4

The More Options button

4. In the Drawing Orientation group that appears in the lower-right corner of the dialog box, select the Landscape or Portrait radio button.

5. To ensure that your drawing prints in black and white instead of color or shades of gray, select monochrome.ctb from the Plot Style Table (Pen Assignments) drop-down list, as shown in Figure 12.5.

Figure 12.5

The Plot Style Table drop-down list showing the monochrome.ctb option

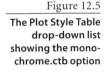

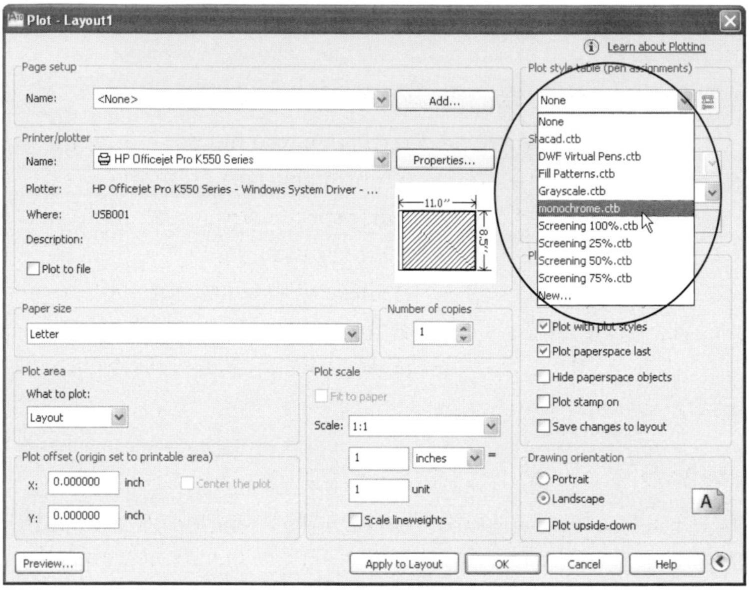

After making your changes, you can save the settings for use in other layout views. This saves you from having to set up each layout that you create and use. Follow these steps:

1. At the top of the Plot dialog box, click the Add button in the Page Setup group, as shown in Figure 12.6.

2. In the Add Page Setup dialog box, you can enter a name for your setup, or you can just accept the default name offered by AutoCAD (see Figure 12.7). Click OK to return to the Plot dialog box.

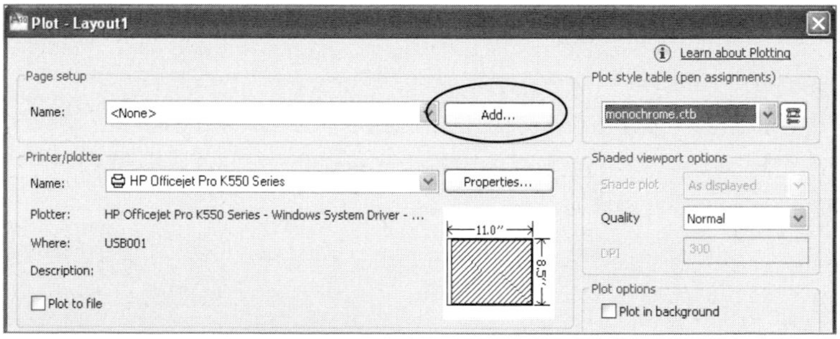

Figure 12.6

The Add button in the Page Setup group

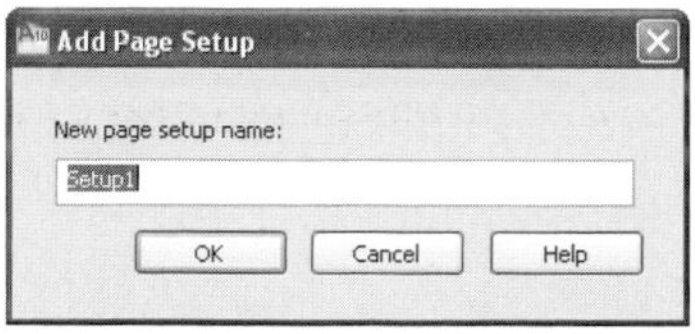

Figure 12.7

The Add Page Setup dialog box

3. Click the Apply to Layout button at the bottom of the Plot dialog box to save the settings you just made.

4. Click Cancel to exit the Plot dialog box without printing your drawing.

When you return to the layout view you've been setting up, you might notice some subtle differences in the dashed line that shows the nonprintable area of your printer. Since every printer is different, this area depends on your specific printer selection.

The next time you open the Plot dialog box, you'll see the same settings you entered in the previous example. You can then click OK to go ahead with your printing.

This section gave you a brief tour of the layout features in AutoCAD. The rest of the chapter describes the methods you'll need to know to fine-tune your printer output, starting with the issue of scale.

Using Layout Views to Scale Down Your Drawing

In the Model tab, you draw everything to full scale. When you're ready to print, you need a way to scale down your drawing to fit on a piece of paper. The layout views are like the staging ground where you can adjust your Model tab drawing to the right size. You can choose from a set of standard scales for your Model tab drawing so that it fits onto the paper size you have selected for your output. If you don't know the scale to use, you can try various ones to find the scale that works.

To set the scale of a viewport in a layout view, take the following steps:

1. In a layout view, click the viewport border to select it, right-click, and choose Properties from the context menu to open the Properties palette for the viewport (Figure 12.8).

2. Select a scale from the Standard Scale option in the Properties palette.

   Or, after selecting the viewport border, click the Viewport Scale drop-down list at the bottom of the AutoCAD window, and select the scale you want to use. The view in the viewport changes to reflect the new scale.

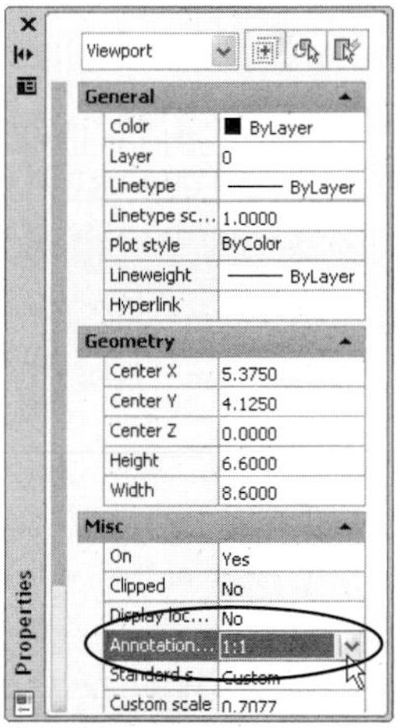

Figure 12.8

You can select a scale from the Standard Scale option in the Properties palette.

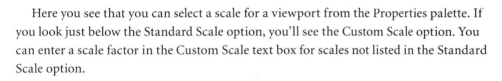

Here you see that you can select a scale for a viewport from the Properties palette. If you look just below the Standard Scale option, you'll see the Custom Scale option. You can enter a scale factor in the Custom Scale text box for scales not listed in the Standard Scale option.

Creating Additional Viewports

Quite often, you'll want several views of your Model tab drawing visible in a layout view. For example, you might have a wall section at one scale and enlarged details at another, and you might want both to appear in a layout view.

Adding a Single Viewport

You can add as many viewports as you need through the Viewports dialog box, but if you need to add only one, here's what you can do:

1. Click the New tool in the View tab's Viewports panel to open the Viewports dialog box.

2. Make sure the New Viewports tab is selected, and then select the Single option in the Standard Viewports list, as shown in Figure 12.9.

3. Click OK.

4. At the `Specify first corner or [Fit] <Fit>:` prompt, click a point in the layout for the first corner of the new viewport.

5. At the `Specify opposite corner:` prompt, you'll see the corner of the new viewport follow the cursor. Click a point to place the other corner of the viewport.

Don't worry if your viewport isn't exactly the size you want it. You can adjust the size of the viewport by selecting its border and then clicking a corner grip to move the corner.

If you want the viewport to cover the entire layout, you can enter **F↵** in step 4 to use the Fit option. This immediately places the viewport in the layout that extends all the way to the edge of the printable area of the layout.

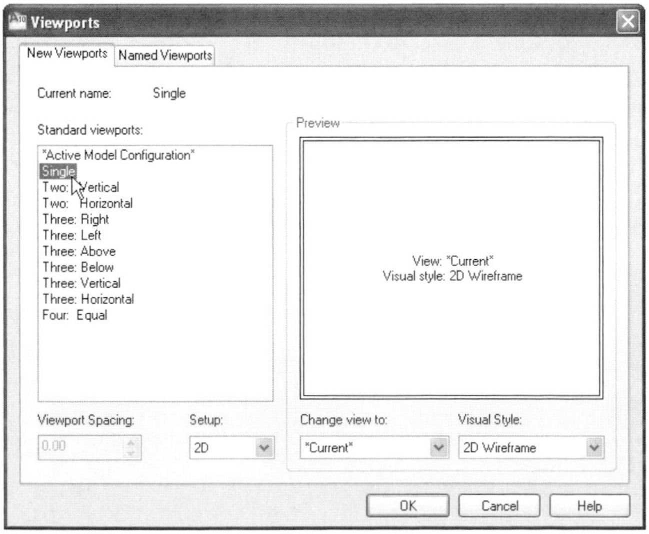

Figure 12.9

The Single option selected in the New Viewports tab

Adding Multiple Viewports at Once

The Viewports dialog box contains several options that let you add multiple viewports at one time. In step 2 of the previous example, you selected the Single option. If you select a different option, such as the Three: Above option, for example, you'll see a preview of the viewport layout in the preview panel to the right (see Figure 12.10). This shows you the arrangement of the selected option as it will appear when you finally place the viewport.

Once you select an option and click OK, you can place the viewports as described in steps 4 and 5 of the previous example. You can also enter **F**↵ in step 4 if you want the viewports to fill the layout.

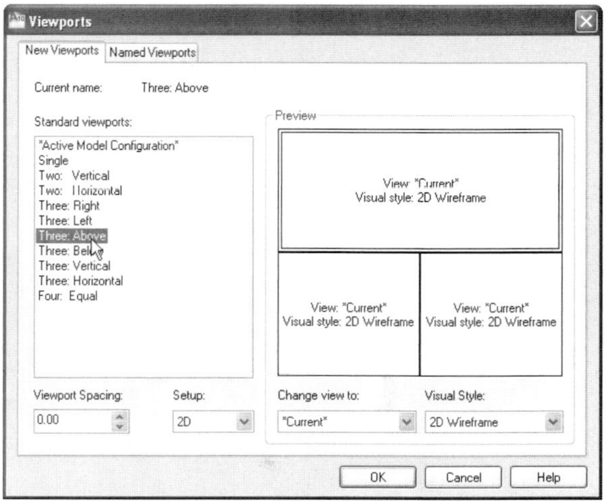

Figure 12.10

The Three: Above option in the Viewports dialog box

Exploring Other Multiple Viewport Options

Some other options also let you control the views that appear in each of the viewports. By default, the current model space view is placed in all the viewports as indicated in the preview area.

You can select between 2D and 3D views from the Setup drop-down list shown in Figure 12.11.

You can then use the Change View To drop-down list shown in Figure 12.12 to select the type of view you want for each viewport.

If you want a viewport to use a visual style, you can select one from the Visual Style drop-down list in the lower-right corner of the dialog box. This is useful if you want to be able to see a conceptual visual style of a 3D model in one viewport while working on that model in a wireframe style.

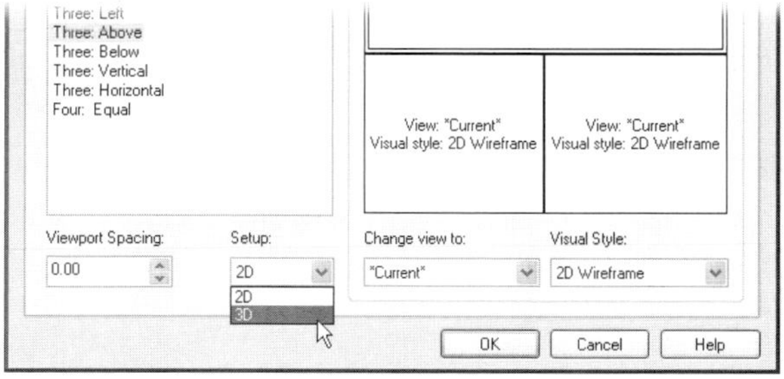

Figure 12.11

The Setup option at the bottom of the Viewports dialog box

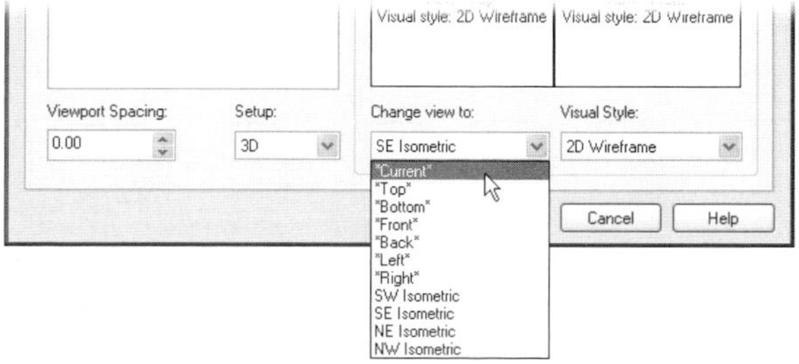

Figure 12.12

The Change View To drop-down list at the bottom of the Viewports dialog box

Controlling How Viewports Display and Print

Several other settings let you control the way viewports display and print your drawing. You can turn the display of your drawing off entirely, lock the view to prevent accidental pans and zooms, and set up a 3D view to plot a hidden line or rendered view.

Locking the Viewport View from Pans and Zooms

You might end up spending a fair amount of time setting up your Viewport view for the proper scale and view area. But you can easily alter the scale accidentally, just by going to floating model space and zooming in to a part of the view. For this reason, AutoCAD offers a way to lock the Viewport view so zooms and pans will not alter the scale or view contents.

To lock the viewport from pans and zooms, click the viewport border to select it, right-click, and choose Display Locked → Yes. Once you've done this, you can use the Pan and Zoom tools to move around in the viewport, but you won't affect the actual Viewport view.

Turning the Viewport Display On or Off

Another lesser-used viewport feature is the ability to turn the view on or off. If you encounter a drawing with empty layout viewports, chances are you can turn on the display by doing the following: click the viewport border to select it, right-click, and choose Display Viewport Objects → Yes.

Printing a 3D Model with Hidden Lines or Shaded

If you have a Viewport view of a 3D model and you want that model to print as a hidden-line view or as a shaded view, you can do the following: click the viewport border to select it, right-click, and choose Shade Plot → Hidden or Shade Plot → Rendered. Your view of the model won't change, but when you plot the layout, the 3D model appears as a hidden-line view or a rendered view.

Setting Layers for Individual Viewports

You can control the layer settings for each individual viewport in a layout view. This can be helpful when you want to show the same view of a drawing in different ways. For example, you can draw a single floor plan in the Model tab with different types of information on different layers. Then in a layout view, you can create multiple viewports showing the same view but with different layer settings in each viewport to show the different elements. If your drawing is a floor plan, you might want a layout that shows one viewport with the furniture layer turned on and another viewport with an electrical layout layer turned on and the furniture turned off, as shown in Figure 12.13.

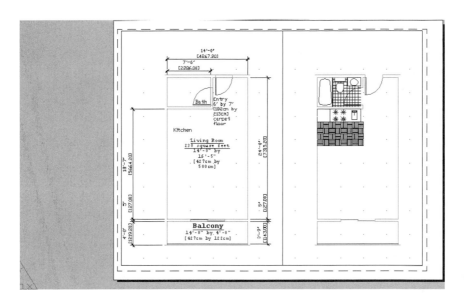

Figure 12.13

A layout with two viewports, each showing the same view with different layer settings

In the Layer Properties Manager dialog box, you're already familiar with the sun icon farthest to the left of any layer. This is the Freeze/Thaw icon that controls the freezing and thawing of layers globally. Several columns to the right of that icon is a sun icon with a transparent rectangle. This icon, called the VP Freeze icon, controls the freezing and thawing of layers in individual viewports. The next exercise shows you firsthand how it works:

1. Double-click in a viewport to go to floating model space.

2. If you have multiple viewports, click in the viewport whose layers you want to control.

3. Open the Layer Properties Manager dialog box.

4. Locate the layer you want to freeze or thaw, and then click its name to isolate this layer in the list (see Figure 12.14).

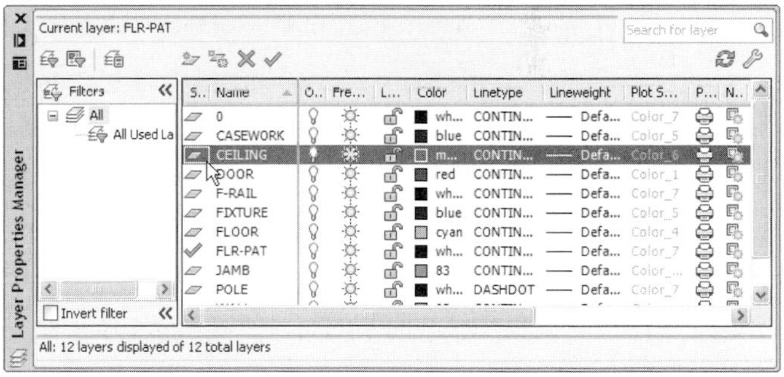

Figure 12.14

A single layer selected in the Layer Properties Manager dialog box

5. Look for the VP Freeze column for the selected layer. You might need to widen the Layer Properties Manager dialog box or use the scroll bar at the bottom of the dialog box to find this column. The VP Freeze column is the twelfth column from the left side of the dialog box. The icon looks like a rectangle behind a sun. The sun tells you the layer is on for the current viewport (see Figure 12.15).

6. Click the VP Freeze icon to turn the layer off for the current viewport. The sun changes to a snowflake. The selected viewport changes to reflect the layer changes you made.

Figure 12.15

The Current VP Freeze option in a layer listing

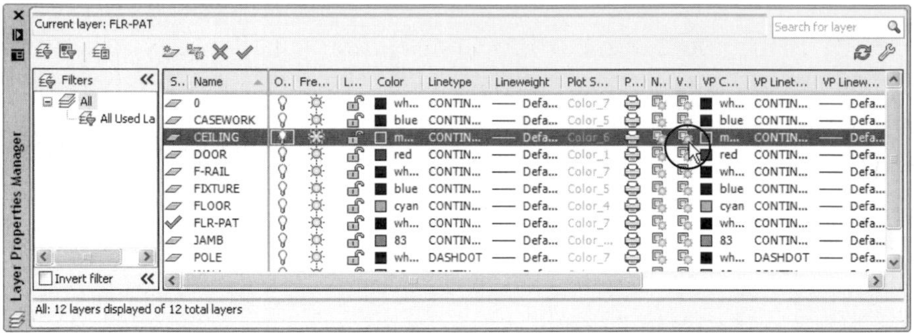

You can also use the Layer Control drop-down list in the Home tab's Layers panel to freeze layers in individual viewports. Proceed with the steps in the previous example, but

Figure 12.16

The Layer Control drop-down list

instead of opening the Layer Properties Manager dialog box in step 3, open the Layer Control drop-down list shown in Figure 12.16.

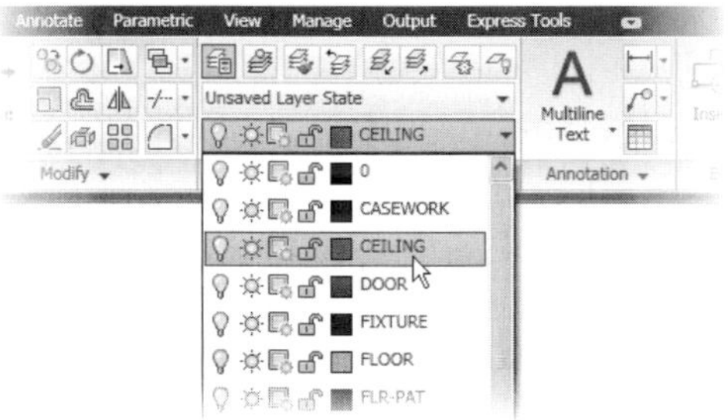

Locate the layer you want to affect from the drop-down list, and then click the sun icon with the small rectangle to turn the layer off.

If you find that a layer does not display in a viewport and you want it turned on, you might need to turn it on or thaw it globally by using the On/Off or Freeze/Thaw column of the Layer Properties Manager dialog box.

Adding Layouts Using the Quick View Layouts Tool

In a new drawing, AutoCAD provides two layout views, labeled Layout1 and Layout2. You're not limited to two layouts. For small projects with only a handful of drawings in the printed set, you can set up a layout for each sheet in the set.

If you need more layout views, you can easily duplicate an existing layout by doing the following:

1. Right-click the Quick View Layouts tool in the status bar and choose Move or Copy from the context menu to open the Move or Copy dialog box.

2. Select the name of the layout you want to copy, and turn on the Create a Copy option at the bottom of the dialog box (see Figure 12.17).

3. Click OK. A new layout view is created. The new view contains the name of the original view from which the copy was made plus a number in parentheses indicating that it is a copy of the original.

To rename the new layout view, or any view for that matter, click the Quick View Layouts tool that you saw in step 1 of the previous exercise. You'll see a set of preview panels showing the contents of each layout.

Right-click in the preview of the layout you want to rename, and choose Rename from the context menu. The name of the layout in the preview panel will highlight, enabling you to type a new name. Once you've changed the name, click in the drawing area to close the preview panels.

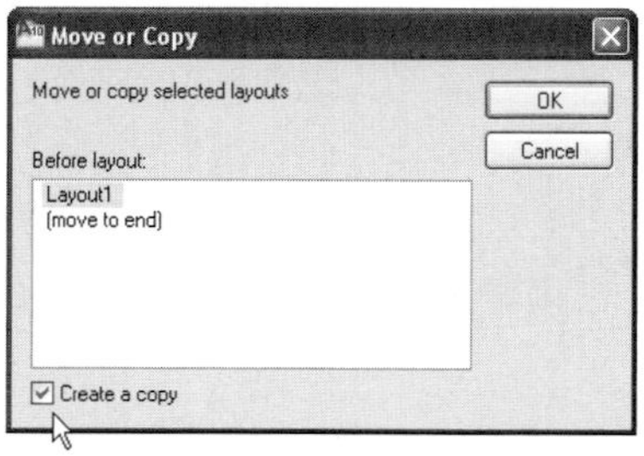

Figure 12.17

The Move or Copy dialog box with the Create a Copy option turned on

Switching Between Layouts

Once you have multiple layouts, you can easily switch between them using the Quick View Layouts tool in the status bar (Figure 12.18).

When you click the Quick View Layouts tool, you see a set of preview panels showing you the model and layout views. You will also see a toolbar with some additional features.

To switch to a different layout, click in a preview panel, and then click in the drawing area.

The toolbar offers additional tools to "pin" the previews to the screen, create a new layout, or start the Publish tool to print a set of layout views.

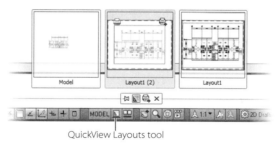

QuickView Layouts tool

Figure 12.18

Quick View Layouts tool

Printing Your Drawing

Once your layout is set up, you're ready to print your drawing. If you read the first part of this chapter, you saw how you can right-click a layout view and choose the Plot option to open the Plot dialog box. From there, you can print your drawing after making a few adjustments. In that first example, you selected a printer, paper size, and paper orientation. These are the most common settings, but eventually, you'll have to use some of the other settings in the Plot dialog box.

In the following sections, you'll find descriptions for each group of options in the Plot dialog box. Some options are fairly common, such as those in the Drawing Orientation group, but others might be new to you, such as those in the Plot Area group. You might want to skim the following sections so you have an idea of what all the options are for, and then later, when you want to make adjustments to your plotter settings, you can refer to the topic you need.

Selecting and Storing Printer Settings

The Printer/Plotter group lets you select a printer and make setting changes to the printer you select. At first glance, these settings look like those of any other Windows program, but an important difference exists. You can save changes you make to a printer's properties and later recall them. Here's how it works:

1. Open the layout view you want to plot and then click the Plot tool in the Quick Access toolbar to open the Plot dialog box. You can also click Plot in the Output tab's Plot panel.

2. From the Name drop-down list in the Printer/Plotter group, select a printer.

3. Click the Properties button to open the Plotter Configuration Editor dialog box.

4. Make a change to any of the properties in this dialog box (see the next section, "Exploring the Printer Configuration Options").

5. Click OK. You'll see the Changes to a Printer Configuration File dialog box, as shown in Figure 12.19.

6. Click the Save Changes to the Following File option; then enter a name for this printer configuration that will remind you of the settings, and finally click OK.

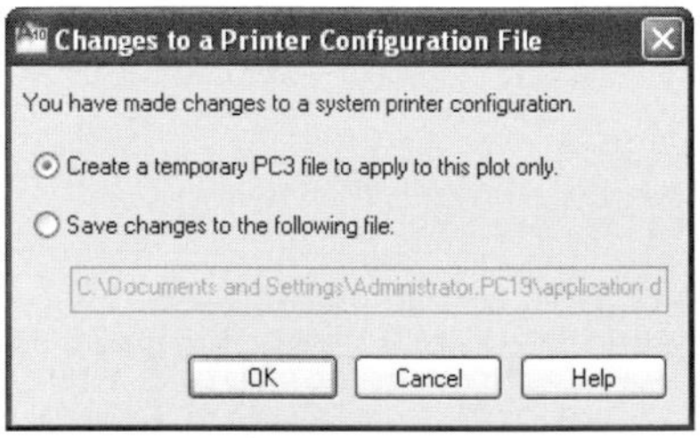

Figure 12.19

The Changes to a Printer Configuration File dialog box

> ### HOW DO I GET MY COLORS TO PRINT IN BLACK AND WHITE?
>
> By default, AutoCAD prints your drawings just as they appear in the AutoCAD window, including the colors you assign to layers or objects. The AutoCAD colors are helpful when you're editing because they can help you visually organize your drawing, but most of the time, you'll want to print your drawings in black and white. You can use plot styles to automatically convert colors to black or shades of gray. You'll find more about plot styles in the section "Using AutoCAD's Predefined Plot Styles" later in this chapter.

The next time you use the Name drop-down list to locate a printer, you'll see the name of the printer configuration file you just created. You can then select that configuration file to use those printer settings. This saves you from having to remember settings you used to print a drawing.

A single printer can have multiple configuration files. You can create a configuration for custom paper sizes or any other settings you find useful in the Plotter Configuration Editor dialog box.

Configuration files end with the .pc3 filename extension. They are usually stored in the Plotters folder under the C:\Documents and Settings*User Name*\Application Data\ Autodesk\AutoCAD 2010\R18.0\enu\ folder. *User Name* is your login name. You can get to this folder quickly by choosing Print → Manage Plotters from the Application menu.

CREATING A PDF OF YOUR DRAWING

AutoCAD lets you create a PDF of your drawing through the Plot tool. Proceed as if you are going to plot your drawing, In the Plot dialog box, select the Adobe PDF option from the Name drop-down list in the Printer/Plotter group. Make other plotter setting adjustments as needed. When you click OK to plot your drawing, AutoCAD will produce a PDF file of your drawing.

Exploring the Printer Configuration Options

The printer configuration options vary somewhat from printer to printer, but this section contains some general guidelines for using the Plotter Configuration Editor dialog box. These options include items such as the port your printer is connected to, the quality of bitmap image printing, custom paper sizes, and printer calibration, which lets you adjust your plotter for any size discrepancies in output.

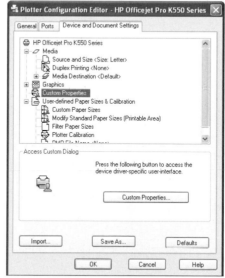

Figure 12.20

The Device and Document Settings tab of the Plotter Configuration Editor dialog box

The Plotter Configuration Editor dialog box has three tabs: General, Ports, and Device and Document Settings. The General tab lists Windows drivers that this configuration uses, if any, and it has a space for your own comments. The Ports tab lets you specify where your plotter data is sent. You can also select AutoSpool, which allows you to direct your plot to an intermediate location for distribution to the appropriate output device. The Device and Document Settings tab is the main part of this dialog box. The main list box contains options in a hierarchical list, similar to a listing in Windows Explorer (see Figure 12.20).

The list has four main categories: Media, Graphics, Custom Properties, and User-Defined Paper Sizes & Calibration. Not all the options under these categories are available for all plotters. When you select an item from this list, the area just below the list displays the options associated with that item.

Media

Many printers offer options for choosing the source and size of printer media and for choosing the media type. If the Source and Size option is available, the Media option lets you select it. Duplex Printing, when available, allows for double-sided printing in printers that support this feature. Media Destination, when available, lets you select a destination for output such as collating or stapling in printers that support such features.

Graphics

These options give you control over color depth, dots per inch, and the rendering of shaded areas. You can adjust your output for better color or faster speed. One popular setting is Merge Control, which controls how overlapping lines are drawn.

Custom Properties

These options are actually the same as those you find when you edit your printer properties through the Windows Start menu. (Choose Start → Settings → Printers and Faxes, right-click the printer whose properties you want to edit, and choose Properties.) The main difference here is that settings you make through this option are saved in a plot configuration file.

User-Defined Paper Sizes & Calibration

Several settings relate to paper sizes that fall under User-Defined Paper Sizes & Calibration. For some printers, the Custom Paper Sizes option offers the ability to create a nonstandard paper size. Another similar option is Modify Standard Paper Size. As the name implies, this option lets you change the standard paper sizes. Filter Paper Sizes is handy for printers that offer a large number of paper sizes. You can limit the sizes shown in the Plot dialog box by selecting the sizes you want to appear from a list.

Another option under the User-Defined Paper Sizes & Calibration heading is Plotter Calibration. This feature is significant because it lets you adjust the aspect ratio of your image on the printed page. If you find that your printer stretches your drawing in one direction, you might need to calibrate your printer. The Plotter Calibration option offers a way to adjust your printer so it produces a properly proportioned print.

If you select Plotter Calibration, the Calibrate Plotter button appears in the lower half of the dialog box. Click this button to start the Calibrate Plotter Wizard. You can follow the instructions in the wizard to fine-tune the width and height ratio of your printer output.

Selecting a Paper Size and Number of Copies

These options are fairly obvious. You can select a paper size from the Paper Size drop-down list and set the number of copies in the Number of Copies text box in the Plot dialog box. One feature of the Paper Size option is not obvious. You can control the paper sizes that are displayed by editing the properties for the current printer. See the preceding "Exploring the Printer Configuration Options" section.

Determining What View Will Print

You can be selective about the part of your drawing that prints. The Plot Area group offers the What to Plot drop-down list. This list contains several options that determine the view that is sent to the printer. Typically, you print from a layout, so you use the Layout option. But at other times, you might want to print from the Model tab and select a specific view. The other options offer different ways to select the area to print. Table 12.1 shows those options and describes their typical use.

The Scale option in the Plot Scale group affects how these options appear in the final printed sheet. Typically, if you're using the Layout option, you can use the default scale of 1:1 in the Plot Scale group. You'll have to calculate the proper scale for the Limits, Extents, Display, and Window options, or if the scale is not important, you can use the Fit to Paper option.

OPTION	USE
Display	Uses the current display as the area to print.
Extents	Uses the extents of the drawing as the area to print. This is the same view that you'll see on the screen if you choose Zoom → Extents.
Layout	Uses the current layout as the print area.
Limits	Available in the Model tab only. It uses the limits of the drawing to determine what to print. This is the same view you'll see in model space when you choose View → Zoom → All.
Window	Asks you to select a window to indicate the area you want to plot. The dialog box temporarily closes to allow you to select points.

Table 12.1

The What to Plot Options

Adjusting the Location of Your Printed Image

You can adjust the position of your drawing on the printed sheet by changing the options in the Plot Offset (Origin Set to Printable Area) group. X and Y options let you adjust the location of the printed image by increasing the X and Y coordinate value. The default zero X and zero Y location is the lower-left corner of the printable area. (Remember that a dashed line represents the printable area in a layout view.)

If you prefer, you can set up AutoCAD to use the corner of the paper as the origin instead of the printable area. The Plot and Publish tab of the Options dialog box (choose Options from the Application menu) offers the Specify Plot Offset Relative To button group. This group offers two radio buttons: Printable Area and Edge of Paper. You can select the option that makes the most sense for you.

Setting the Print Scale

If you're printing from a layout view, you can usually keep this setting at 1:1. You can alter that scale using the options in the Plot Scale group. For example, if you want to print a drawing at half its intended size, you can specify a scale of 1:2 in the Scale drop-down list. Or if you're printing a 3D view from the Model tab, you can use the Fit to Paper option.

For the most part, you need to set the plot scale only if you're plotting from model space and are using one of the options in Table 12.1 other than the Layout option. If that is what you're doing, be sure that the scale you select allows your drawing to fit on the paper size you select in the Paper Size group. You can use the Preview button in the lower-left corner of the Plot dialog box to check.

Selecting a Scale

To use the Scale options, open the Scale drop-down list, and select a scale. The proportions of the scale then appear in the text boxes directly below the Scale drop-down list. You can select inches or mm from the drop-down list below and to the right of the Scale drop-down list. If you want to use a scale that is not listed in the Scale drop-down list, select Custom, and then enter the appropriate values in the text boxes below the Scale drop-down list.

Adjusting Lineweights to Your Scale

AutoCAD lets you set lineweights in your drawing. When you plot your drawing through a layout view, AutoCAD faithfully prints the lineweights you've selected. But often, you want to print a half-size view or your layout, and you want the lineweights reduced to half their specified size. To ensure your lineweights are scaled to your half-size prints, make sure the Scale Lineweights setting is turned on. AutoCAD then applies the selected scale to lineweights.

Options for Printing 3D Views

When you're working with 3D models in AutoCAD, you can view them as 2D or 3D wireframe, hidden-line, or conceptual or realistic shaded views. A *wireframe* view shows all the lines in the model as if you could see through it. A *hidden* view gives you a more realistic view by hiding the parts you usually wouldn't see. A *shaded* view adds a bit more realism by giving the surfaces of the model a solid, colored appearance.

You can apply these view options to your printed output through the Shaded Viewport Options group in the Plot dialog box and the Properties palette for the Layout viewport. The Shaded Viewport Options group offers three main options:

- The Shade Plot drop-down list
- The Quality drop-down list
- The dpi (which stands for *dots per inch*) text box

If you don't see the Shaded Viewport Options group, click the More Options button in the lower-right corner of the Plot dialog box.

The Shade Plot options in the Plot dialog box are not available if you're plotting from a layout view. Instead, you can control this value by doing the following:

1. Go to the layout showing your 3D view.

2. Select the viewport containing the 3D view.

3. Right-click, and then choose Shade Plot from the context menu.

4. From the cascading menu, select the option you want to apply to the viewport. The choices are As Displayed, Wireframe, Hidden, 3D Hidden, 3D Wireframe, Conceptual, Realistic, and Rendered. You can also select the quality settings of Draft, Low, Medium, High, and Presentation. (LT users will not have the Rendered or other 3D options.)

The As Displayed option plots the 3D view as it appears in the viewport. Hidden plots your 3D view with hidden lines removed. Rendered renders your 3D view before plotting. The Conceptual and Realistic options plot the drawing as they appear with these visual styles (see Chapter 6 for more about visual styles). The quality settings of Draft, Low, Medium, High, and Presentation control the resolution of the image. Draft is the lowest resolution, and Presentation is the highest resolution.

Plot Options

The Plot Options group contains some general settings that you can use to control your printer output.

Plot in Background   If you're printing a fairly large file that will take some time, you can use this option to print in the background. You can then get back to work while AutoCAD prints.

Plot Object Lineweights   If you set lineweights by object or layer, this option prints lineweights as you specified them.

Plot with Plot Styles   Plot styles give you control over the way colors, lineweights, area fills, and the corners of lines print. You can use this setting to specify whether to use plot style settings. See the section "Controlling Color, Lines, and Fills Through Plot Styles" later in this chapter.

Plot Paperspace Last   When you're printing from a layout view, this option determines whether objects in paper space are drawn before or after objects in model space.

Hide Paperspace Objects   AutoCAD offers controls over 3D hidden-line views in viewports through the context menu or the Properties palette for a selected viewport. In the event that a 3D model has been drawn in the layout view in paper space, this option prints paper space objects using hidden lines.

Plot Stamp On   You can add a plot stamp to your printer output using this option. The plot stamp prints information about the current drawing that can be helpful to anyone viewing the printed copy. When you activate Plot Stamp On, the Plot Stamp Settings button appears (Figure 12.21).

You can click this button to gain access to the Plot Stamp dialog box (Figure 12.22). This dialog box lets you determine the information included in the plot stamp. Clicking the Advanced button opens the Advanced Options dialog box (Figure 12.23), which lets you specify the location and orientation of the plot stamp. It also lets you adjust font and text size.

Save Changes to Layout When this option is turned on, the changes you make to the Plot dialog box settings are saved with the current layout.

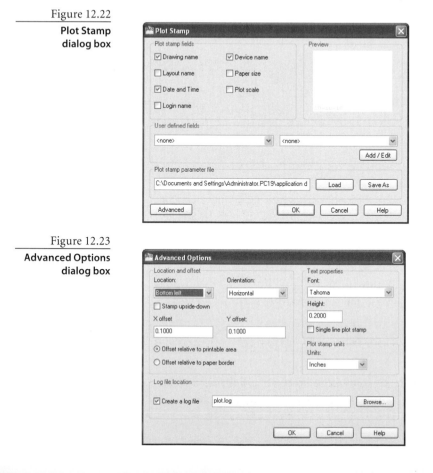

Drawing Orientation

As with most programs, you can control the orientation of the document you're printing. In the Drawing Orientation group, you have the typical Landscape and Portrait options plus the Plot Upside-Down option.

Storing Your Printer Settings

Figure 12.24

The Page Setup Manager dialog box

You'll most likely have to print an AutoCAD drawing many times over the course of a project. Not only that, but each time you print a drawing, you might want to use the same settings. To help you keep consistency in your printing, AutoCAD offers the Page Setup Manager dialog box.

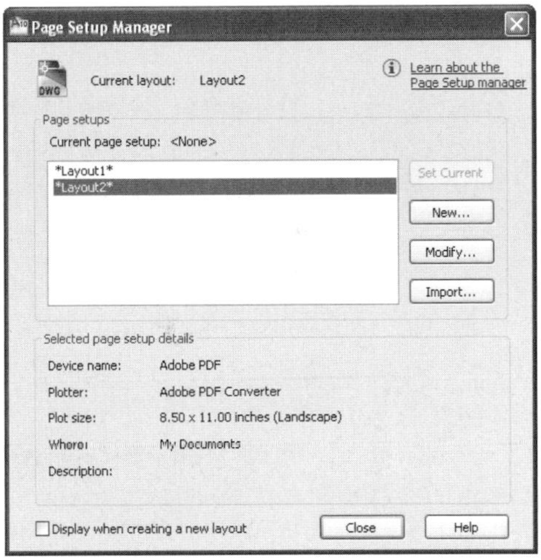

If you did the exercise at the beginning of this chapter, you encountered the Page Setup option in the Plot dialog box. There, you made some plotter settings and then saved the settings as a page setup called Setup1. You don't have to save your printer settings in a setup, but doing so can be a real time-saver.

The Page Setup group at the top of the Plot dialog box lets you select from a drop-down list of setups you've created. You can also create and manage setups through the Page Setup Manager dialog box. You can get to the Page Setup Manager and edit or create new setups by doing the following:

1. In the status bar, click the Quick View Layouts tool, and then right-click in a preview panel for a layout whose settings you want to edit.

2. Select Page Setup Manager from the context menu. This opens the Page Setup Manager dialog box, as shown in Figure 12.24.

3. Click the New button to open the New Page Setup dialog box, as shown in Figure 12.25.

Figure 12.25

The New Page Setup dialog box

4. To create a new page setup, enter a name in the New Page Setup Name input box, and then select a prototype setup from the Start With list box. AutoCAD offers the name of Setup1 as a default for a new setup, but it will be helpful to give your setup a name to help you remember the purpose of the setup.

5. Click OK when you're finished. The Page Setup dialog box opens. This dialog box is nearly identical to the Plot dialog box, with a few options made unavailable.

6. Make your custom settings, and then click OK. You return to the Page Setup Manager dialog box. You'll see your new page setup in the Current Page Setup list box.

7. You can select a page setup from the list box and then click the Set Current button to make it the current page setup for the layout. You can also select a page setup from the Page Setup group of the Plot dialog box (see Figure 12.26).

Figure 12.26

Select a page setup from the Page Setup group of the Plot dialog box.

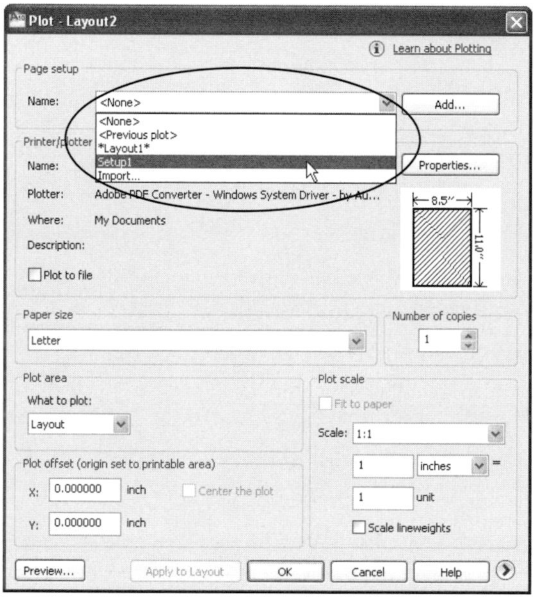

Page setups are stored with the drawing, but if you want to import a setup from another drawing, you can do so by clicking the Import option in the Page Setup Manager dialog box. A standard file dialog box opens in which you can select a drawing file that contains the page setup you want to import. Here, the trick is to remember the drawing in which you stored the desired setup.

The current page setup applies to the current layout view, but once you create a new page setup, it is displayed as an option in the Page Setup Manager dialog box for all other layout views.

Controlling Color, Lines, and Fills Through Plot Styles

When you print, AutoCAD attempts to reproduce your drawing's appearance in a layout view or in the Model tab. However, you might want to change the way certain parts of the drawing appear in the printed output. For example, you might want all line work in black instead of the AutoCAD colors, or you might want filled areas in shades of gray instead of solid fills. To produce these effects without actually converting all your objects to the color black, you need to employ plot styles.

You can think of plot styles as a way to translate the colors and fills in an AutoCAD drawing into different colors or patterns. You can control whether the color red on your AutoCAD screen is printed in black or gray or even green, or you can control whether an area filled solid black is screened to 30 percent. The plot styles also let you specify whether the lines forming the corners of a rectangle are rounded or square, as shown in Figure 12.27.

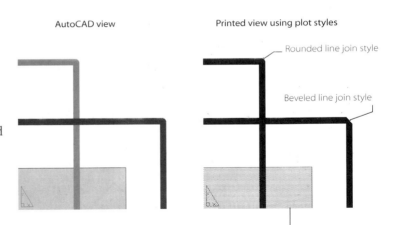

AutoCAD view

Printed view using plot styles

Rounded line join style

Beveled line join style

30% screen

Figure 12.27

Plot styles can translate colors and fills into shades of gray and halftone screens.

You can use two types of plot styles: color and named. *Color* plot styles let you control printer output based on the color you assigned to the objects in your drawing. For example, you can tell AutoCAD to print the color red as black using a 50 percent screen or as a line width of 0.5mm. This is a method similar to the one used by early versions of AutoCAD, and it persists today, mainly because many old drawings are still in use.

Named plot styles operate in a different way. They let you give a name to a set of printer parameters including the lineweight, the color, the percent screen, or the corner condition of line work. You can then apply that named set of parameters, called a *plot style*, to objects or layers. If you're coming from another CAD program, you might be more familiar with this method of assigning printer parameters to objects in a drawing.

Using AutoCAD's Predefined Plot Styles

AutoCAD comes with a set of plot styles you can use right away. These plot styles are stored in database-like files called *plot-style tables*. There are two sets—one for color plot styles and another for named plot styles. You can select the plot styles from the Plot Style Table drop-down list of the Plot or Page Setup dialog box (see Figure 12.28).

Figure 12.28

Selecting a plot style from the Plot Style Table drop-down list of the Page Setup dialog box

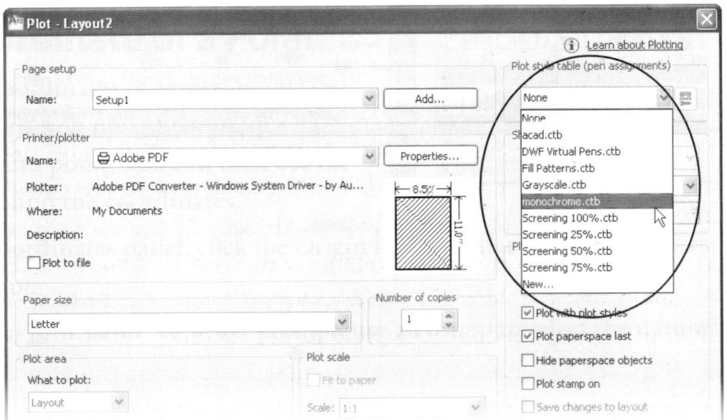

Table 12.2 describes the predefined color plot styles available in AutoCAD. Table 12.3 describes the predefined named plot styles tables.

You might find that you can do most of your work with these standard plot-style tables. At other times, you'll be required by your employer to use custom plot-style tables that have been set up for your projects.

	PLOT STYLE	PURPOSE
Table 12.2 **The Standard Color Plot-Style Tables**	Acad.ctb	Converts the first eight AutoCAD colors to black when printing.
	DWF Virtual Pens.ctb	Converts AutoCAD colors to virtual pens of the same color in DWF files.
	Fill Patterns.ctb	Converts the first nine AutoCAD colors into fill patterns.
	Grayscale.ctb	Converts all AutoCAD colors into grayscale equivalents on printers that support this feature.
	monochrome.ctb	Converts all AutoCAD colors into black.
	Screening xxx%.ctb	Converts all AutoCAD colors into a screened value indicated by the Plot Style name (*xxx* is the screen percentage).
	New	Starts the Add Color Dependent Plot Style Table Wizard to allow you to create a new plot style.
	None	No plot styles are applied to the drawing.

	PLOT STYLE	PURPOSE
Table 12.3 **The Standard Named Plot-Style Tables**	Acad.stb	Plots AutoCAD colors as they are displayed in the drawing area.
	Autodesk-Color.stb	Includes screened "colors" from solid (100 percent) to 10 percent. This uses object color for printed color.
	Autodesk-MONO.stb	Same as Autodesk-Color.stb but converts colors to black, white, and shades of gray.
	Monochrome.stb	Converts all AutoCAD colors to black.
	New	Starts the Add Name Dependent Plot Style Table Wizard to allow you to create a new plot style.

Choosing Between Color and Named Plot-Style Tables

If you need to create your own plot-style tables, decide which type of plot-style table you want to use. Named plot styles are more flexible than color plot styles, but if you already have a library of AutoCAD drawings set up for a specific set of plotter settings, color plot styles are a better choice. Color plot styles are the most familiar to users of the older method of assigning AutoCAD colors to plotter pens.

The type of plot-style table assigned to a drawing depends on the template you use to start a new drawing. The acad.dwt template file uses color plot-style tables, and the acad-Named Plot Styles.dwt template file uses named plot styles.

You can also set up AutoCAD to use color or named plot-style tables for the default drawing that appears when you start AutoCAD. The Options dialog box provides controls over the default plot style used for the drawing*x*.dwg default drawing (*x* is the drawing number). Here's how to make those settings:

1. Right-click in the drawing area and select Options from the context menu to open the Options dialog box. Then click the Plot and Publish tab.

2. Click the Plot Style Table Settings button to open the Plot Style Table Settings dialog box.

3. In the Default Plot Style Behavior for New Drawings button group, click the Use Color Dependent Plot Styles radio button.

4. Click OK, and then click OK again to return to the drawing.

Once you've set up AutoCAD for color plot-style tables, any new drawings you create are allowed to use only color plot-style tables. You can change this setting at any time for new files, but once you save a file, the type of plot style that is current when the file is created is the only type of plot style available to that file. If you find that you need to change a color plot style to a named plot style drawing, see the section "Converting a Drawing from Color Plot Styles to Named Plot Styles" later in this chapter.

Creating a Plot-Style Table

If you're using color plot-style tables, you can create a plot-style table file (with the .ctb filename extension) for different styles of drawings. You might create one for presentation drawings in which certain colors and screened solid fills are assigned to colors in your drawing. Or you might have specific screen settings you use frequently when printing monochrome prints. The following steps describe how you can create your own color plot-style table:

1. Open a drawing, and then click the Quick View Layouts tool in the status bar.

2. Right-click a layout preview panel, choose Page Setup Manager to open the Page Setup Manager dialog box, and then click Modify.

3. In the Plot Style Table group in the upper-right corner, open the drop-down list, and select New. If the current drawing uses color plot-style tables, you'll see the Add Color-Dependent Plot Style Table Wizard, as shown in Figure 12.29. If it uses a named plot style, you'll see the Add Name-Dependent Plot Style Table Wizard.

Figure 12.29

The first screen of the Add Color-Dependent Plot Style Table Wizard

4. Click the Start from Scratch radio button, and then click Next.

5. The next screen of the wizard asks for a filename. Enter a name for the file, and click Next.

6. The next screen of the wizard lets you edit your plot style and assign the plot style to your current, new, or old drawings. You'll learn about editing plot styles a bit later.

7. Click Finish to return to the Page Setup dialog box. Once you have created a color plot style, you can make setting changes.

Add Color-Dependent Plot Style Table - Begin

- Begin
- Browse File
- File Name
- Finish

This wizard provides you with the ability to either create a color-dependent plot style table from scratch, or by importing settings from a PCP, PC2, or Release 14 CFG file. The new plot style table can be assigned to any color-dependent drawing.

○ Start from scratch

Create a new plot style table from scratch.

○ Use a CFG file

Import R14 pen settings that were saved automatically to a CFG file.

○ Use a PCP or PC2 file

Import R14 pen settings that were saved in a PCP or PC2 file.

< Back   Next >   Cancel

Editing and Using Plot Style Tables

Once you've created a plot style, you'll can set it up the way you want. In the Page Setup dialog box, open the Plot Style Table drop-down list in the upper-right corner of the dialog box, and select the plot style you want to edit (see Figure 12.28 earlier in this chapter). Click the Edit button to open the Plot Style Table Editor dialog box.

The Edit button is just to the right of the Plot Style Table drop-down list. Click the Form View tab, which is shown at the top of Figure 12.30.

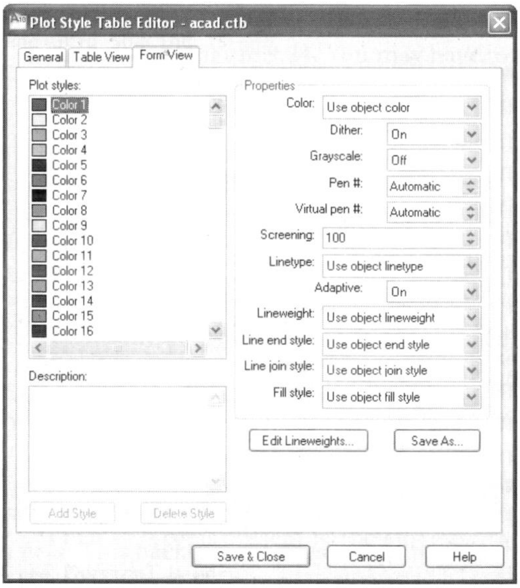

Figure 12.30

The Form View tab of the Plot Style Table Editor dialog box

You can find plot-style table files in C:\Documents and Settings\Username\Application Data\Autodesk\AutoCAD 2010\R18.0\enu\Plot Styles. To edit a plot-style file, just double-click it.

The Plot Style Table Editor dialog box has three tabs that give you control over how each color in AutoCAD is plotted. The Form View tab lets you select a color from a list box and then set the properties of that color using the options on the right side of the tab.

Understanding the Options in the Plot Style Table Editor

Once you get to the Plot Style Table Editor dialog box, you'll see quite a few options. These options are the same for both the named and color plot-style tables. The main difference is that the color plot-style table lists all 256 of the AutoCAD colors as plot styles. Named plot-style tables list only a single plot style. You can add other plot styles and name them.

The General Tab

The General tab contains information regarding the plot style you're currently editing. You can enter a description of the style in the Description box. This can be useful if you plan to include the plot style with a drawing you're sending to someone else for plotting.

The File Information group gives you the basic information about the file location and name, as well as the number of color styles included in the plot-style table.

The Apply Global Scale Factor to Non-ISO Linetypes check box lets you determine whether ISO linetype scale factors are applied to all linetypes. When this item is checked, the Scale Factor input box becomes active, allowing you to enter a scale factor.

The Table View Tab

The Table View tab offers the same settings as the Form View tab (described next), only in a different format (see Figure 12.31). Each plot style appears as a column with the properties of each plot style listed along the left side of the tab. To change a property, click the property in the column.

To apply the same setting to all plot styles at once, right-click a setting you want to use from a single plot style, and choose Copy from the context menu. Right-click the setting again, and then choose Apply to All Styles from the context menu.

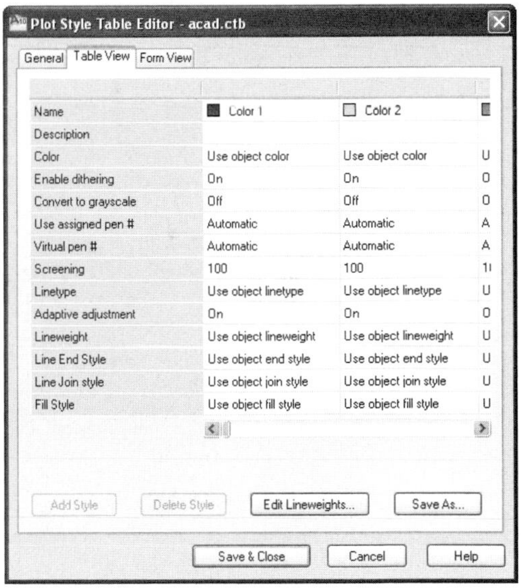

The Form View Tab

To modify the properties of a plot style or color, select it from the list at the left side of the Form View tab, and then edit the values in the Properties button group on the right side of the dialog box (see the Form View tab in Figure 12.30 earlier in this chapter). For example, to change the screen value of the Color 3 style in a color plot-style table, highlight Color 3 in the Plot Styles list, double-click the Screening input box, and enter a new value.

You can select several plot styles at once from the list by selecting the first plot style and then Shift+clicking the last one in a group. Or you can Ctrl+click individual plot styles.

The following describes the settings in the Form View tab:

Figure 12.31

The Table View tab of the Plot Style Table Editor dialog box

Description This option allows you to enter a description for each individual color.

Color This option allows you to select a print color that is different from the display color.

Dither Dithering enables your plotter to simulate colors beyond the basic 256 available in AutoCAD. Although this option is desirable when you want to create a wider range of colors in your plots, it can also create some distortions, including broken, fine lines and false colors. For this reason, dithering is usually turned off. This option is not available in all plotters.

Grayscale This option converts colors to grayscale.

Pen # This option lets you specify what pen number is assigned to each color in your drawing. This option applies only to pen plotters.

Virtual Pen # Many ink-jet and laser plotters offer "virtual pens" to simulate the processes of the old-style pen plotters. Frequently, such plotters offer as many as 255 virtual pens, with each pen offering a different lineweight or pattern. Plotters with virtual pens often let you assign AutoCAD colors to a virtual pen number. This is significant if the virtual pens of your plotter can be assigned screening width, end style, and joint styles. You can then use the Virtual Pen settings instead of the settings in the Plot Style Table Editor dialog box. This option is most beneficial to users who already have a library of drawings that are set up for plotters with virtual pen settings.

You can set up your ink-jet printer for virtual pens under the Vector Graphics listing of the Device and Documents Setting tab of the Plotter Configuration Editor dialog box.

Screening Lets you set the screening value for a color. A screening value of 50 will print a color that is half, or 50 percent, of its value. For example, black with a screening value of 50 will print as gray. Black with a screening value of 20 will be a lighter gray than if set to a 50 percent value.

Linetype If you prefer, you can use this setting to control linetypes in AutoCAD based on the color of the object. By default, this option is set to Use Object Linetype. I recommend you leave this option at its default.

Adaptive This option is on by default. The Adaptive option controls how noncontinuous linetypes begin and end. Noncontinuous lines have gaps so this option forces linetypes to begin and end in a line segment. With this option turned off, a noncontinuous linetype is drawn without regard for its ending. This can cause the line to appear as though its end is missing because it can end on the gap portion of the noncontinuous line.

Lineweight This option lets you specify the thickness of lines. You can select a lineweight from a drop-down list. If you need to modify a lineweight, you can do so using the Edit Lineweights button near the bottom of the Plot Style Table Editor dialog box.

Line End Style This option lets you specify the shape of the ends of simple lines that have a lineweight greater than zero.

Line Join Style You can determine the shape of the corners of polylines (see Figure 12.32).

Fill Style This option lets you set up a color to be drawn as a pattern when used in a solid-filled area. The patterns appear in the drop-down list, as shown in Figure 12.33.

Add Style Clicking this button lets you add more plot styles or colors.

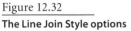

Figure 12.32
The Line Join Style options

Figure 12.33
The Fill Style patterns

Delete Style   Clicking this button deletes the selected style.

Edit Lineweights   When you click this option, the Edit Lineweights dialog box appears. This dialog box lets you change the lineweights offered in the Lineweight option. This dialog box also lets you specify whether to show lineweights in inches or millimeters.

Save As   Clicking this button lets you save the current plot-style table.

Assigning Named Plot Styles Directly to Layers and Objects

With color plot-style tables, you have to rely on the AutoCAD colors to control how objects are printed. But with named plot styles, you're not limited to object colors to control the way an object prints. Color plot styles are easier to manage for the beginning user, but if you're an advanced user or if you're used to a CAD program that allows you to control printing properties of each individual object, you'll want to know how to use named plot styles.

> The instructions in the following sections require that your drawing is set up to use named plot styles. See "Choosing Between Color and Named Plot-Style Tables" earlier in this chapter to learn how to set up new drawings for named plot styles. If you have an existing drawing that is set up for color plot styles, see "Converting a Drawing from Color Plot Styles to Named Plot Styles" later in this chapter to learn how to convert your drawing to use named plot styles.

Assigning Plot Styles to Objects

If you've set up AutoCAD to use named plot styles (see "Choosing Between Color and Named Plot-Style Tables" earlier in this chapter), you can begin to assign plot styles to objects through the Properties palette. Here are the steps to take to assign plot styles to objects while in a layout view:

1. Click the Quick View Layouts tool in the status bar.

2. Right-click a layout preview panel and then choose Page Setup Manager to open the Page Setup Manager dialog box.

3. Select a layout or page setup to edit, and click Modify.

4. In the Page Setup dialog box, select a named plot-style table from the drop-down list in the Plot Style Table group. Make sure the Display Plot Styles check box is selected, and then click OK.

5. Click Close to close the Page Setup Manager dialog box.

Once you've selected a named plot-style table, you can begin to apply plot styles to individual objects. Next, make sure the plot styles will be displayed in the drawing:

1. In the Home tab's Properties panel, choose Lineweight Settings from the Lineweight drop-down list (Figure 12.34).

2. Make sure the Display Lineweight check box is selected in the Lineweight Settings dialog box, and click OK (see Figure 12.35).

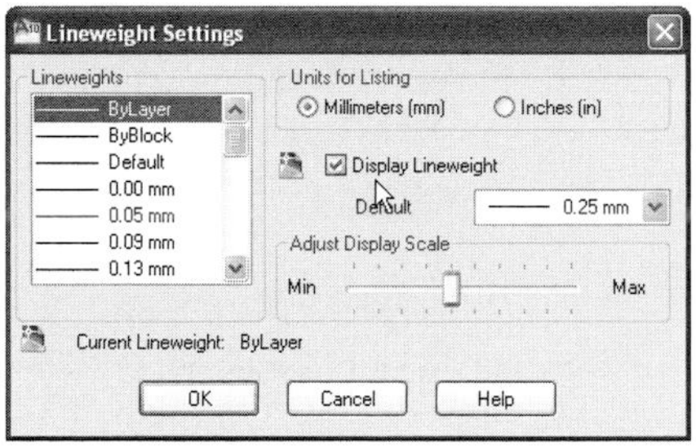

Figure 12.35

The Lineweight Settings dialog box with the Display Lineweight option checked

Figure 12.34

Choosing Lineweight Settings

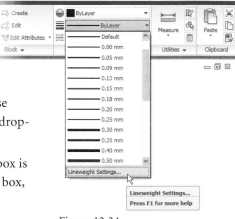

3. In the layout view drawing area, double-click in a viewport to switch to floating model space. This lets you select objects in the drawing while in a layout view.

4. Select the objects to which you want to assign a plot style, right-click, and choose Properties from the context menu.

5. In the Properties palette, click the Plot Style option. The option turns into a drop-down list

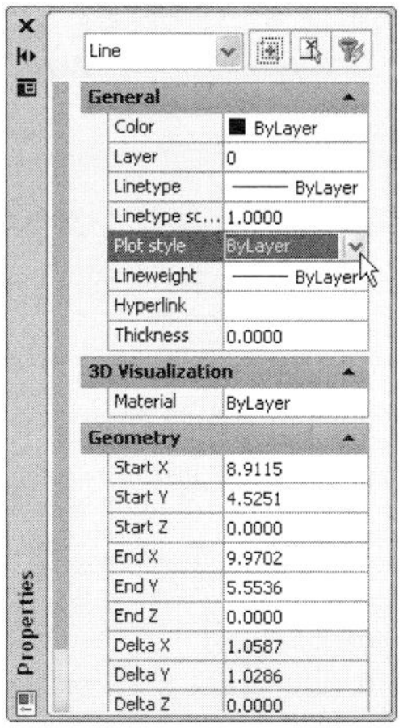

Figure 12.36

The Plot Style drop-down list in the Properties palette

with a down-pointing arrow to the far right (see Figure 12.36). Click the arrow, and then select Other from the list to open the Select Plot Style dialog box, as shown in Figure 12.37.

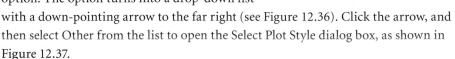

6. Select the name of the plot style you want to use from the Active plot style table drop-down list toward the bottom of the dialog box, and click OK. Notice that the style you selected now appears as the value for the plot style in the Properties palette. Close the Properties palette.

7. Type **Rea↵**. If you have the lineweight visibility turned on, you'll see the results in the drawing editor.

   You can also assign a plot style to individual objects using the Plot Style drop-down list in the Properties palette.

8. Select the objects, and then select the plot style from the Select a Plot Style drop-down list in the Home tab's Properties panel. If you're using a color plot-style table like the one you created in earlier exercises, the Select a Plot Style drop-down list is unavailable.

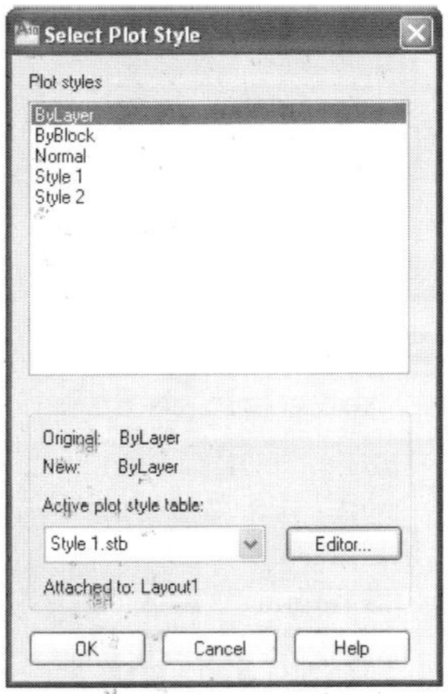

Figure 12.37

The Select Plot Style dialog box

Assigning Named Plot Style Tables to Layers

If you prefer, you can assign named plot styles to layers. This has a similar effect to using the color plot-style tables. The main difference is that with named plot-style tables, you assign the plot-style tables directly to the layer instead of assigning a plot style to the color of a layer. Here's how to assign a plot-style table to a layer:

1. Click the Layer Properties Manager tool (shown in Figure 12.38) to open the Layer Properties Manager dialog box.

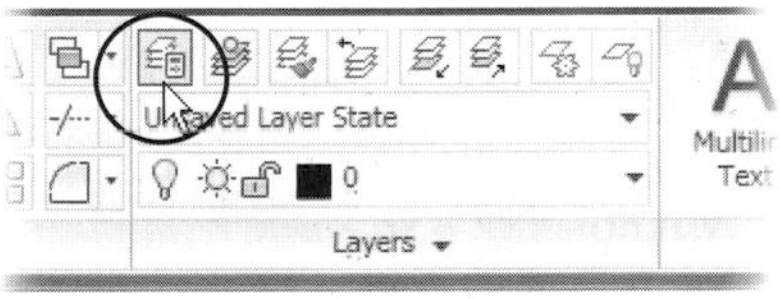

2. Select a layer or set of layers whose plot style you want to change.

3. Click Normal in the Plot Style column of the selected layers (see Figure 12.39). You might have to scroll to the right to see the Plot Style column. The Select Plot Style dialog box opens, as shown in Figure 12.40.

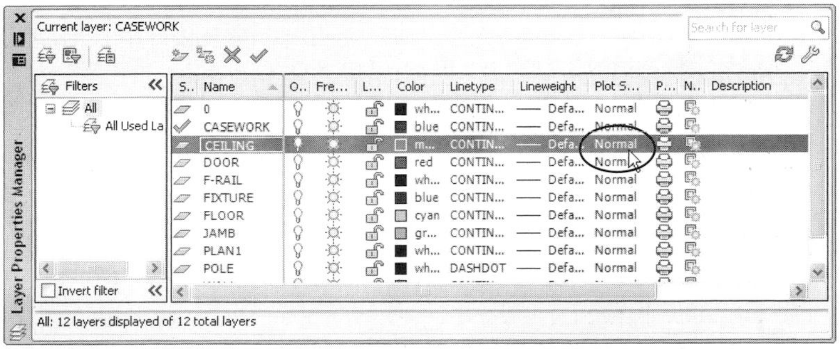

Figure 12.38

The Layer Properties Manager tool in the Layers panel

Figure 12.39

Click Normal in the Plot Style column of the selected layer.

Figure 12.40

The Select Plot Style dialog box

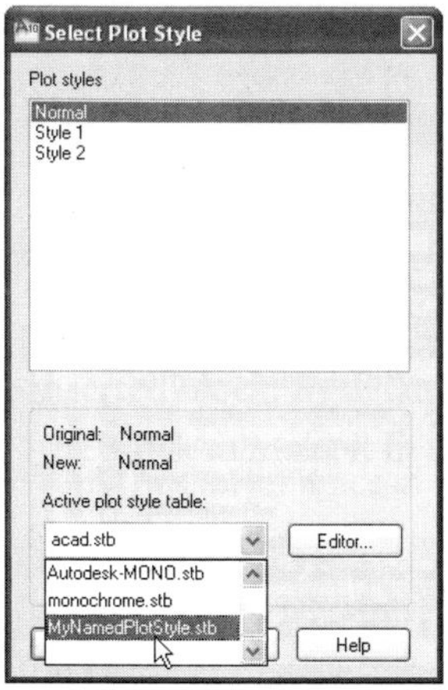

4. Select the plot style you want to use from the Active Plot Style Table drop-down list toward the bottom of the dialog box. The selected style appears in the Plot Style list.

5. Select the plot style you want to assign to the layer or layers from the Plot Style list, and then click OK. The Layer Properties Manager dialog box opens again.

6. Close the Layer Properties Manager dialog box, and then type **Re↵**. Your view of the plan changes to reflect the new plot style assignment to the layers you modified.

Converting a Drawing from Color Plot Styles to Named Plot Styles

If you work in an office where drawings from other offices frequently cross your desk, you might eventually need to convert a drawing from a color plot style to named, or vice versa.

To convert a color plot-style drawing to a named plot-style drawing, you need to use the Convertctb and Convertpstyles commands. This conversion is a two-part process. In the first part, which is needed only the first time you perform the conversion, you convert a color plot-style table file into a named plot-style table file. You can then convert the drawing file. Follow these steps:

1. Open the AutoCAD drawing you want to convert.

2. At the command prompt, enter **Convertctb↵** to open the Select File dialog box, in which you can select a color plot-style table file; these files have the filename extension `.ctb`.

3. Select the color plot style you want to convert with the drawing, and then click Open to open the Create File dialog box. This dialog box allows you to provide a name for the converted file. For example, if you opened the Acad.ctb file in step 1, you might

want to give the new file the name **AcadConvert** so you know that it is a converted .ctb file. AutoCAD automatically adds the .stb filename extension. Click Save. AutoCAD creates a new named plot-style table file.

Once a color plot-style table is converted, you can convert the drawing, as described next:

1. Open the file you want to convert, and enter **Convertpstyles↵** at the command prompt. You'll see a warning message to make sure you've converted a .ctb file to an .stb file.

2. Click OK. The Select File dialog box opens.

3. Select the converted .stb file you created using the Convertctb command. The current drawing is converted to use a named plot-style table.

The process for converting a drawing that uses named plot styles to one that uses color plot styles is a bit simpler. You need only to use the Convertpstyles command. When you do, you'll see a warning message telling you that all the named plot styles will be removed from the drawing. Click OK to convert the drawing.

Summary

There is a lot to learn when it comes to printing in AutoCAD, but it's worth the effort to become as familiar as you can with the process. By mastering the printing process, you'll have better control over the appearance of your drawings. You'll be able to organize your drawings in a clearer fashion, and you'll get more consistent output from print to print.

The documents you produce in AutoCAD will most likely be used to convey detailed information. Someone might rely on your work to construct a building or to manufacture a crucial part, so mastering these printing tools is essential.

Index

Note to reader: **Bold** page references indicates definitions and main discussions of a topic. *Italicized* page references indicates illustrations.

DISCARDED